Ranma 1/2

VOL. 9 — Action Edition

STORY & ART BY
RUMIKO TAKAHASHI

RANMA 1/2

VOL. 5
Action Edition

Story and Art by
RUMIKO TAKAHASHI

English Adaptation/Gerard Jones and Toshifumi Yoshida
Touch-Up Art & Lettering/Wayne Truman
Cover and Interior Design & Graphics/Yuki Ameda
Editor (1st Edition)/Trish Ledoux
Editor (Action Edition)/Avery Gotoh
Supervising Editor (Action Edition)/Michelle Pangilinan

Managing Editor/Annette Roman
Editorial Director/Alvin Lu
Director of Production/Noboru Watanabe
Sr. Dir. of Licensing & Acquisitions/Rika Inouye
VP of Sales & Marketing/Liza Coppola
Executive VP/Hyoe Narita
Publisher/Seiji Horibuchi

RANMA 1/2 is rated "T+" for Older Teens. It may contain violence, language, alcohol or tobacco use, or suggestive situations.

The stories, characters, and incidents mentioned in this publication are entirely fictional. For the purposes of publication in English, the artwork in this publication is printed in reverse from the original Japanese version.

Printed in Canada.

Published by VIZ, LLC
P.O. Box 77010
San Francisco, CA 94107

1st Edition Published 1997

Action Edition
10 9 8 7 6 5 4 3 2
First Printing, April 2004
Second printing, October 2004

store.viz.com

STORY THUS FAR

The Tendos are an average, run-of-the-mill Japanese family—on the surface, that is. Soun Tendo is the owner and proprietor of the Tendo Dojo, where "Anything-Goes Martial Arts" is practiced. Like the name says, anything goes, and usually does.

When Soun's old friend Genma Saotome comes to visit, Soun's three lovely young daughters—Akane, Nabiki, and Kasumi—are told that it's time for one of them to become the fiancée of Genma's teenaged son, as per an agreement made between the two fathers years ago. Youngest daughter Akane—who says she hates boys—is quickly nominated for bridal duty by her sisters.

Unfortunately, Ranma and his father have suffered a strange accident. While training in China, both plunged into one of many "cursed" springs at the legendary martial arts training ground of Jusenkyo. These springs transform the unlucky dunkee into whoever—or whatever—drowned there hundreds of years ago.

From now on, a splash of cold water turns Ranma's father into a giant panda, and Ranma becomes a beautiful, busty young woman. Hot water reverses the effect...but only until next time. As it turns out, Ranma and Genma aren't the only ones who have taken the Jusenkyo plunge—and it isn't long before they meet several other members of the Jusenkyo "cursed."

Although their parents are still determined to see Ranma and Akane marry and carry on the training hall, Ranma seems to have a strange talent for accumulating surplus fiancées...and Akane has a few stubbornly determined suitors of her own. Will the two ever work out their differences, get rid of all these "extra" people, or will they just call the whole thing off? What's a half-boy, half-girl (not to mention all-girl, *angry* girl) to do...?

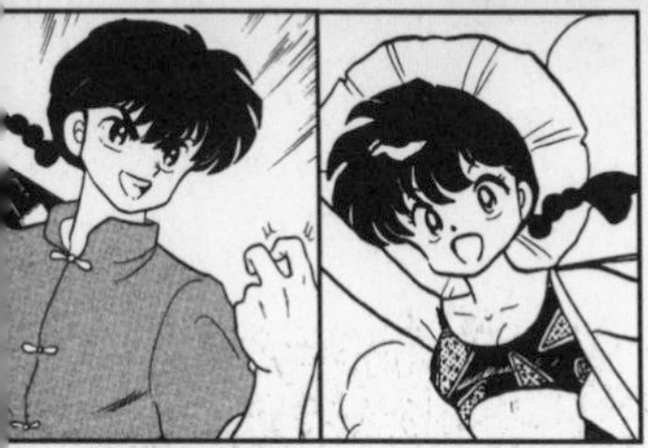

RYOGA HIBIKI
Melancholy martial artist with no sense of direction, a hopeless crush on Akane, and a stubborn grudge against Ranma. Changes into a small, black pig Akane's named "P-chan."

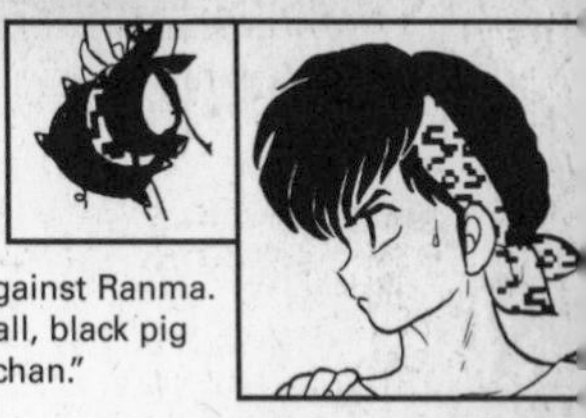

RANMA SAOTOME
Martial artist with far too many fiancées, and an ego that won't let him take defeat. Changes into a girl when splashed with cold water.

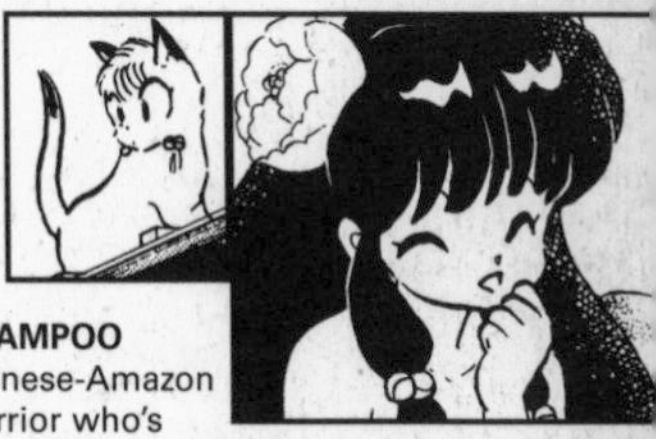

SHAMPOO
Chinese-Amazon warrior who's gone from wanting to kill Ranma to wanting to marry him.

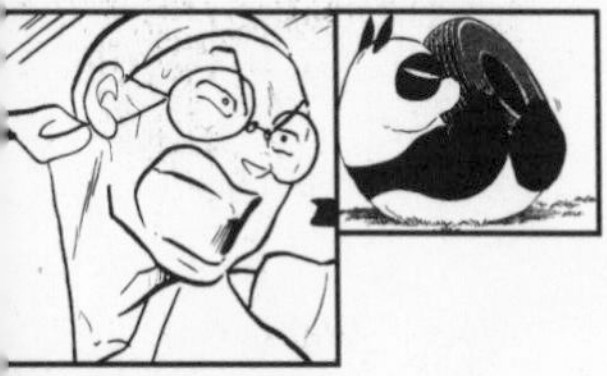

GENMA SAOTOME
Ranma's lazy father, who left his wife and home years ago with his young son (Ranma) to train in the martial arts. Changes into a panda.

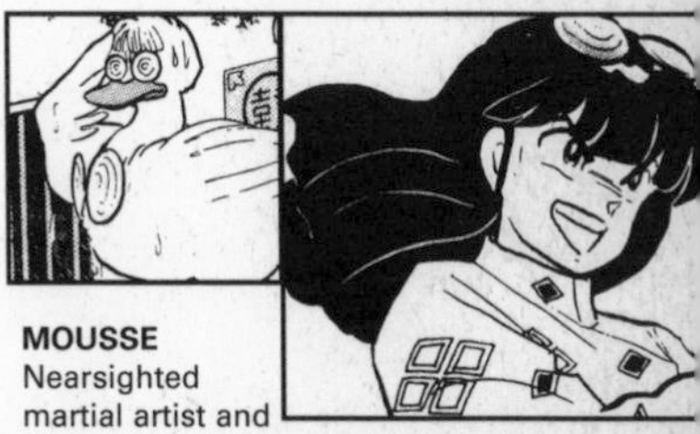

MOUSSE
Nearsighted martial artist and Shampoo's childhood suitor. Master of hidden weapons.

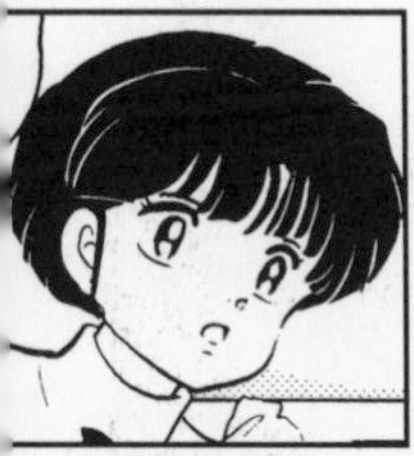

AKANE TENDO
Martial artist, tomboy, and Ranma's reluctant fiancée. Has no clue how much Ryoga likes her, or what relation he might have to her pet black pig, P-chan.

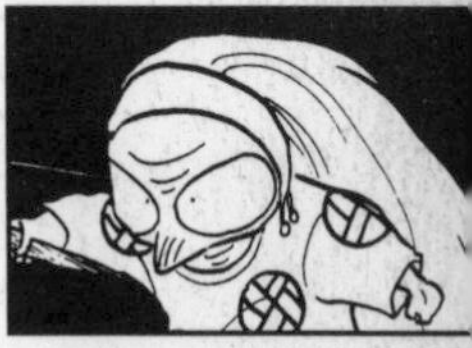

COLOGNE
Shampoo's great-grandmother, a martial artist, and matchmaker.

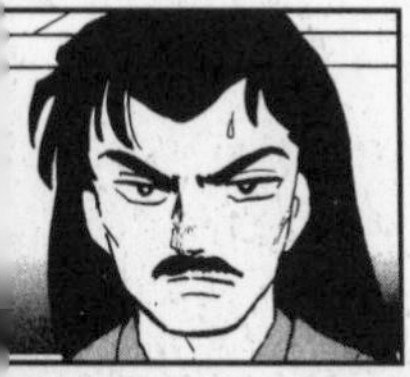

SOUN TENDO
Head of the Tendo household and owner of the Tendo Dojo.

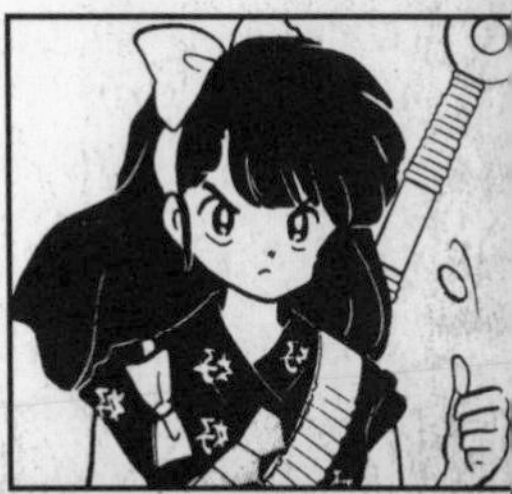

UKYO KUONJI
Ranma's childhood friend. Has a flair for cooking and a dislike of Akane. Also weilds a mean spatula.

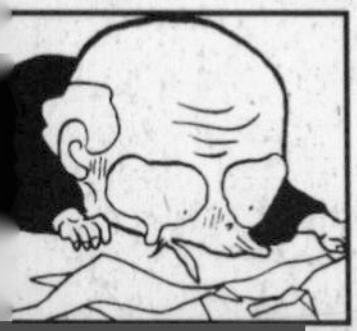

HAPPOSAI
Martial arts master who trained both Genma and Soun. Also a world-class pervert.

CONTENTS

Part 1

AKANE BECOMES A DUCK

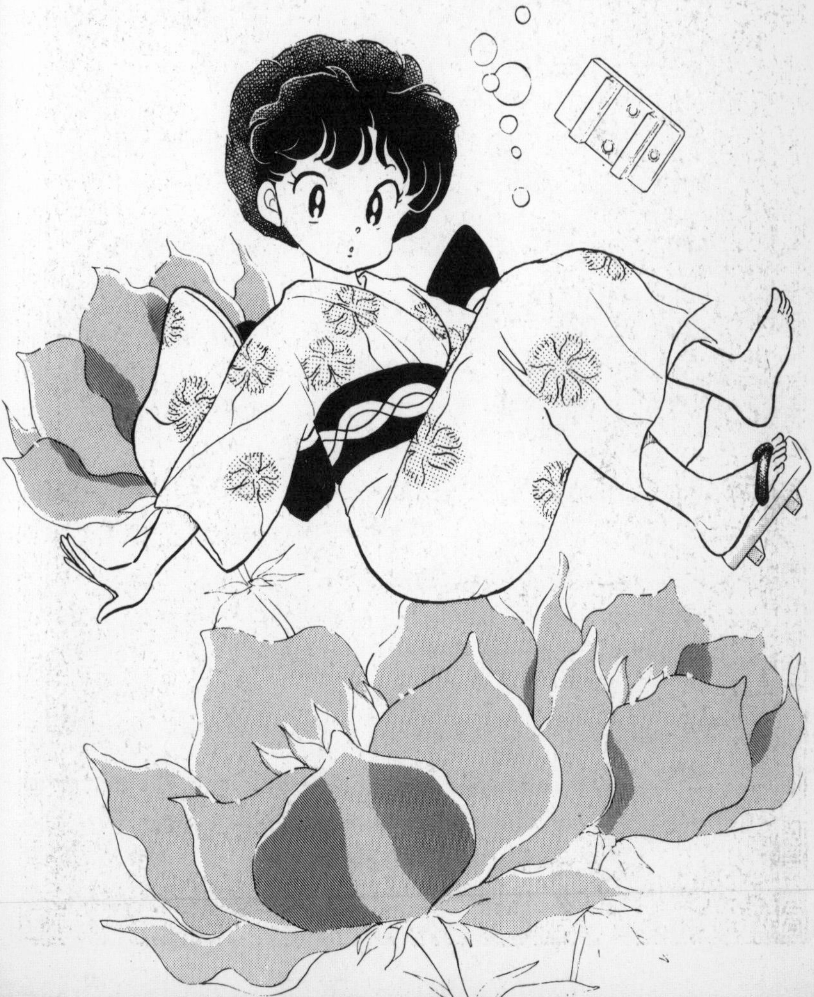

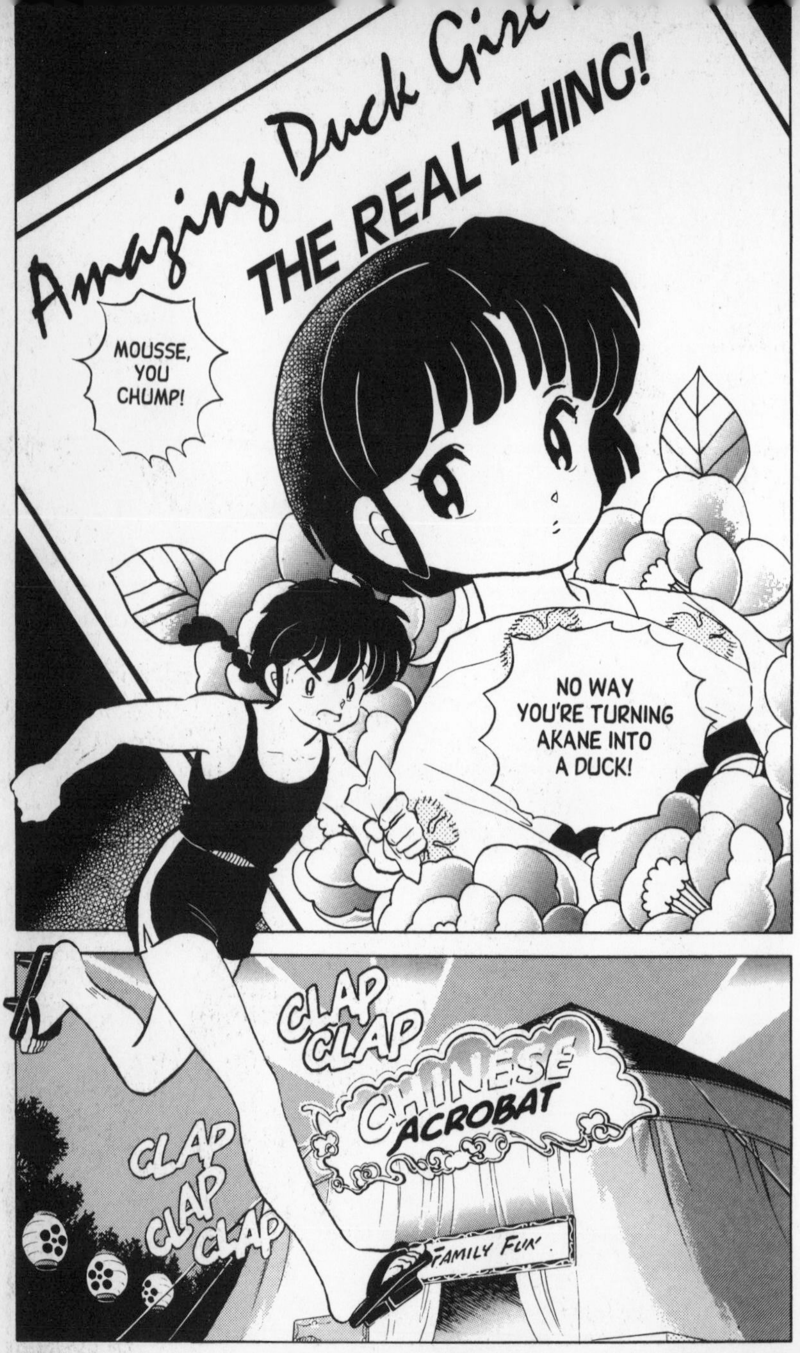
Amazing Duck Girl
THE REAL THING!
MOUSSE, YOU CHUMP!
NO WAY YOU'RE TURNING AKANE INTO A DUCK!
CLAP CLAP
CHINESE ACROBAT
CLAP CLAP CLAP
FAMILY FUN

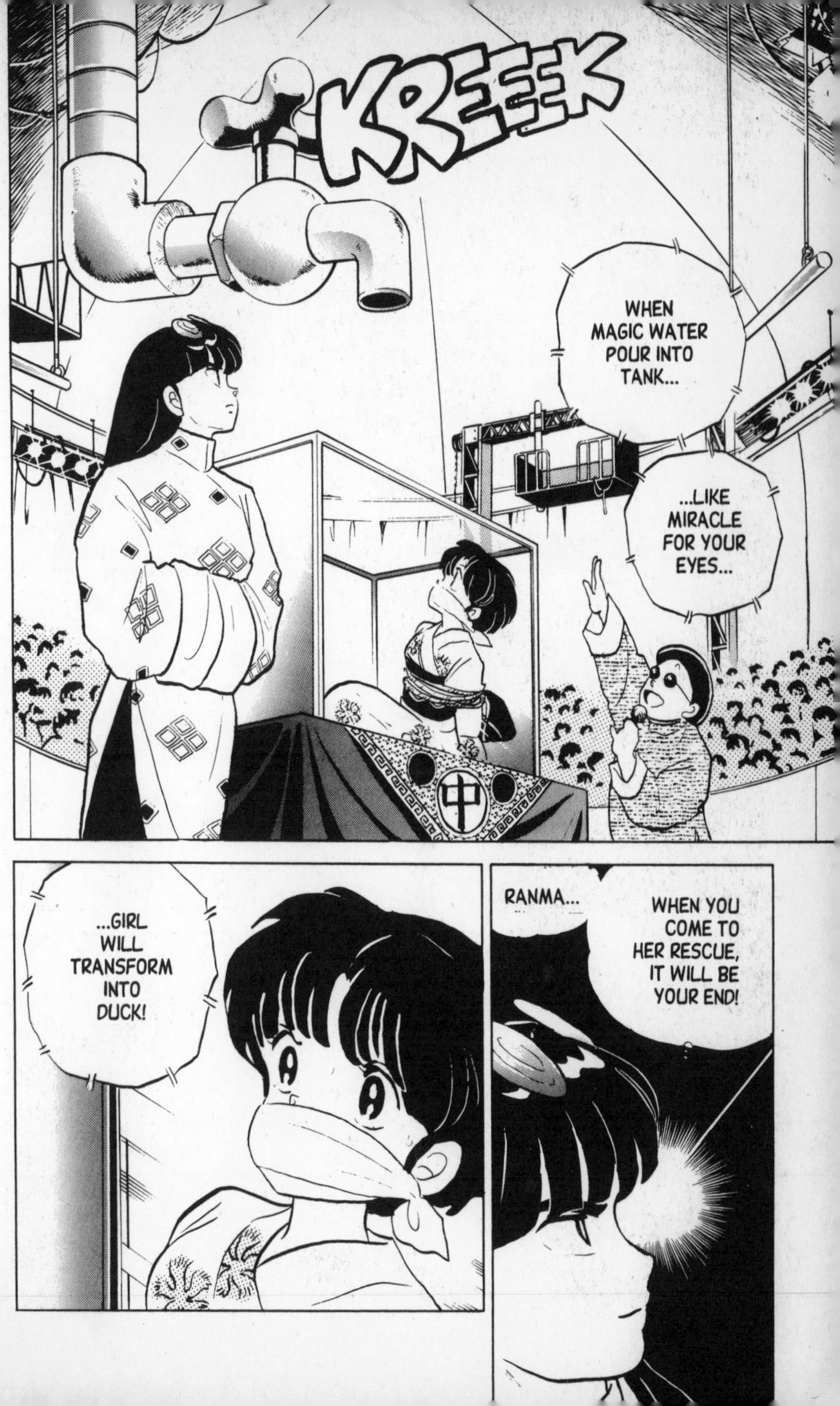
KREEEK
WHEN MAGIC WATER POUR INTO TANK...
...LIKE MIRACLE FOR YOUR EYES...
...GIRL WILL TRANSFORM INTO DUCK!
RANMA...
WHEN YOU COME TO HER RESCUE, IT WILL BE YOUR END!

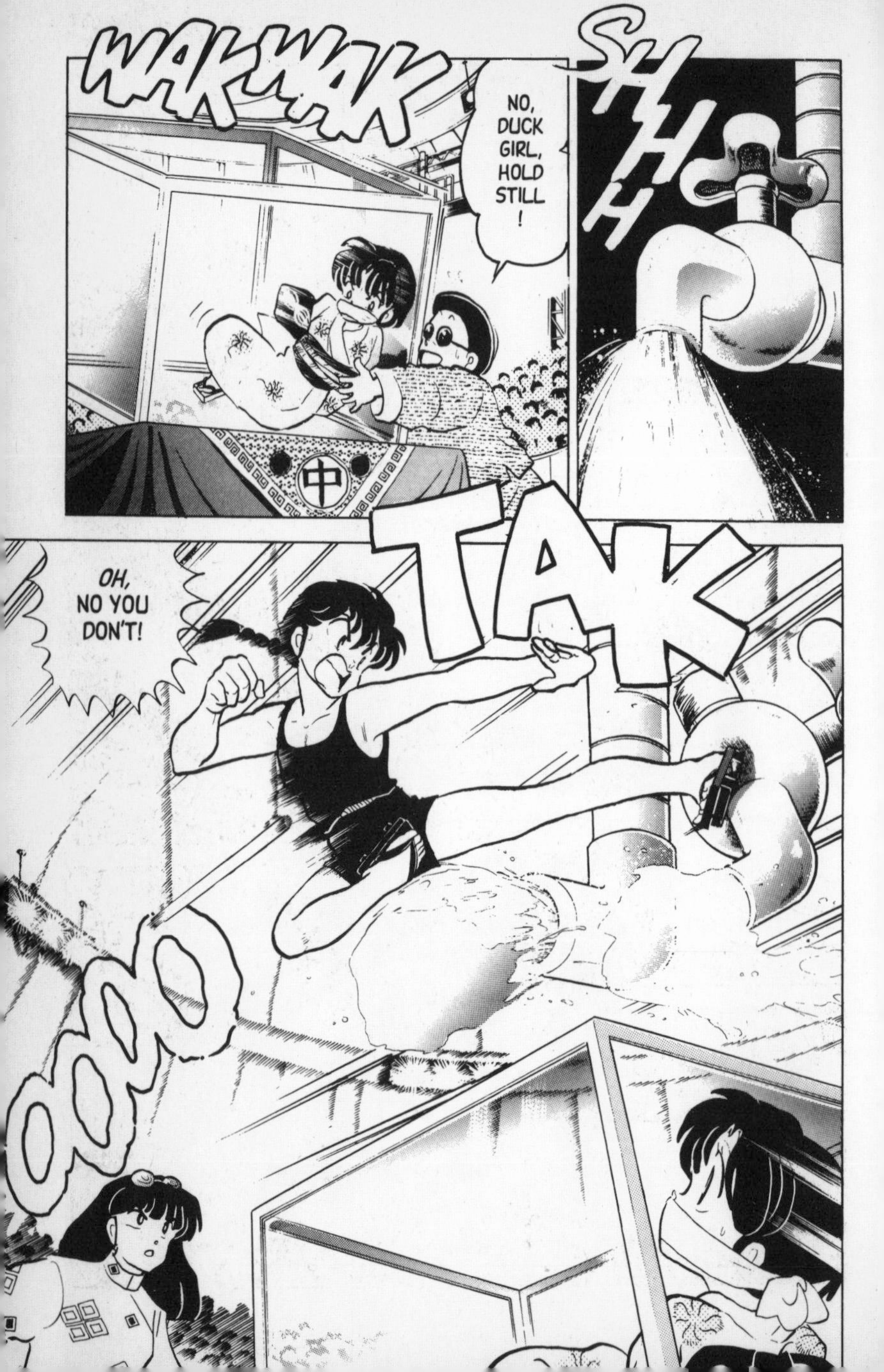

WAK WAK
NO, DUCK GIRL, HOLD STILL!
SHHH
OH, NO YOU DON'T!
TAK
OOOO

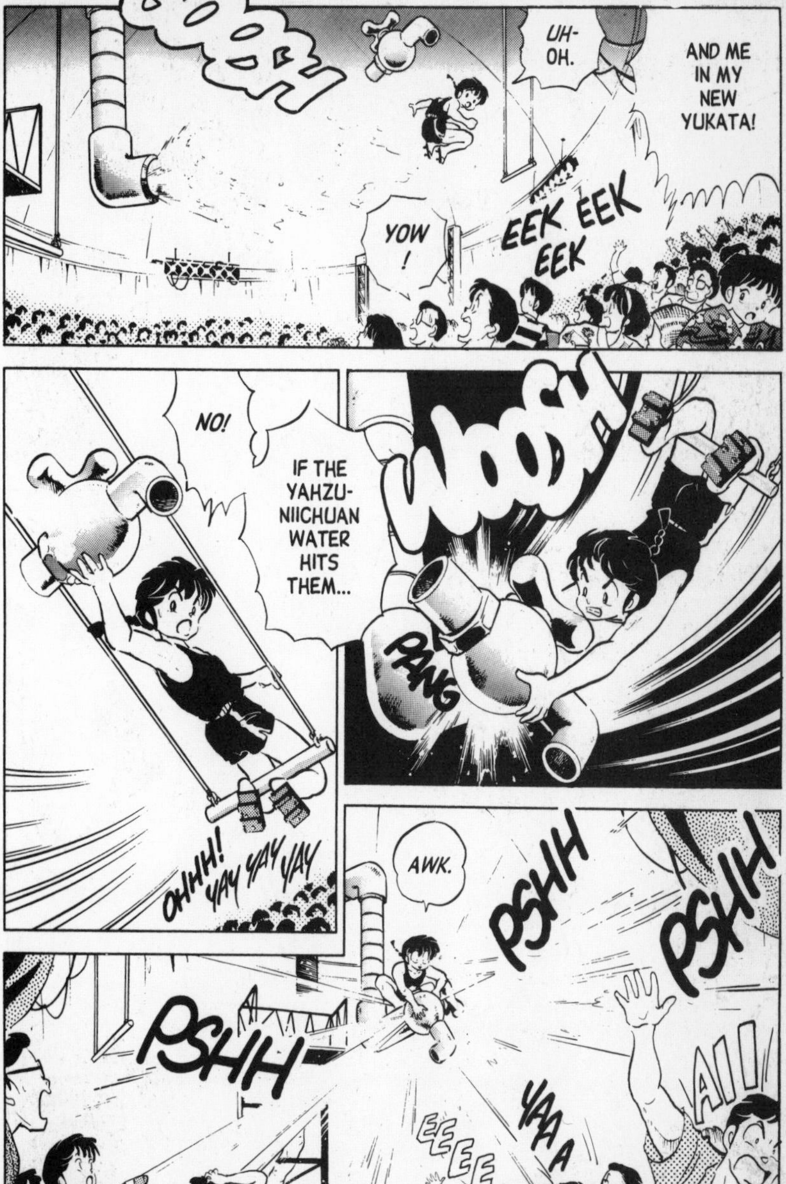
GOOSH
UH-OH.
AND ME IN MY NEW YUKATA!
YOW!
EEK EEK EEK
NO!
IF THE YAHZUNIICHUAN WATER HITS THEM...
OHHH! YAY YAY YAY
WOOSH
PANG
AWK.
PSHH
PSHH
PSHH
AII
YAAA
EEEE

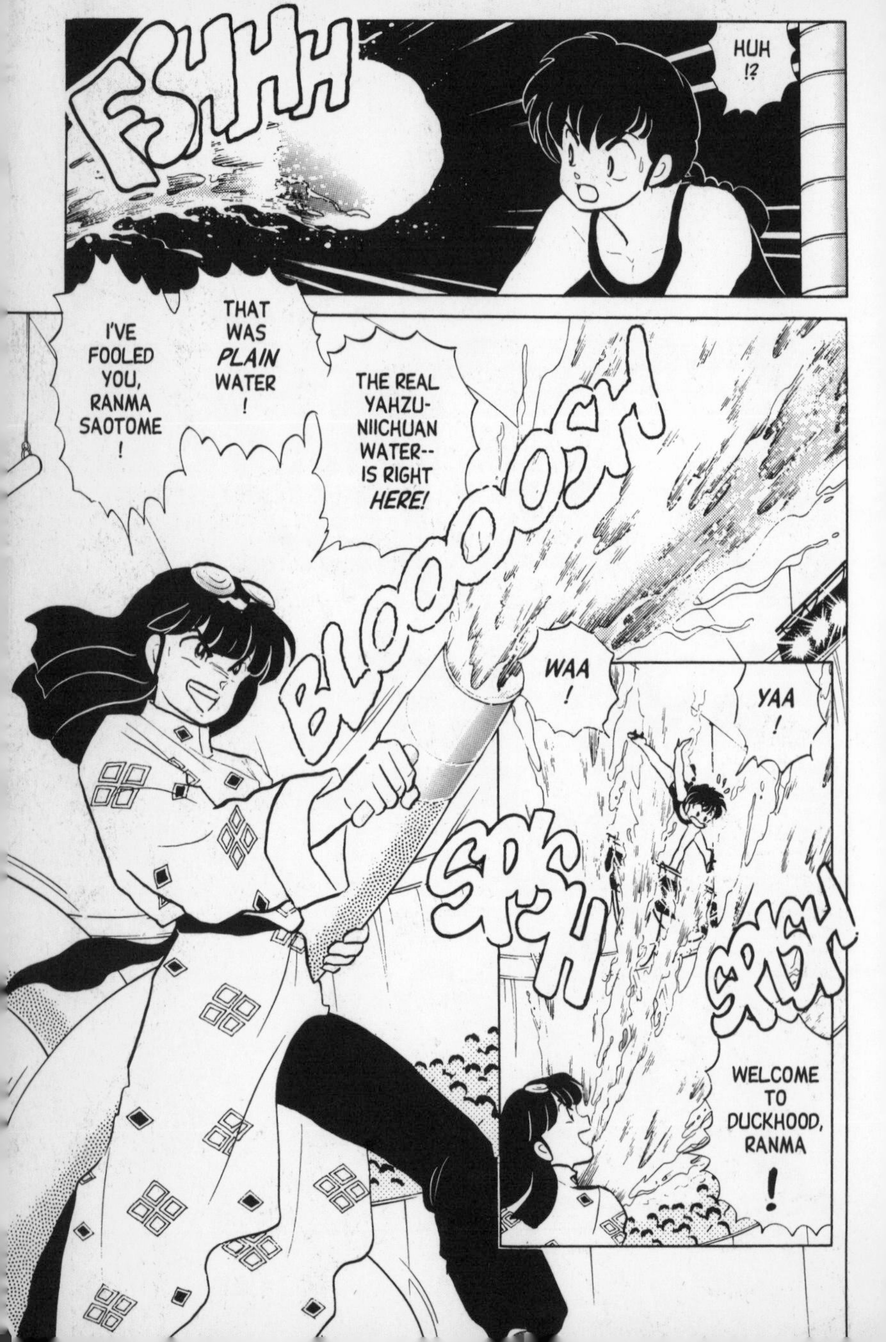
FSHHH
HUH !?
I'VE FOOLED YOU, RANMA SAOTOME !
THAT WAS *PLAIN* WATER !
THE REAL YAHZU-NIICHUAN WATER-- IS RIGHT *HERE!*
BLOOOOOSH!
WAA !
YAA !
SPLSH
SPLSH!
WELCOME TO DUCKHOOD, RANMA !

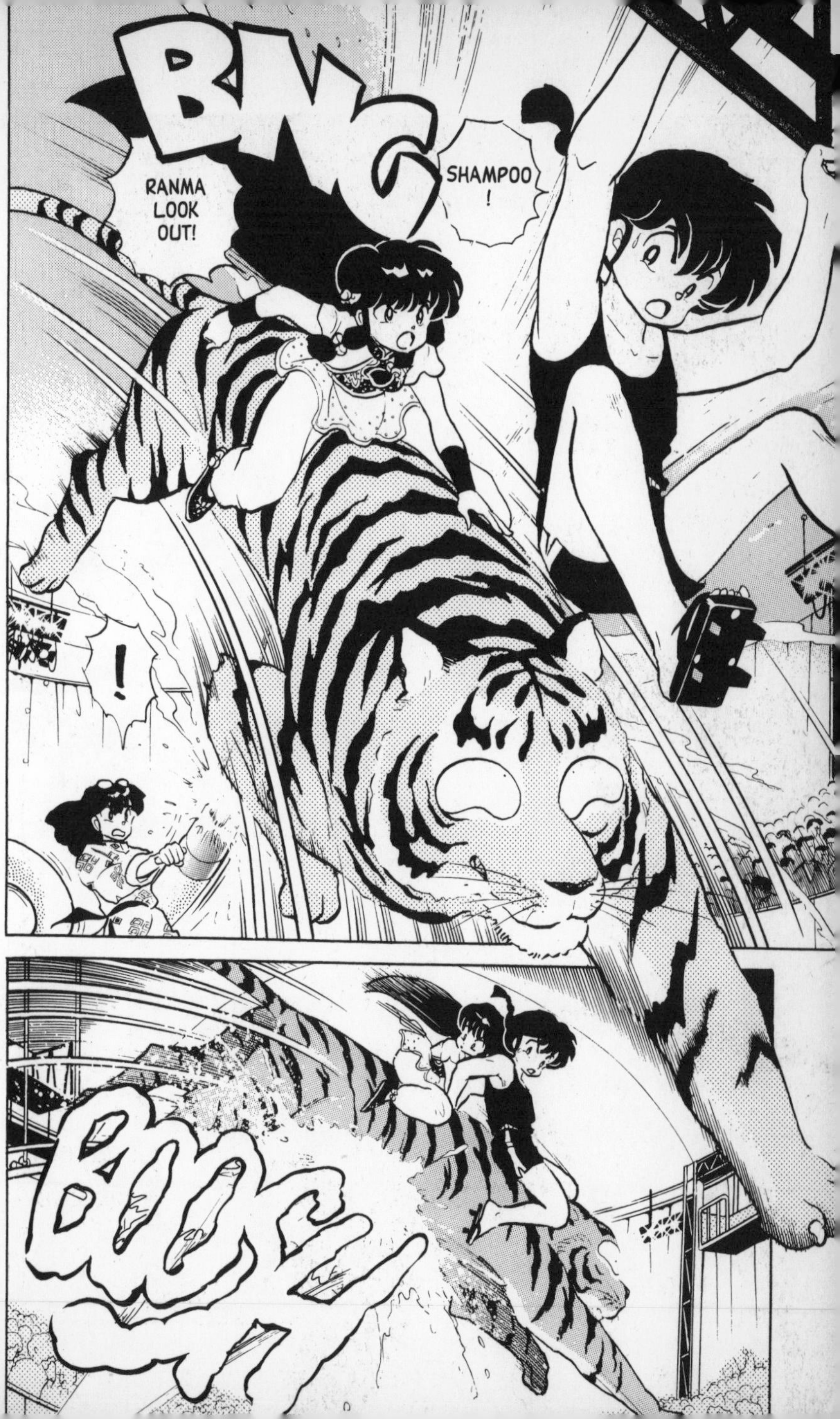
RANMA LOOK OUT!
SHAMPOO!
!

SHAMPOO....

AMAZING!

CLAP CLAP

HE TURNED THAT TIGER INTO A DUCK!

CLAP CLAP CLAP CLAP

OHHHH

THOP

QUAK QUAK

WHY!?

WHY DO YOU PROTECT RANMA?!

ANSWER ME, SHAMPOO!

WHY DON'T YOU...

OOBLE-OOBLE-OOBLE

ASK *HER*, MR. NEAR-SIGHTED!?

BOOT

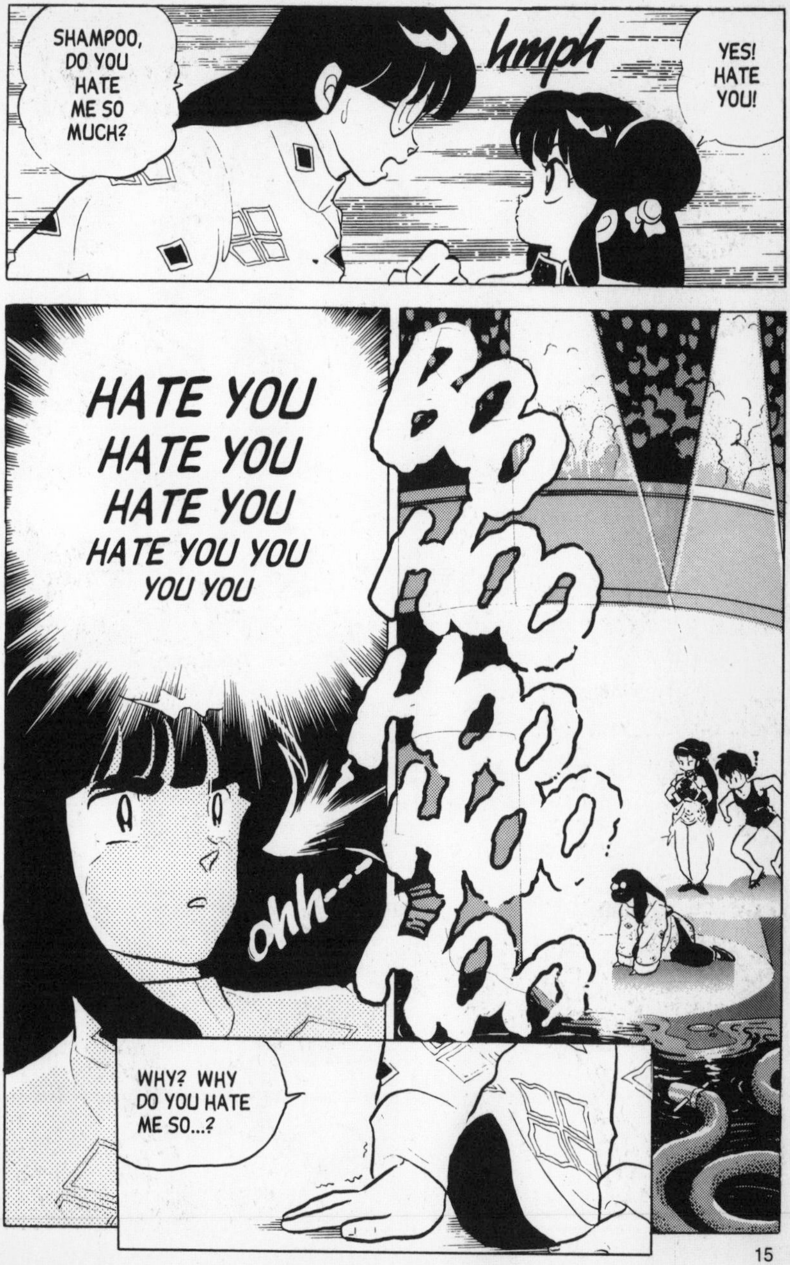
SHAMPOO, DO YOU HATE ME SO MUCH?
hmph
YES! HATE YOU!
HATE YOU HATE YOU HATE YOU HATE YOU YOU YOU YOU
BOO HOO HOO HOO
ohh
WHY? WHY DO YOU HATE ME SO...?

SINCE WE WERE CHILDREN, I'VE WATCHED OVER YOU...

SHAMPOO

WHERE YOU LOOKING, MOUSSE!?

DREAMED OF WHEN WE'D BE ONE...

SHAMPOO, MARRY ME...

RNK

OH, HOW HEARTBREAKING... SOB SOB SOB SOB SOB SOB SOB SOB SOB SOB SOB SOB

CHEER UP, MOUSSE.

SPAP

RANMA...?

YOU'RE IN LOVE WITH SHAMPOO, RIGHT?

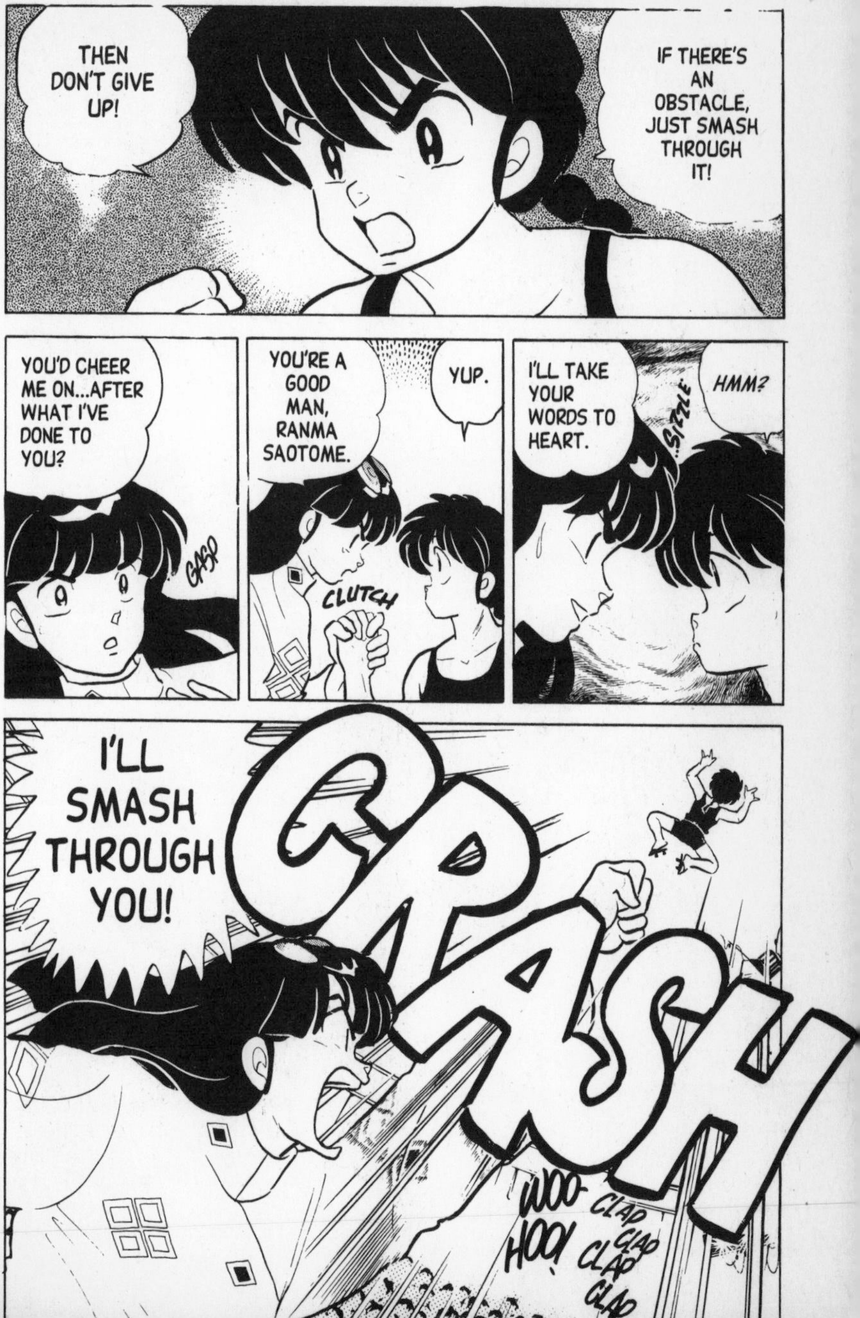
THEN DON'T GIVE UP!
IF THERE'S AN OBSTACLE, JUST SMASH THROUGH IT!
YOU'D CHEER ME ON...AFTER WHAT I'VE DONE TO YOU?
GASP
YOU'RE A GOOD MAN, RANMA SAOTOME.
YUP.
CLUTCH
I'LL TAKE YOUR WORDS TO HEART.
...SIZZLE
HMM?
I'LL SMASH THROUGH YOU!
CRASH
WOO-HOO!
CLAP CLAP CLAP CLAP

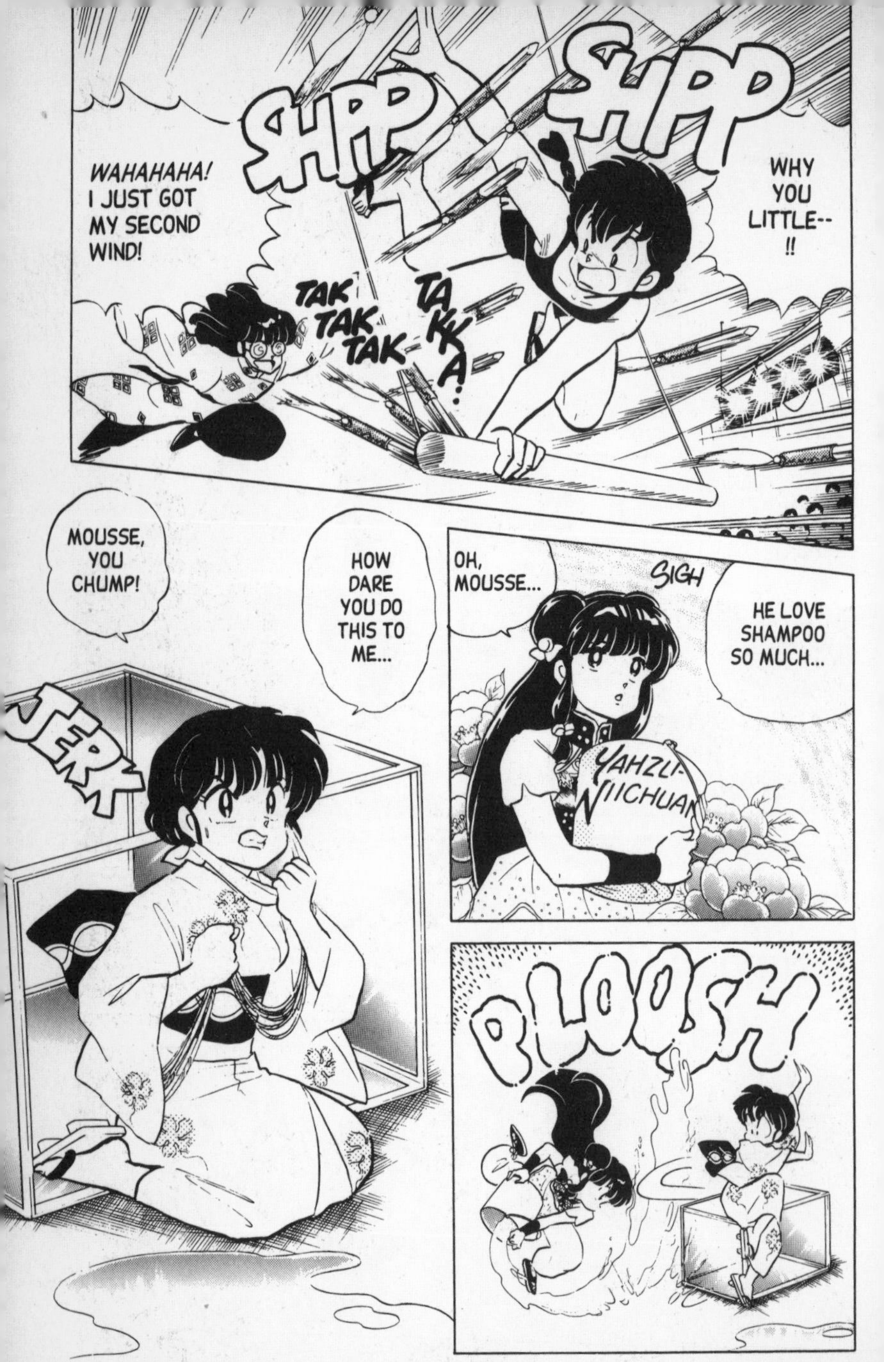

SHPP SHPP
WAHAHAHA! I JUST GOT MY SECOND WIND!
WHY YOU LITTLE-- !!
TAK TAK TAK
TAKKA!
MOUSSE, YOU CHUMP!
HOW DARE YOU DO THIS TO ME...
JERK
OH, MOUSSE...
SIGH
HE LOVE SHAMPOO SO MUCH...
YAHZLI-NIICHUAN
PLOOSH

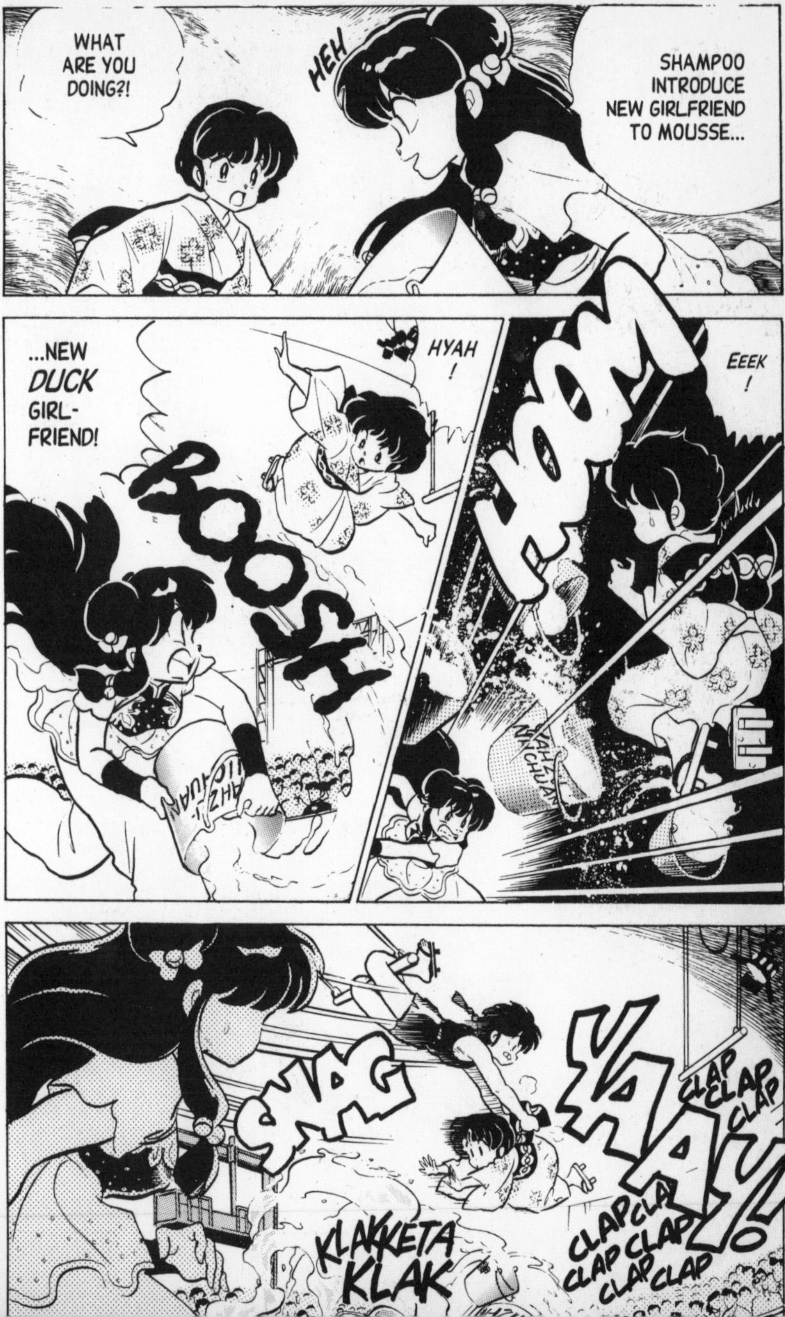
WHAT ARE YOU DOING?!
HEH
SHAMPOO INTRODUCE NEW GIRLFRIEND TO MOUSSE...
...NEW DUCK GIRL-FRIEND!
HYAH!
BOOSH
WHOOM
EEEK!
SMAG
YAY!
CLAP CLAP CLAP
KLAKKETA KLAK
CLAP CLAP CLAP CLAP CLAP CLAP CLAP

YOUR
DAYS
ARE
DONE
!!

GYAKK!

BANG

OOO

SORRY,
MOUSSE...

VP

...FEATHERS
DON'T
SUIT
ME!

VVVIP

VVLOP

SPHOOOOO
OOOO

TONK

HUH
?!

BOING

UH-OH!
GOTTA
STOP IT
BEFORE--

SKINCH

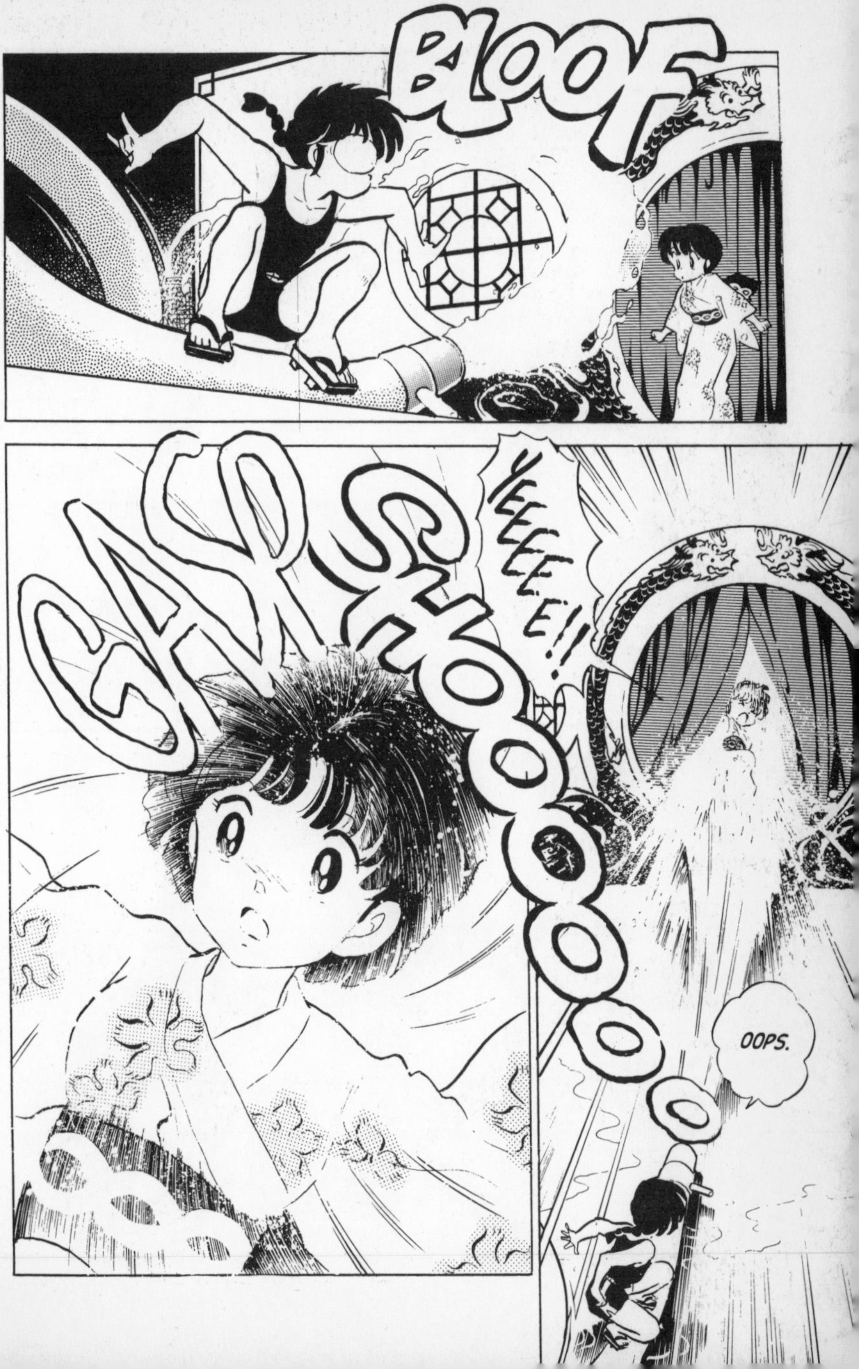
BLOOF
YEEEEE!!
GASHOOOOOOOOO
OOPS.

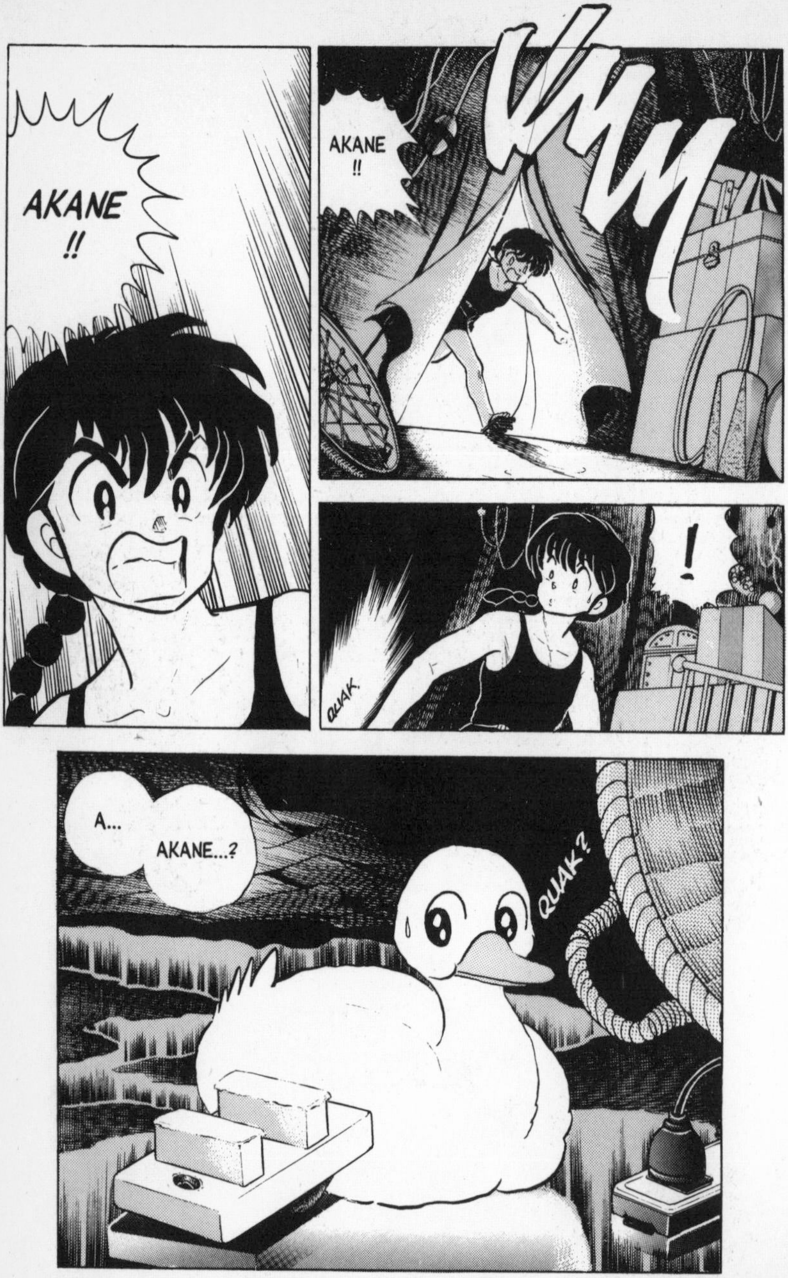
AKANE !!
AKANE !!
VMM
!
QUAK
A... AKANE...?
QUAK?

Part 2

FOWL PLAY

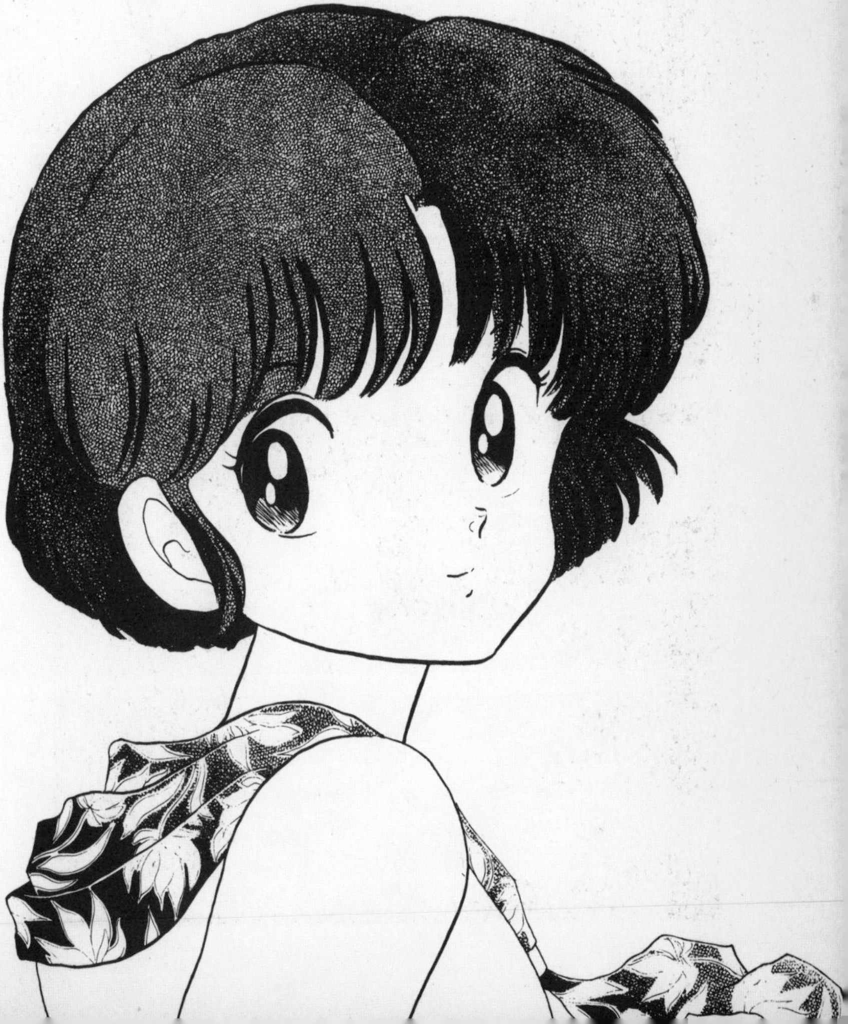

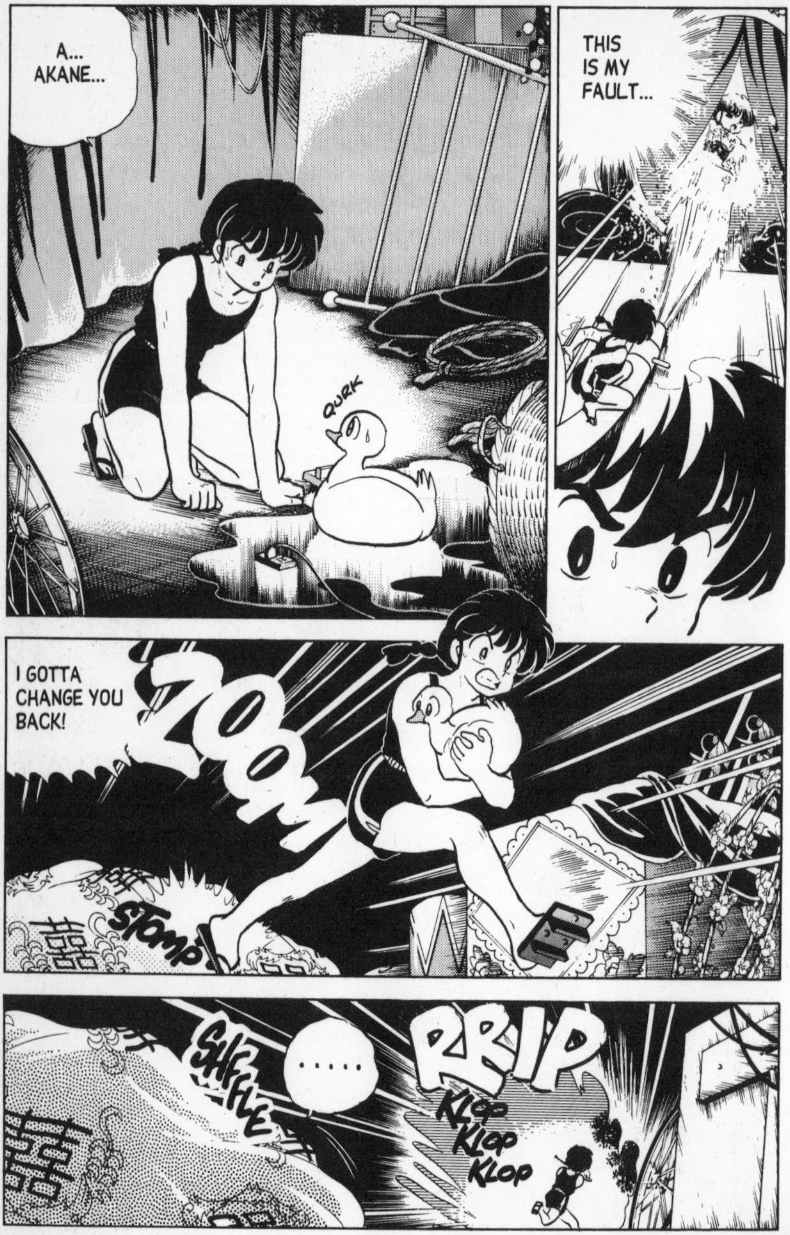
A... AKANE...
QURK
THIS IS MY FAULT...
I GOTTA CHANGE YOU BACK!
ZOOM
STOMP
SHFFLE
......
RRIP
KLOP KLOP KLOP

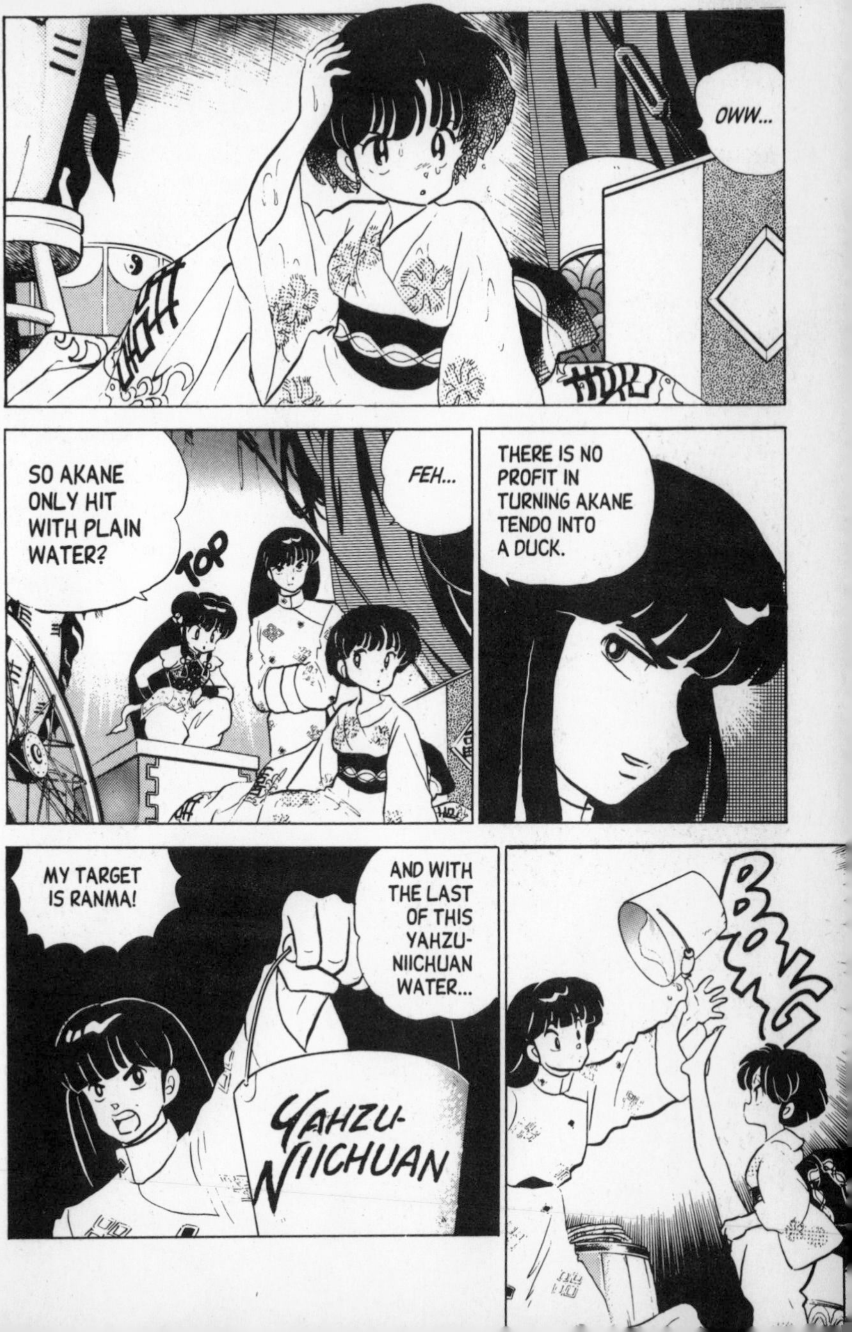
OWW...
SO AKANE ONLY HIT WITH PLAIN WATER?
TOP
FEH...
THERE IS NO PROFIT IN TURNING AKANE TENDO INTO A DUCK.
MY TARGET IS RANMA!
AND WITH THE LAST OF THIS YAHZU-NIICHUAN WATER...
YAHZU-NIICHUAN

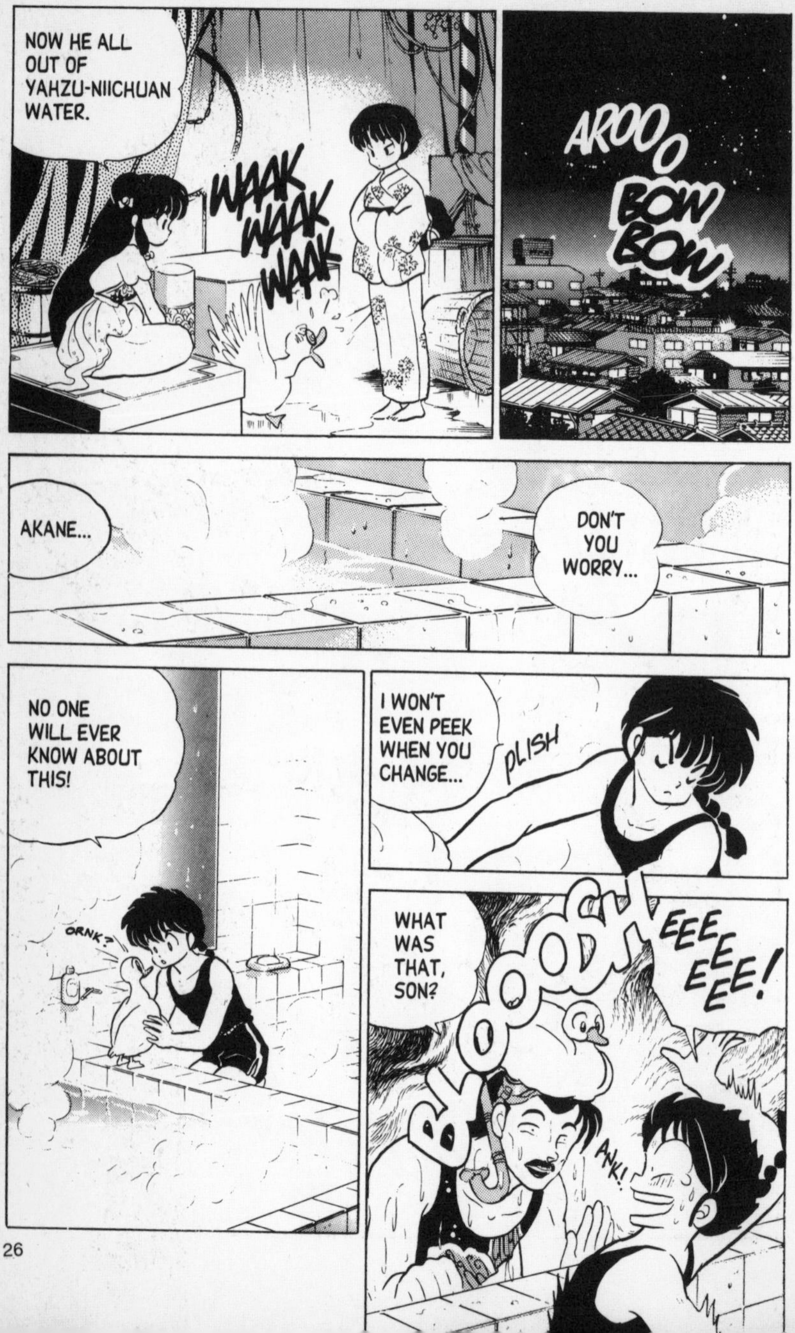

NOW HE ALL OUT OF YAHZU-NIICHUAN WATER.
WAAK WAAK WAAK
AROOOO BOW BOW
AKANE...
DON'T YOU WORRY...
NO ONE WILL EVER KNOW ABOUT THIS!
ORNK?
I WON'T EVEN PEEK WHEN YOU CHANGE...
PLISH
WHAT WAS THAT, SON?
BLOOOOSH
EEEEEEEE!
ANK!

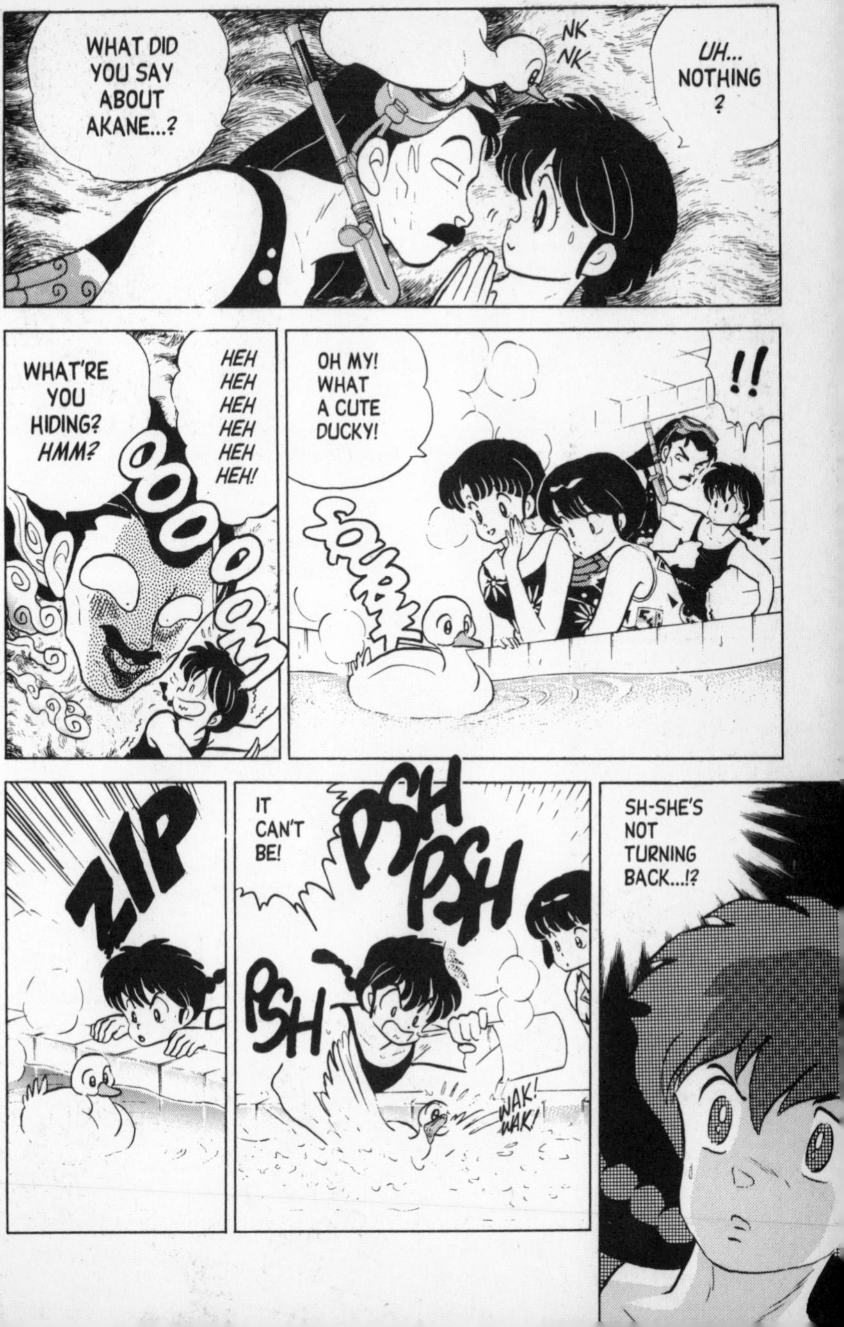
WHAT DID YOU SAY ABOUT AKANE...?
NK NK
UH... NOTHING ?
WHAT'RE YOU HIDING? HMM?
HEH HEH HEH HEH HEH HEH!
OOOOOOM
OH MY! WHAT A CUTE DUCKY!
SQUEAK
!!
ZIP
IT CAN'T BE!
PSH PSH
PSH
WAK! WAK!
SH-SHE'S NOT TURNING BACK...!?

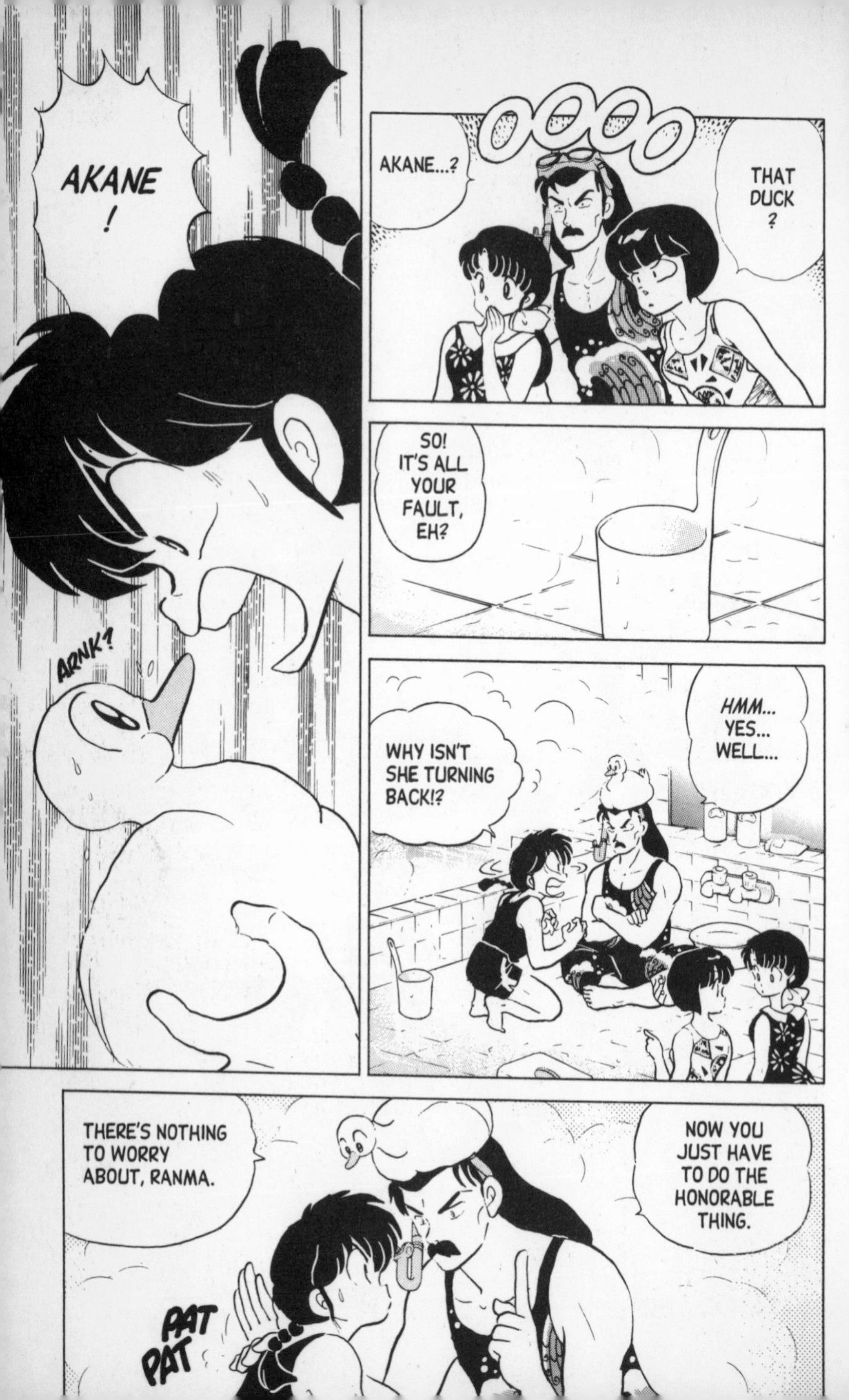
AKANE!
ARNK?
AKANE...?
THAT DUCK?
SO! IT'S ALL YOUR FAULT, EH?
WHY ISN'T SHE TURNING BACK!?
HMM... YES... WELL...
THERE'S NOTHING TO WORRY ABOUT, RANMA.
NOW YOU JUST HAVE TO DO THE HONORABLE THING.
PAT PAT

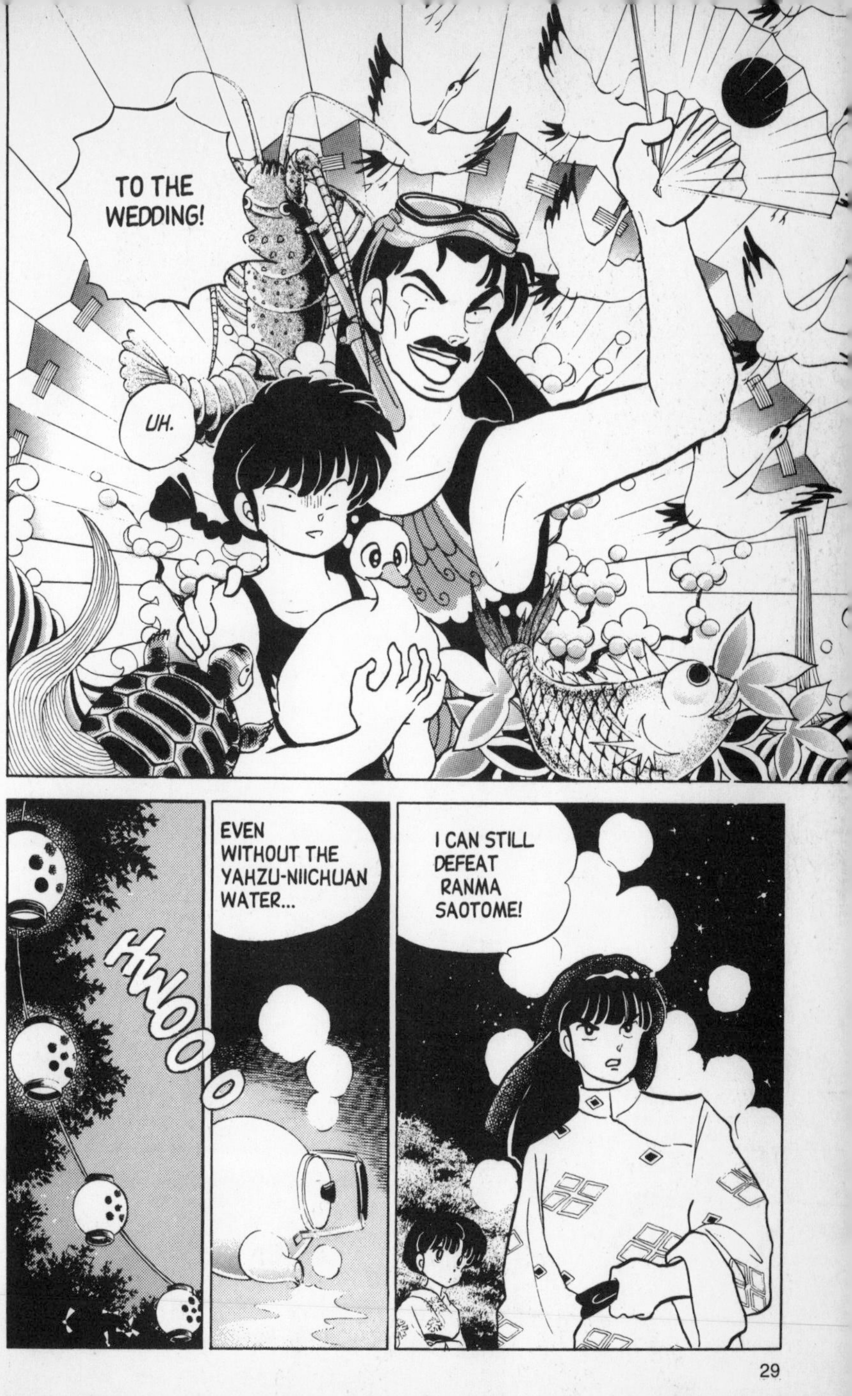
TO THE WEDDING!
UH.
HWOOO
EVEN WITHOUT THE YAHZU-NIICHUAN WATER...
I CAN STILL DEFEAT RANMA SAOTOME!

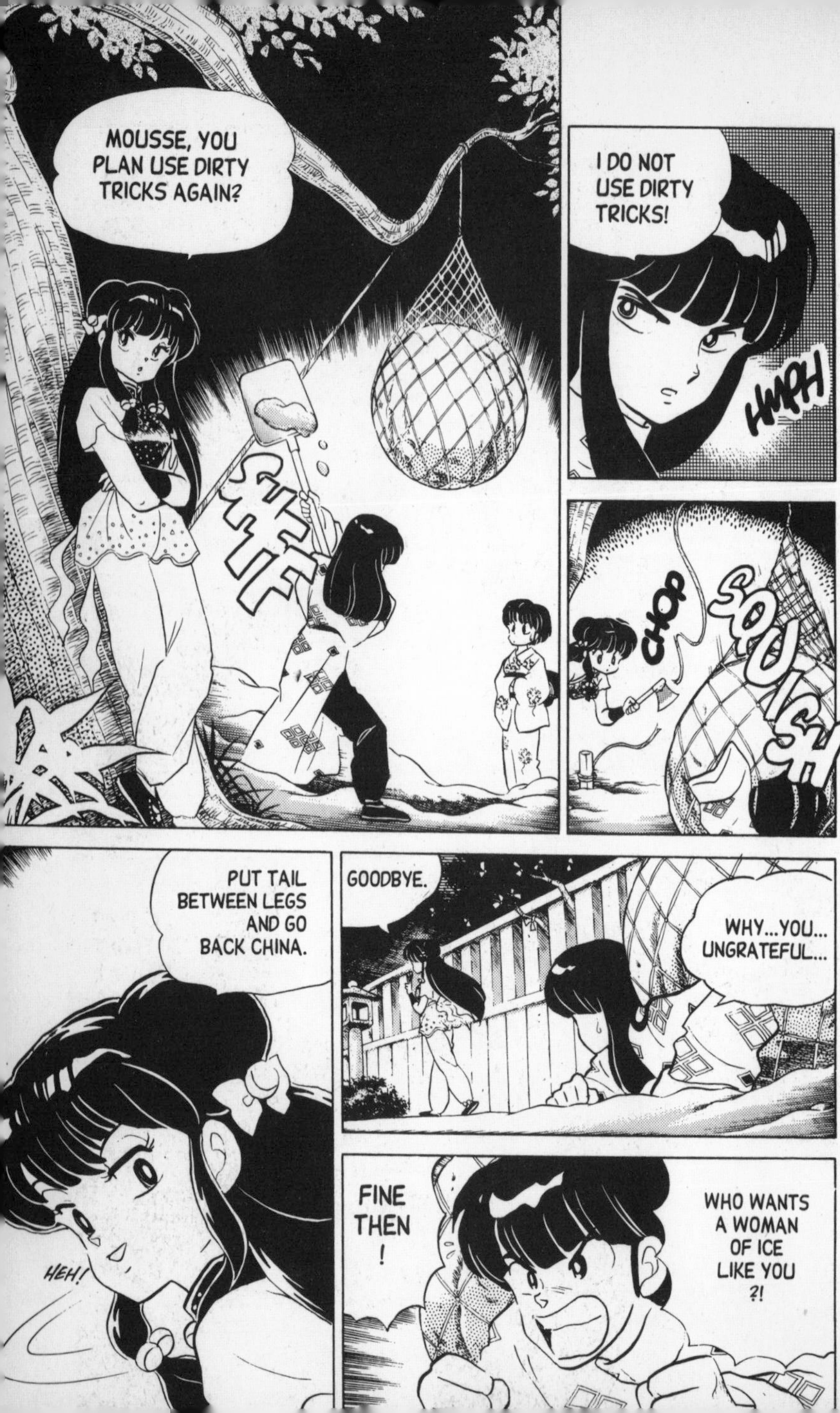
MOUSSE, YOU PLAN USE DIRTY TRICKS AGAIN?
SHFF
I DO NOT USE DIRTY TRICKS!
HMPH
CHOP
SQUISH
PUT TAIL BETWEEN LEGS AND GO BACK CHINA.
HEH!
GOODBYE.
WHY...YOU... UNGRATEFUL...
FINE THEN !
WHO WANTS A WOMAN OF ICE LIKE YOU ?!

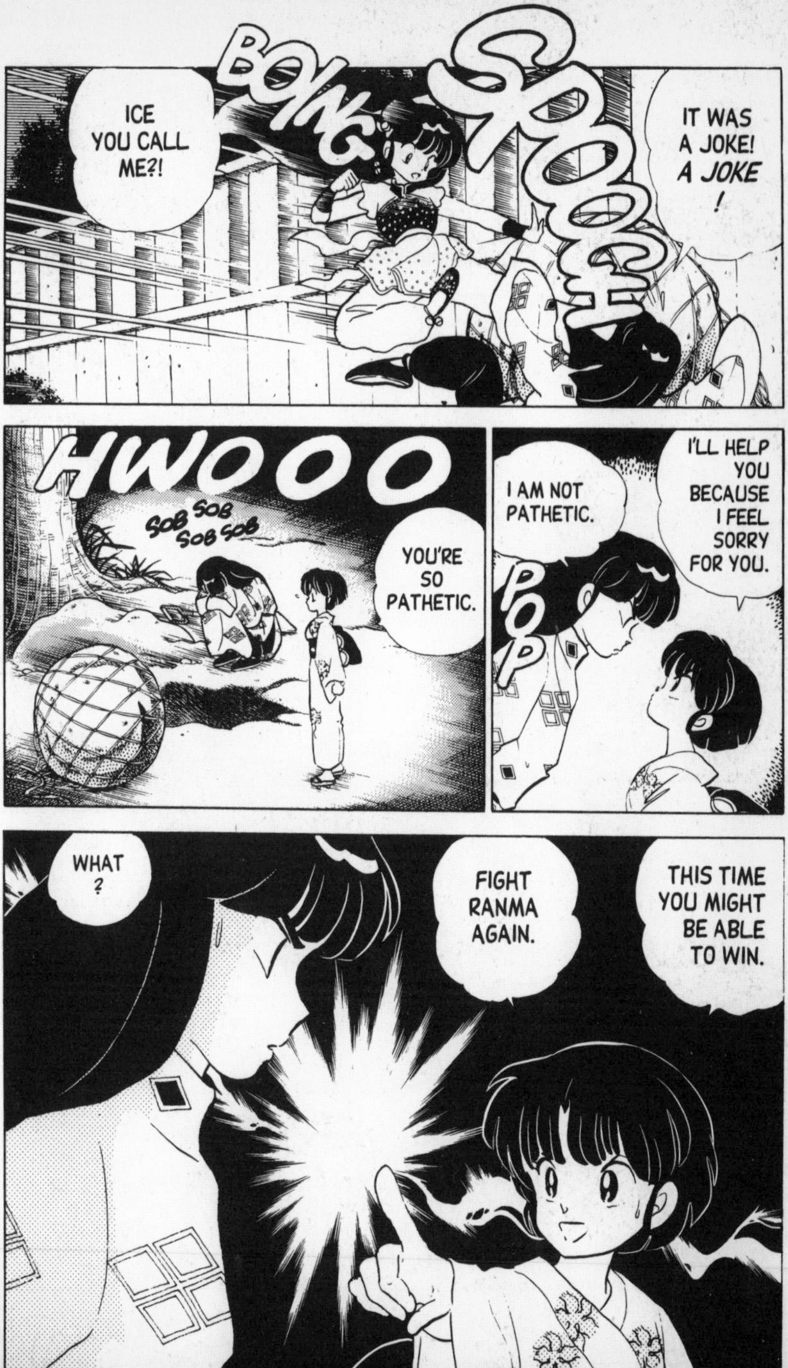
BOING
ICE YOU CALL ME?!
SQOOCH
IT WAS A JOKE! A JOKE!
HWOOO
SOB SOB SOB SOB
YOU'RE SO PATHETIC.
I AM NOT PATHETIC.
POP
I'LL HELP YOU BECAUSE I FEEL SORRY FOR YOU.
WHAT?
FIGHT RANMA AGAIN.
THIS TIME YOU MIGHT BE ABLE TO WIN.

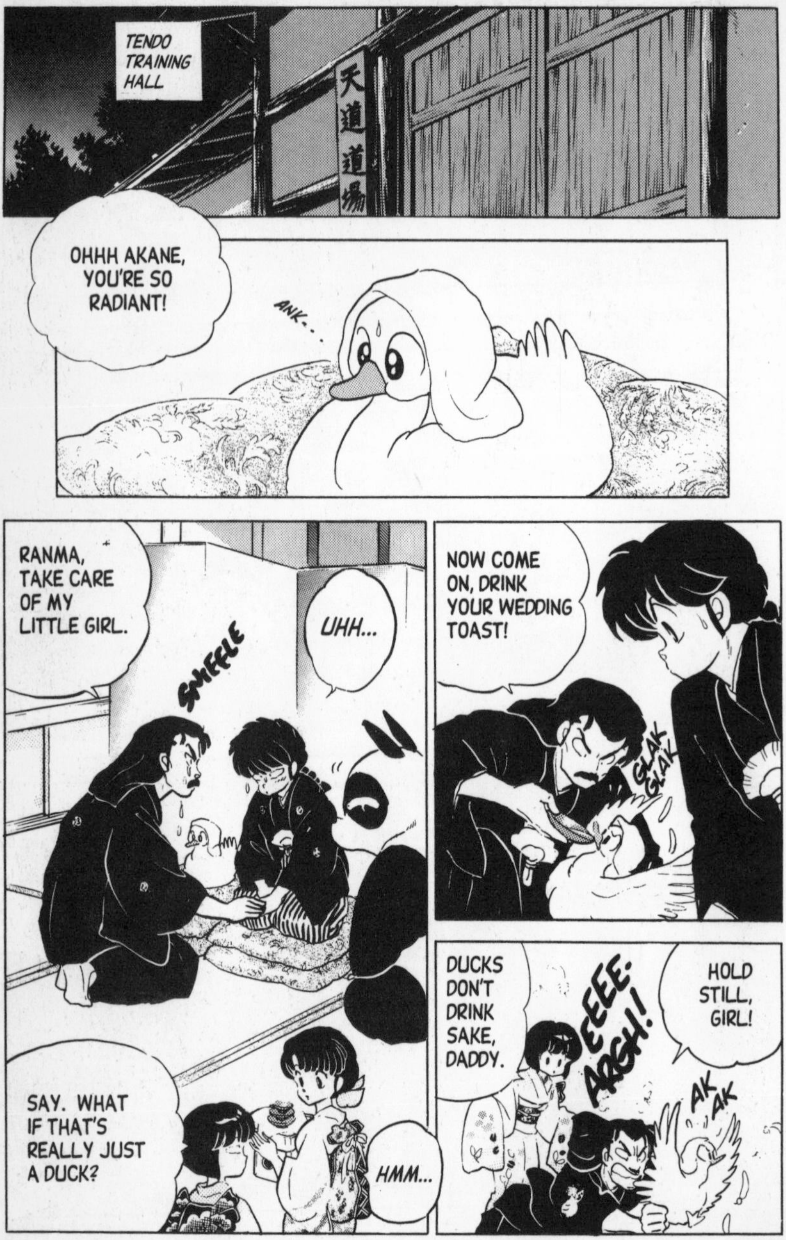
TENDO TRAINING HALL
天道道場
OHHH AKANE, YOU'RE SO RADIANT!
ANK...
RANMA, TAKE CARE OF MY LITTLE GIRL.
SHUFFLE
UHH...
SAY. WHAT IF THAT'S REALLY JUST A DUCK?
HMM...
NOW COME ON, DRINK YOUR WEDDING TOAST!
GLAK GLAK
DUCKS DON'T DRINK SAKE, DADDY.
EEEE- ARGH!
HOLD STILL, GIRL!
AK AK

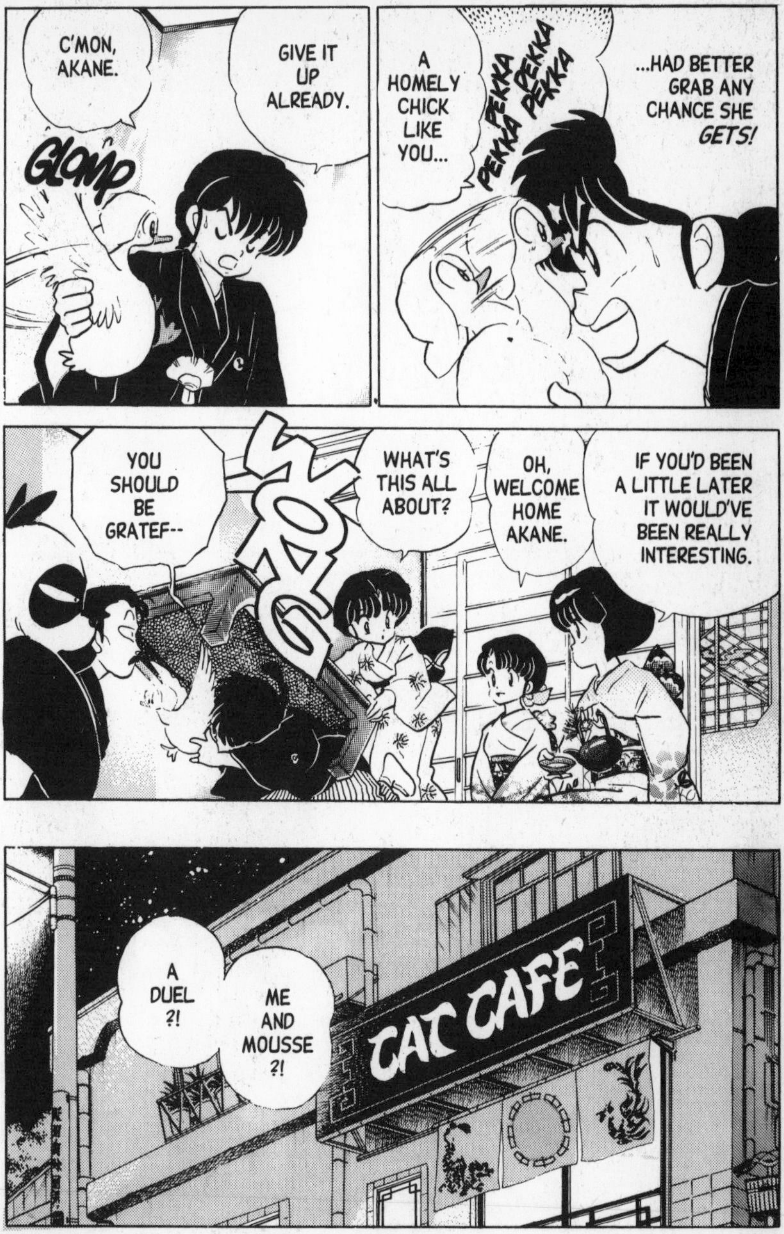
C'MON, AKANE.
GLOMP
GIVE IT UP ALREADY.
A HOMELY CHICK LIKE YOU...
PEKKA PEKKA PEKKA PEKKA
...HAD BETTER GRAB ANY CHANCE SHE GETS!
YOU SHOULD BE GRATEF--
YOINK
WHAT'S THIS ALL ABOUT?
OH, WELCOME HOME AKANE.
IF YOU'D BEEN A LITTLE LATER IT WOULD'VE BEEN REALLY INTERESTING.
A DUEL ?!
ME AND MOUSSE ?!
CAT CAFE

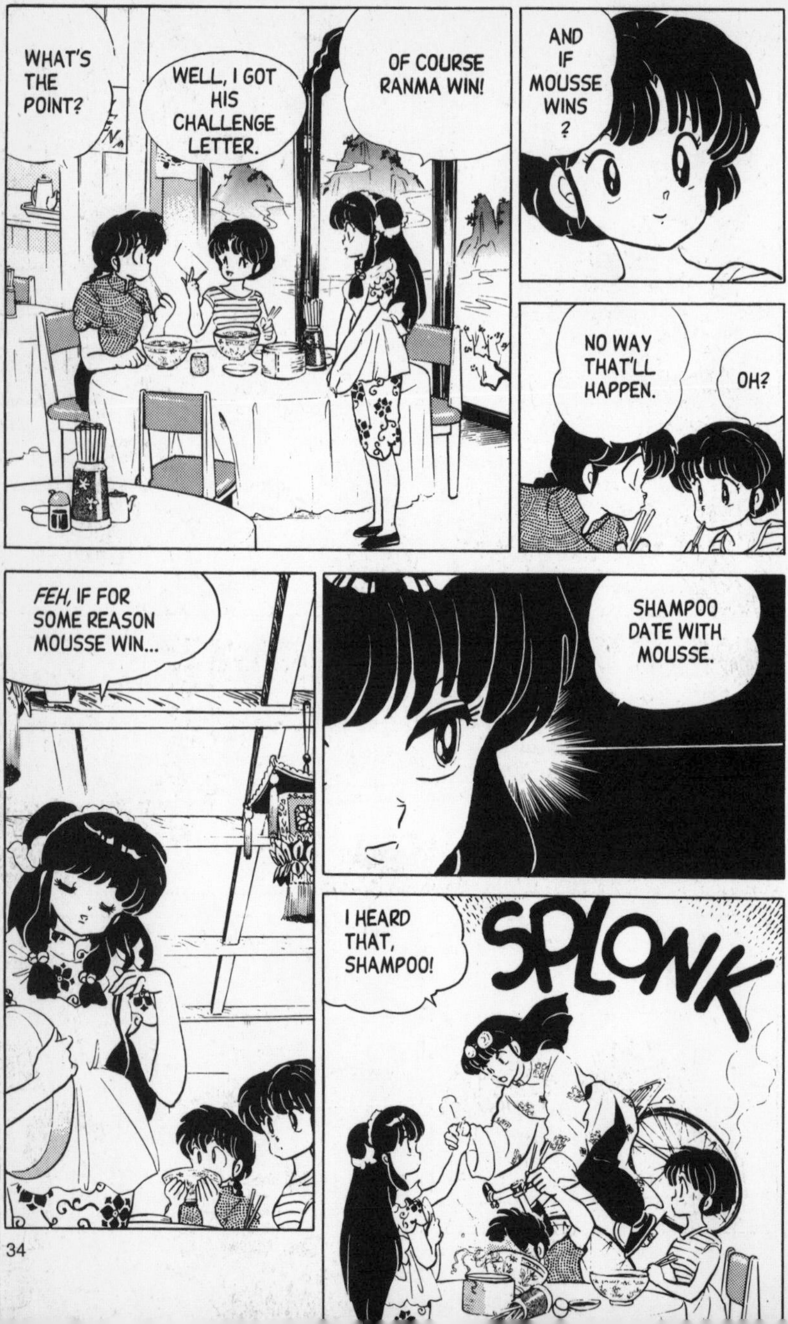
WHAT'S THE POINT?
WELL, I GOT HIS CHALLENGE LETTER.
OF COURSE RANMA WIN!
AND IF MOUSSE WINS?
NO WAY THAT'LL HAPPEN.
OH?
FEH, IF FOR SOME REASON MOUSSE WIN...
SHAMPOO DATE WITH MOUSSE.
I HEARD THAT, SHAMPOO!
SPLONK

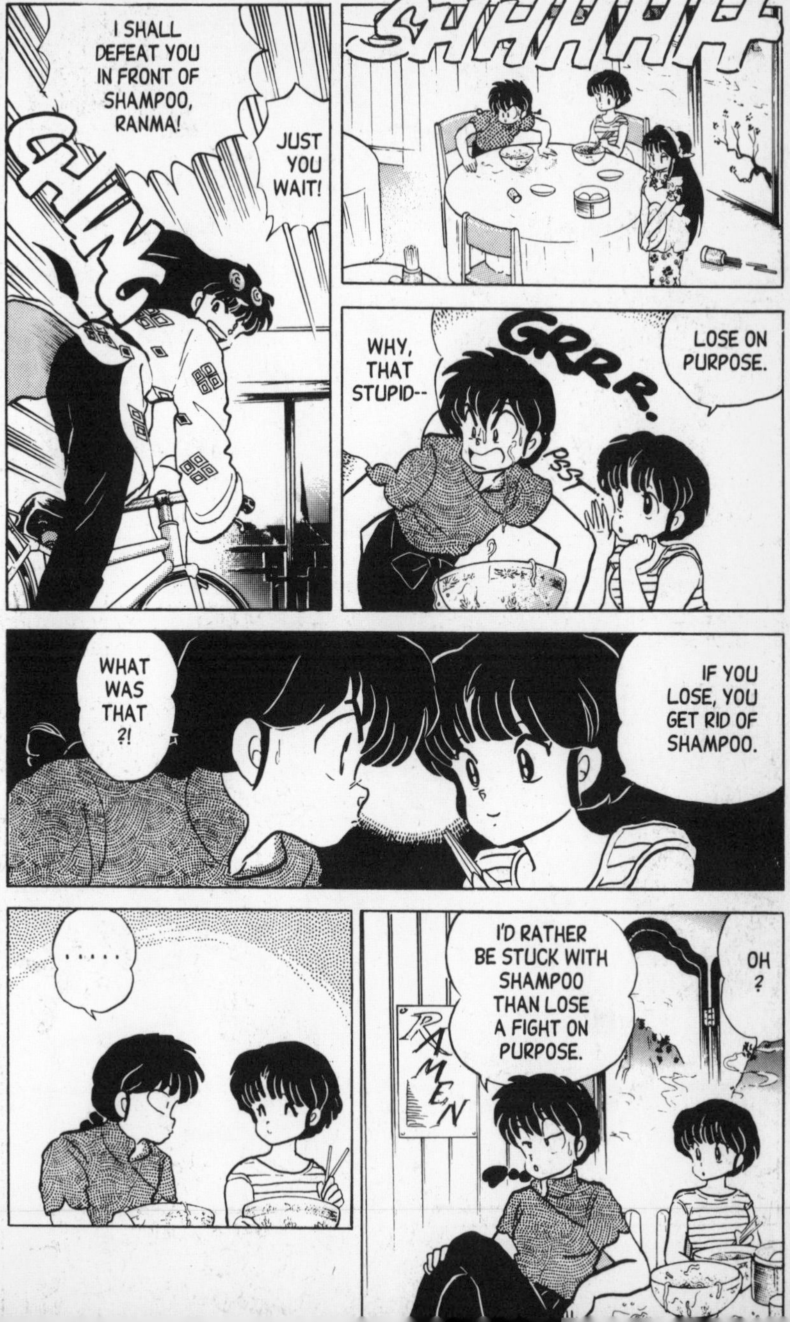
I SHALL DEFEAT YOU IN FRONT OF SHAMPOO, RANMA!
JUST YOU WAIT!
CHING
SHHHHHH
WHY, THAT STUPID--
GRRR.
LOSE ON PURPOSE.
PSST
WHAT WAS THAT ?!
IF YOU LOSE, YOU GET RID OF SHAMPOO.
......
I'D RATHER BE STUCK WITH SHAMPOO THAN LOSE A FIGHT ON PURPOSE.
RAMEN
OH ?

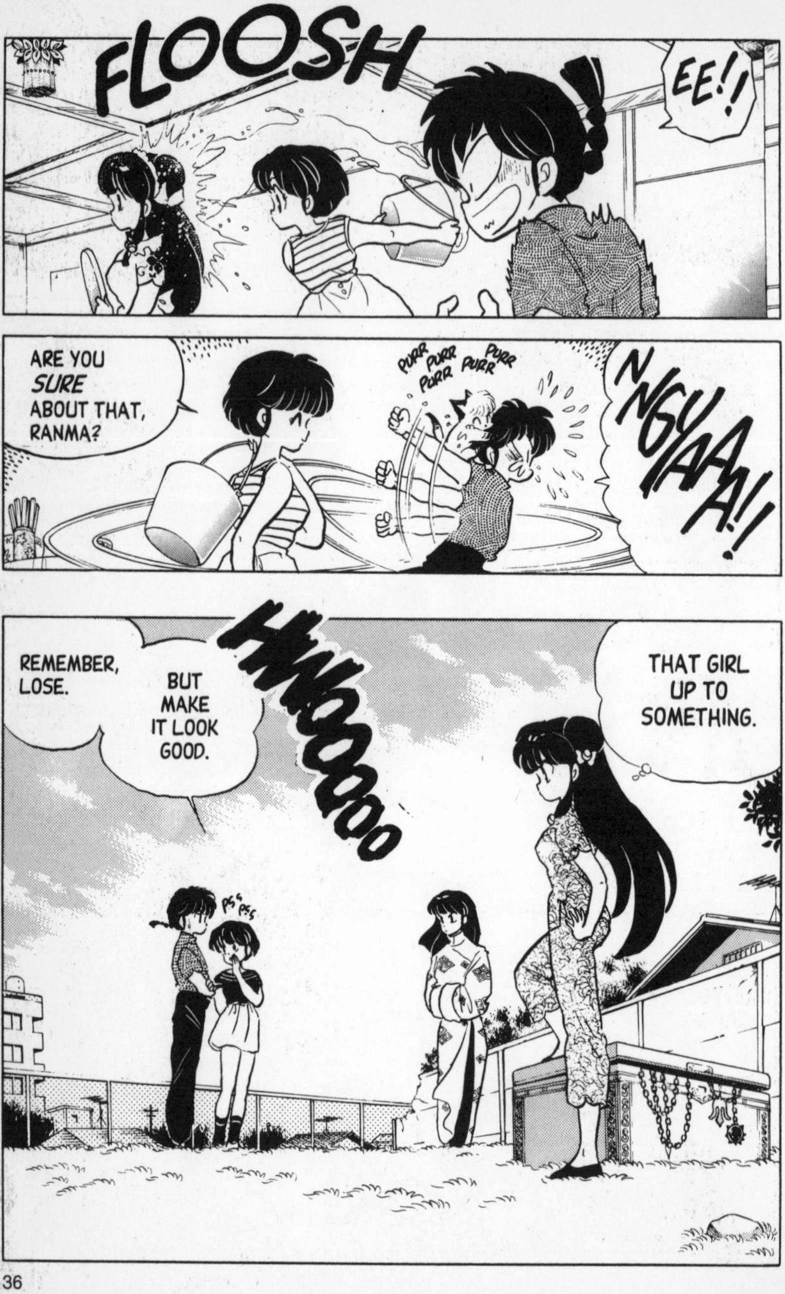
FLOOSH
EE!!
ARE YOU SURE ABOUT THAT, RANMA?
PURR PURR PURR PURR PURR
NNGYAAAA!!
REMEMBER, LOSE.
BUT MAKE IT LOOK GOOD.
HWOOOOOO
THAT GIRL UP TO SOMETHING.

NO LET YOU LOSE, RANMA.

SH

MOUSSE!

THOP

WH-WHAT'S THIS...?

I AM INVINCIBLE!

BOO HOO

GOOD LUCK MOUSSE!

SHAMPOO MAKE SPECIAL WEAPON FOR MOUSSE.

SH-SHAMPOO... YOU...YOU MADE THIS FOR ME...?

SOB

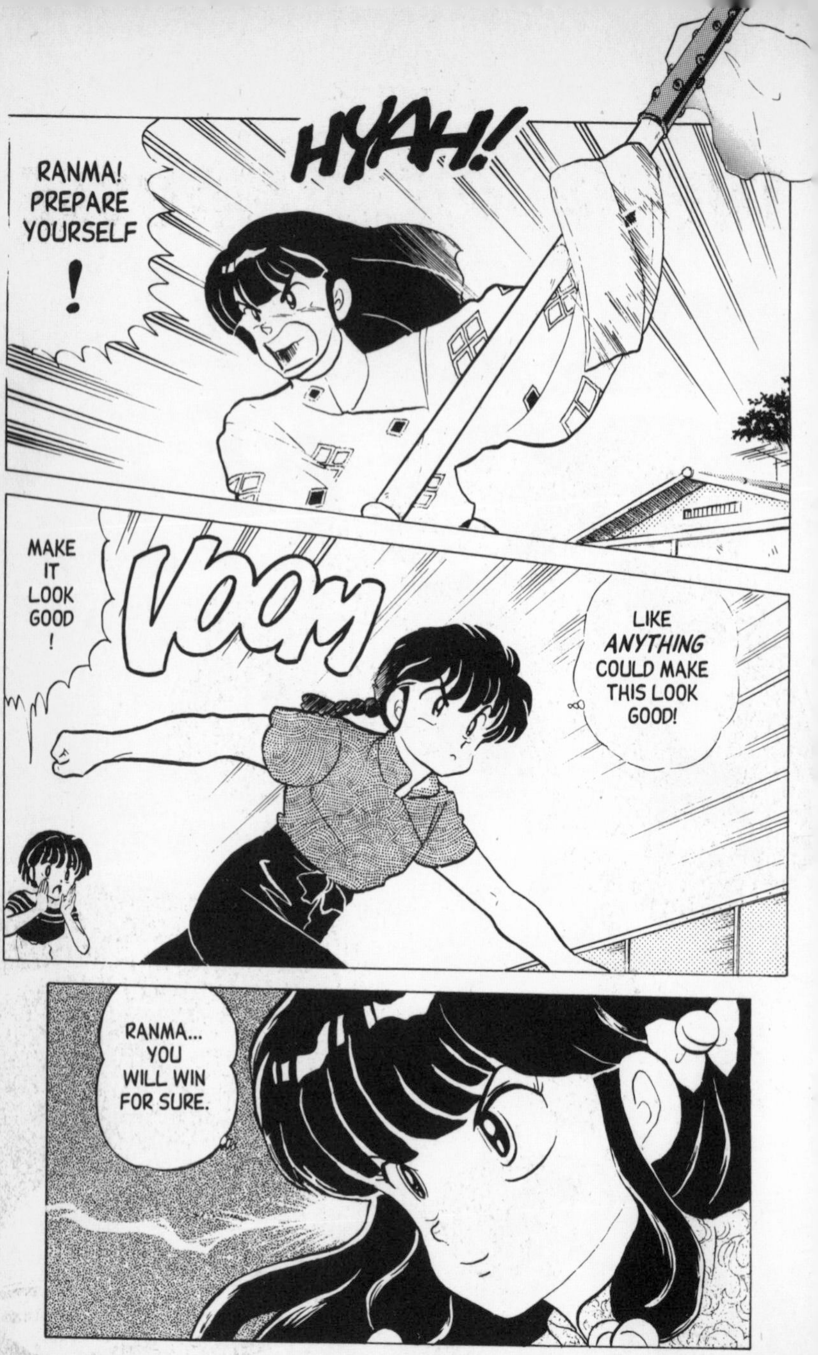
HYAH!
RANMA! PREPARE YOURSELF !
MAKE IT LOOK GOOD !
VOOM
LIKE ANYTHING COULD MAKE THIS LOOK GOOD!
RANMA... YOU WILL WIN FOR SURE.

Part 3

THE HAPPIEST MOUSSE

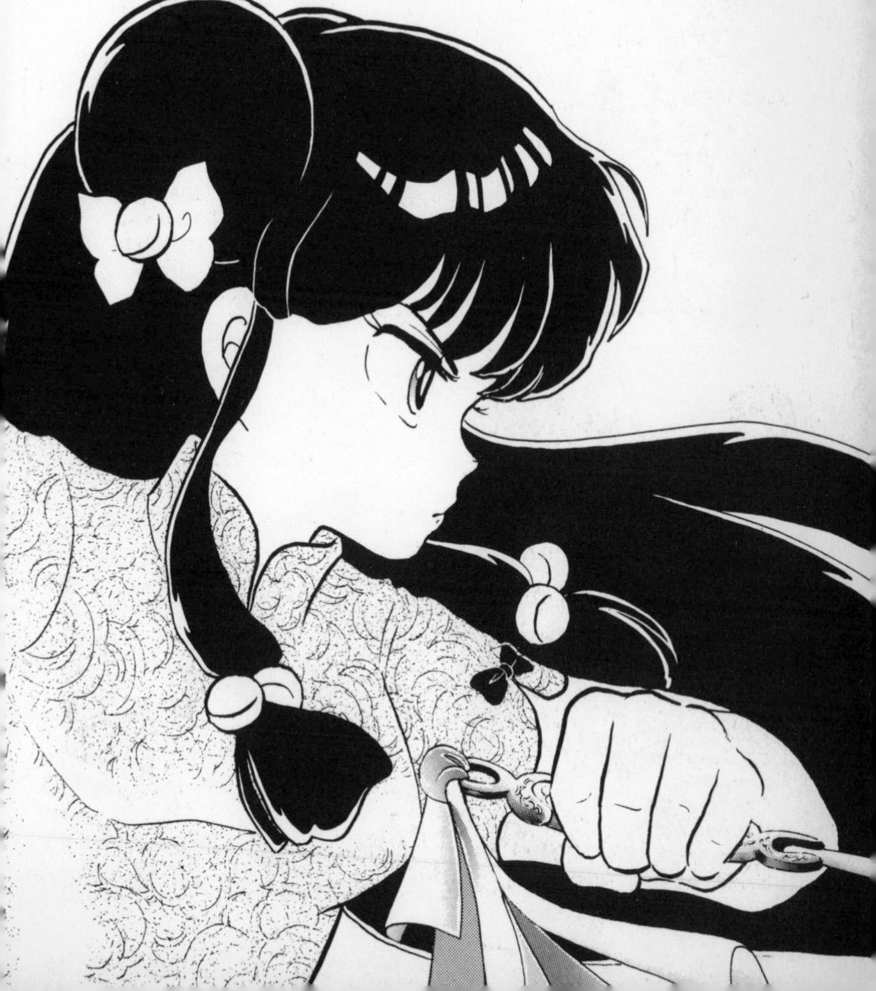

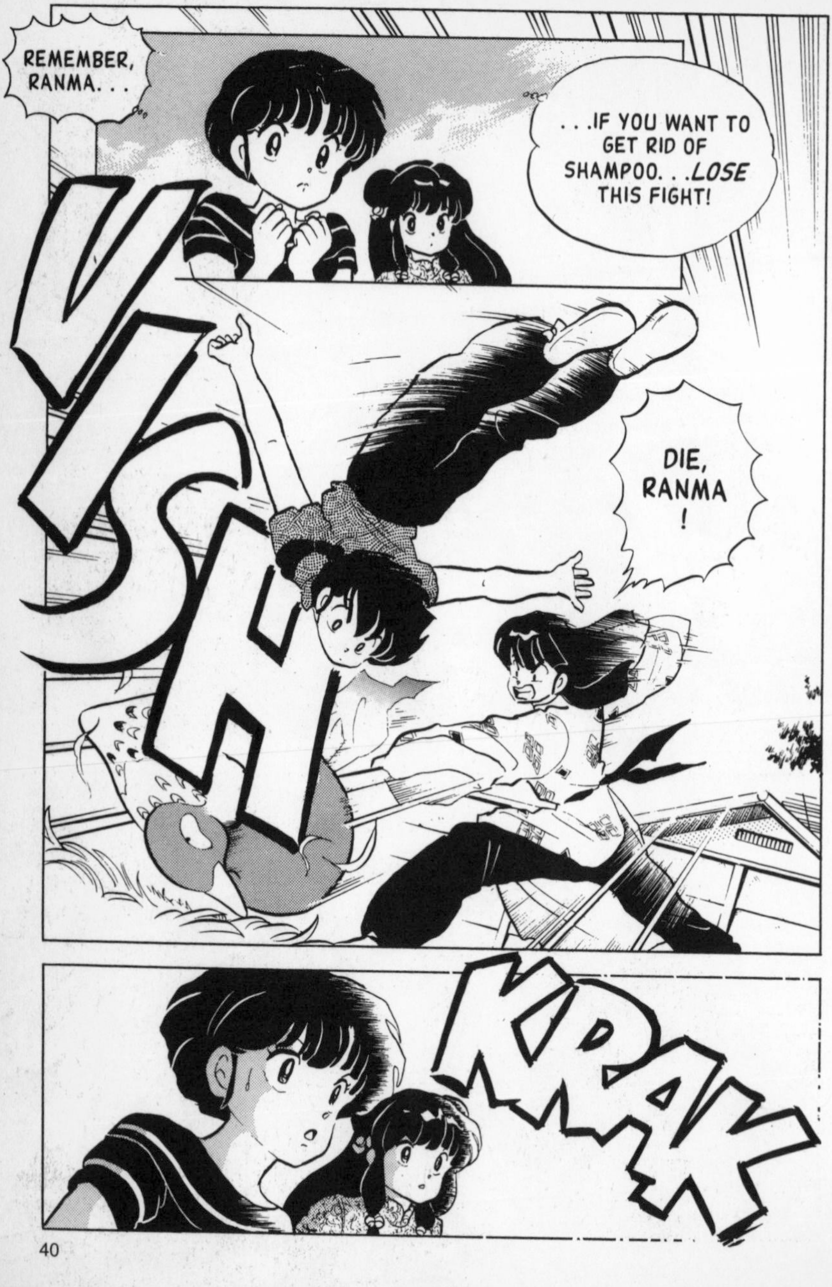
REMEMBER, RANMA. . .
. . .IF YOU WANT TO GET RID OF SHAMPOO. . .*LOSE* THIS FIGHT!
DIE, RANMA!
KRAK

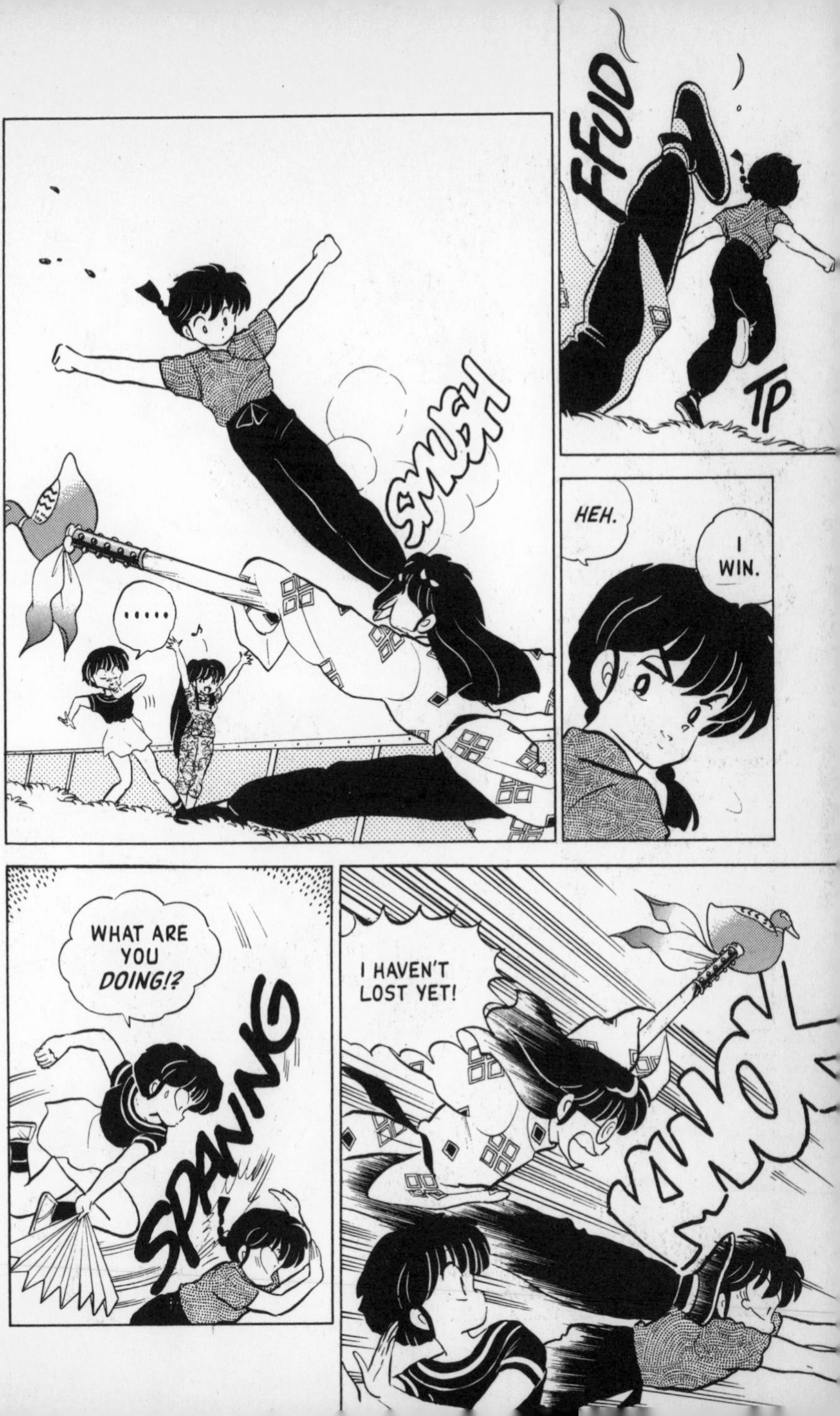

SMUSH
.....
FFUD
TP
HEH.
I WIN.
WHAT ARE YOU *DOING!?*
SPANNG
I HAVEN'T LOST YET!

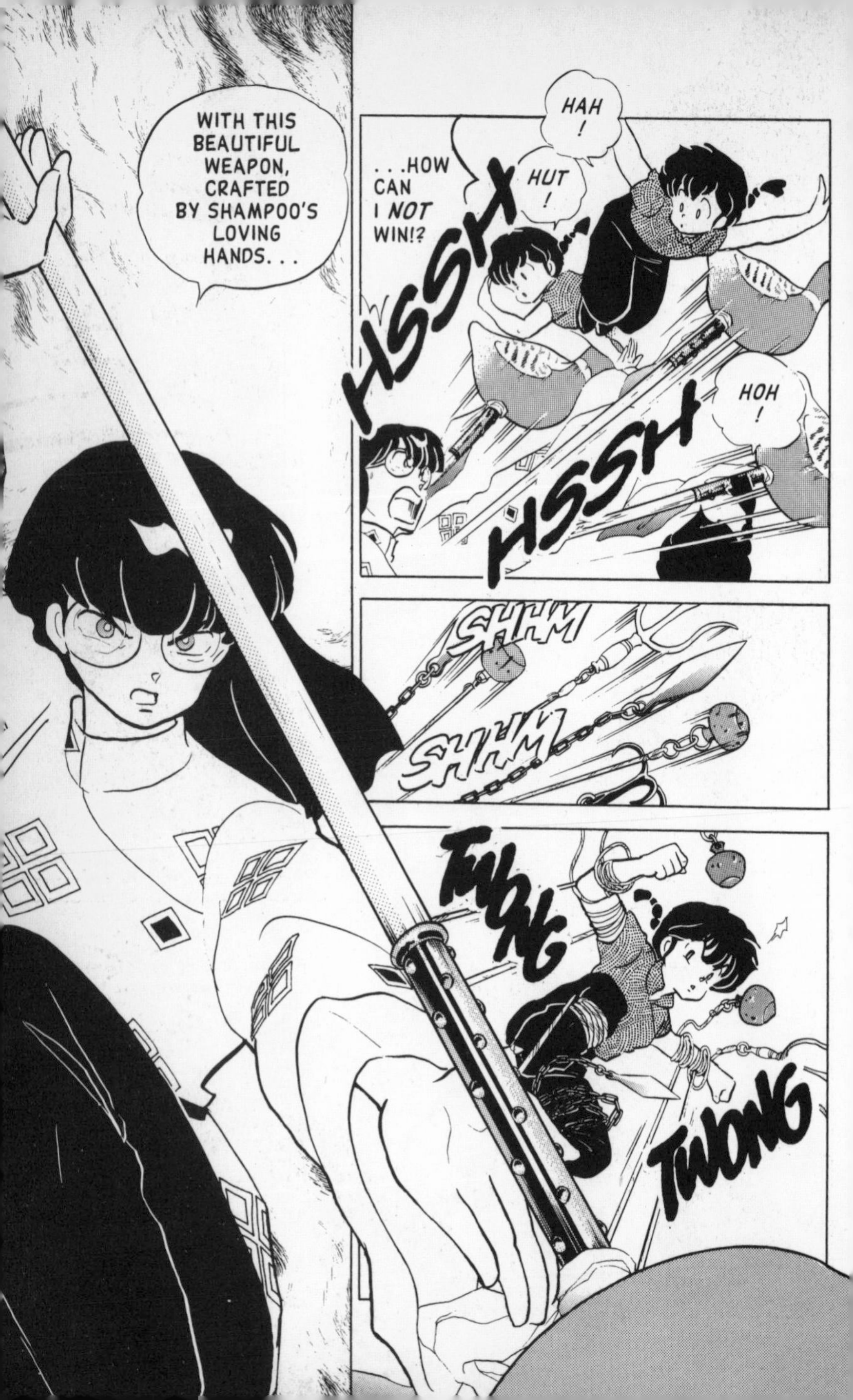
WITH THIS BEAUTIFUL WEAPON, CRAFTED BY SHAMPOO'S LOVING HANDS. . .
. . .HOW CAN I *NOT* WIN!?
HSSH
HUT!
HAH!
HSSH
HOH!
SHHM
SHHM
TWONG
TWONG

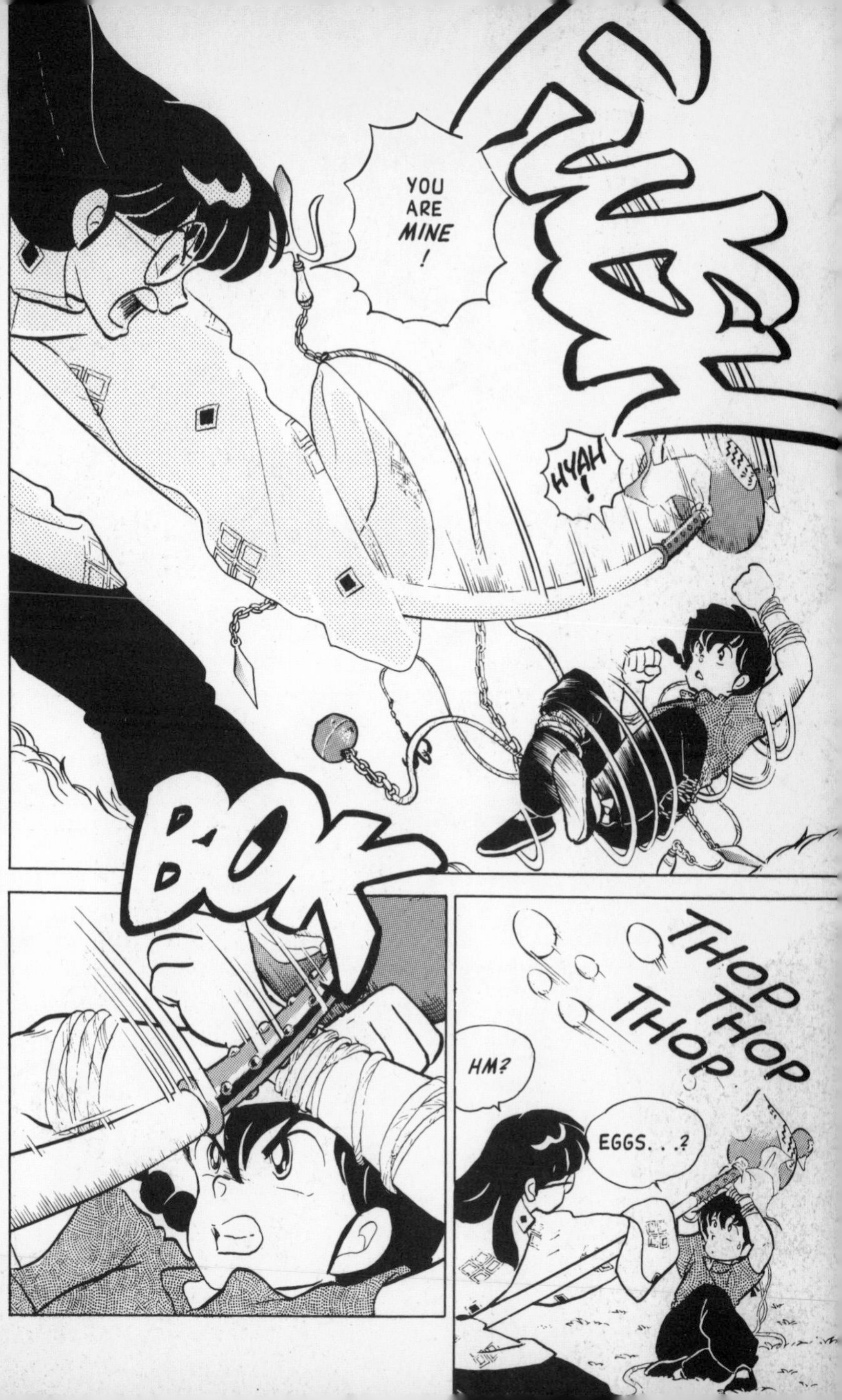
YOU ARE MINE!
HYAH!
BOK
THOP THOP THOP
HM?
EGGS...?

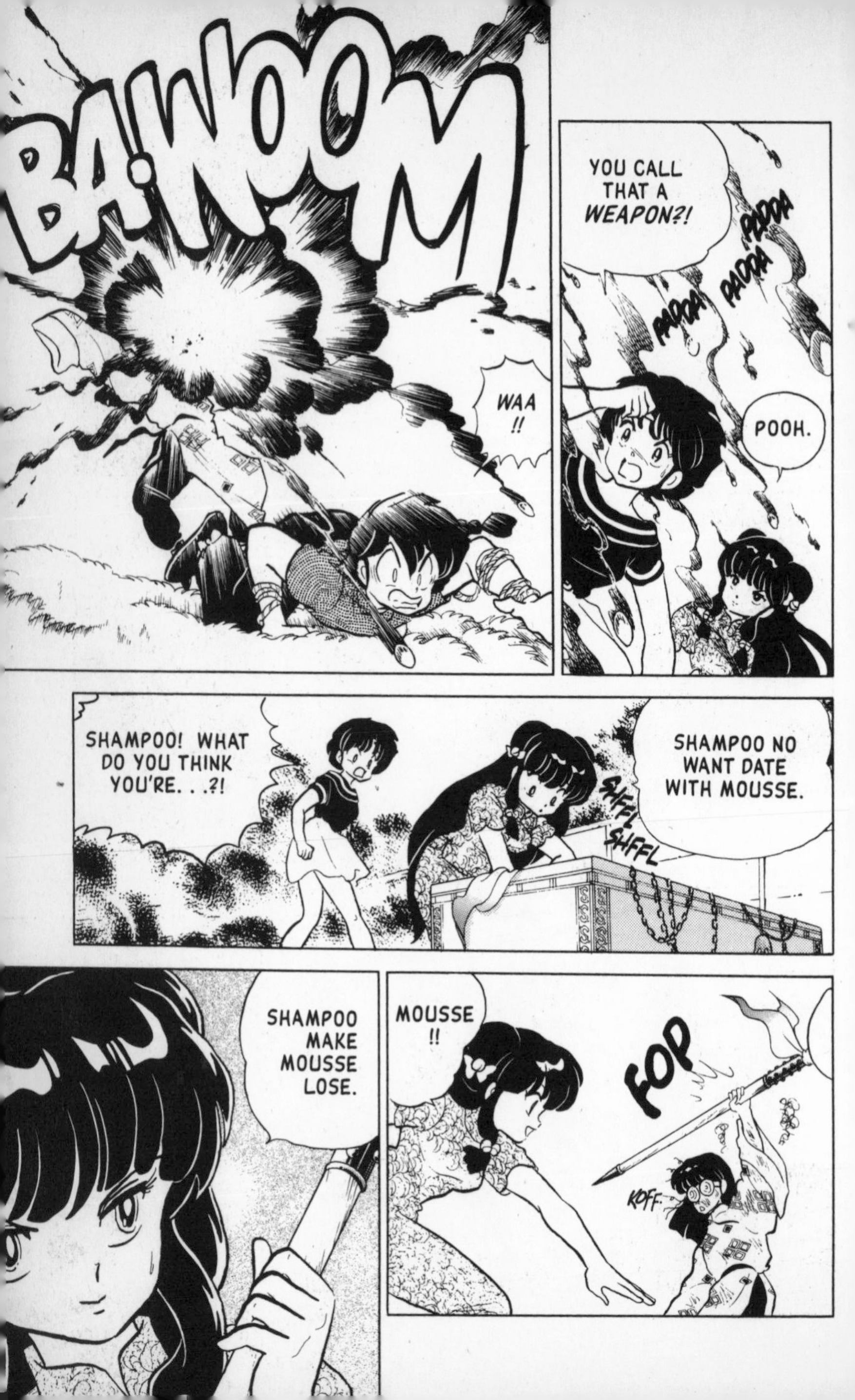
BAWOOM
WAA !!
YOU CALL THAT A WEAPON?!
PADDA PADDA PADDA PADDA
POOH.
SHAMPOO! WHAT DO YOU THINK YOU'RE. . .?!
SHFFL SHFFL
SHAMPOO NO WANT DATE WITH MOUSSE.
SHAMPOO MAKE MOUSSE LOSE.
MOUSSE !!
FOP
KOFF

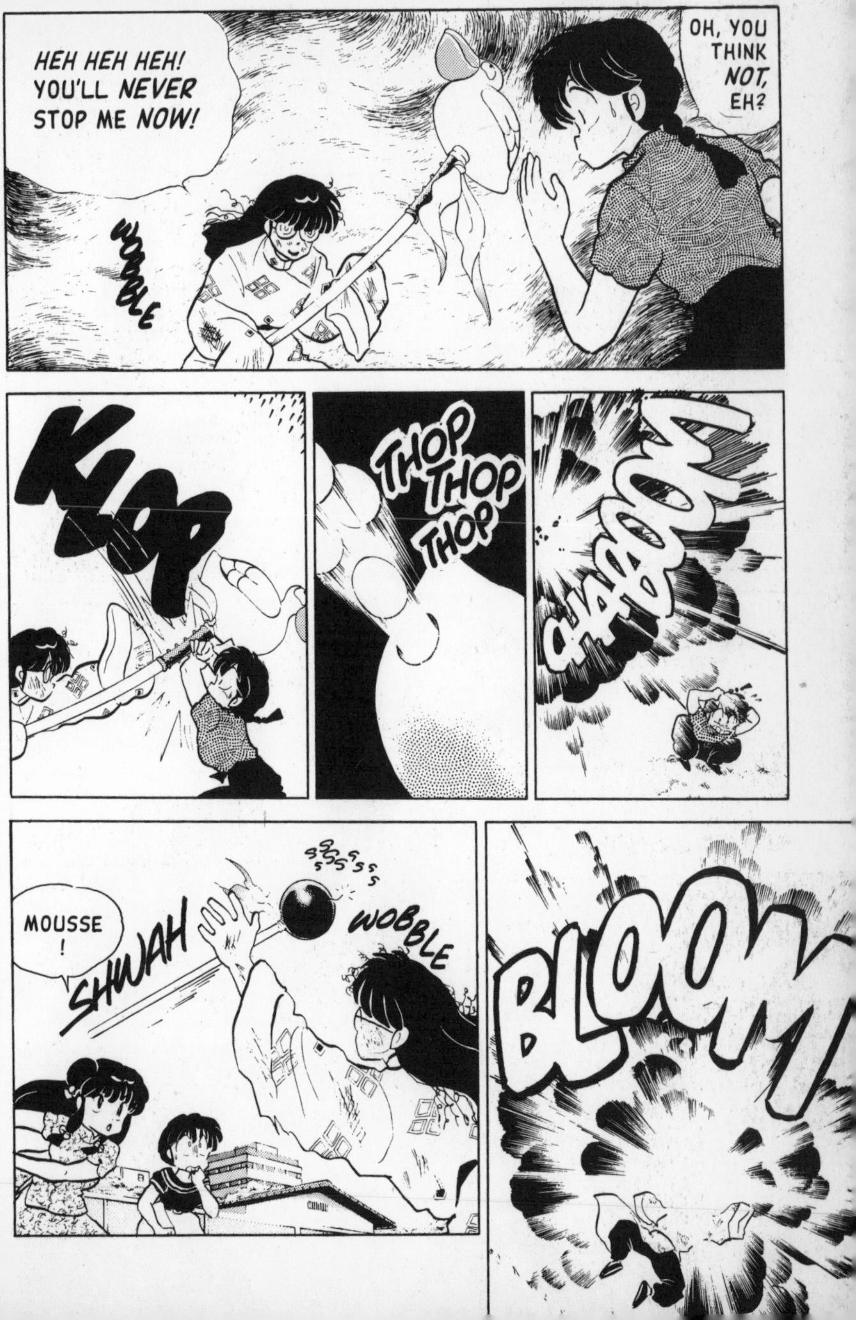
HEH HEH HEH! YOU'LL NEVER STOP ME NOW!
WOBBLE
OH, YOU THINK NOT, EH?
KLOP
THOP THOP THOP
CHABOOM
MOUSSE !
SHWAH
WOBBLE
BLOOM

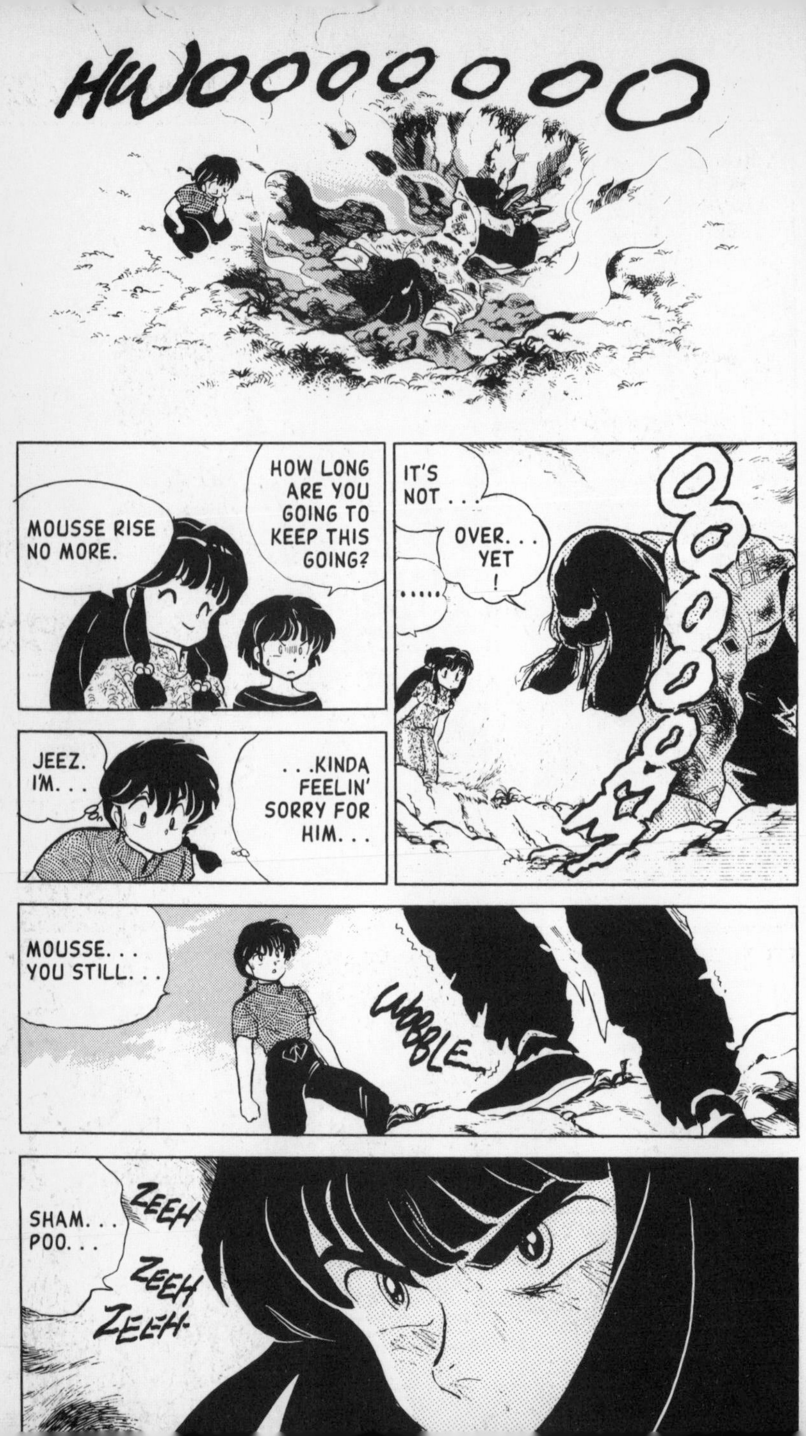
HWOOOOOOOO
MOUSSE RISE NO MORE.
HOW LONG ARE YOU GOING TO KEEP THIS GOING?
JEEZ. I'M. . .
. . .KINDA FEELIN' SORRY FOR HIM. . .
IT'S NOT . . .
OVER. . . YET !
. . . . .
OOOOOOOOM
MOUSSE. . . YOU STILL. . .
WOBBLE
SHAM. . . POO. . .
ZEEH
ZEEH
ZEEH

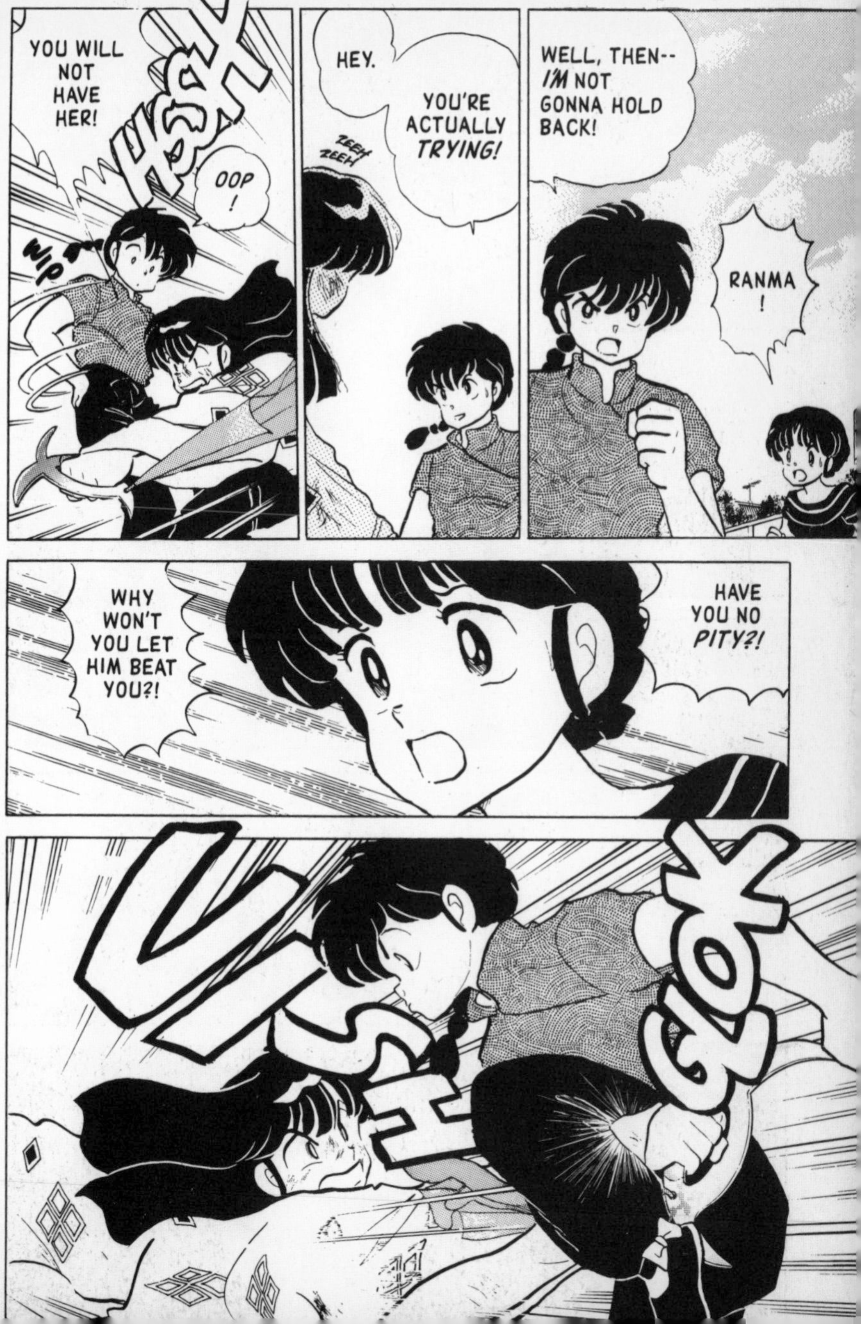
YOU WILL NOT HAVE HER!
OOP!
WIP
HEY.
ZEEH ZEEH
YOU'RE ACTUALLY TRYING!
WELL, THEN-- I'M NOT GONNA HOLD BACK!
RANMA!
WHY WON'T YOU LET HIM BEAT YOU?!
HAVE YOU NO PITY?!
CLOK

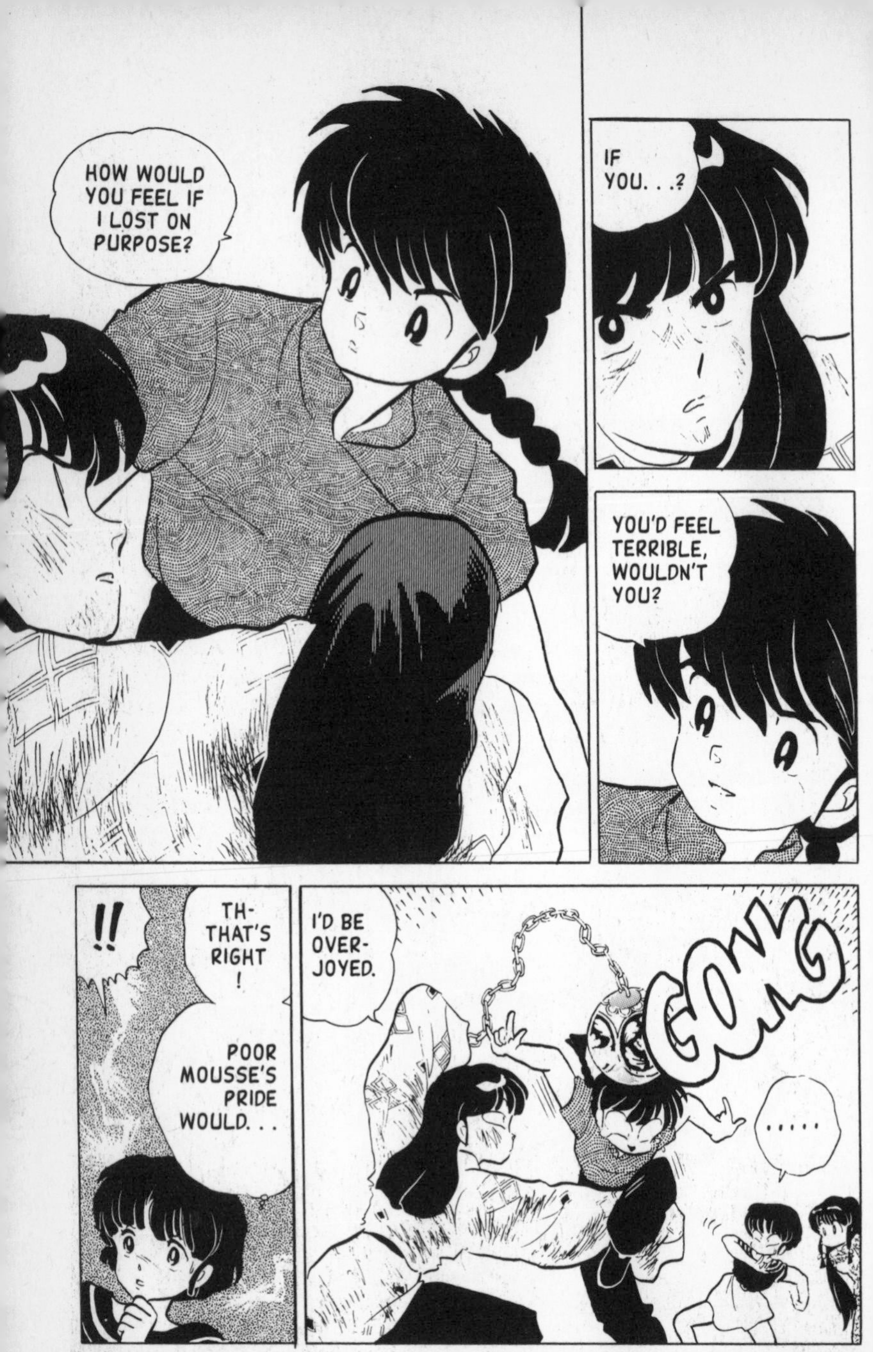
HOW WOULD YOU FEEL IF I LOST ON PURPOSE?
IF YOU. . .?
YOU'D FEEL TERRIBLE, WOULDN'T YOU?
!!
TH- THAT'S RIGHT !
POOR MOUSSE'S PRIDE WOULD. . .
I'D BE OVER-JOYED.
GONG
. . . . .

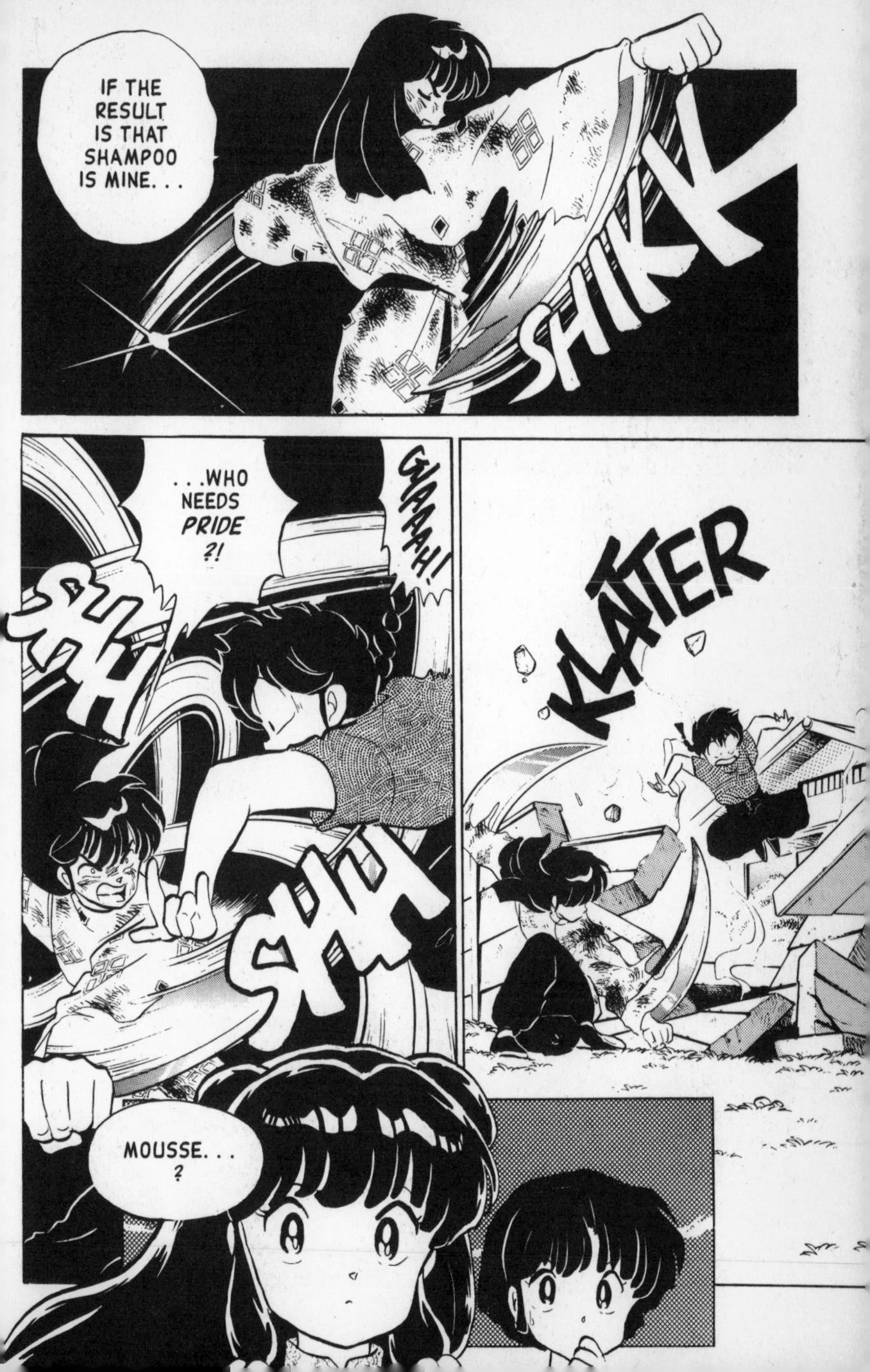
IF THE RESULT IS THAT SHAMPOO IS MINE. . .
SHIKK
. . .WHO NEEDS PRIDE ?!
GUAAAAH!
SHH
SHH
KLATTER
MOUSSE. . . ?

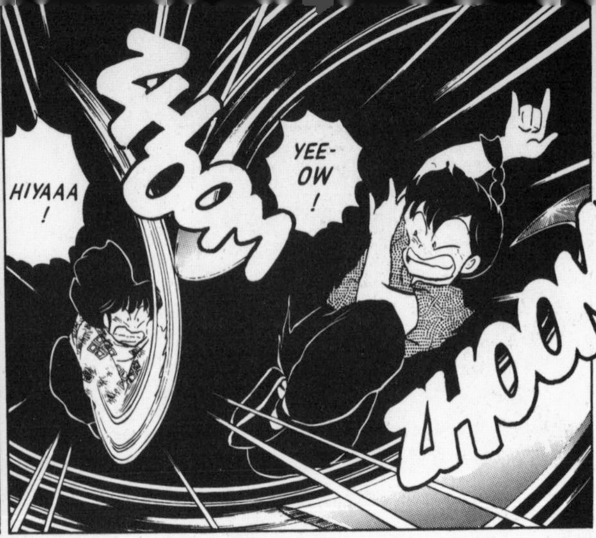
YEE-OW!
HIYAAA!
ZHOOM
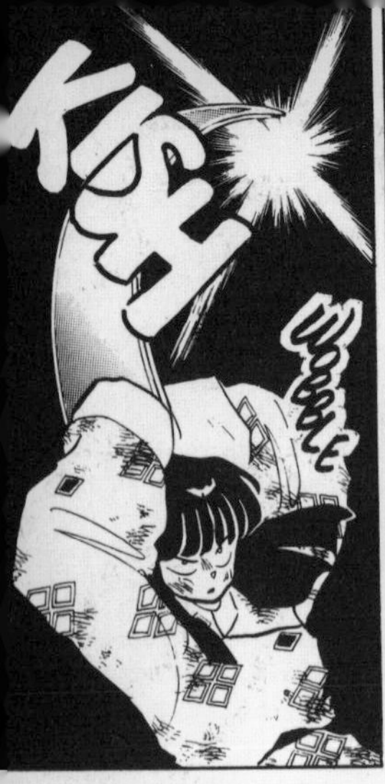
KISH
WOBBLE
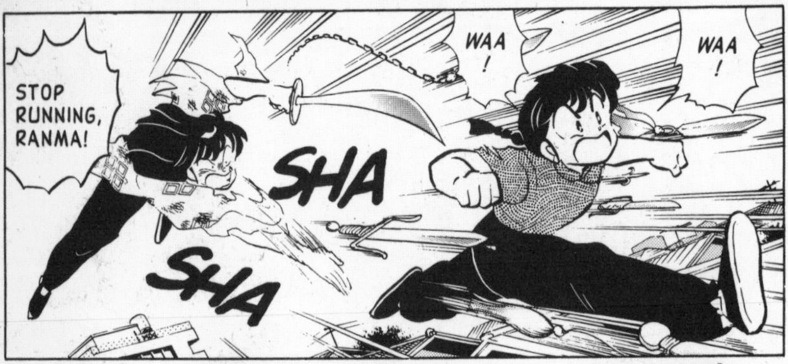
WAA!
WAA!
STOP RUNNING, RANMA!
SHA
SHA
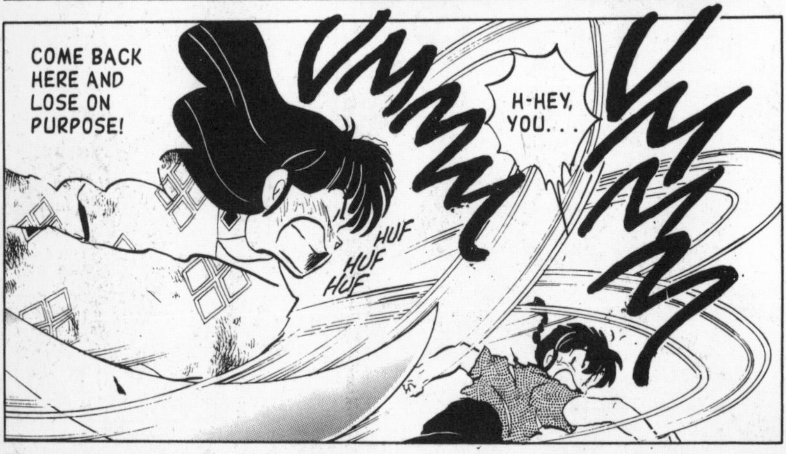
H-HEY, YOU. . .
COME BACK HERE AND LOSE ON PURPOSE!
HUF
HUF
HUF

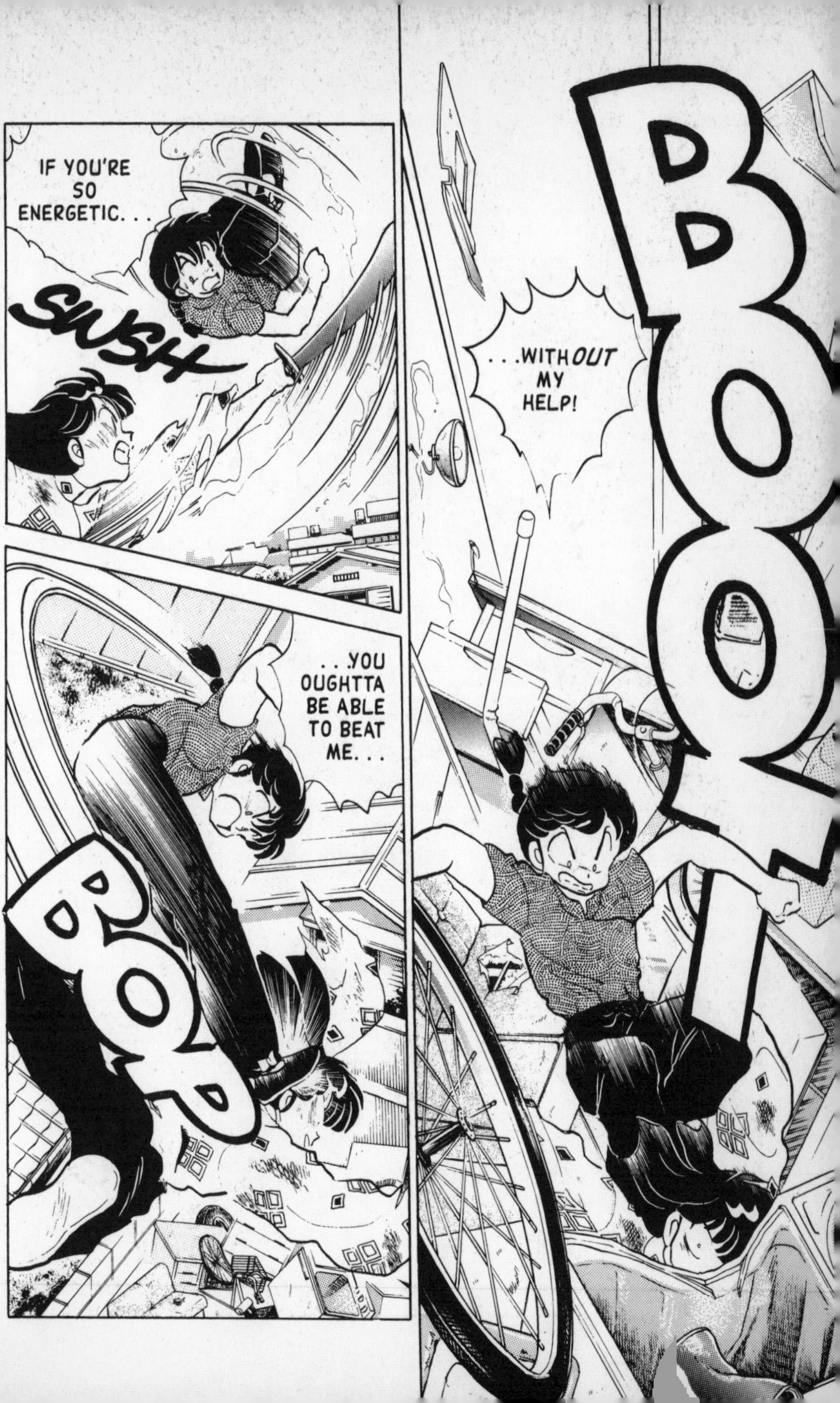
IF YOU'RE SO ENERGETIC. . .
SWSH
. . .YOU OUGHTTA BE ABLE TO BEAT ME. . .
BOP
. . .WITHOUT MY HELP!
BOO!

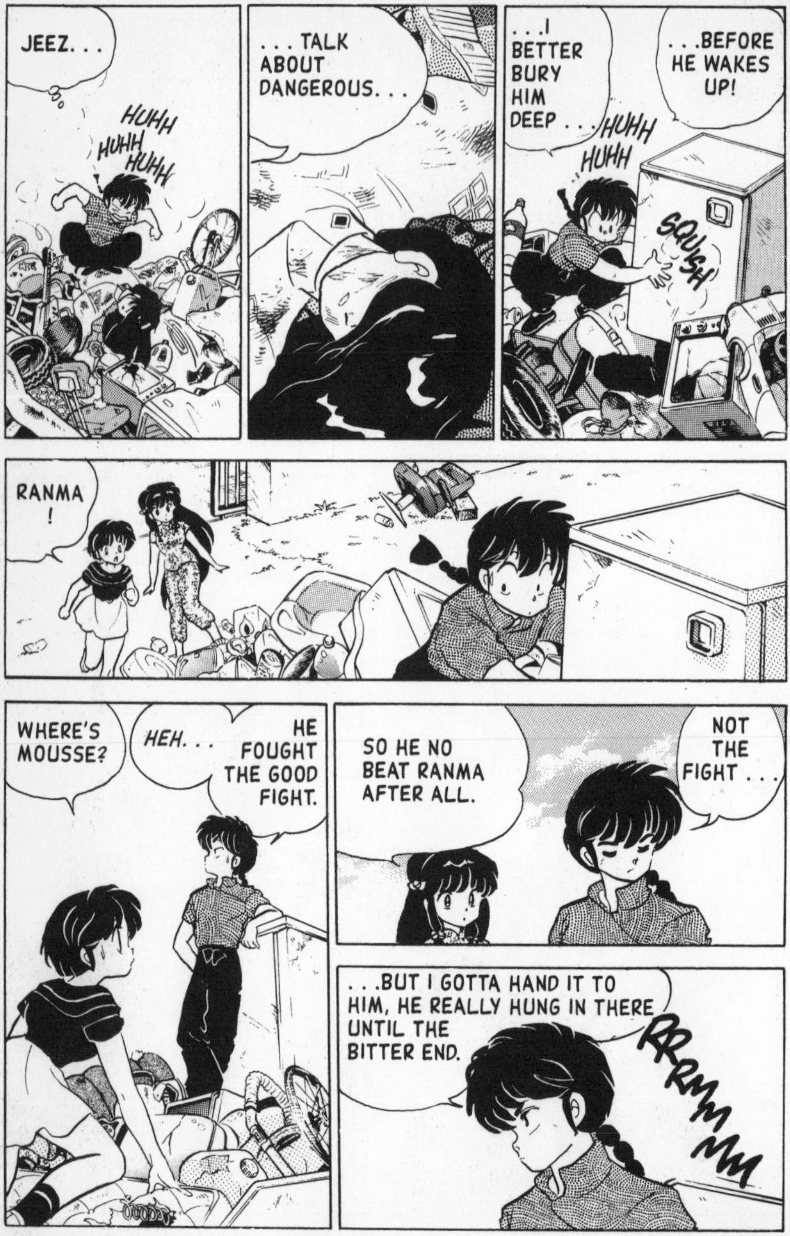
JEEZ. . .
HUHH HUHH HUHH
. . . TALK ABOUT DANGEROUS. . .
. . .I BETTER BURY HIM DEEP . . .
. . .BEFORE HE WAKES UP!
HUHH HUHH
SQUISH
RANMA!
WHERE'S MOUSSE?
HEH. . .
HE FOUGHT THE GOOD FIGHT.
SO HE NO BEAT RANMA AFTER ALL.
NOT THE FIGHT . . .
. . .BUT I GOTTA HAND IT TO HIM, HE REALLY HUNG IN THERE UNTIL THE BITTER END.
RRRMMMMM

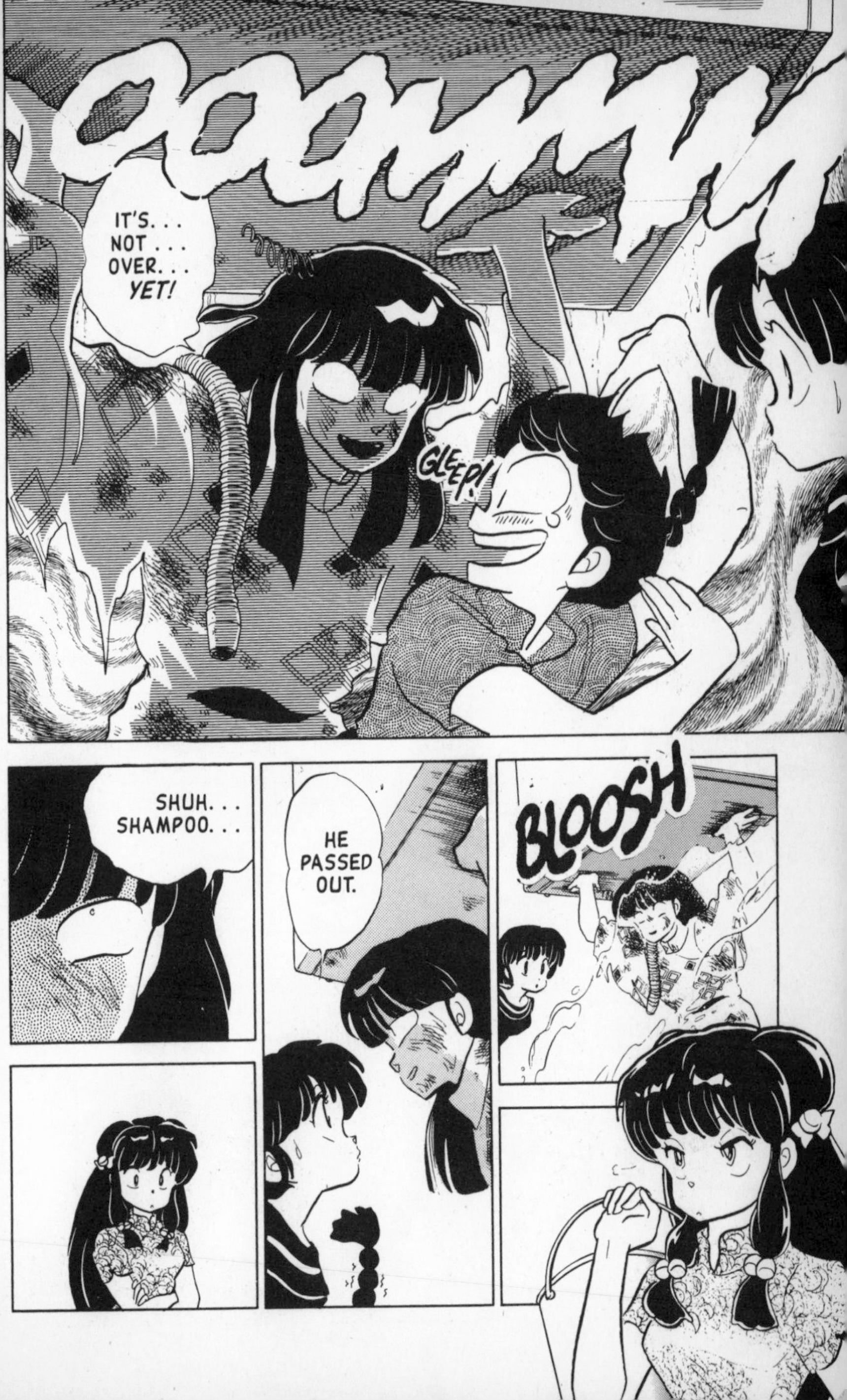
IT'S... NOT... OVER... YET!
GLEEP!
SHUH... SHAMPOO...
HE PASSED OUT.
BLOOSH

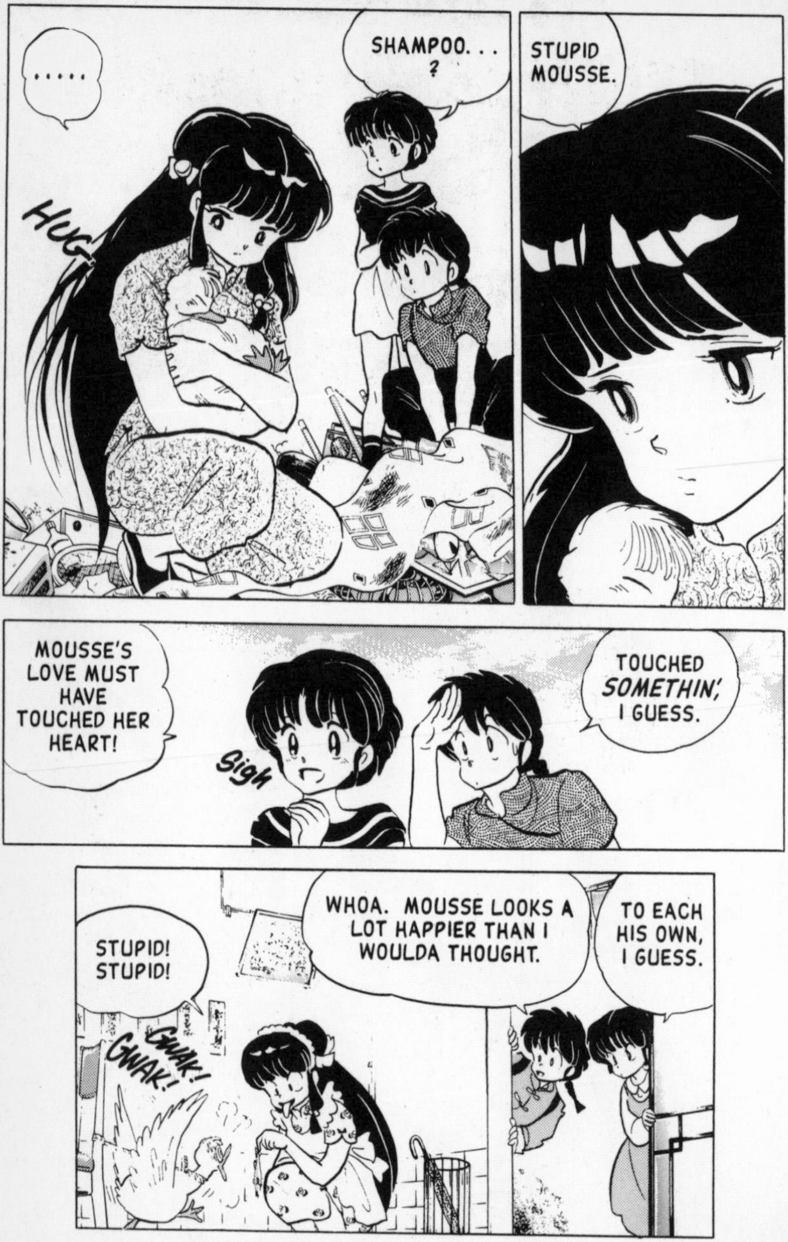
......
SHAMPOO...?
HUG!
STUPID MOUSSE.
MOUSSE'S LOVE MUST HAVE TOUCHED HER HEART!
Sigh
TOUCHED *SOMETHIN',* I GUESS.
STUPID! STUPID!
GWAK! GWAK!
WHOA. MOUSSE LOOKS A LOT HAPPIER THAN I WOULDA THOUGHT.
TO EACH HIS OWN, I GUESS.

Part 4

TSUBASA KURENAI BUSTS LOOSE!

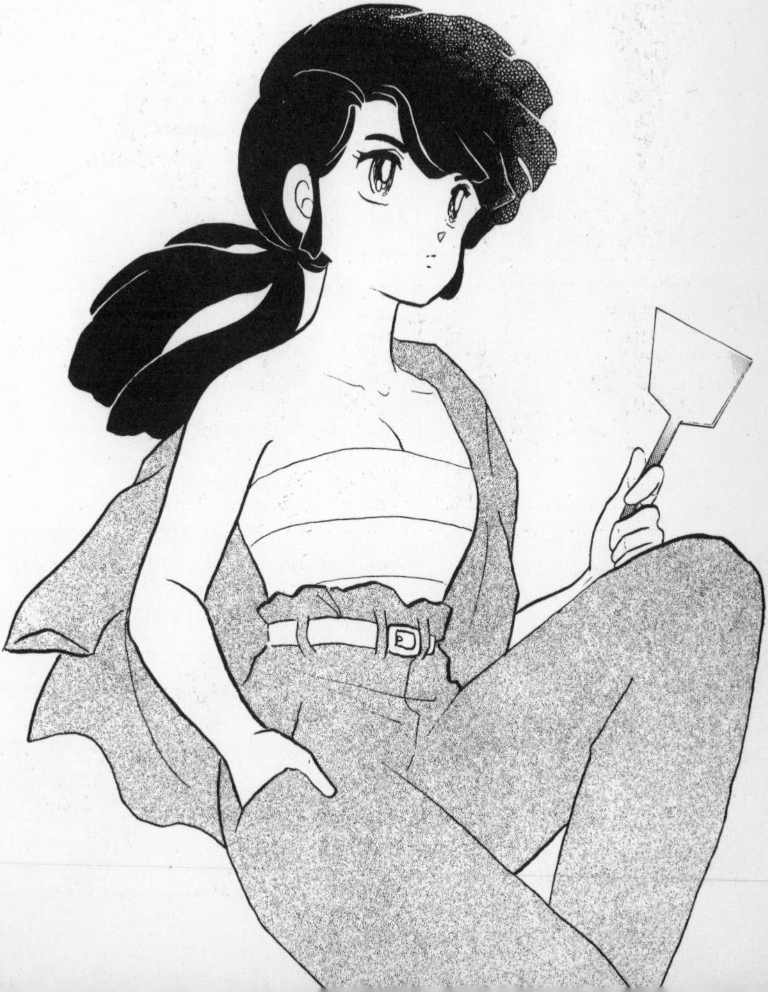

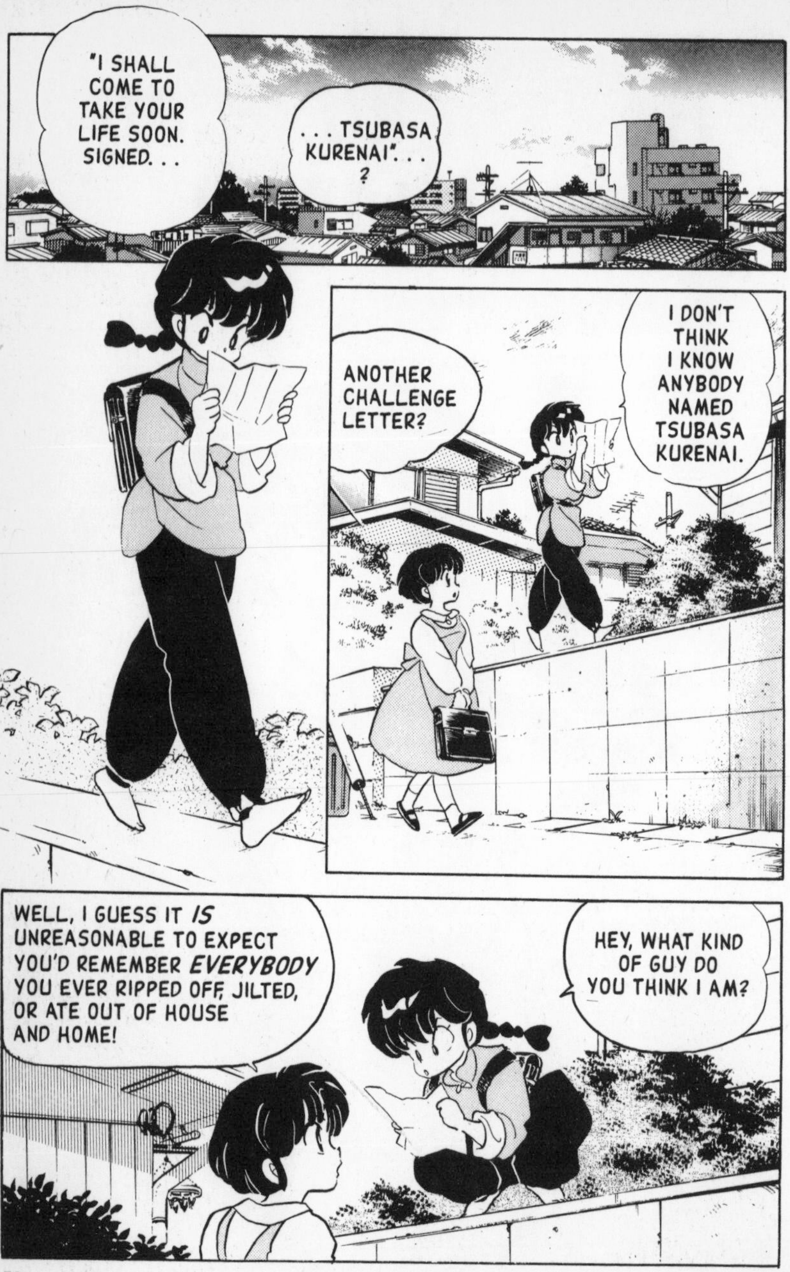
"I SHALL COME TO TAKE YOUR LIFE SOON. SIGNED. . .
. . . TSUBASA KURENAI". . . ?
ANOTHER CHALLENGE LETTER?
I DON'T THINK I KNOW ANYBODY NAMED TSUBASA KURENAI.
WELL, I GUESS IT *IS* UNREASONABLE TO EXPECT YOU'D REMEMBER *EVERYBODY* YOU EVER RIPPED OFF, JILTED, OR ATE OUT OF HOUSE AND HOME!
HEY, WHAT KIND OF GUY DO YOU THINK I AM?

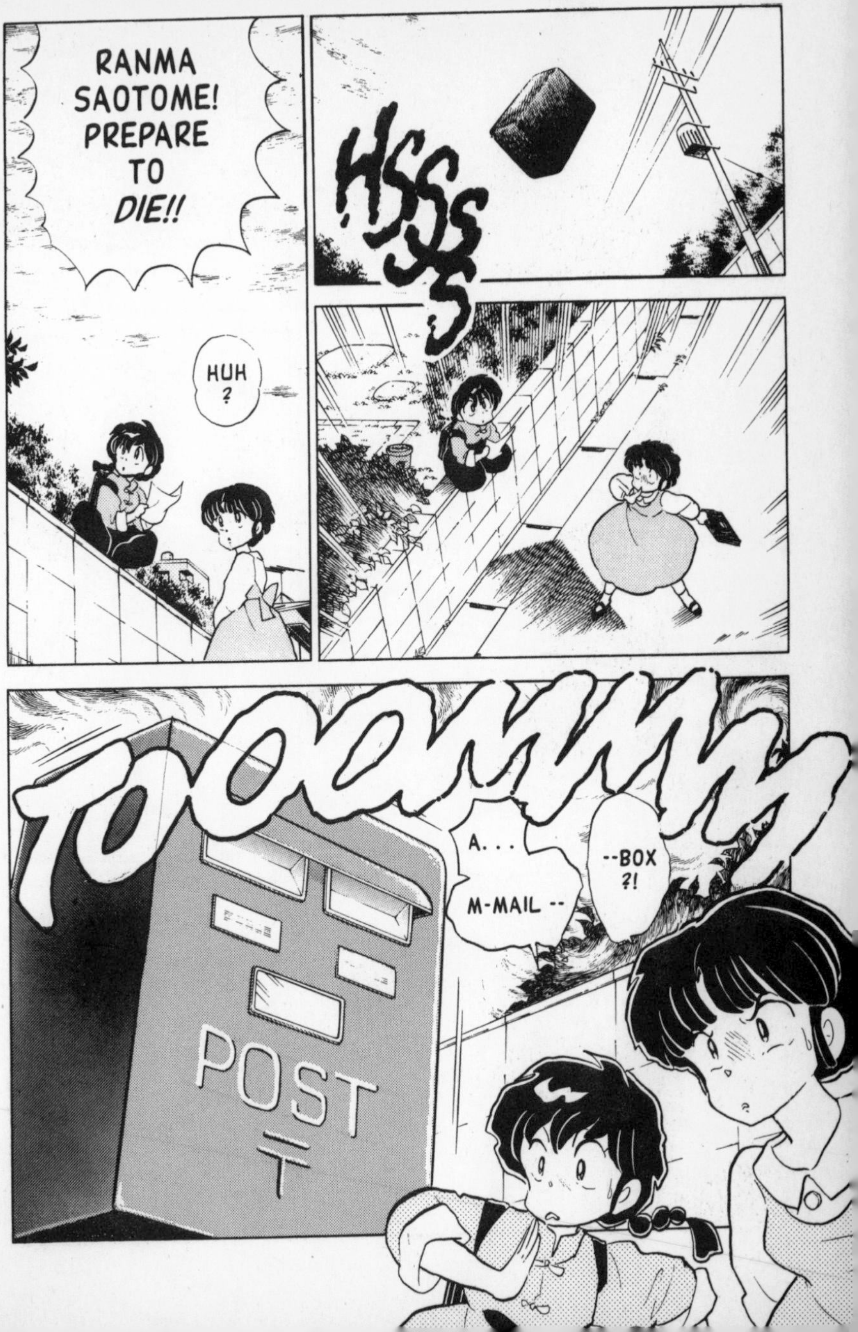
RANMA SAOTOME! PREPARE TO *DIE!!*
HUH?
HSSSS
TOOMMM
A. . . M-MAIL --
--BOX?!
POST

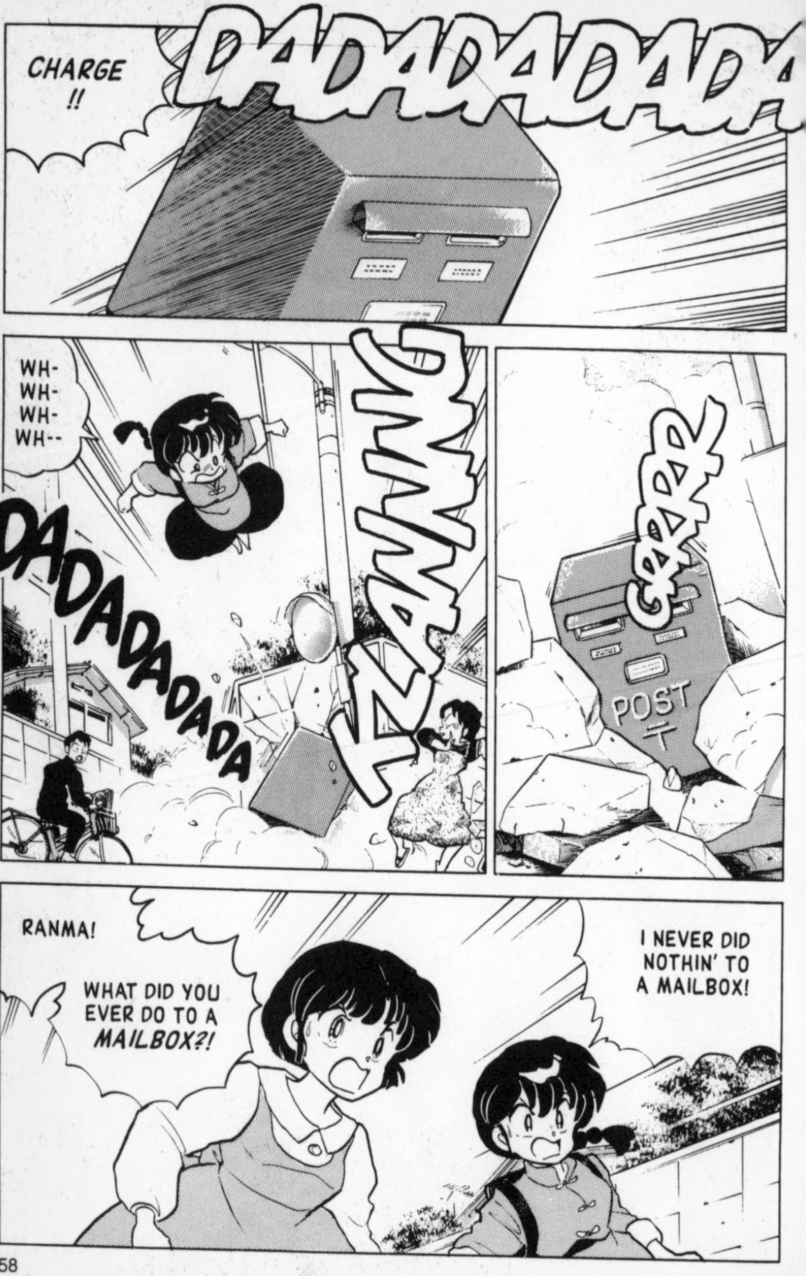
CHARGE !!
DADADADADADA
WH- WH- WH- WH--
DADADADADADA
ZZAWNG
GRRRR
POST 〒
RANMA!
WHAT DID YOU EVER DO TO A MAILBOX?!
I NEVER DID NOTHIN' TO A MAILBOX!

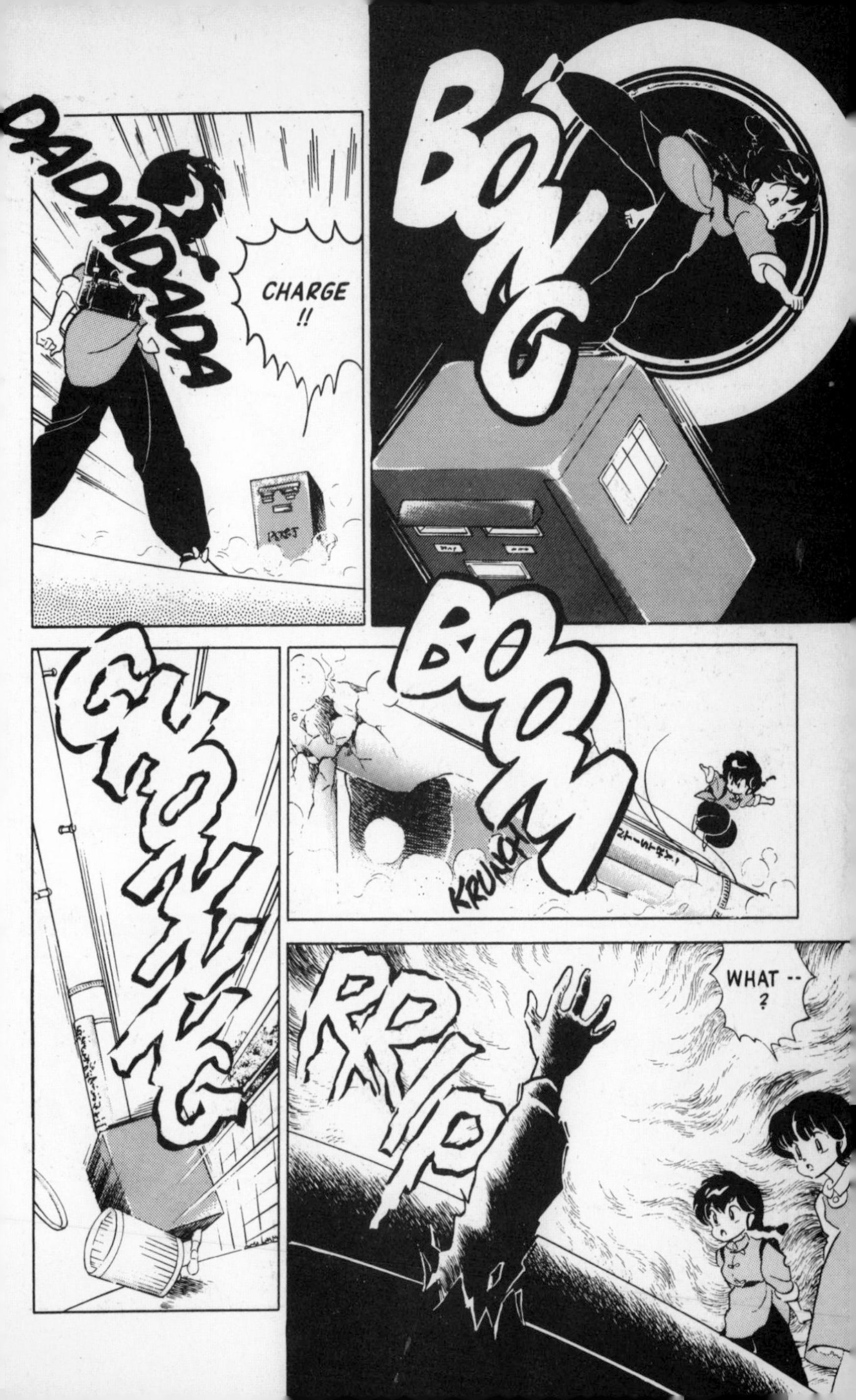
DADADADADA
CHARGE !!
BOING
CLANG
BOOM
KRUNCH
RRIP
WHAT -- ?

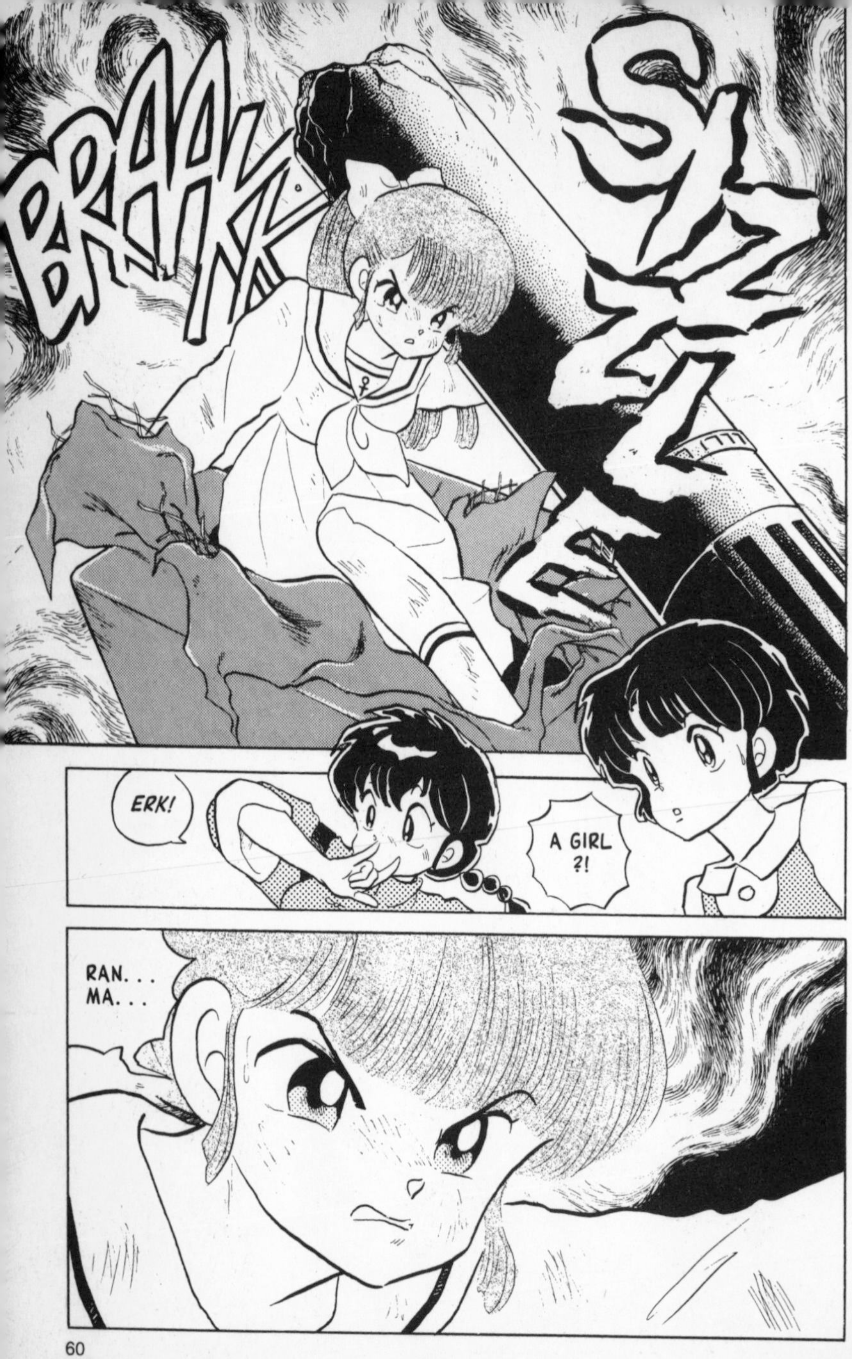
BRAAAK
SKZZZ
ERK!
A GIRL ?!
RAN. . .
MA. . .

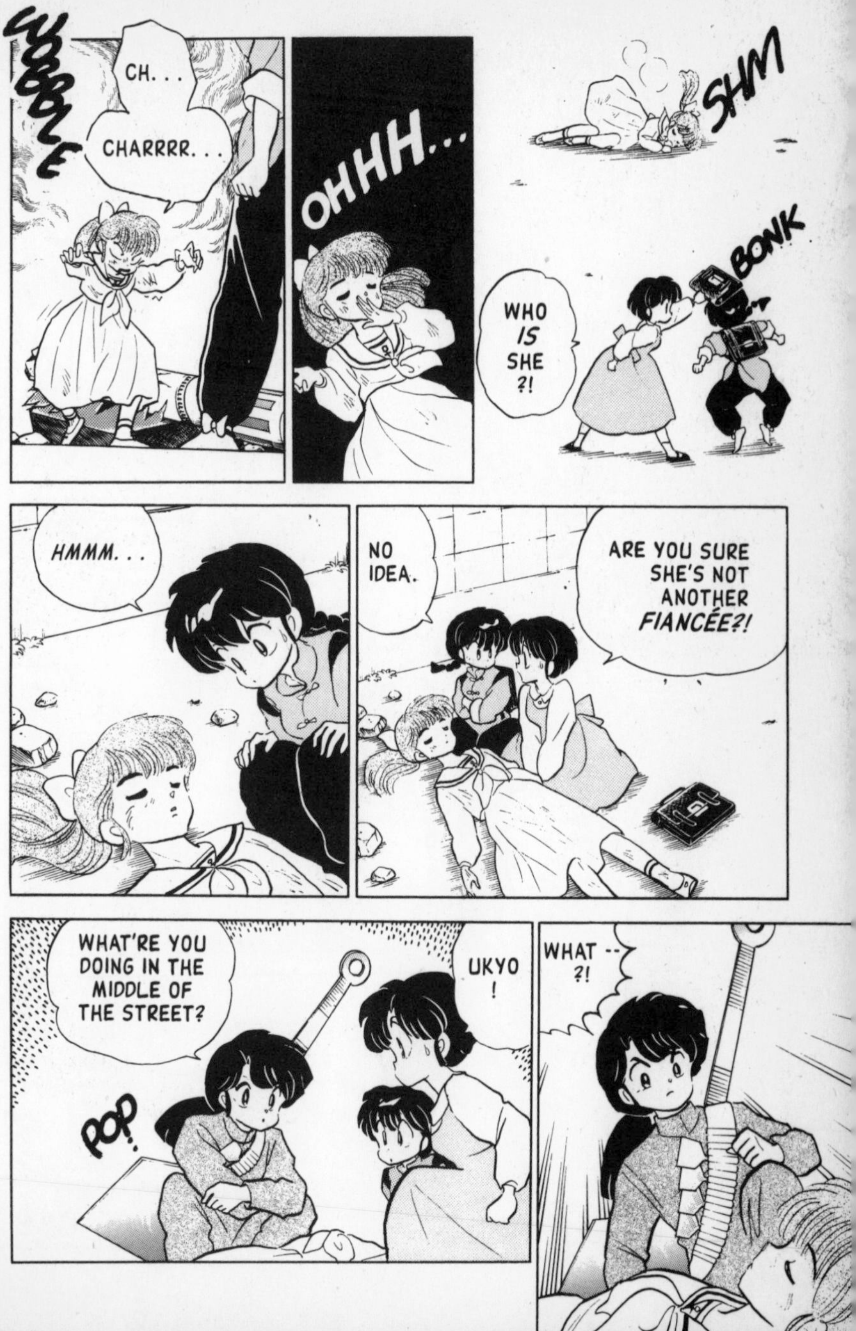
WOBBLE
CH. . .
CHARRRR. . .
OHHH. . .
SHM
BONK
WHO *IS* SHE ?!
HMMM. . .
NO IDEA.
ARE YOU SURE SHE'S NOT ANOTHER *FIANCÉE?!*
WHAT'RE YOU DOING IN THE MIDDLE OF THE STREET?
POP
UKYO !
WHAT -- ?!

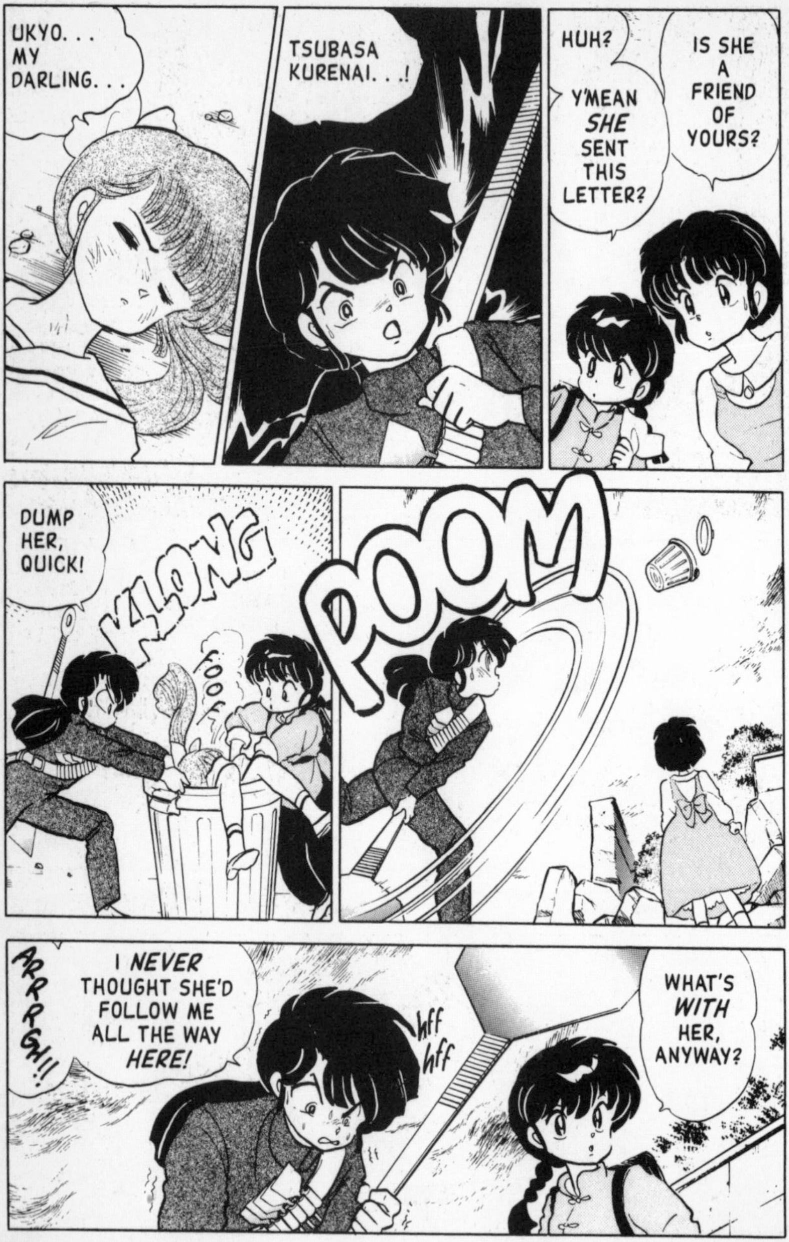
UKYO. . . MY DARLING. . .
TSUBASA KURENAI. . .!
HUH?
Y'MEAN SHE SENT THIS LETTER?
IS SHE A FRIEND OF YOURS?
DUMP HER, QUICK!
KLONG
FOOF
POOM
ARRRGH!!
I NEVER THOUGHT SHE'D FOLLOW ME ALL THE WAY HERE!
hff hff
WHAT'S WITH HER, ANYWAY?

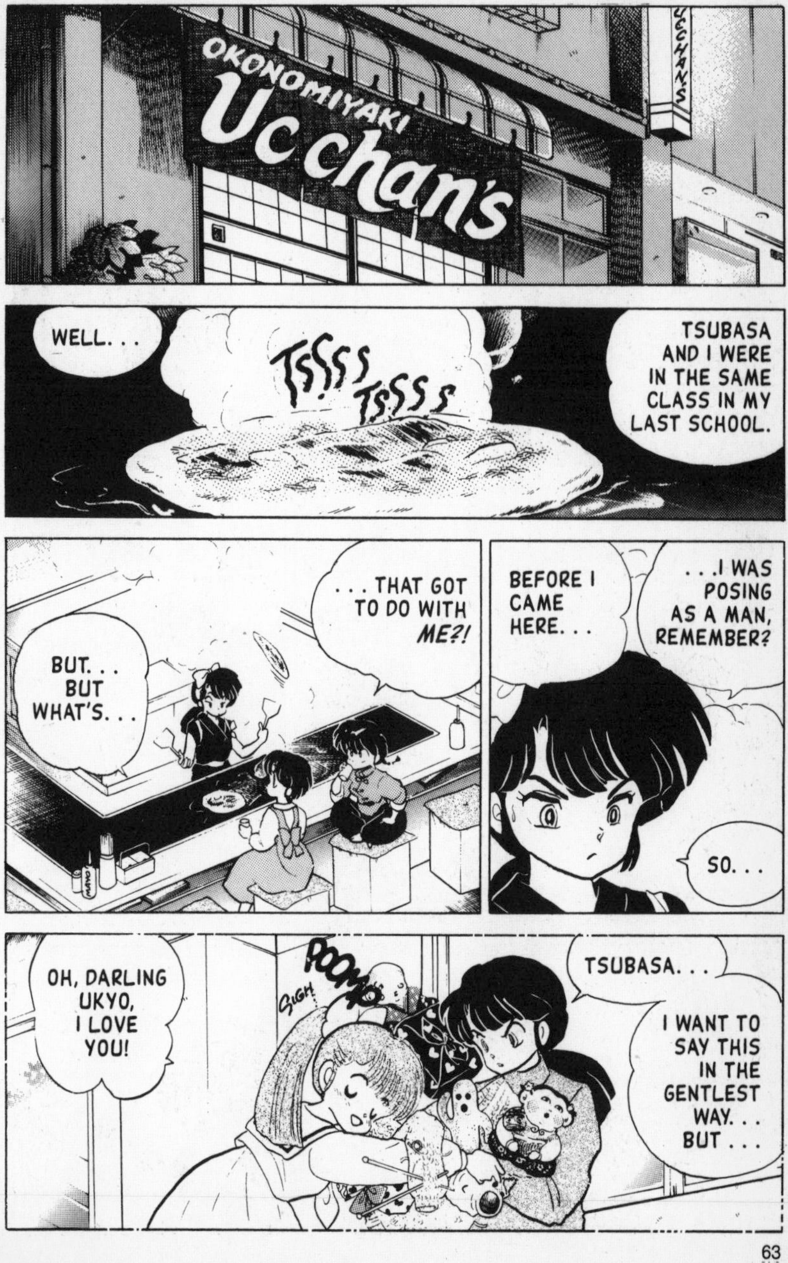
OKONOMIYAKI
Ucchan's
UCCHAN'S
WELL...
TSSSS TSSSS
TSUBASA AND I WERE IN THE SAME CLASS IN MY LAST SCHOOL.
BUT... BUT WHAT'S...
...THAT GOT TO DO WITH ME?!
MAYO
BEFORE I CAME HERE...
...I WAS POSING AS A MAN, REMEMBER?
SO...
OH, DARLING UKYO, I LOVE YOU!
SIGH
POOMP
TSUBASA...
I WANT TO SAY THIS IN THE GENTLEST WAY... BUT ...

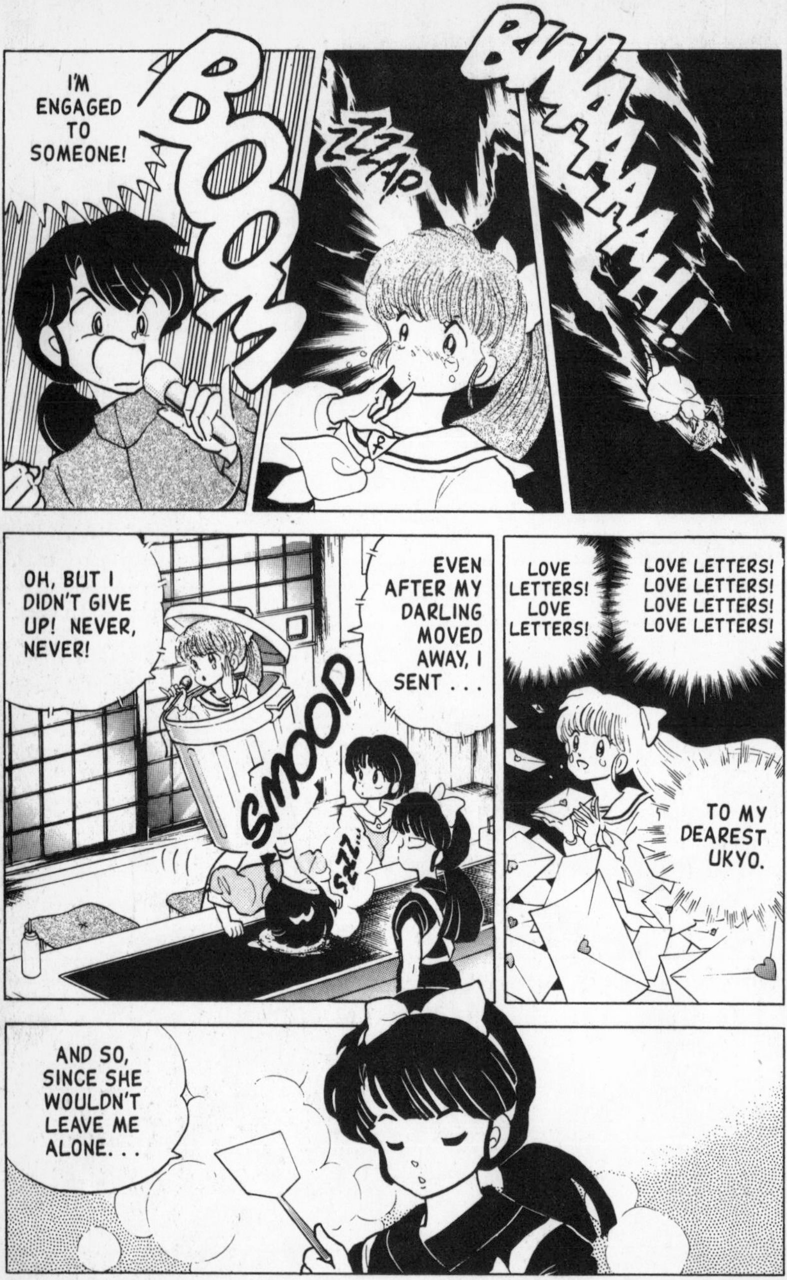
I'M ENGAGED TO SOMEONE!
BOOM
ZZZAP
BWAAAAAH!!
OH, BUT I DIDN'T GIVE UP! NEVER, NEVER!
EVEN AFTER MY DARLING MOVED AWAY, I SENT . . .
SMOOP
LOVE LETTERS! LOVE LETTERS!
LOVE LETTERS! LOVE LETTERS! LOVE LETTERS! LOVE LETTERS!
TO MY DEAREST UKYO.
AND SO, SINCE SHE WOULDN'T LEAVE ME ALONE. . .

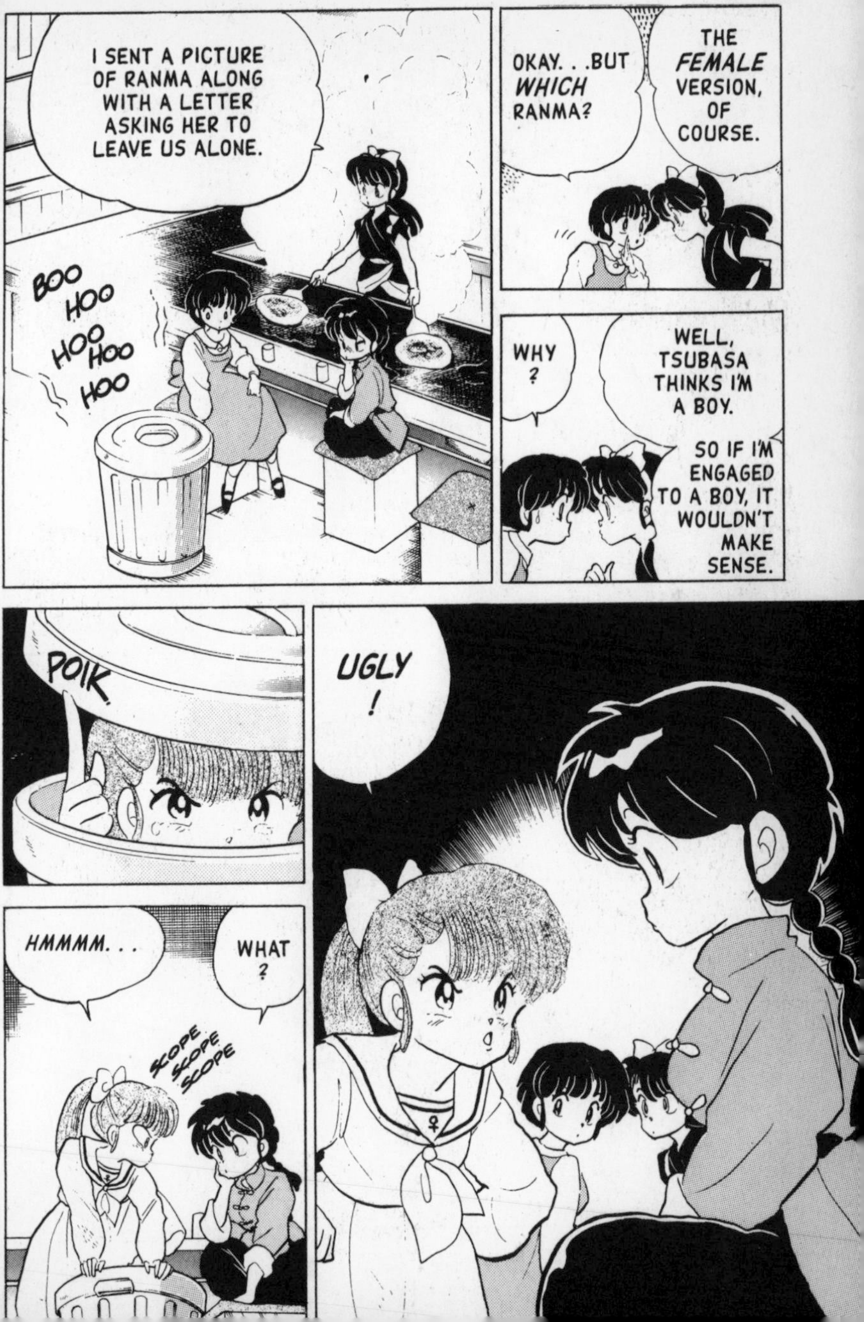
I SENT A PICTURE OF RANMA ALONG WITH A LETTER ASKING HER TO LEAVE US ALONE.
BOO HOO HOO HOO HOO
OKAY. . .BUT WHICH RANMA?
THE FEMALE VERSION, OF COURSE.
WHY?
WELL, TSUBASA THINKS I'M A BOY.
SO IF I'M ENGAGED TO A BOY, IT WOULDN'T MAKE SENSE.
POIK
HMMMM. . .
WHAT?
SCOPE SCOPE SCOPE
UGLY!

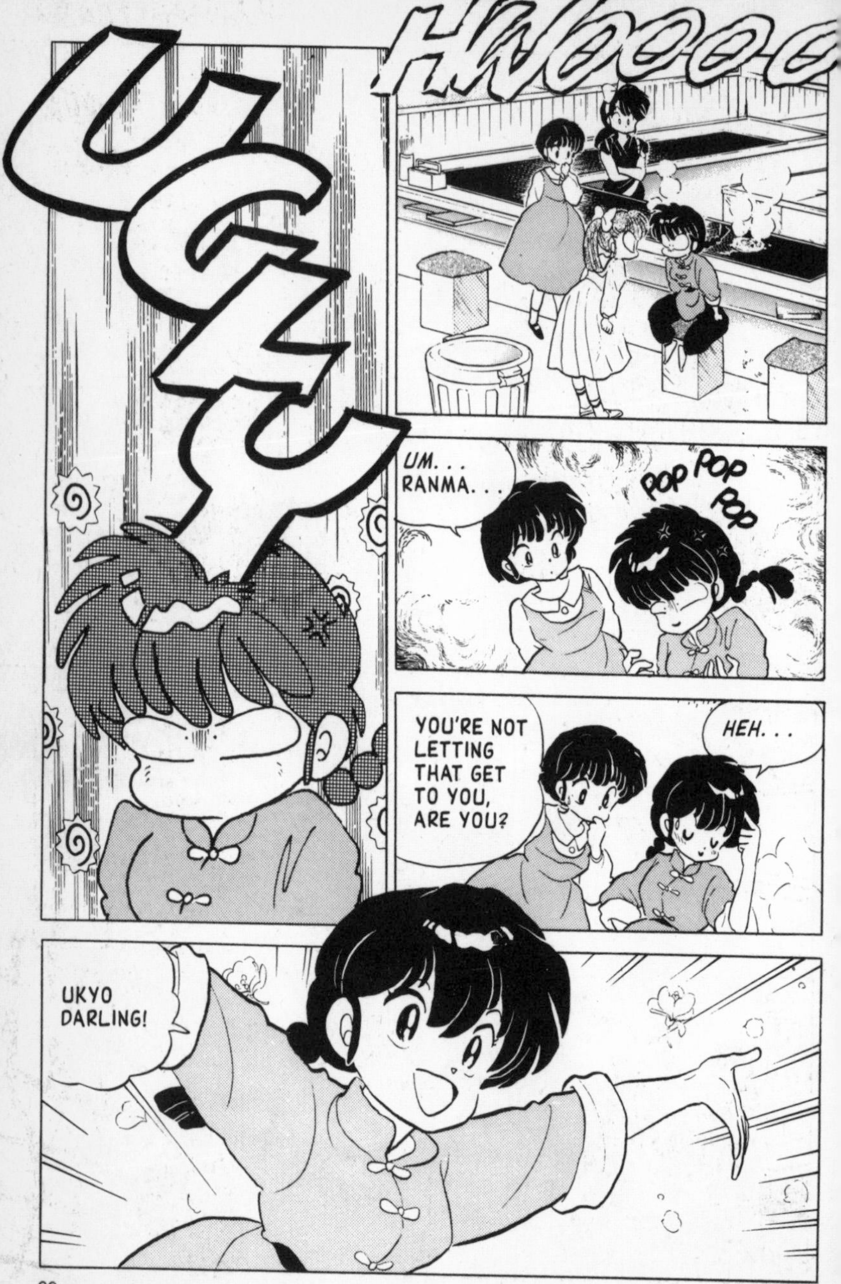
UGZU
HWOOOO
UM... RANMA...
POP POP POP POP
YOU'RE NOT LETTING THAT GET TO YOU, ARE YOU?
HEH...
UKYO DARLING!

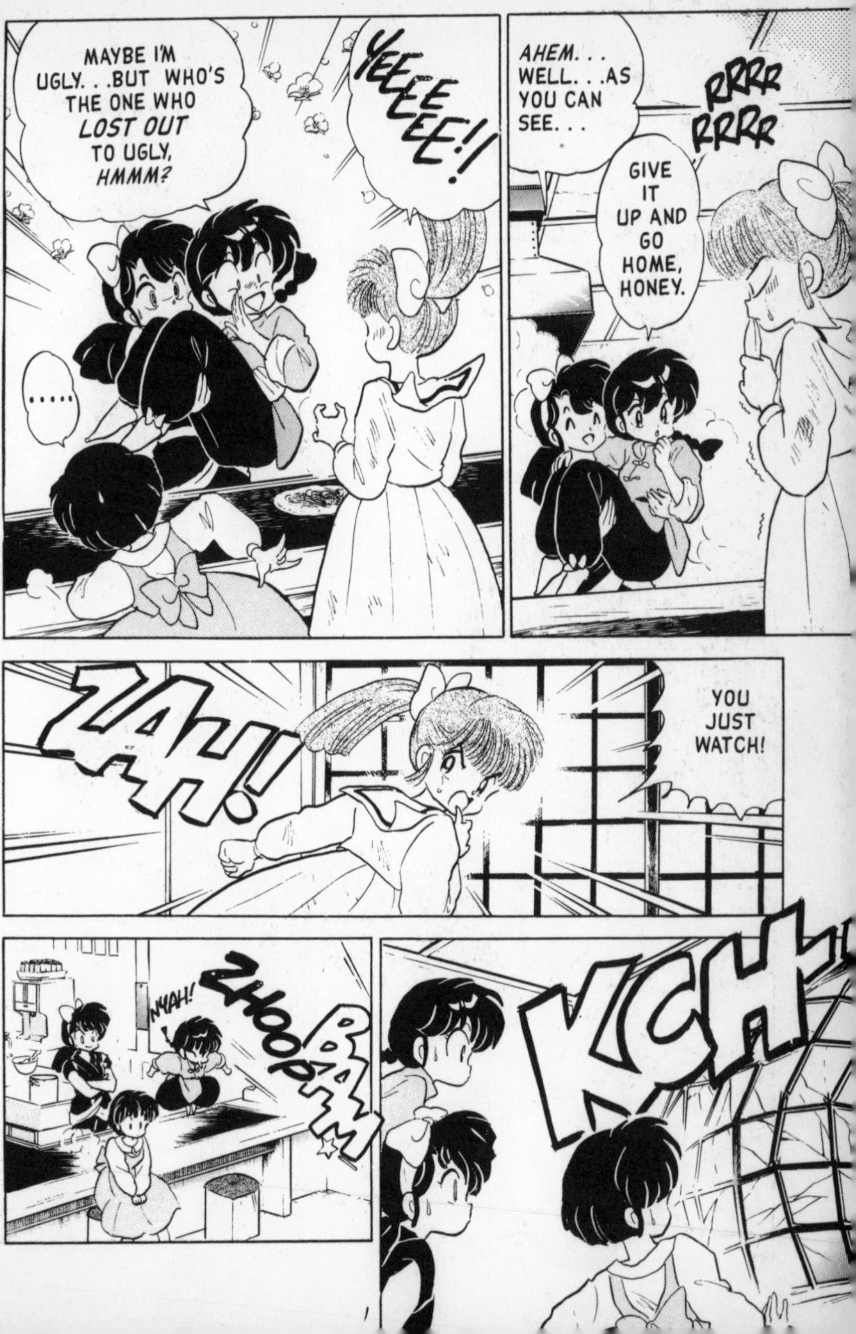
MAYBE I'M UGLY. . .BUT WHO'S THE ONE WHO *LOST OUT* TO UGLY, *HMMM?*
YEEEEEEE!!
. . . . .
AHEM. . . WELL. . .AS YOU CAN SEE. . .
RRRR RRRR
GIVE IT UP AND GO HOME, HONEY.
ZAH!
YOU JUST WATCH!
N'YAH!
ZHOOP

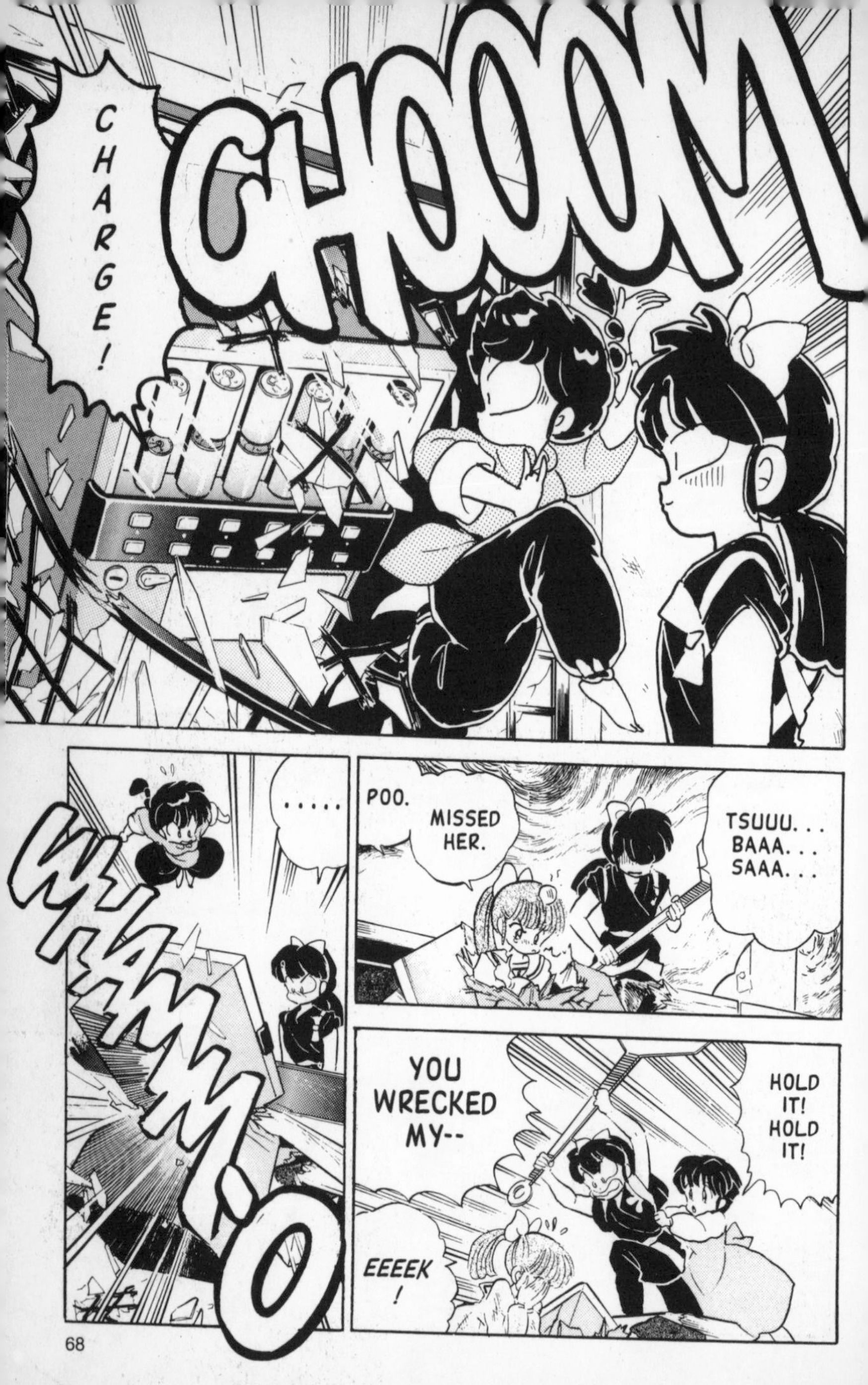
CHARGE!
CHOOOM
WHAMMO
.....
POO.
MISSED HER.
TSUUU... BAAA... SAAA...
YOU WRECKED MY--
HOLD IT! HOLD IT!
EEEEK!

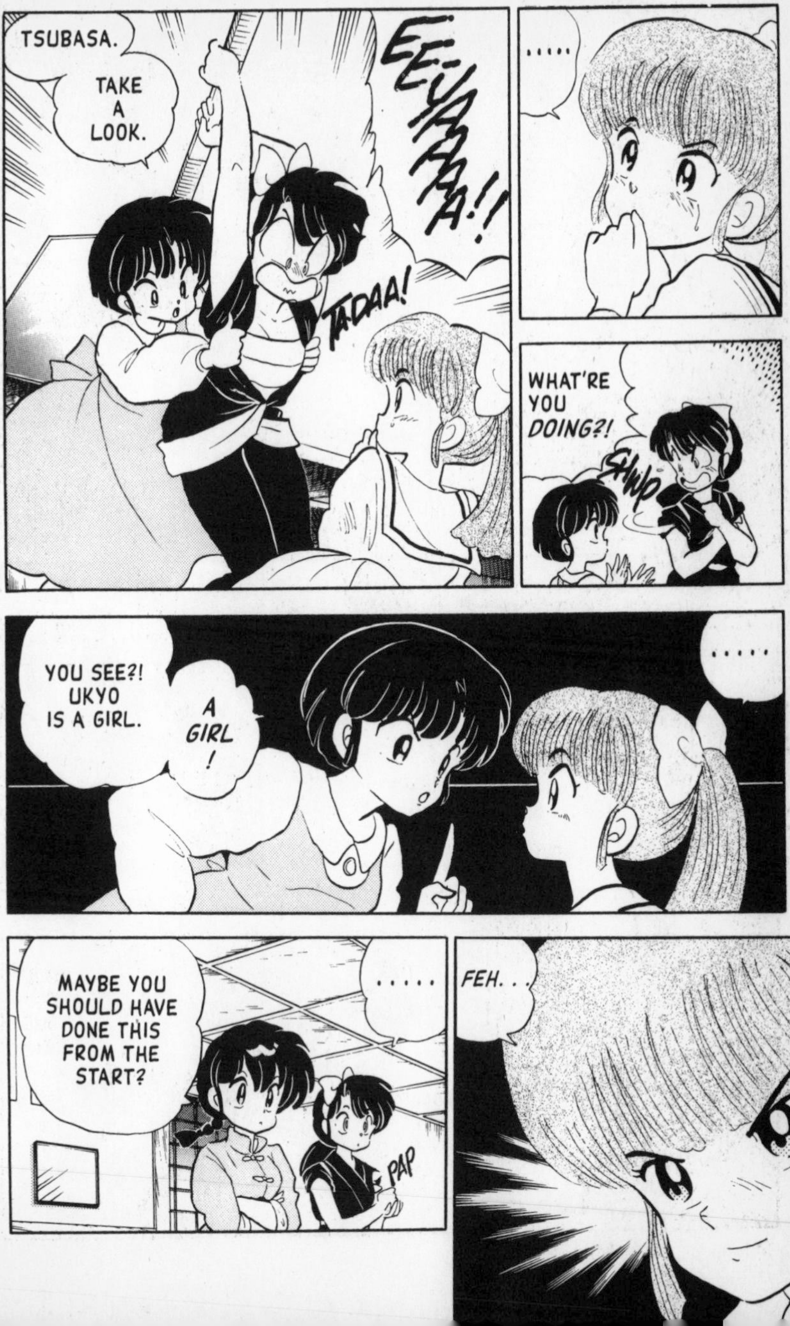
TSUBASA.
TAKE A LOOK.
EE-YAAAAA!!
TA-DAA!
.....
WHAT'RE YOU DOING?!
SHWUP
YOU SEE?! UKYO IS A GIRL.
A GIRL!
.....
MAYBE YOU SHOULD HAVE DONE THIS FROM THE START?
.....
PAP
FEH...

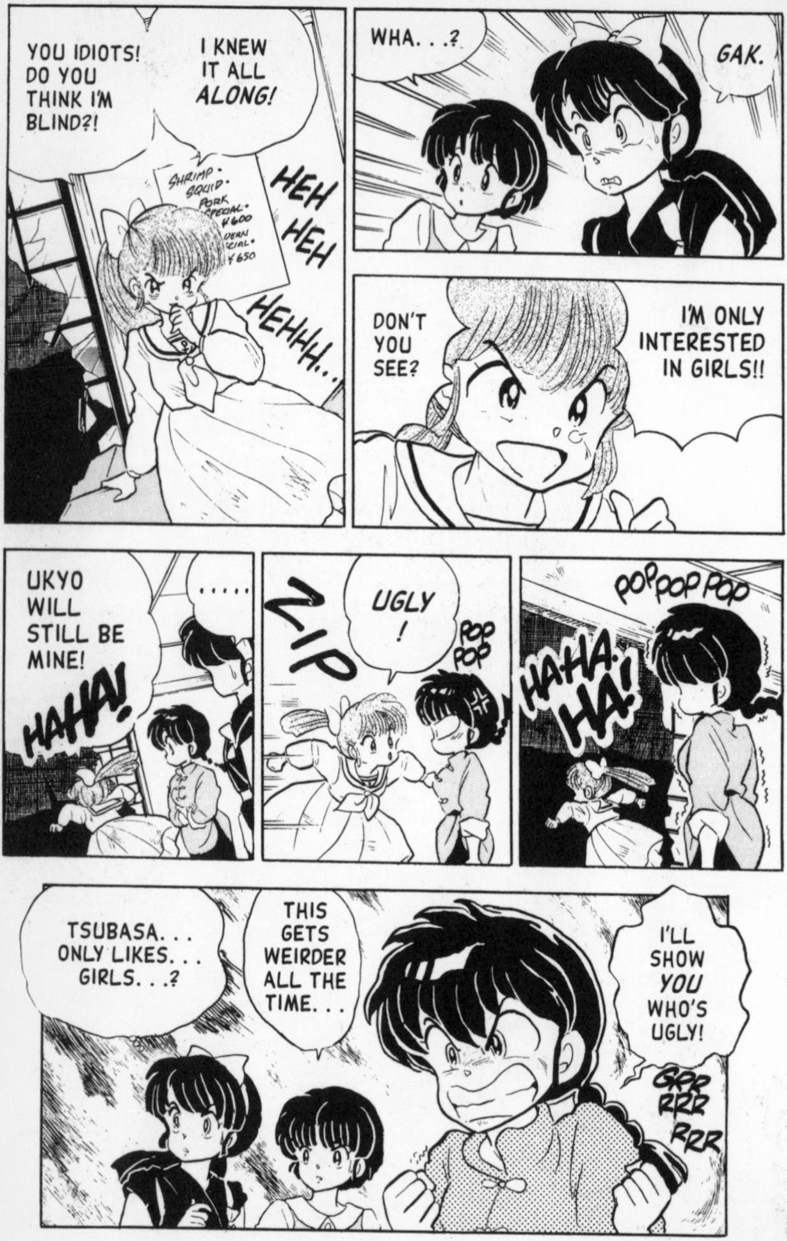
YOU IDIOTS! DO YOU THINK I'M BLIND?!
I KNEW IT ALL ALONG!
SHRIMP • SQUID • PORK SPECIAL • ¥600
¥650
HEH HEH
HEHHH...
WHA. . .?
GAK.
DON'T YOU SEE?
I'M ONLY INTERESTED IN GIRLS!!
UKYO WILL STILL BE MINE!
HAHA!
. . . . .
ZIP
UGLY!
POP POP
POP POP POP
HAHA HA!
TSUBASA. . . ONLY LIKES. . . GIRLS. . .?
THIS GETS WEIRDER ALL THE TIME. . .
I'LL SHOW YOU WHO'S UGLY!
GRR RRR RRR

Part 5
LUNCHTIME LUNACY

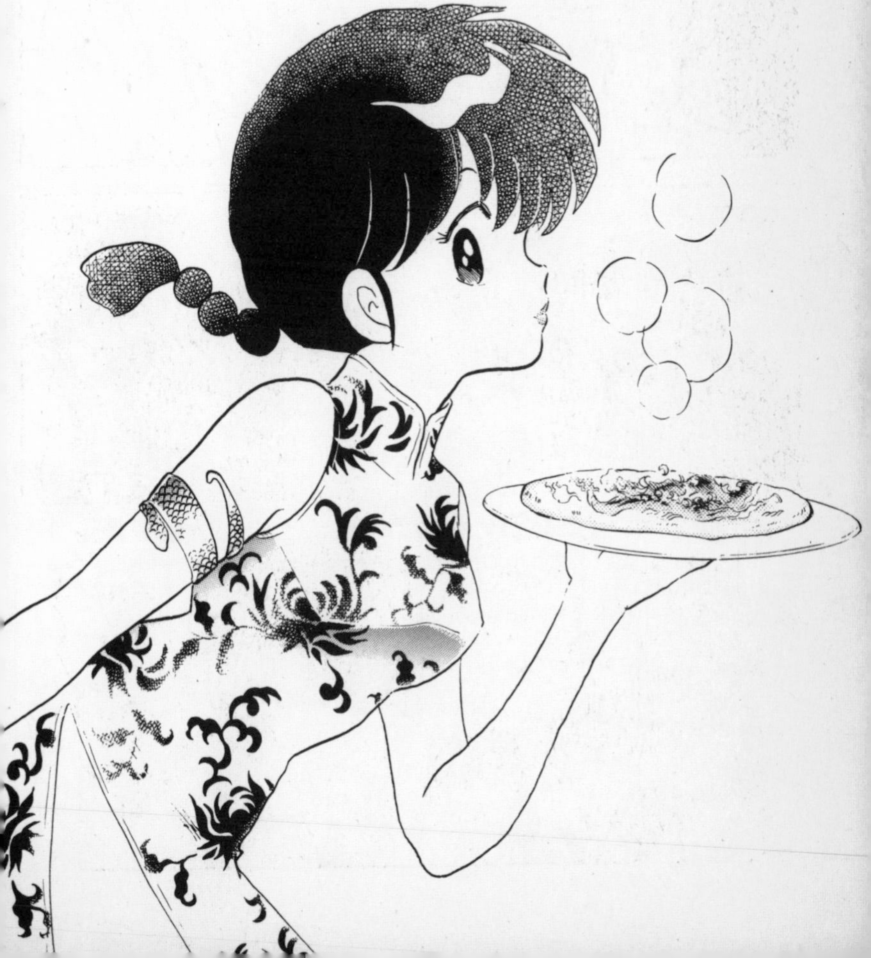

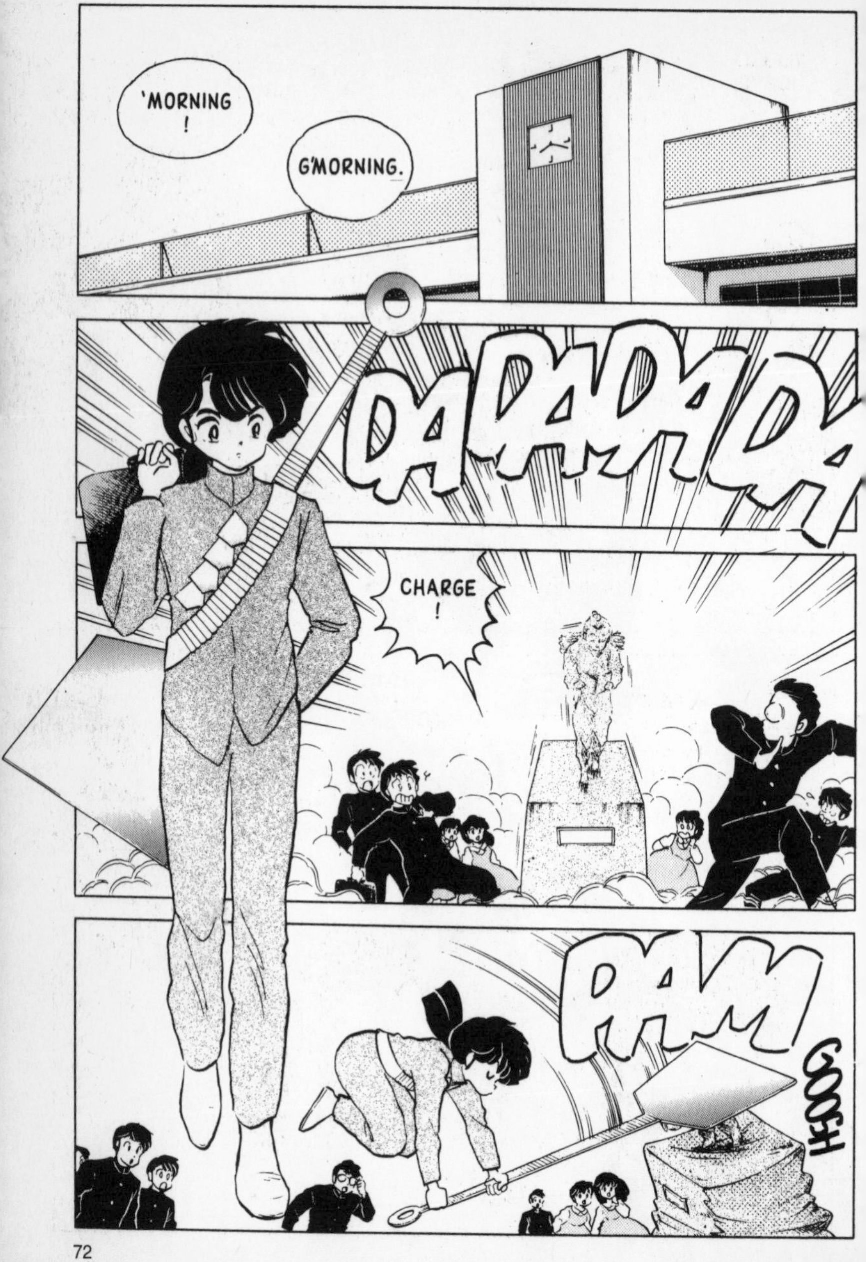
'MORNING !
G'MORNING.
DADADADA
CHARGE !
PAM
GOOSH

OH. DEAREST UKYO, HOW COULD YOU?

WHOA! SHE'S CUTE!

TSUBASA-- I THOUGHT I TOLD YOU TO LEAVE ME ALONE.

SNF SNF

RRRIP

HUH.

TSUBASA KURENAI...

MURMUR MURMUR

DON'T YOU GET IT?

I'M ALREADY ENGAGED TO RAN-CHAN!

THAT... *UGLY* GIRL?!

YOU CAN'T BE ENGAGED TO *HER!*

I'VE BEEN TRYING TO TELL YOU, RANMA IS A B--

OHOHO-HOHO-HO, GOOD MORNING.

VVVUP

OO-OO-OO!

SO. YOU COME AGAIN... UGLY.

PERVERT.

HWOOOOOO

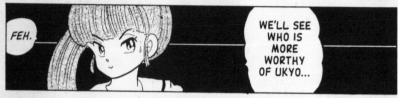

FEH.

WE'LL SEE WHO IS MORE WORTHY OF UKYO...

...LIKE GENTLEMEN!!

SHA

HUH ?!

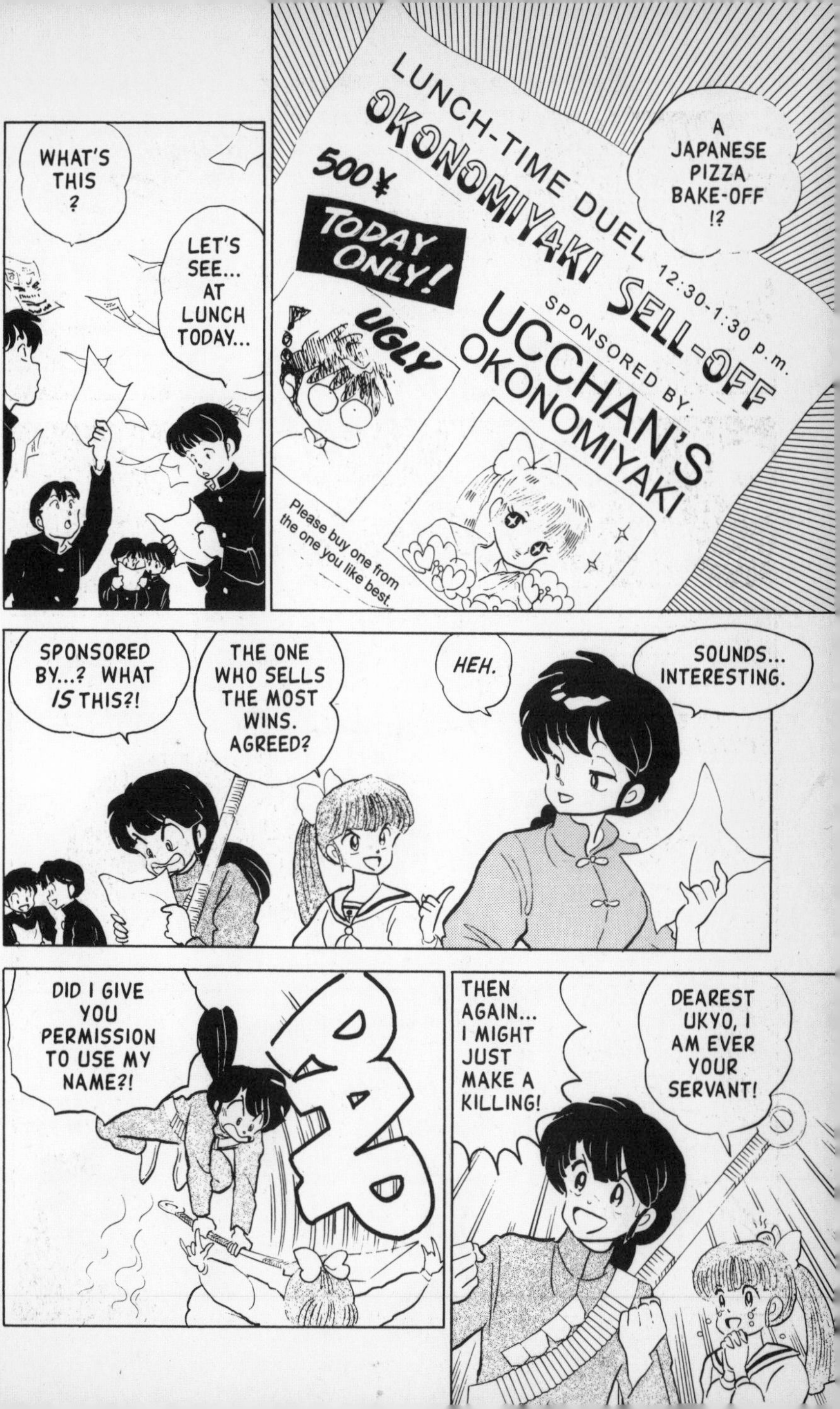
WHAT'S THIS ?
LET'S SEE... AT LUNCH TODAY...
LUNCH-TIME DUEL 12:30-1:30 p.m.
OKONOMIYAKI SELL-OFF
500¥
TODAY ONLY!
UGLY
SPONSORED BY:
UCCHAN'S OKONOMIYAKI
Please buy one from the one you like best.
A JAPANESE PIZZA BAKE-OFF !?
SPONSORED BY...? WHAT IS THIS?!
THE ONE WHO SELLS THE MOST WINS. AGREED?
HEH.
SOUNDS... INTERESTING.
DID I GIVE YOU PERMISSION TO USE MY NAME?!
BAP
THEN AGAIN... I MIGHT JUST MAKE A KILLING!
DEAREST UKYO, I AM EVER YOUR SERVANT!

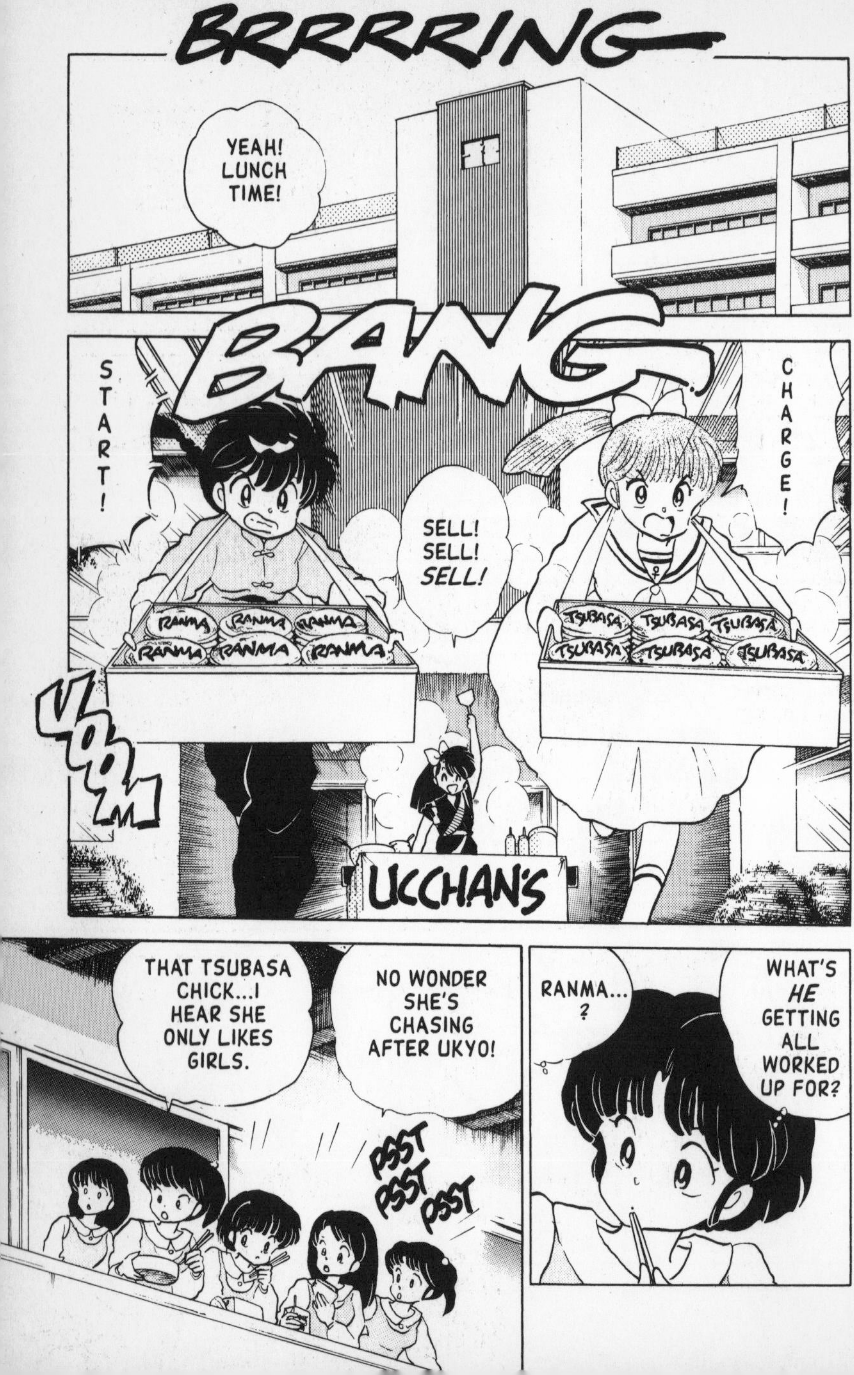
BRRRRING
YEAH! LUNCH TIME!
BANG
START!
SELL! SELL! SELL!
CHARGE!
RANMA RANMA RANMA RANMA RANMA RANMA
TSUBASA TSUBASA TSUBASA TSUBASA TSUBASA TSUBASA
VOOOM
UCCHAN'S
THAT TSUBASA CHICK...I HEAR SHE ONLY LIKES GIRLS.
NO WONDER SHE'S CHASING AFTER UKYO!
PSST PSST PSST
RANMA...?
WHAT'S *HE* GETTING ALL WORKED UP FOR?

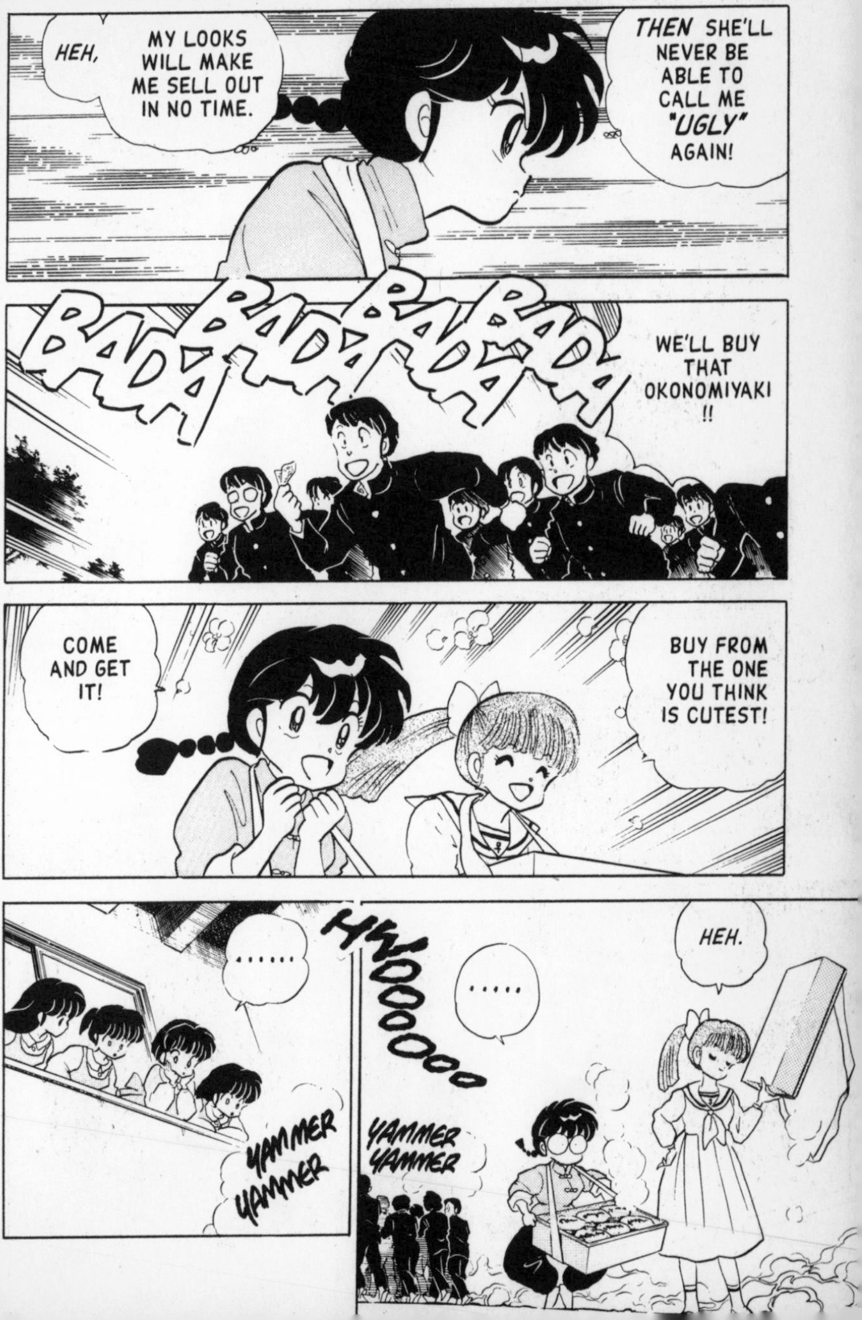
HEH,
MY LOOKS WILL MAKE ME SELL OUT IN NO TIME.
THEN SHE'LL NEVER BE ABLE TO CALL ME "UGLY" AGAIN!
BADA BADA BADA BADA
WE'LL BUY THAT OKONOMIYAKI !!
COME AND GET IT!
BUY FROM THE ONE YOU THINK IS CUTEST!
......
YAMMER YAMMER
HWOOOOOOO
.....
YAMMER YAMMER
HEH.

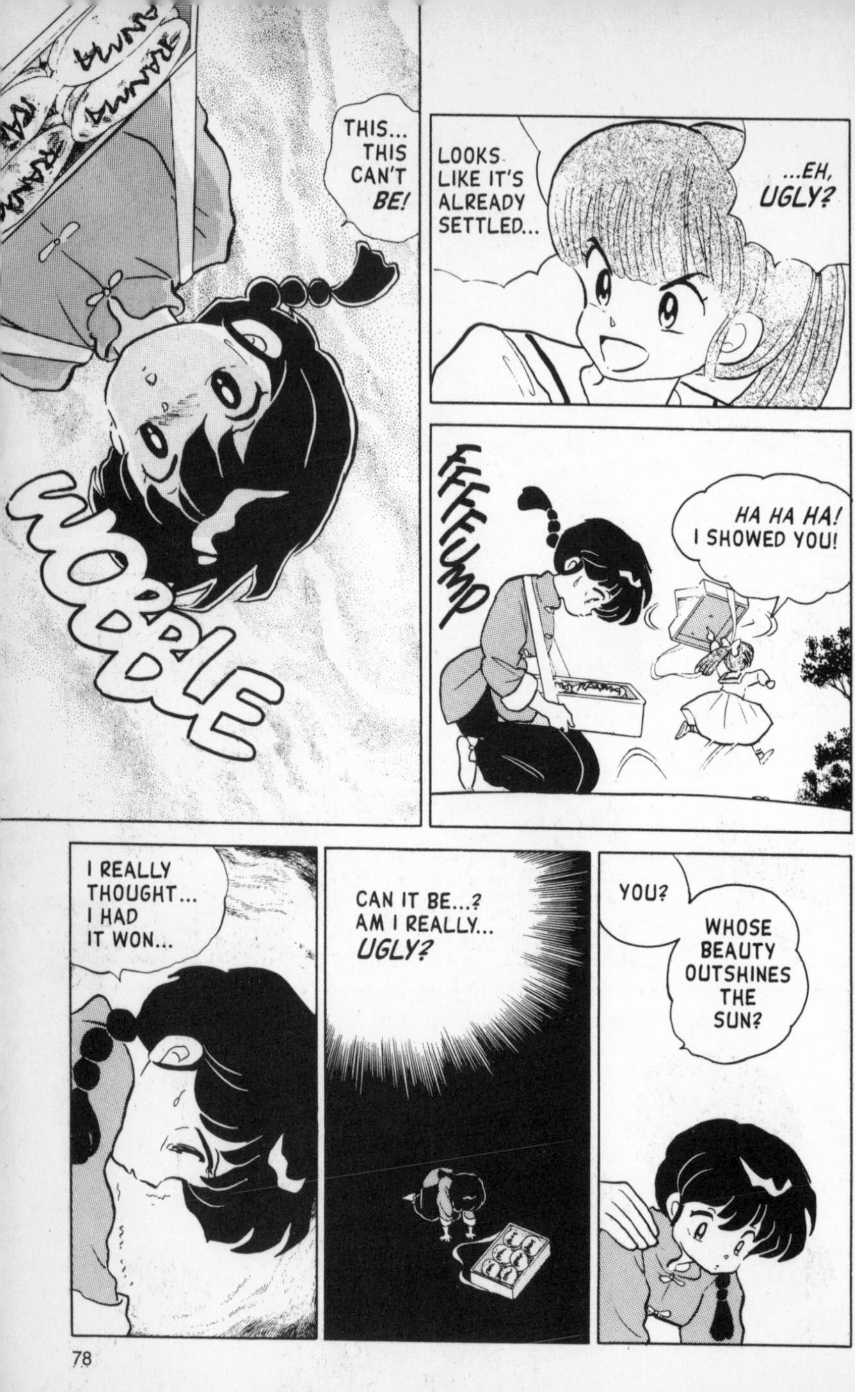
THIS... THIS CAN'T BE!
WOBBLE
LOOKS LIKE IT'S ALREADY SETTLED...
...EH, UGLY?
FFFFUMP
HA HA HA! I SHOWED YOU!
I REALLY THOUGHT... I HAD IT WON...
CAN IT BE...? AM I REALLY... UGLY?
YOU?
WHOSE BEAUTY OUTSHINES THE SUN?

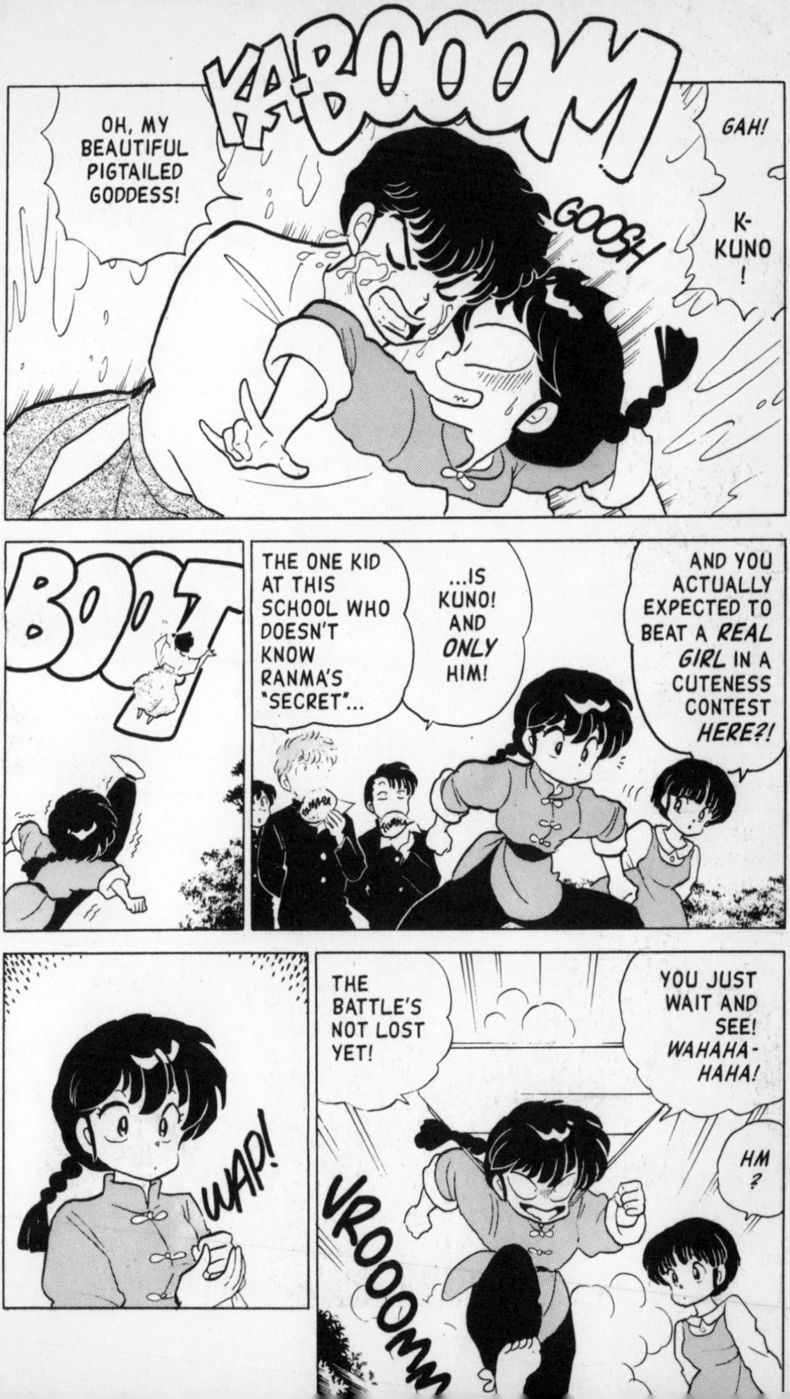
KA-BOOOM
OH, MY BEAUTIFUL PIGTAILED GODDESS!
GOOSH
GAH!
K-KUNO!
BOOT
THE ONE KID AT THIS SCHOOL WHO DOESN'T KNOW RANMA'S "SECRET"...
...IS KUNO! AND *ONLY* HIM!
AND YOU ACTUALLY EXPECTED TO BEAT A *REAL GIRL* IN A CUTENESS CONTEST *HERE?!*
WAP!
THE BATTLE'S NOT LOST YET!
YOU JUST WAIT AND SEE! *WAHAHA-HAHA!*
HM?
VROOOMM

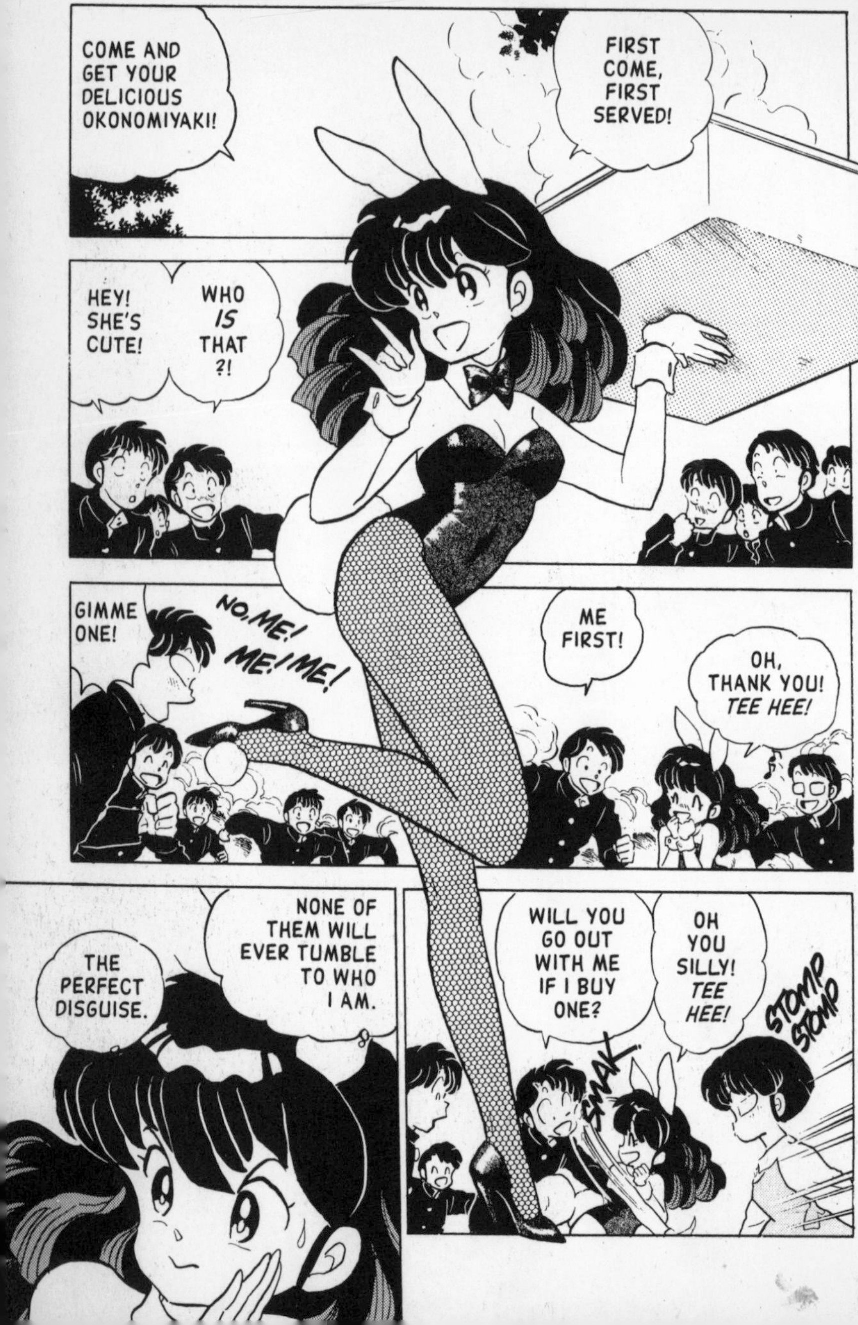
COME AND GET YOUR DELICIOUS OKONOMIYAKI!
FIRST COME, FIRST SERVED!
HEY! SHE'S CUTE!
WHO *IS* THAT ?!
GIMME ONE!
NO, ME! ME! ME!
ME FIRST!
OH, THANK YOU! *TEE HEE!*
THE PERFECT DISGUISE.
NONE OF THEM WILL EVER TUMBLE TO WHO I AM.
WILL YOU GO OUT WITH ME IF I BUY ONE?
OH YOU SILLY! *TEE HEE!*
SMAK
STOMP STOMP

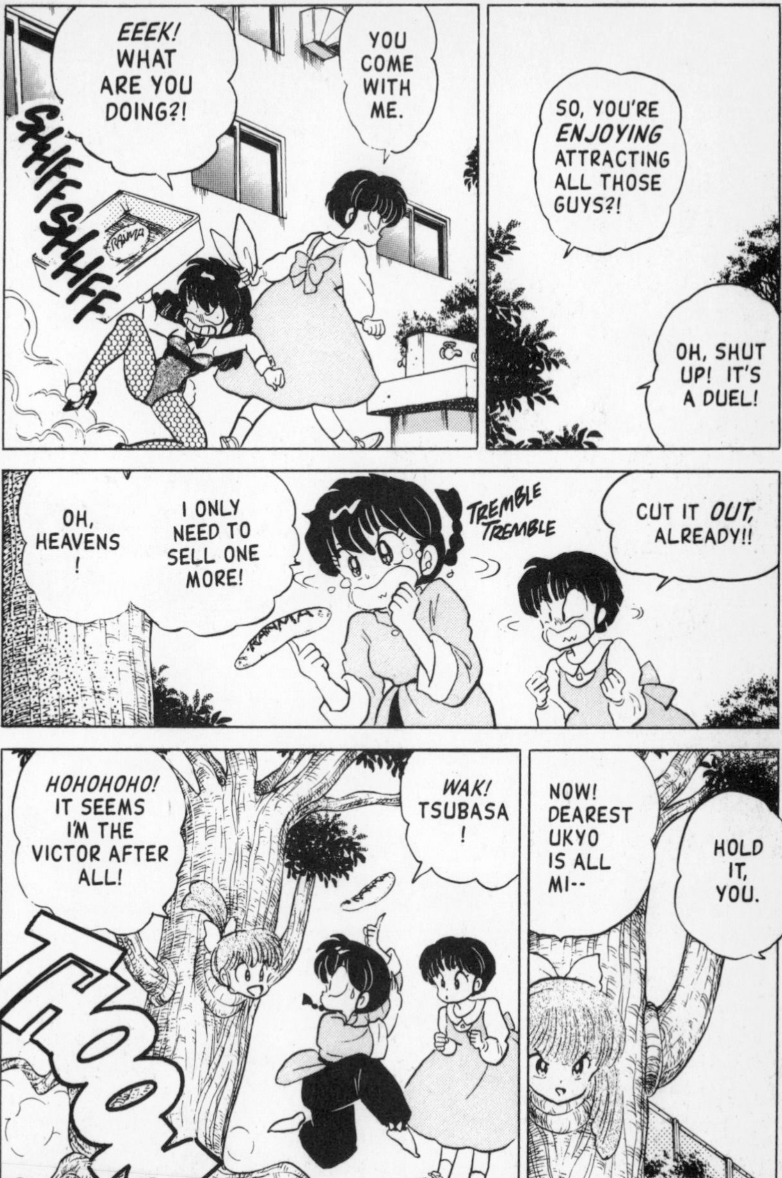
EEEK! WHAT ARE YOU DOING?!
YOU COME WITH ME.
SHHFSHHFF
RANMA
SO, YOU'RE *ENJOYING* ATTRACTING ALL THOSE GUYS?!
OH, SHUT UP! IT'S A DUEL!
OH, HEAVENS!
I ONLY NEED TO SELL ONE MORE!
RANMA
TREMBLE TREMBLE
CUT IT *OUT*, ALREADY!!
HOHOHOHO! IT SEEMS I'M THE VICTOR AFTER ALL!
WAK! TSUBASA!
THOOM
NOW! DEAREST UKYO IS ALL MI--
HOLD IT, YOU.

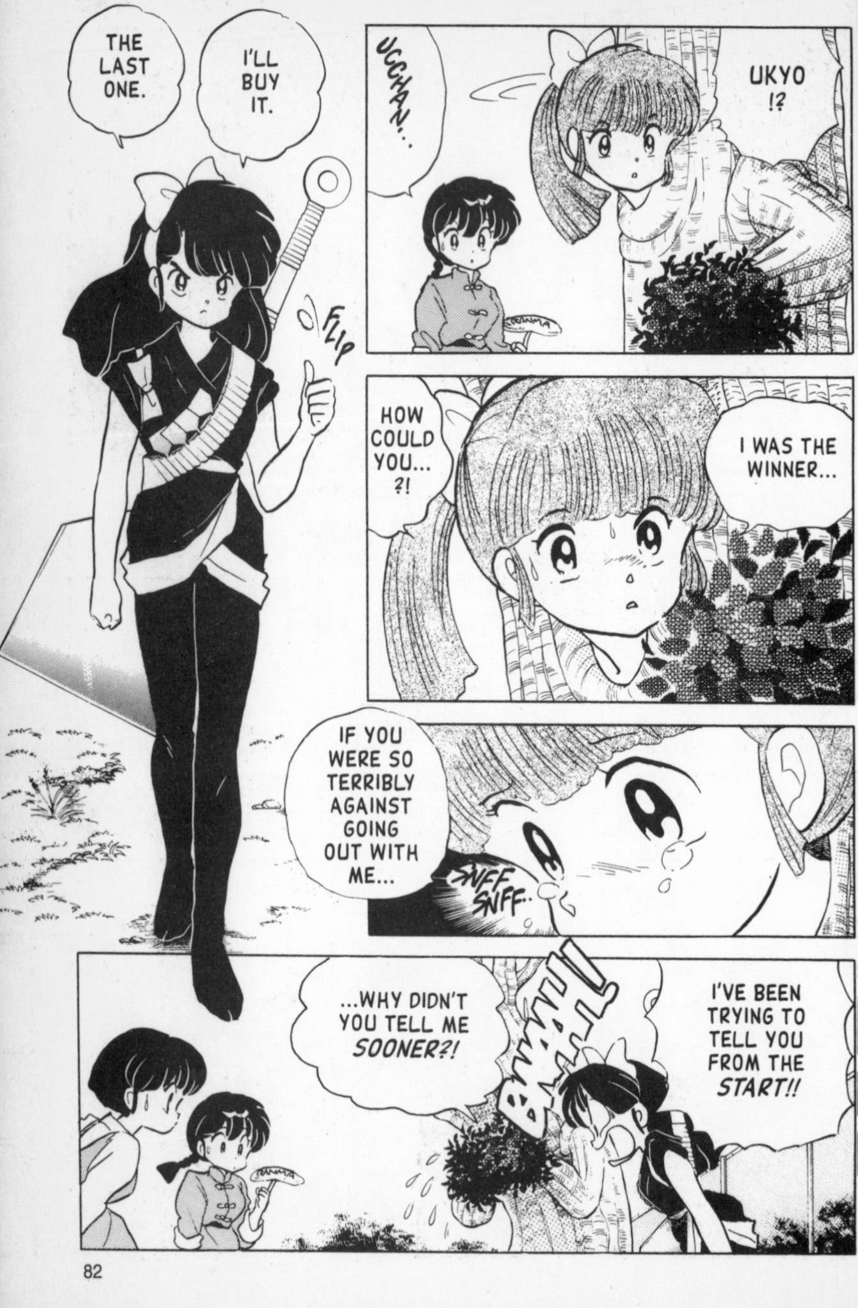
THE LAST ONE.
I'LL BUY IT.
FLIP
UCCHAN...
UKYO!?
HOW COULD YOU...?!
I WAS THE WINNER...
IF YOU WERE SO TERRIBLY AGAINST GOING OUT WITH ME...
SNIFF SNIFF
...WHY DIDN'T YOU TELL ME SOONER?!
I'VE BEEN TRYING TO TELL YOU FROM THE START!!

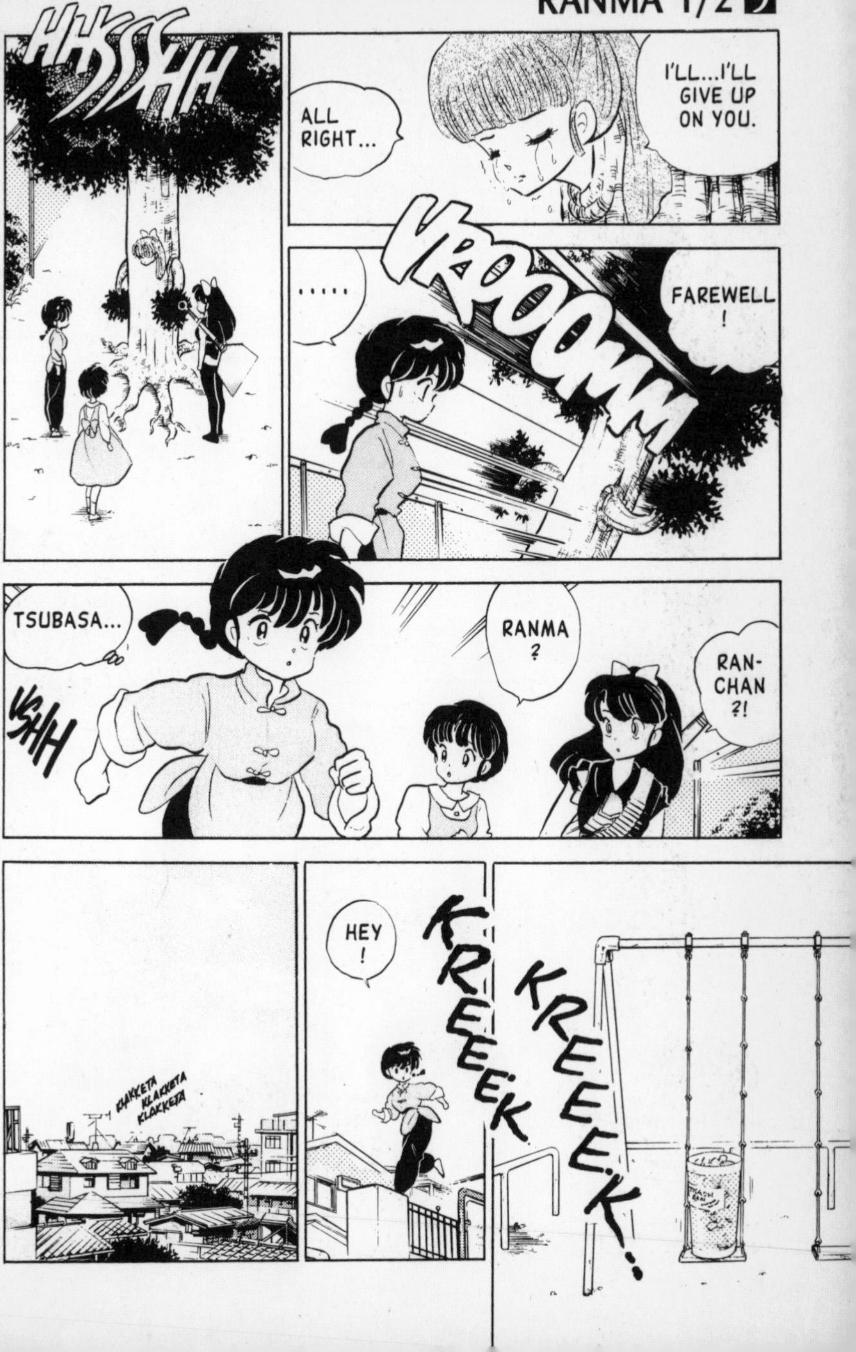
HHSSHH
ALL RIGHT...
I'LL...I'LL GIVE UP ON YOU.
.....
VROOOMM
FAREWELL!
TSUBASA...
VSHH
RANMA?
RAN-CHAN?!
KLAKKETA KLAKKETA KLAKKETA
HEY!
KREEEEK
KREEEEK...

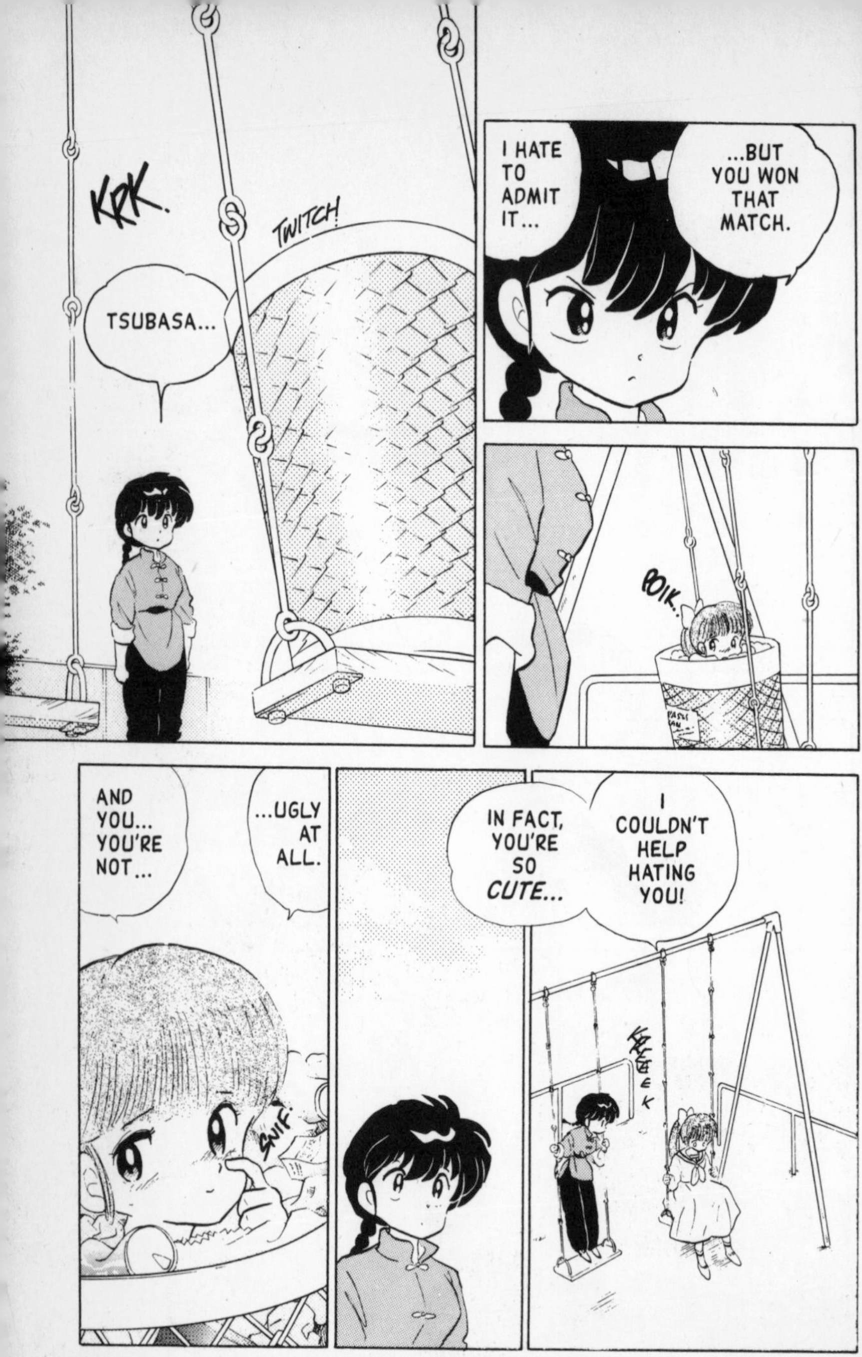
KRK.
TWITCH!
TSUBASA...
I HATE TO ADMIT IT...
...BUT YOU WON THAT MATCH.
POIK..
AND YOU... YOU'RE NOT...
...UGLY AT ALL.
SNIF.
IN FACT, YOU'RE SO *CUTE*...
I COULDN'T HELP HATING YOU!

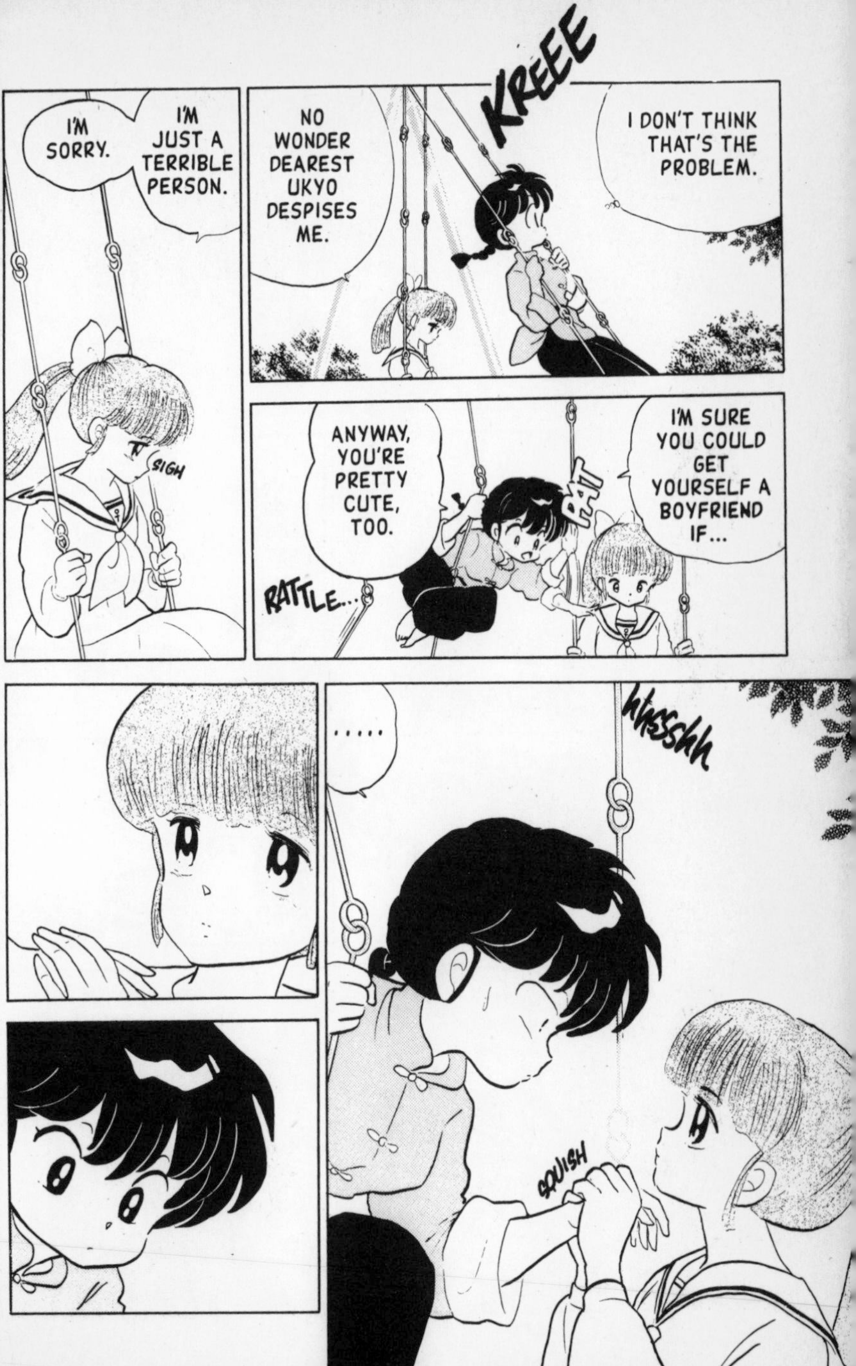
I'M SORRY.
I'M JUST A TERRIBLE PERSON.
SIGH
NO WONDER DEAREST UKYO DESPISES ME.
KREEE
I DON'T THINK THAT'S THE PROBLEM.
ANYWAY, YOU'RE PRETTY CUTE, TOO.
PAT
I'M SURE YOU COULD GET YOURSELF A BOYFRIEND IF...
RATTLE...
.....
SQUISH

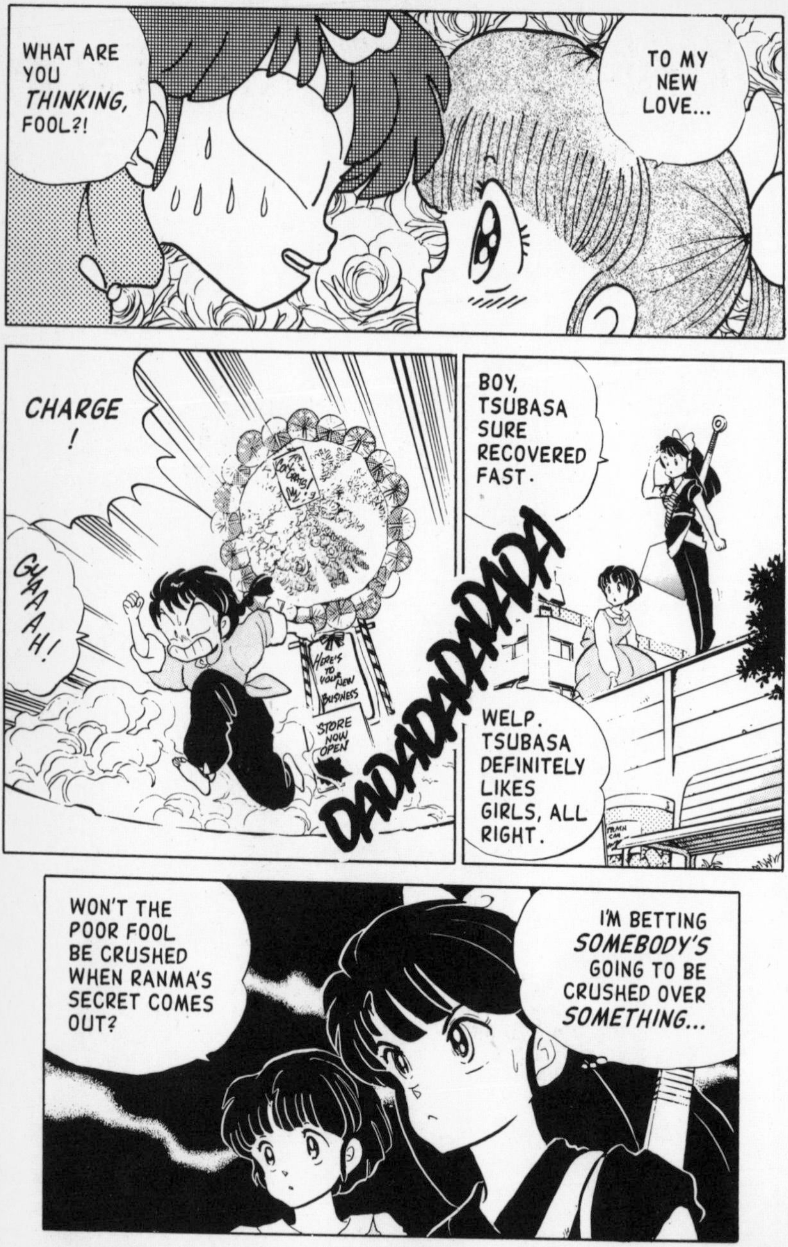
WHAT ARE YOU *THINKING,* FOOL?!
TO MY NEW LOVE...
CHARGE!
GYAAAAH!
CONGRATS!
HERE'S TO YOUR NEW BUSINESS
STORE NOW OPEN
DADADADADADA
BOY, TSUBASA SURE RECOVERED FAST.
WELP. TSUBASA DEFINITELY LIKES GIRLS, ALL RIGHT.
WON'T THE POOR FOOL BE CRUSHED WHEN RANMA'S SECRET COMES OUT?
I'M BETTING *SOMEBODY'S* GOING TO BE CRUSHED OVER *SOMETHING...*

Part 6
THE PERFECT MATCH

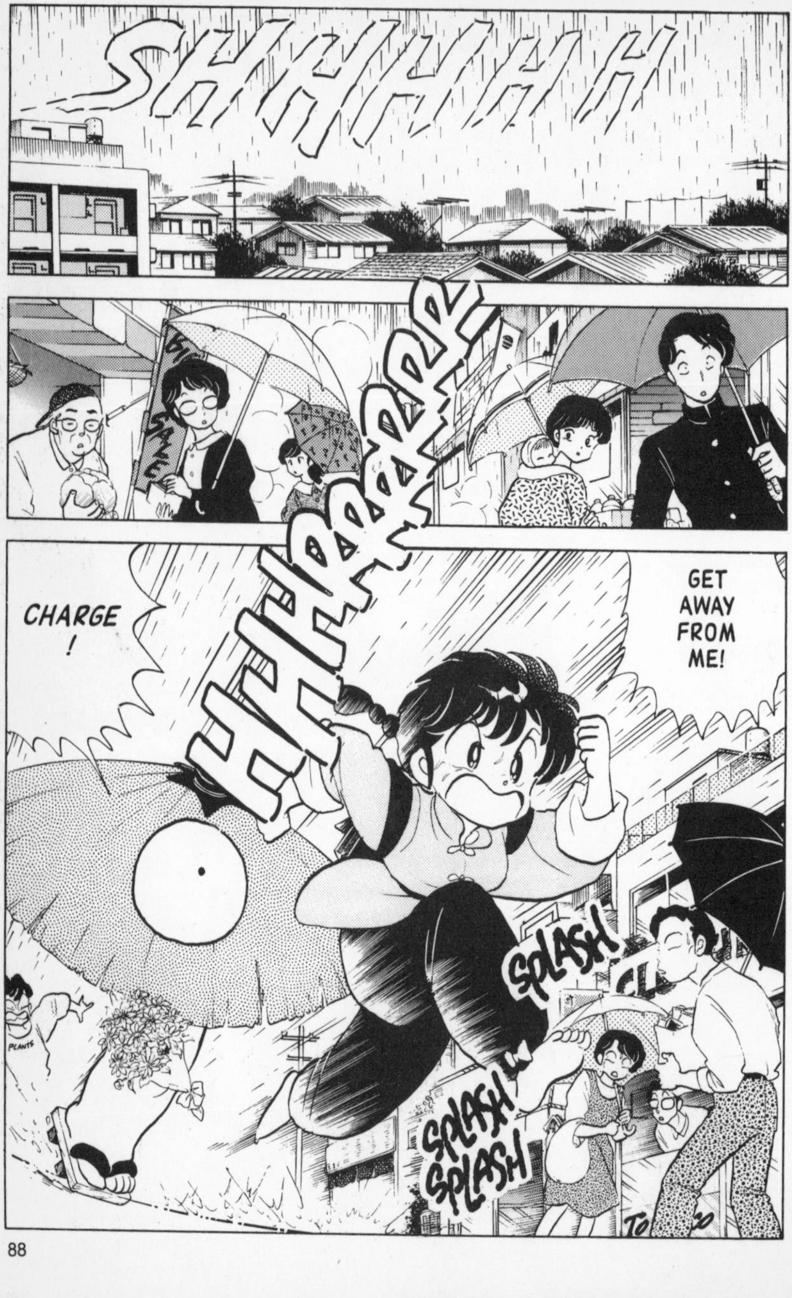
CHARGE
!
GET AWAY FROM ME!
SPLASH
SPLASH
SPLASH

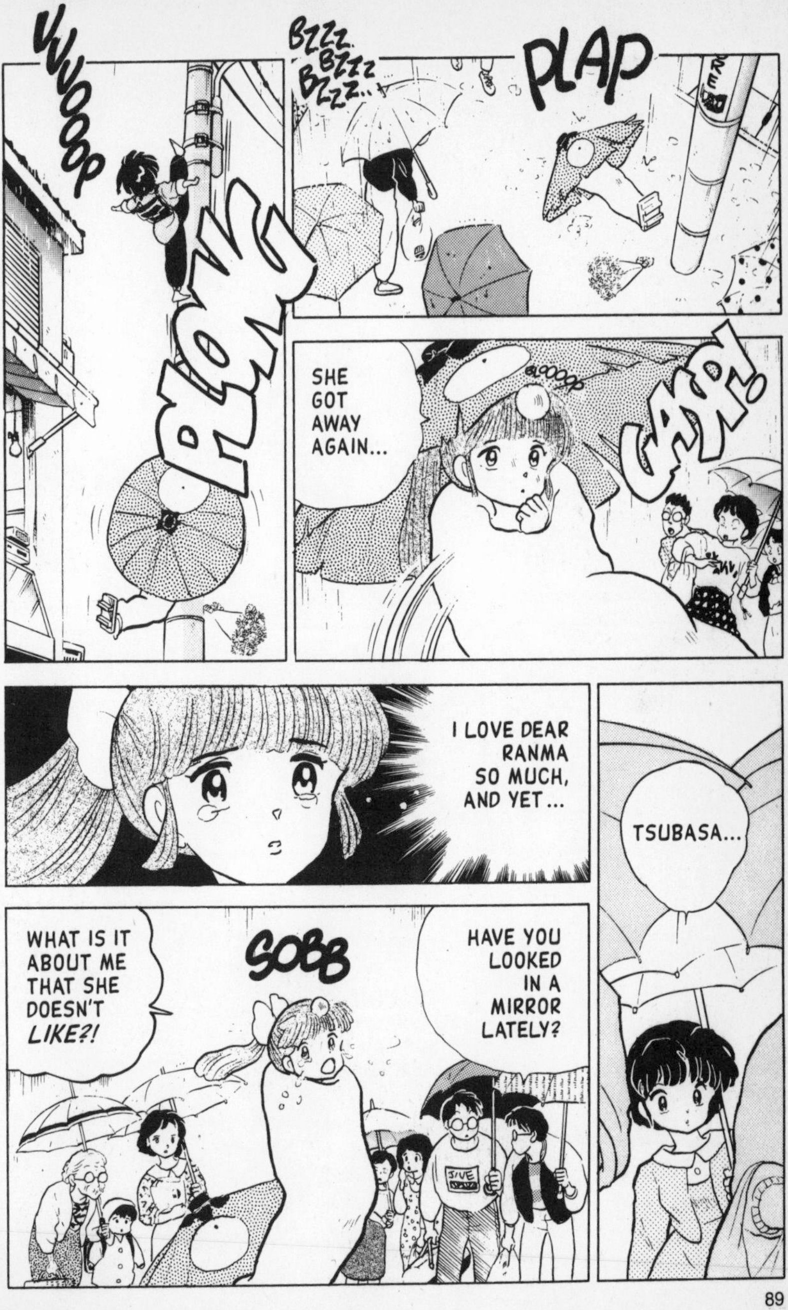
VVVOOOOP
PLOW
BZZZ BZZZ BZZZ...
PLAP
SHE GOT AWAY AGAIN...
BLOOOP
GASP!
I LOVE DEAR RANMA SO MUCH, AND YET...
TSUBASA...
WHAT IS IT ABOUT ME THAT SHE DOESN'T *LIKE?!*
SOBB
HAVE YOU LOOKED IN A MIRROR LATELY?

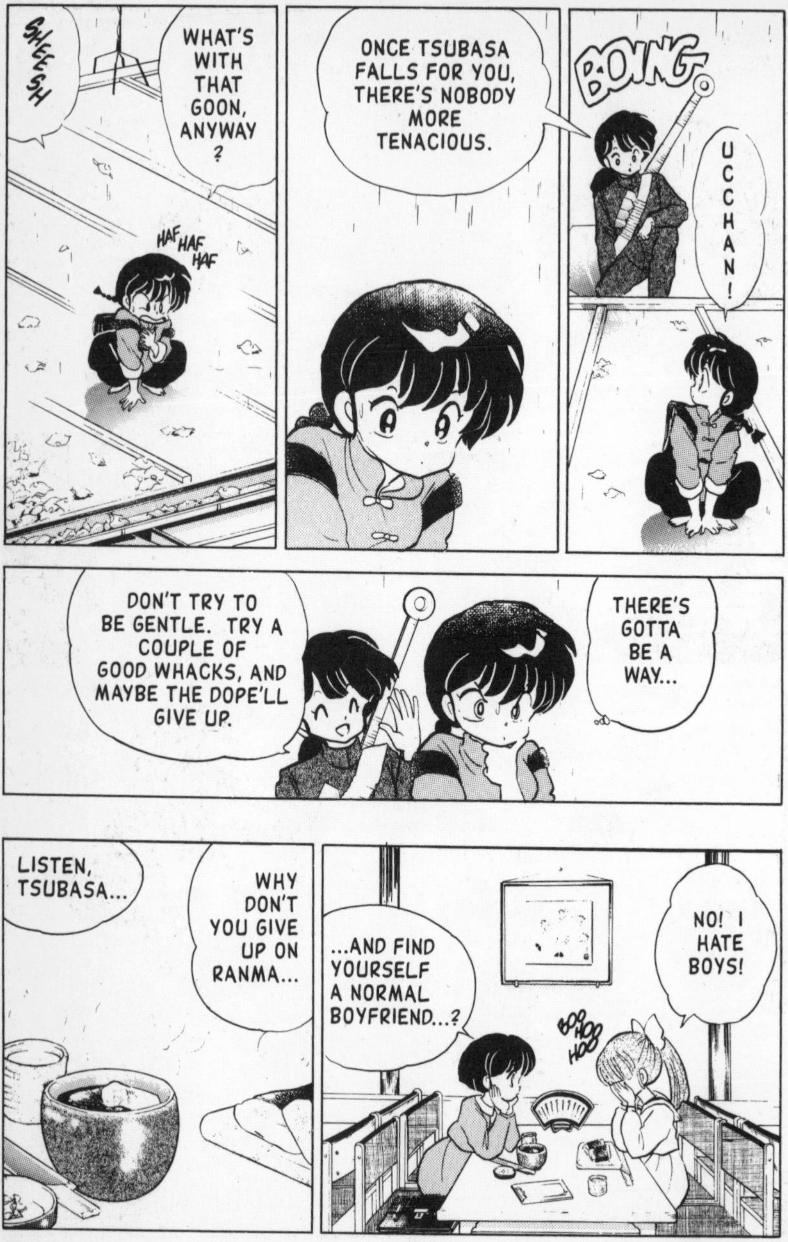
SHEESH
WHAT'S WITH THAT GOON, ANYWAY?
HAF HAF HAF
ONCE TSUBASA FALLS FOR YOU, THERE'S NOBODY MORE TENACIOUS.
BOING
UCCHAN!
DON'T TRY TO BE GENTLE. TRY A COUPLE OF GOOD WHACKS, AND MAYBE THE DOPE'LL GIVE UP.
THERE'S GOTTA BE A WAY...
LISTEN, TSUBASA...
WHY DON'T YOU GIVE UP ON RANMA...
...AND FIND YOURSELF A NORMAL BOYFRIEND...?
NO! I HATE BOYS!
BOO HOO HOO

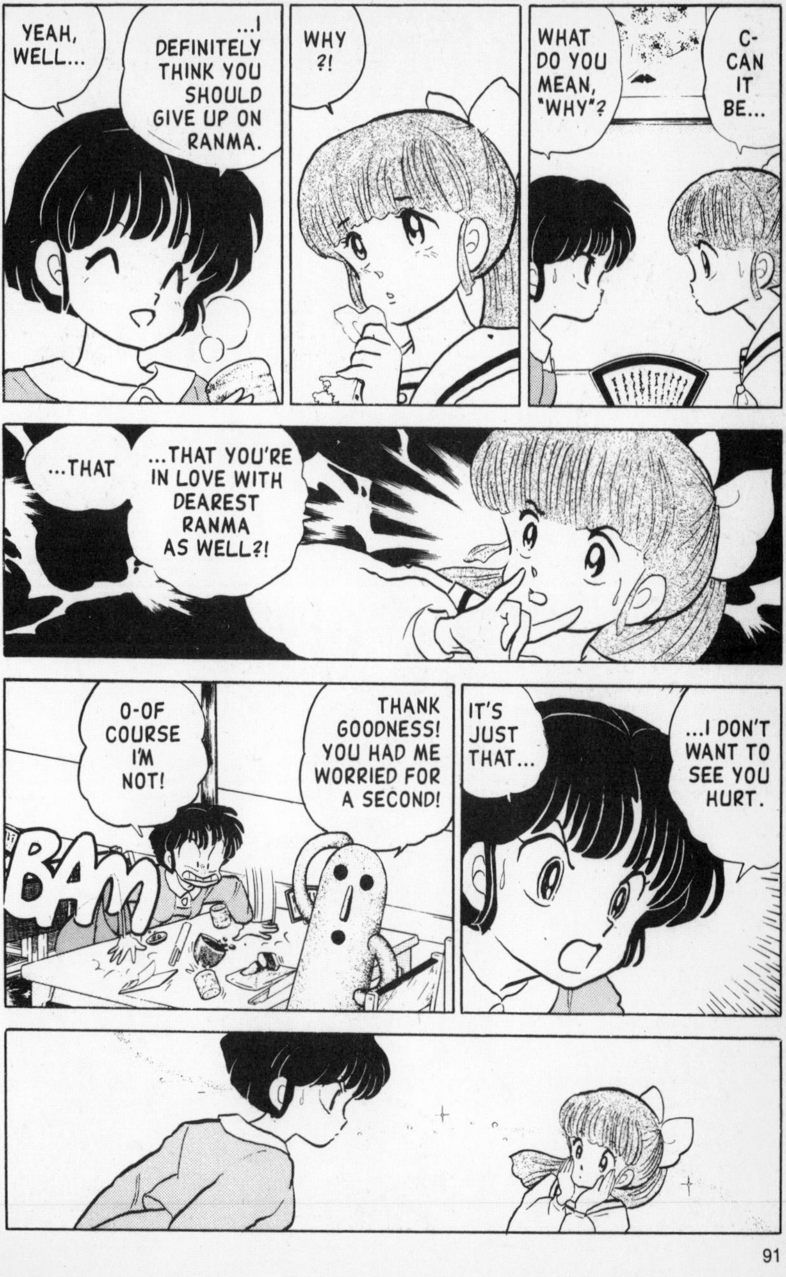
YEAH, WELL...
...I DEFINITELY THINK YOU SHOULD GIVE UP ON RANMA.
WHY?!
WHAT DO YOU MEAN, "WHY"?
C-CAN IT BE...
...THAT
...THAT YOU'RE IN LOVE WITH DEAREST RANMA AS WELL?!
O-OF COURSE I'M NOT!
BAM
THANK GOODNESS! YOU HAD ME WORRIED FOR A SECOND!
IT'S JUST THAT...
...I DON'T WANT TO SEE YOU HURT.

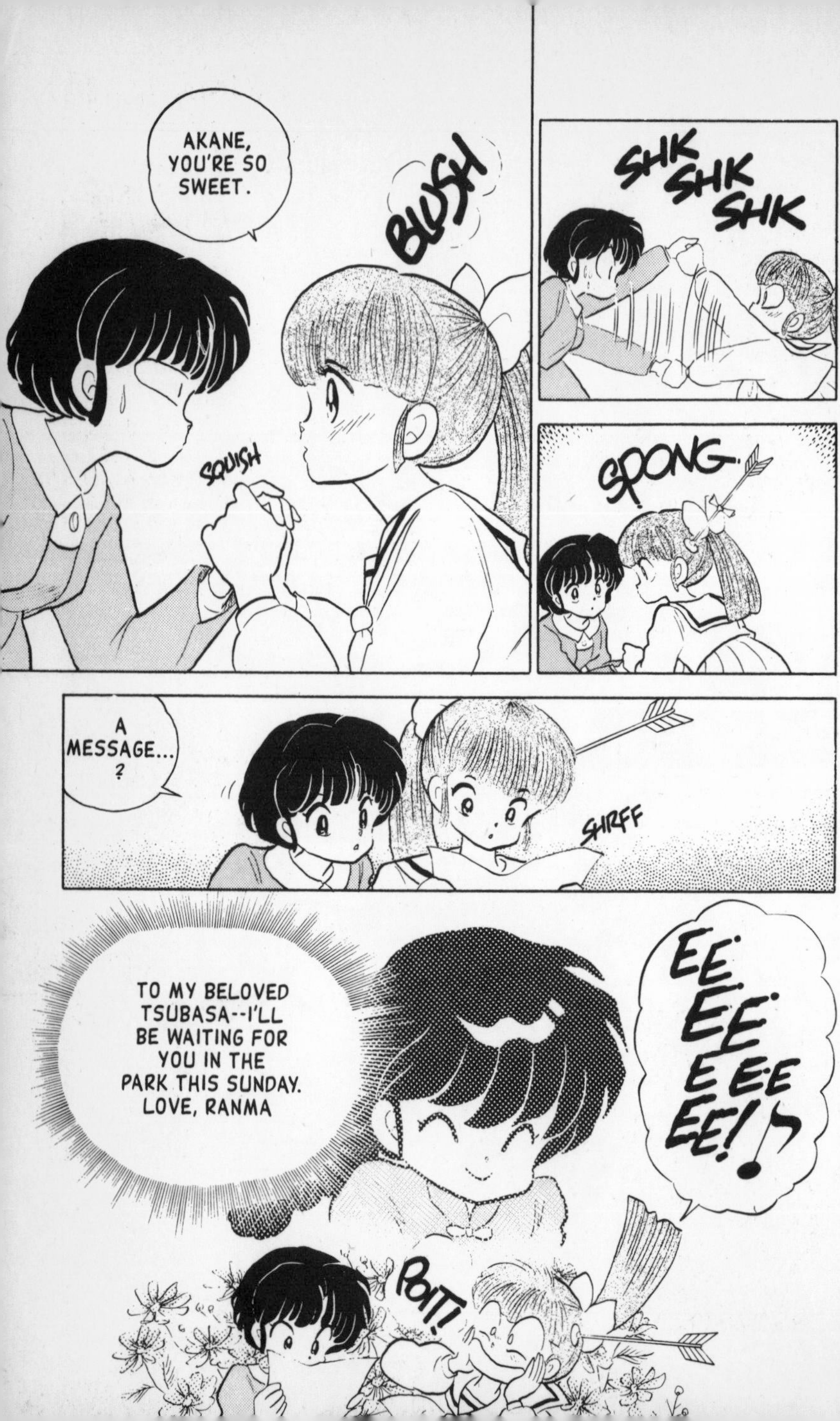
AKANE, YOU'RE SO SWEET.
BLUSH
SQUISH
SHK SHK SHK
SPONG
A MESSAGE...?
SHRFF
TO MY BELOVED TSUBASA--I'LL BE WAITING FOR YOU IN THE PARK THIS SUNDAY. LOVE, RANMA
EEEEEEEEEE!♪
POIT!

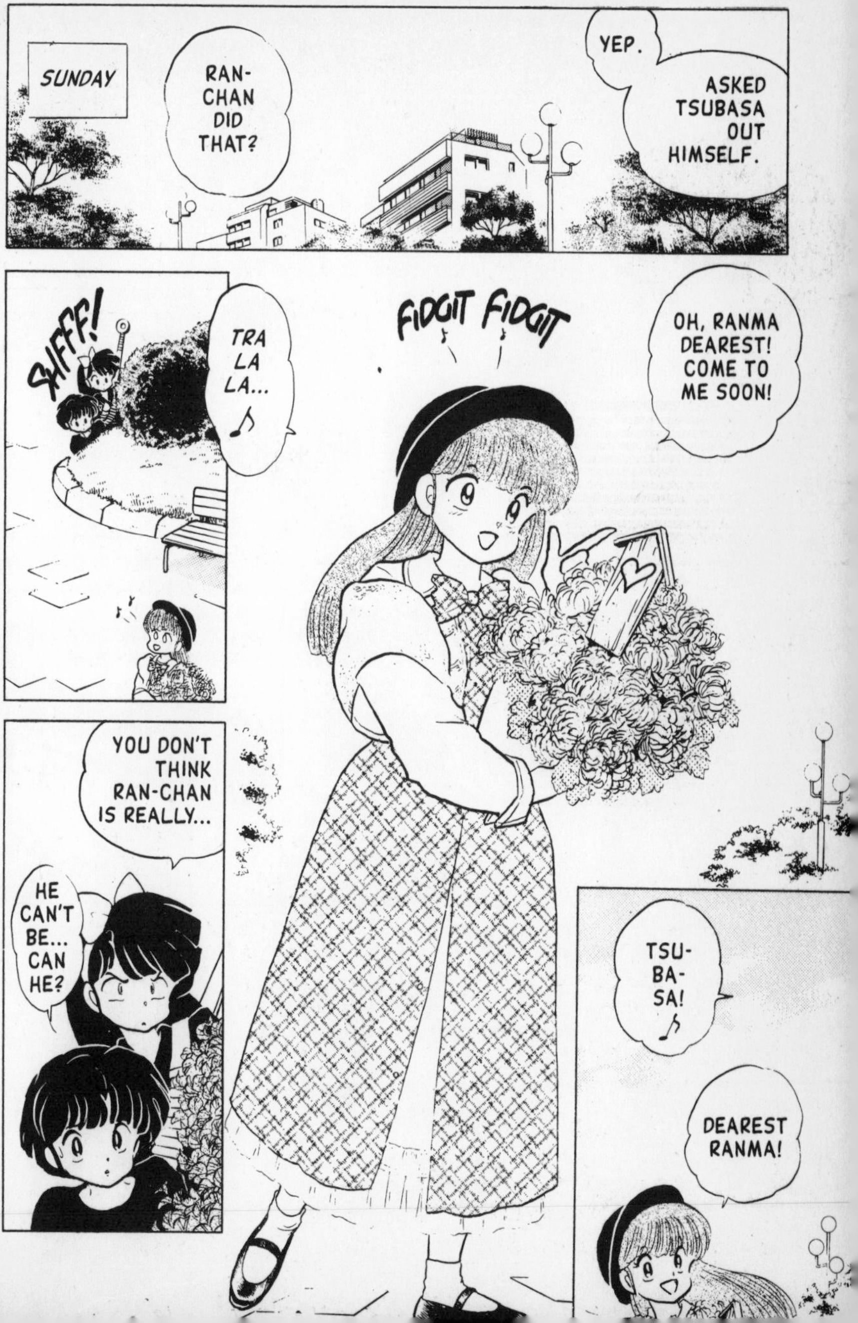
SUNDAY
RAN-CHAN DID THAT?
YEP.
ASKED TSUBASA OUT HIMSELF.
SHFFF!
TRA LA LA... ♪
YOU DON'T THINK RAN-CHAN IS REALLY...
HE CAN'T BE... CAN HE?
FIDGIT FIDGIT
OH, RANMA DEAREST! COME TO ME SOON!
TSU-BA-SA! ♪
DEAREST RANMA!

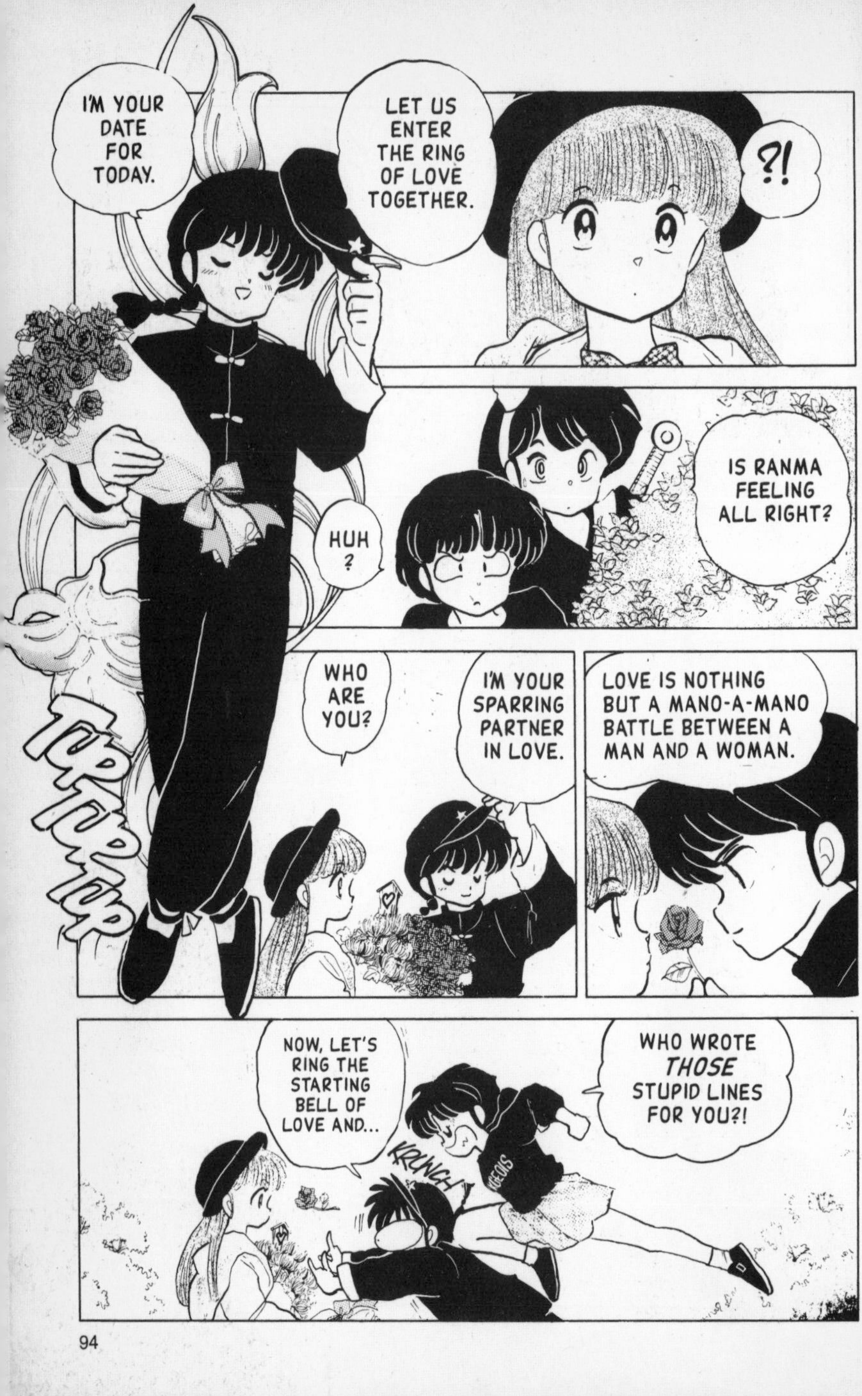
I'M YOUR DATE FOR TODAY.
LET US ENTER THE RING OF LOVE TOGETHER.
?!
TUP TUP TUP
HUH?
IS RANMA FEELING ALL RIGHT?
WHO ARE YOU?
I'M YOUR SPARRING PARTNER IN LOVE.
LOVE IS NOTHING BUT A MANO-A-MANO BATTLE BETWEEN A MAN AND A WOMAN.
NOW, LET'S RING THE STARTING BELL OF LOVE AND...
KRUNCH
WHO WROTE *THOSE* STUPID LINES FOR YOU?!

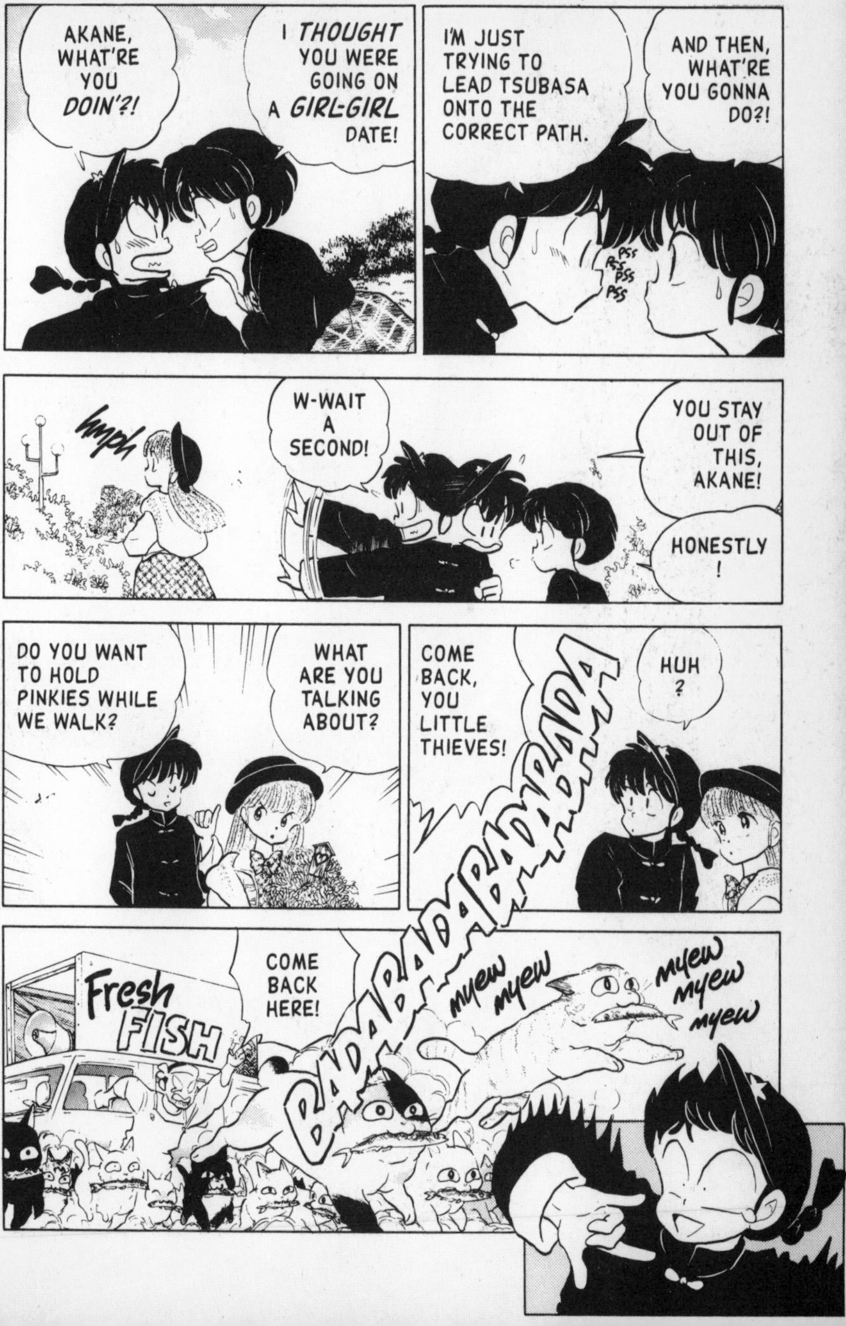
AKANE, WHAT'RE YOU *DOIN'?!*
I *THOUGHT* YOU WERE GOING ON A *GIRL-GIRL* DATE!
I'M JUST TRYING TO LEAD TSUBASA ONTO THE CORRECT PATH.
AND THEN, WHAT'RE YOU GONNA DO?!
PSS PSS PSS PSS
humph
W-WAIT A SECOND!
YOU STAY OUT OF THIS, AKANE!
HONESTLY!
DO YOU WANT TO HOLD PINKIES WHILE WE WALK?
WHAT ARE YOU TALKING ABOUT?
COME BACK, YOU LITTLE THIEVES!
BADABADABADA
HUH?
Fresh FISH
COME BACK HERE!
BADABADABADA
myew myew
myew myew myew

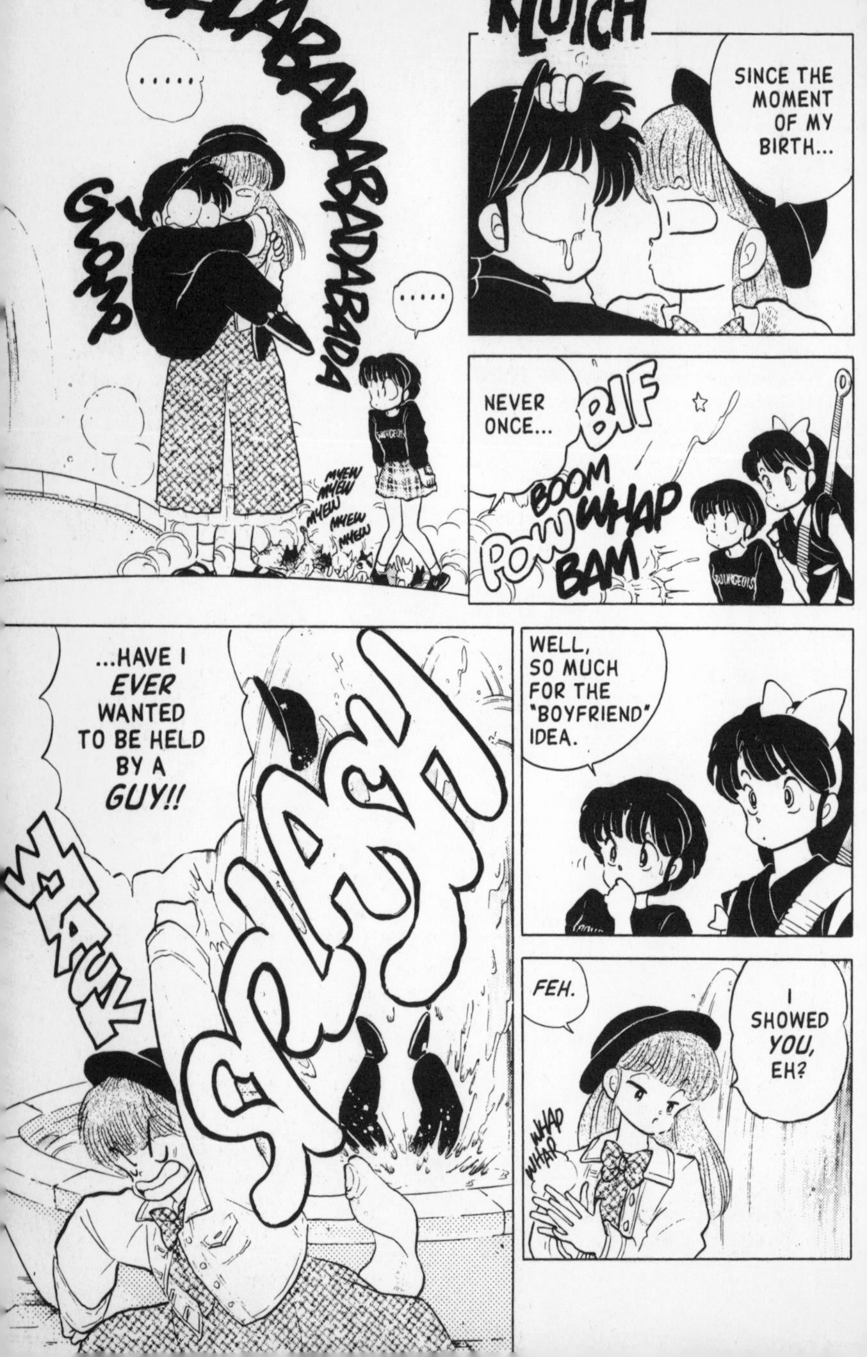

BADABADABADABADABADA
......
GLOMP
......
MYEW MYEW MYEW MYEW MYEW
KLUTCH
SINCE THE MOMENT OF MY BIRTH...
NEVER ONCE...
BIF
BOOM
POW
WHAP
BAM
...HAVE I *EVER* WANTED TO BE HELD BY A *GUY!!*
SPLASH
WELL, SO MUCH FOR THE "BOYFRIEND" IDEA.
FEH.
I SHOWED *YOU,* EH?
WHAP WHAP

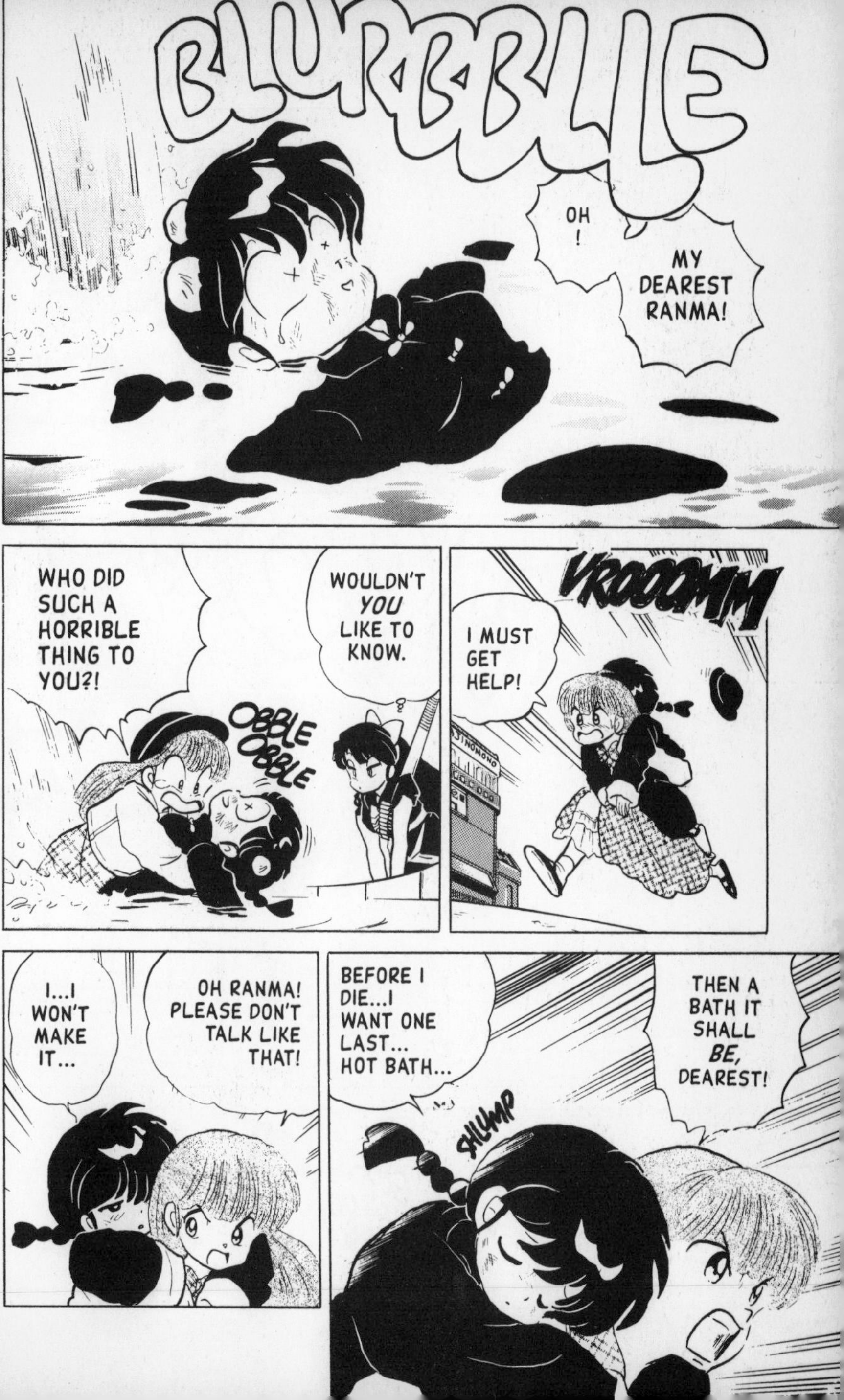
BLUBBLE
OH!
MY DEAREST RANMA!
WHO DID SUCH A HORRIBLE THING TO YOU?!
OBBLE OBBLE
WOULDN'T *YOU* LIKE TO KNOW.
VROOOMM
I MUST GET HELP!
I...I WON'T MAKE IT...
OH RANMA! PLEASE DON'T TALK LIKE THAT!
BEFORE I DIE...I WANT ONE LAST... HOT BATH...
SHLUMP
THEN A BATH IT SHALL *BE*, DEAREST!

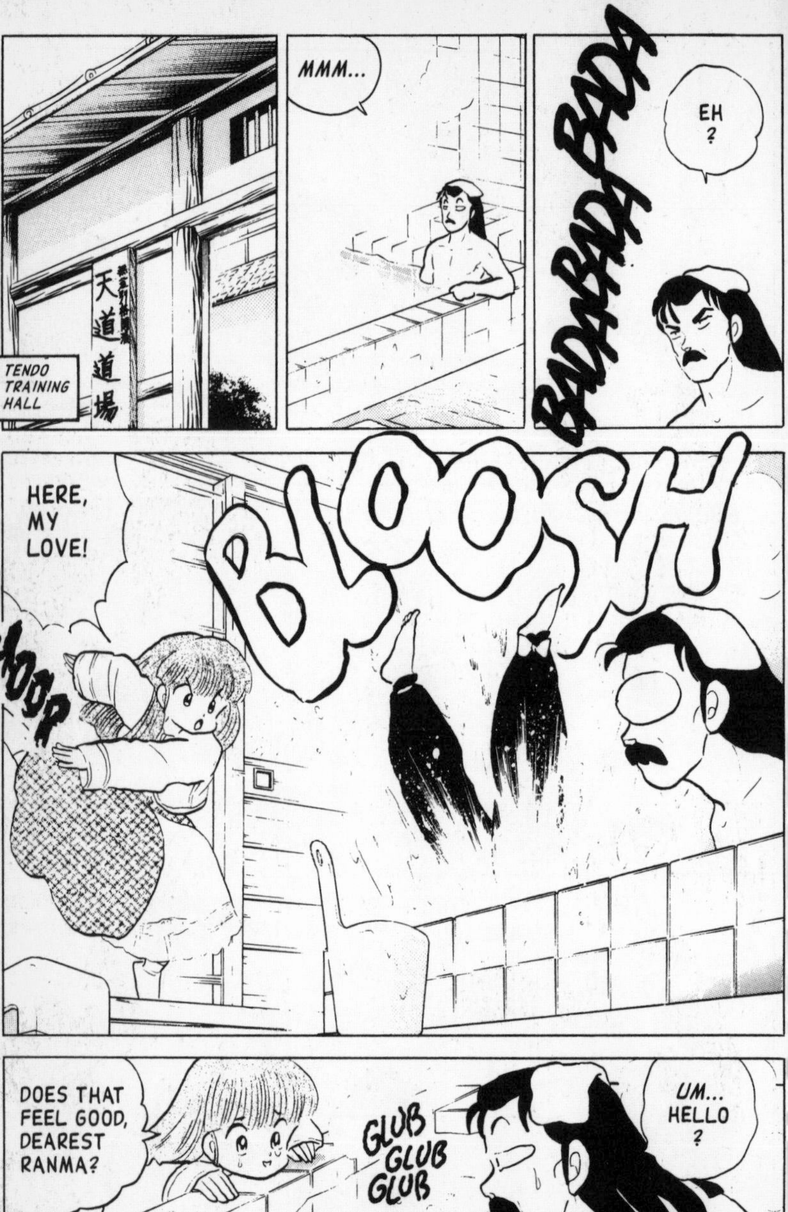
TENDO TRAINING HALL
天道道場
MMM...
BADABADABADA
EH?
HERE, MY LOVE!
ZHOOOP
BLOOSH
DOES THAT FEEL GOOD, DEAREST RANMA?
GLUB GLUB GLUB
UM... HELLO?

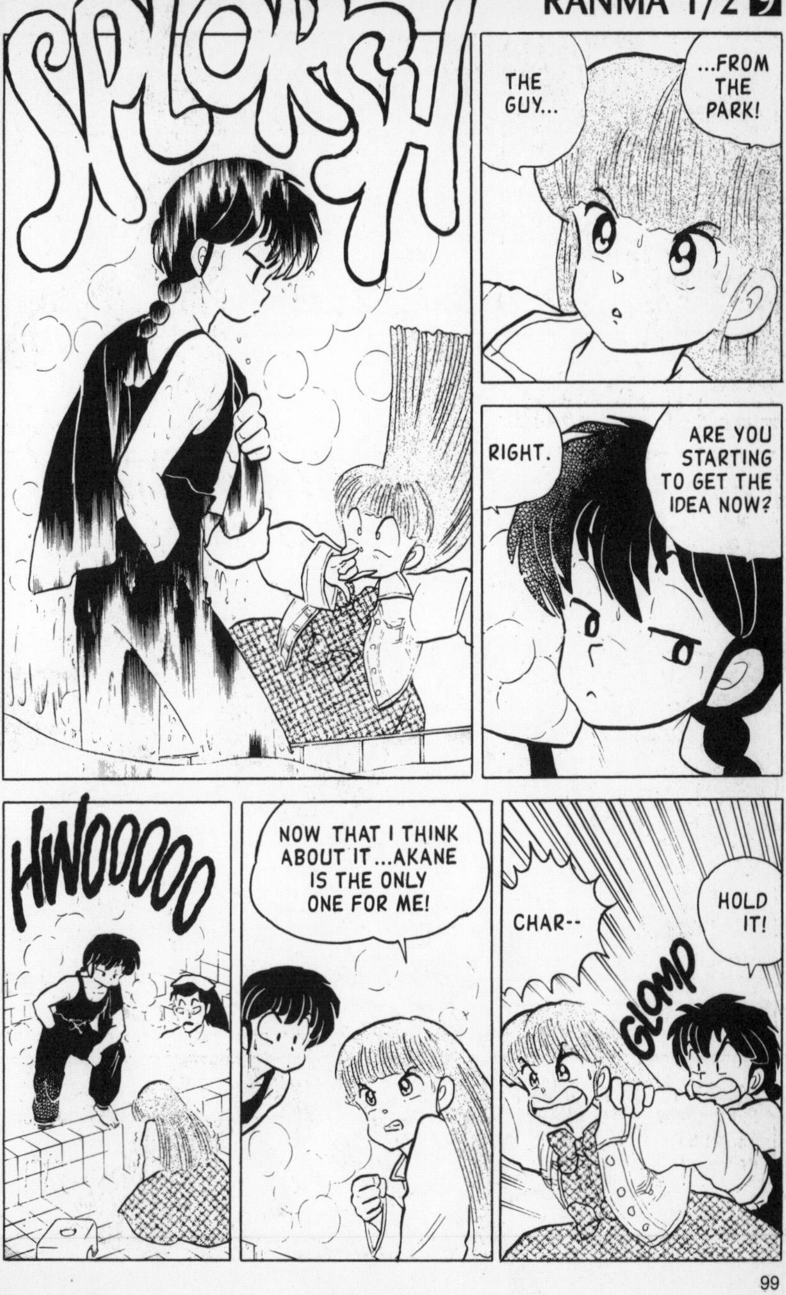
SPLORSH
THE GUY...
...FROM THE PARK!
RIGHT.
ARE YOU STARTING TO GET THE IDEA NOW?
HWOOOOO
NOW THAT I THINK ABOUT IT...AKANE IS THE ONLY ONE FOR ME!
CHAR--
HOLD IT!
GLOMP

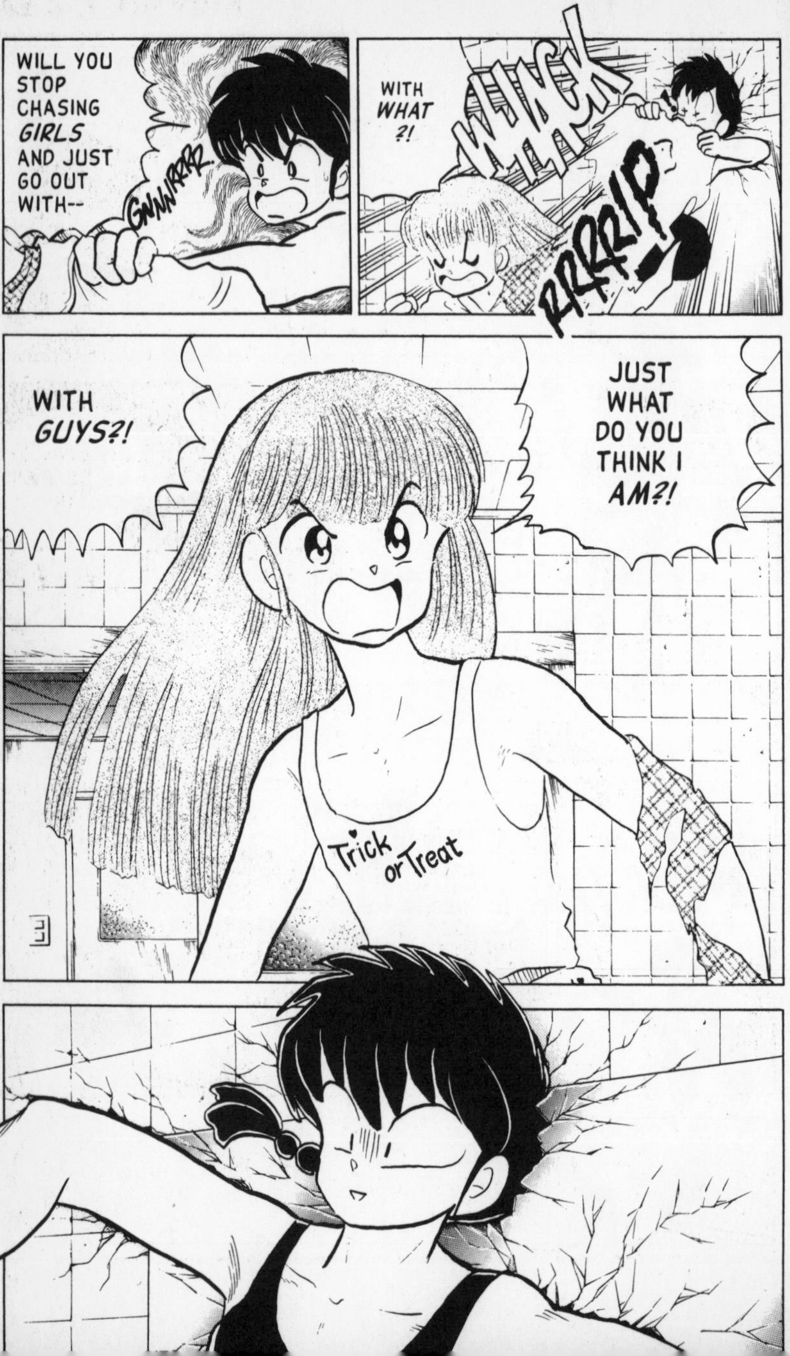
WILL YOU STOP CHASING GIRLS AND JUST GO OUT WITH--
GNNRRRR
WITH WHAT?!
WHACK
RRRRIP!
WITH GUYS?!
JUST WHAT DO YOU THINK I AM?!
Trick or Treat

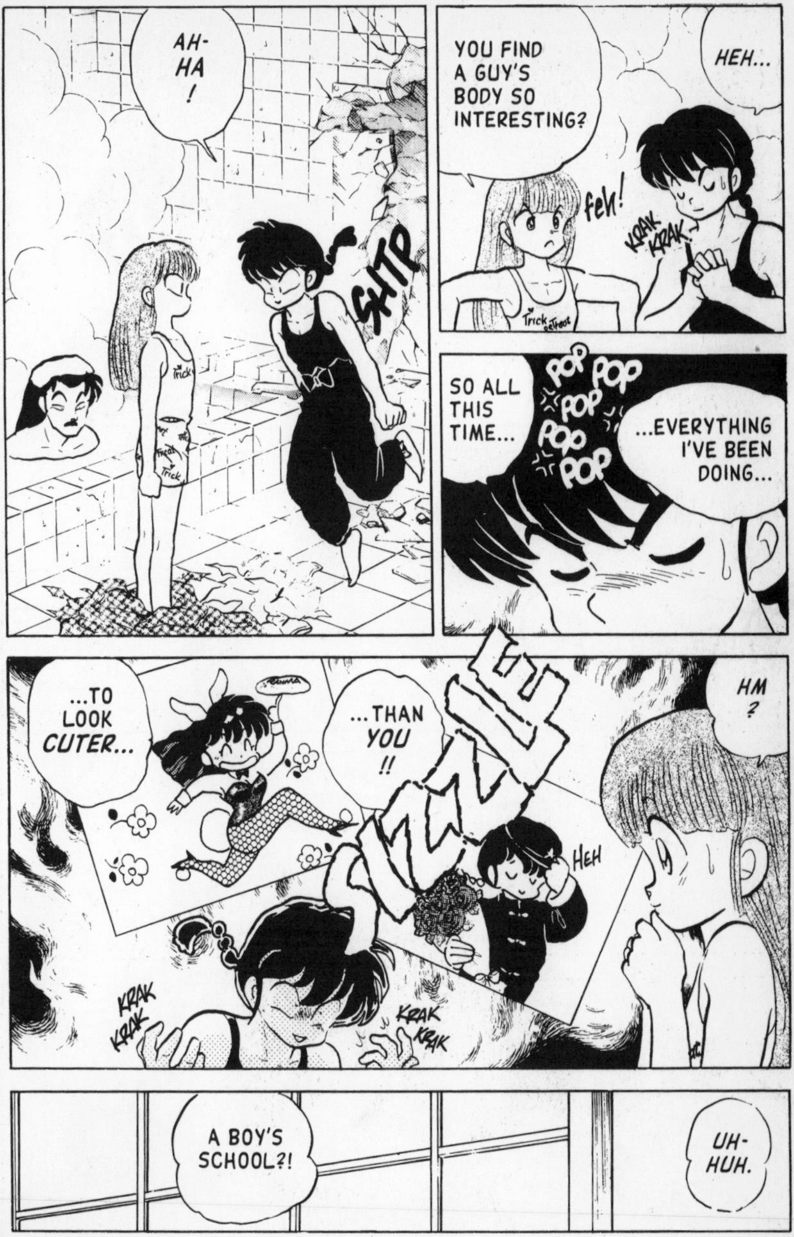
AH-
HA
!
SHTP
YOU FIND
A GUY'S
BODY SO
INTERESTING?
HEH...
feh!
KRAK
KRAK
SO ALL
THIS
TIME...
POP POP
POP
POP
POP
...EVERYTHING
I'VE BEEN
DOING...
...TO
LOOK
CUTER...
...THAN
YOU
!!
HEH
HM
?
KRAK
KRAK
KRAK
KRAK
A BOY'S
SCHOOL?!
UH-
HUH.

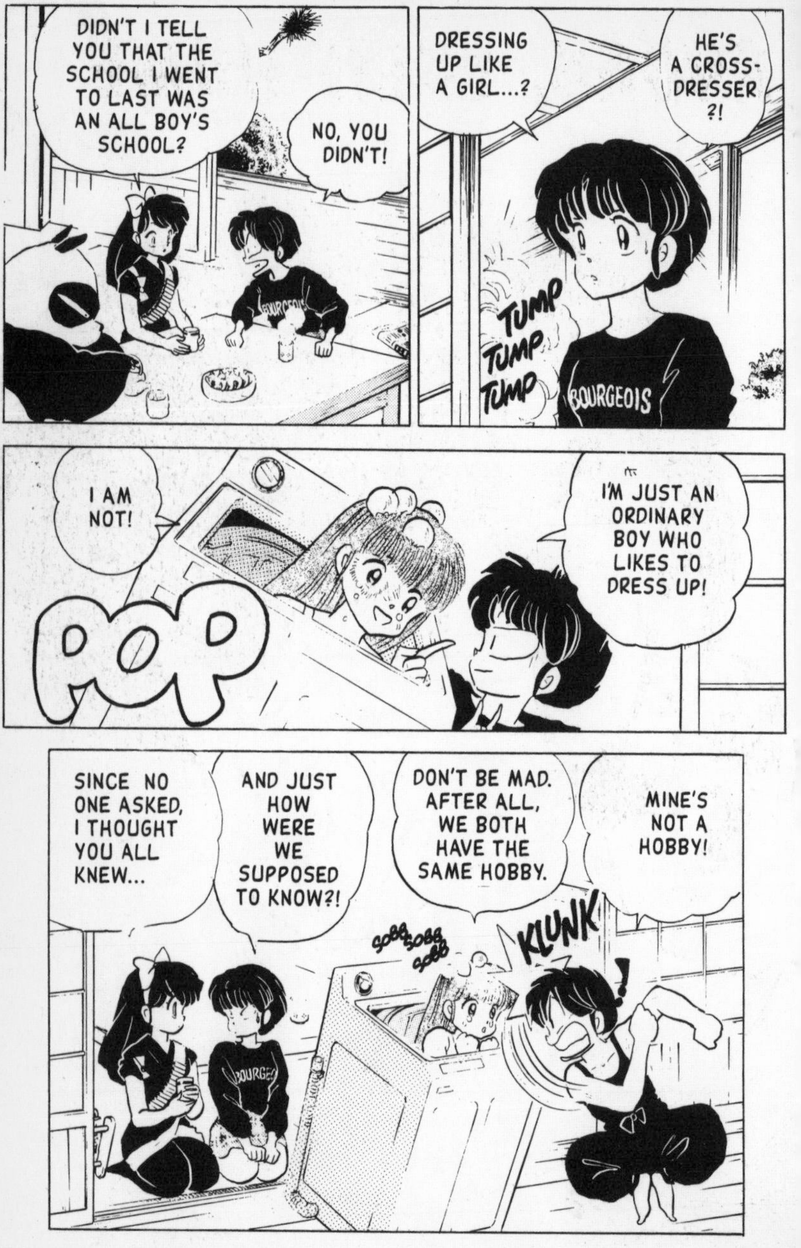
DIDN'T I TELL YOU THAT THE SCHOOL I WENT TO LAST WAS AN ALL BOY'S SCHOOL?
NO, YOU DIDN'T!
DRESSING UP LIKE A GIRL...?
HE'S A CROSS-DRESSER ?!
TUMP TUMP TUMP
BOURGEOIS
I AM NOT!
POP
I'M JUST AN ORDINARY BOY WHO LIKES TO DRESS UP!
SINCE NO ONE ASKED, I THOUGHT YOU ALL KNEW...
AND JUST HOW WERE WE SUPPOSED TO KNOW?!
DON'T BE MAD. AFTER ALL, WE BOTH HAVE THE SAME HOBBY.
MINE'S NOT A HOBBY!
SOBB SOBB SOBB
KLUNK

Part 7

RYOGA, COME HOME

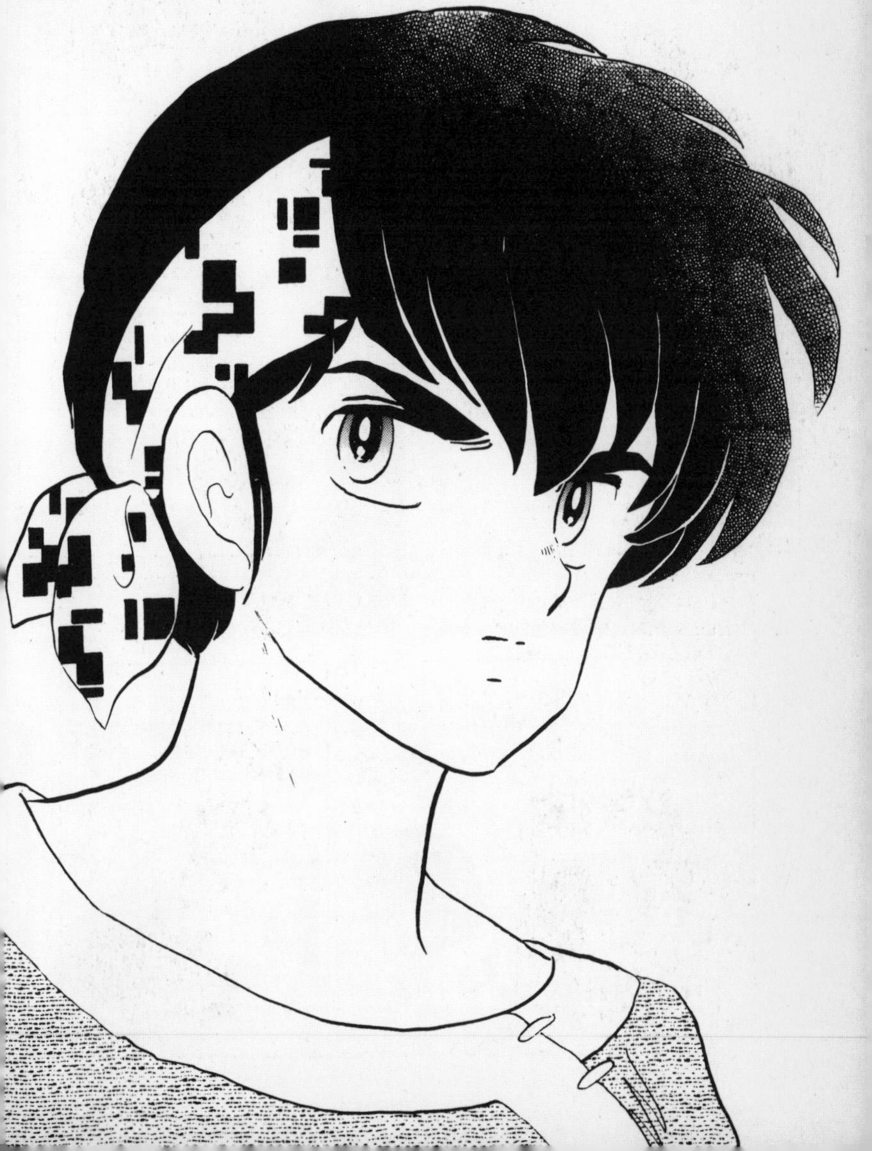

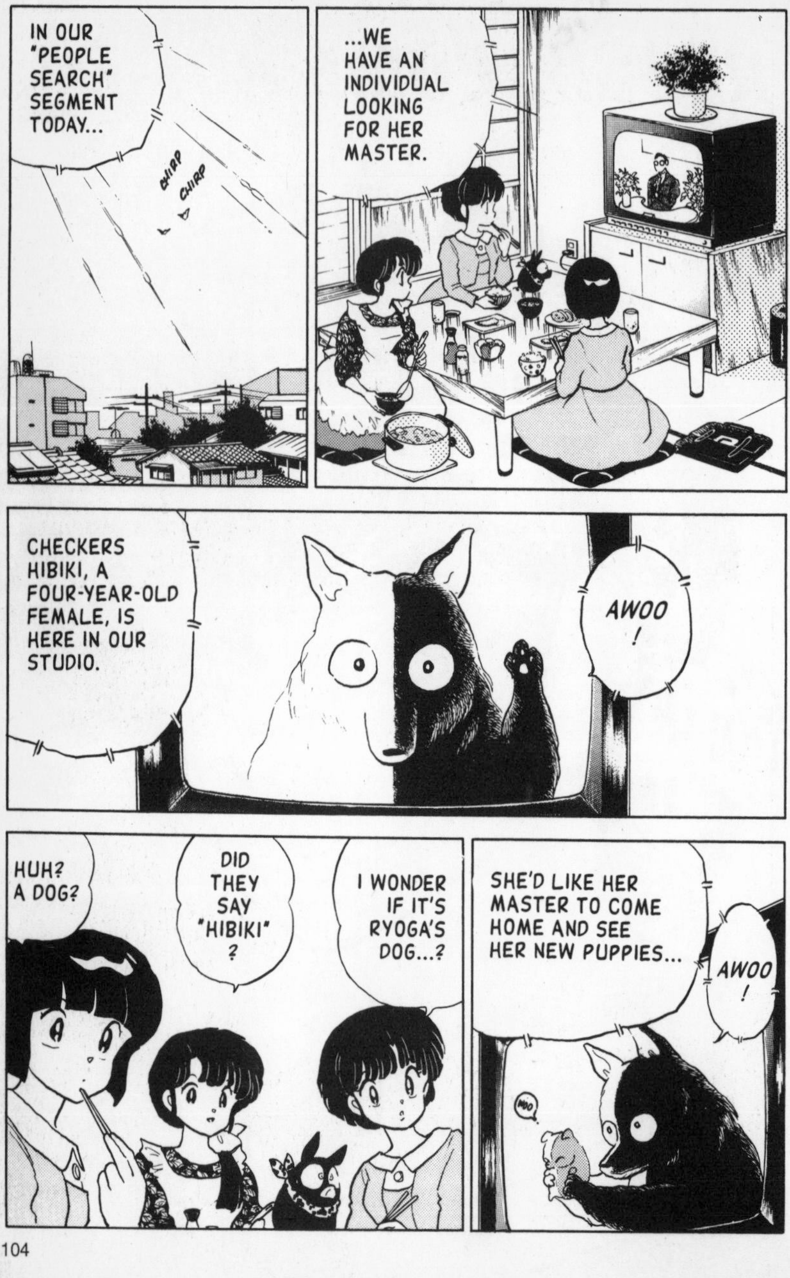
IN OUR "PEOPLE SEARCH" SEGMENT TODAY...
CHIRP
CHIRP
...WE HAVE AN INDIVIDUAL LOOKING FOR HER MASTER.
CHECKERS HIBIKI, A FOUR-YEAR-OLD FEMALE, IS HERE IN OUR STUDIO.
AWOO!
HUH? A DOG?
DID THEY SAY "HIBIKI"?
I WONDER IF IT'S RYOGA'S DOG...?
SHE'D LIKE HER MASTER TO COME HOME AND SEE HER NEW PUPPIES...
AWOO!

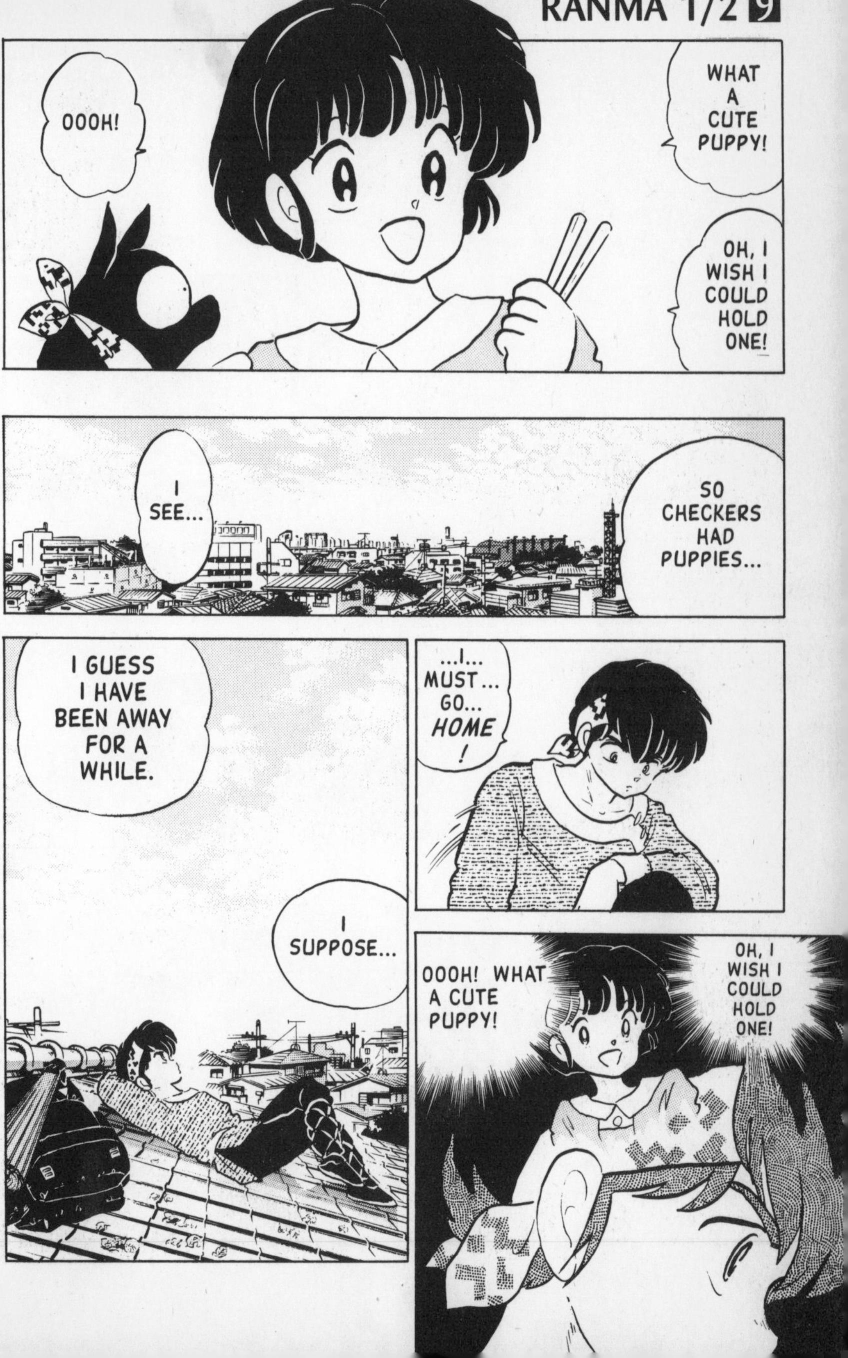
OOOH!
WHAT A CUTE PUPPY!
OH, I WISH I COULD HOLD ONE!
I SEE...
SO CHECKERS HAD PUPPIES...
I GUESS I HAVE BEEN AWAY FOR A WHILE.
I SUPPOSE...
...I... MUST... GO... *HOME*!
OOOH! WHAT A CUTE PUPPY!
OH, I WISH I COULD HOLD ONE!

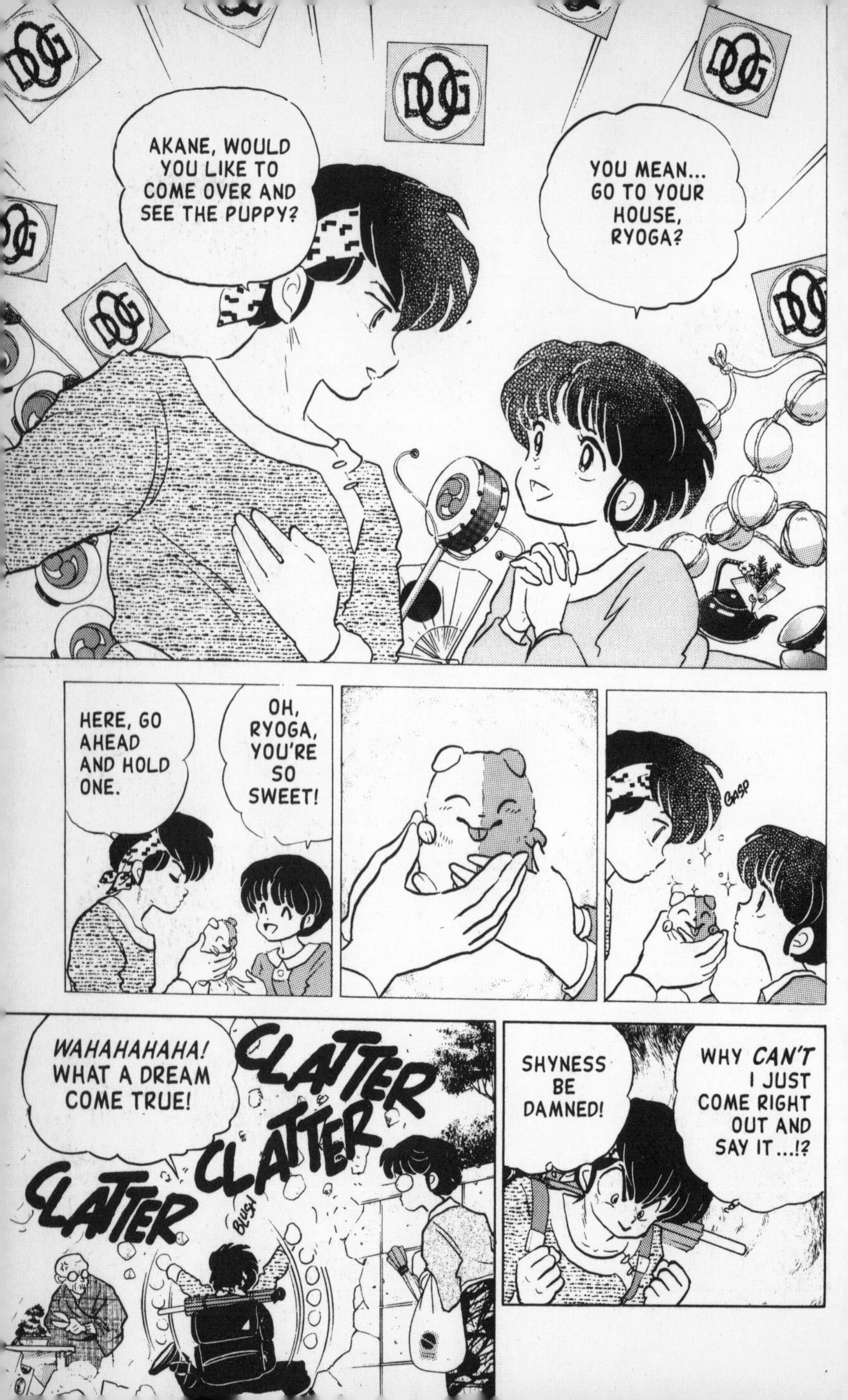
AKANE, WOULD YOU LIKE TO COME OVER AND SEE THE PUPPY?
YOU MEAN... GO TO YOUR HOUSE, RYOGA?
HERE, GO AHEAD AND HOLD ONE.
OH, RYOGA, YOU'RE SO SWEET!
GASP
WAHAHAHAHA! WHAT A DREAM COME TRUE!
CLATTER
CLATTER
CLATTER
BLUSH
SHYNESS BE DAMNED!
WHY CAN'T I JUST COME RIGHT OUT AND SAY IT...!?

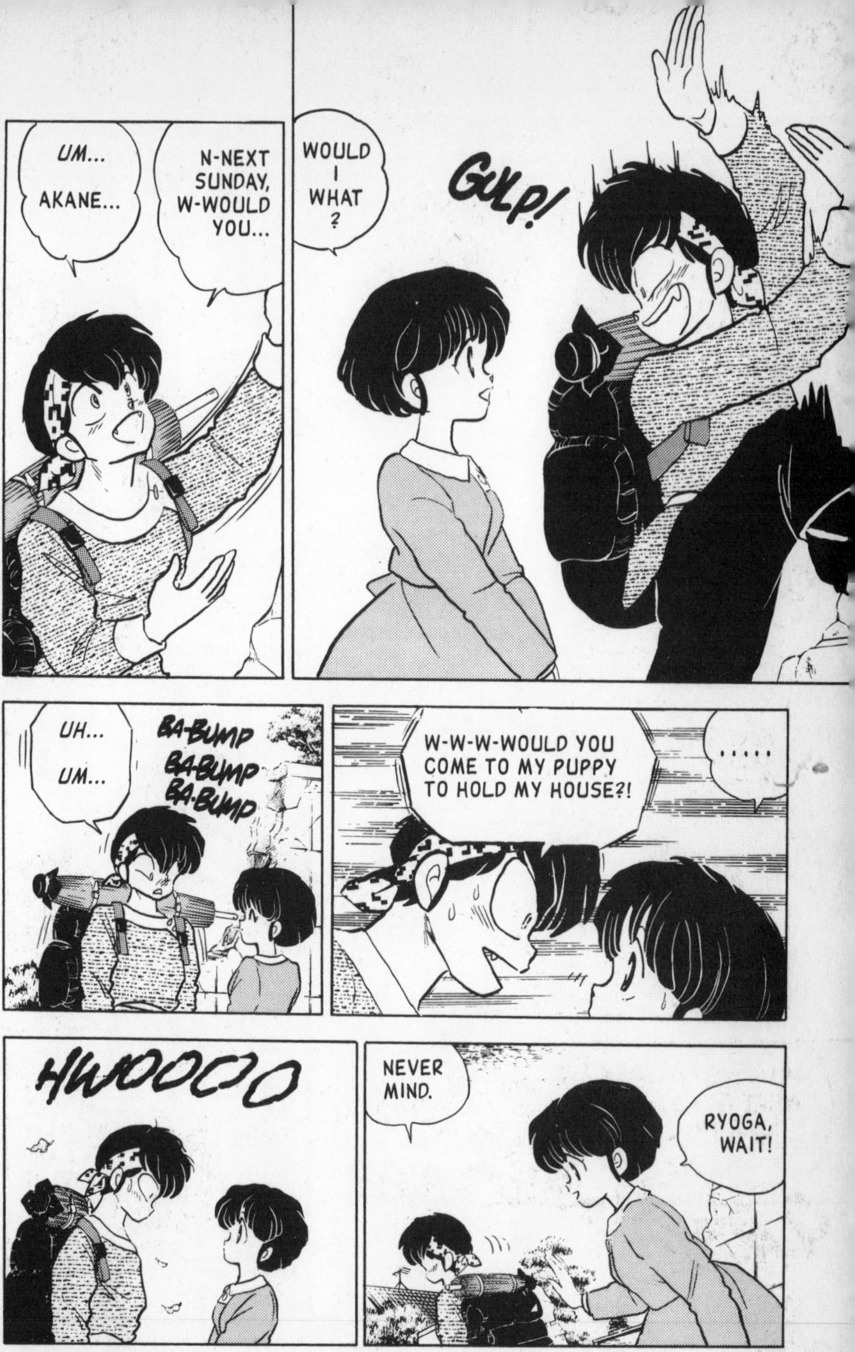

UM... AKANE...
N-NEXT SUNDAY, W-WOULD YOU...
WOULD I WHAT?
GULP!
UH... UM...
BA-BUMP BA-BUMP BA-BUMP
W-W-W-WOULD YOU COME TO MY PUPPY TO HOLD MY HOUSE?!
.....
HWOOOO
NEVER MIND.
RYOGA, WAIT!

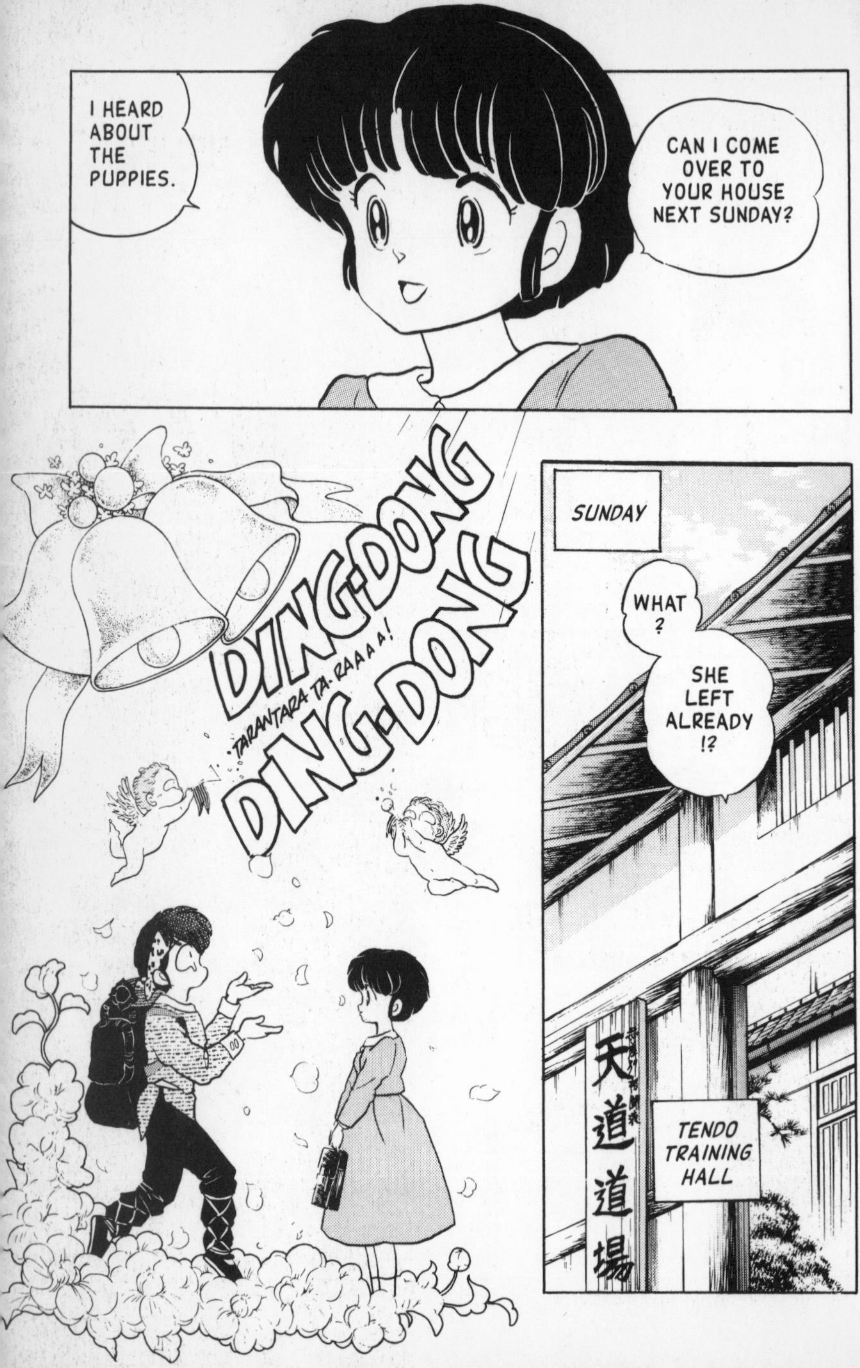
I HEARD ABOUT THE PUPPIES.
CAN I COME OVER TO YOUR HOUSE NEXT SUNDAY?
DING-DONG
TARANTARA TA-RAAAA!
DING-DONG
SUNDAY
WHAT?
SHE LEFT ALREADY!?
天道道場
TENDO TRAINING HALL

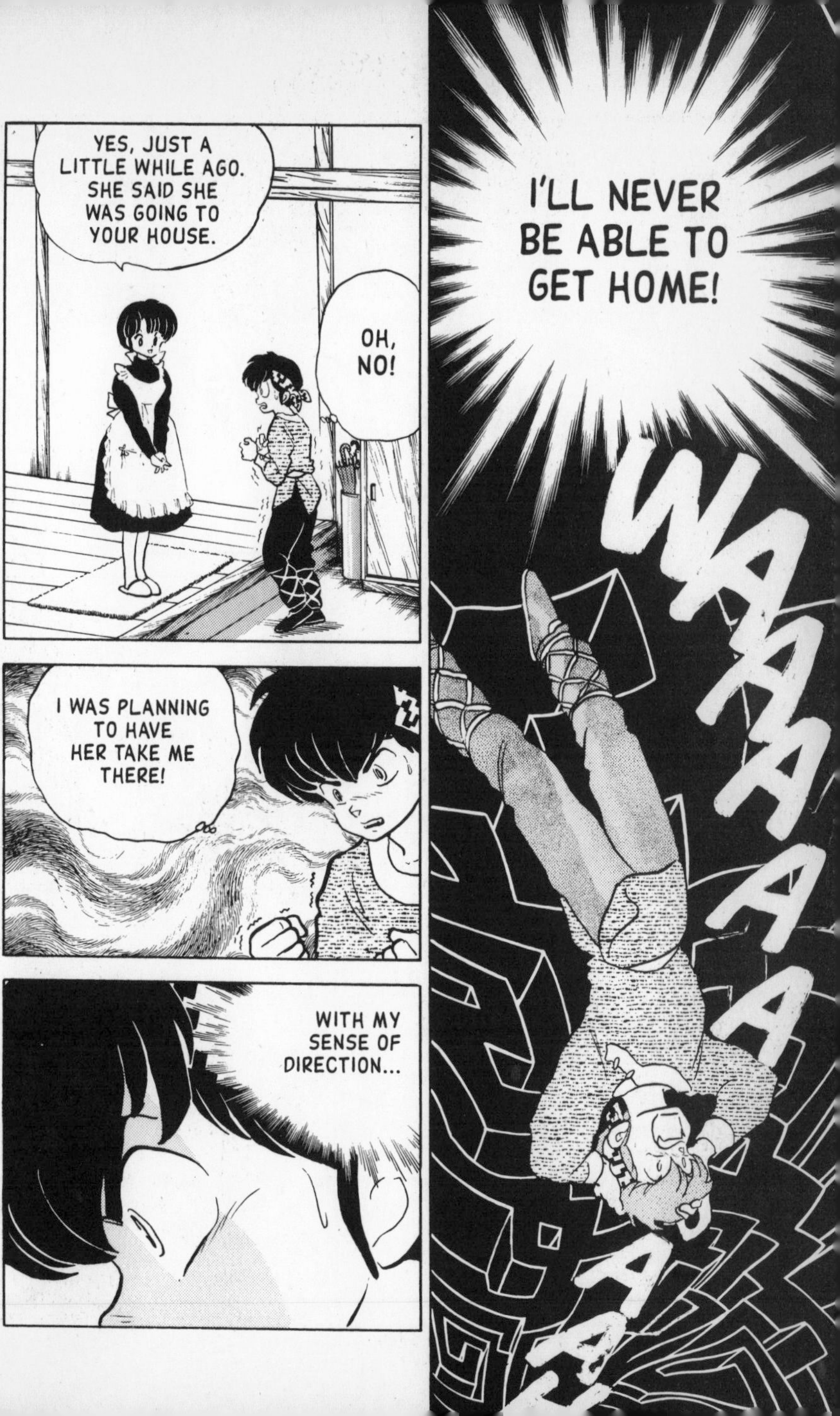
YES, JUST A LITTLE WHILE AGO. SHE SAID SHE WAS GOING TO YOUR HOUSE.
OH, NO!
I WAS PLANNING TO HAVE HER TAKE ME THERE!
WITH MY SENSE OF DIRECTION...
I'LL NEVER BE ABLE TO GET HOME!
WAAAAAAAA!

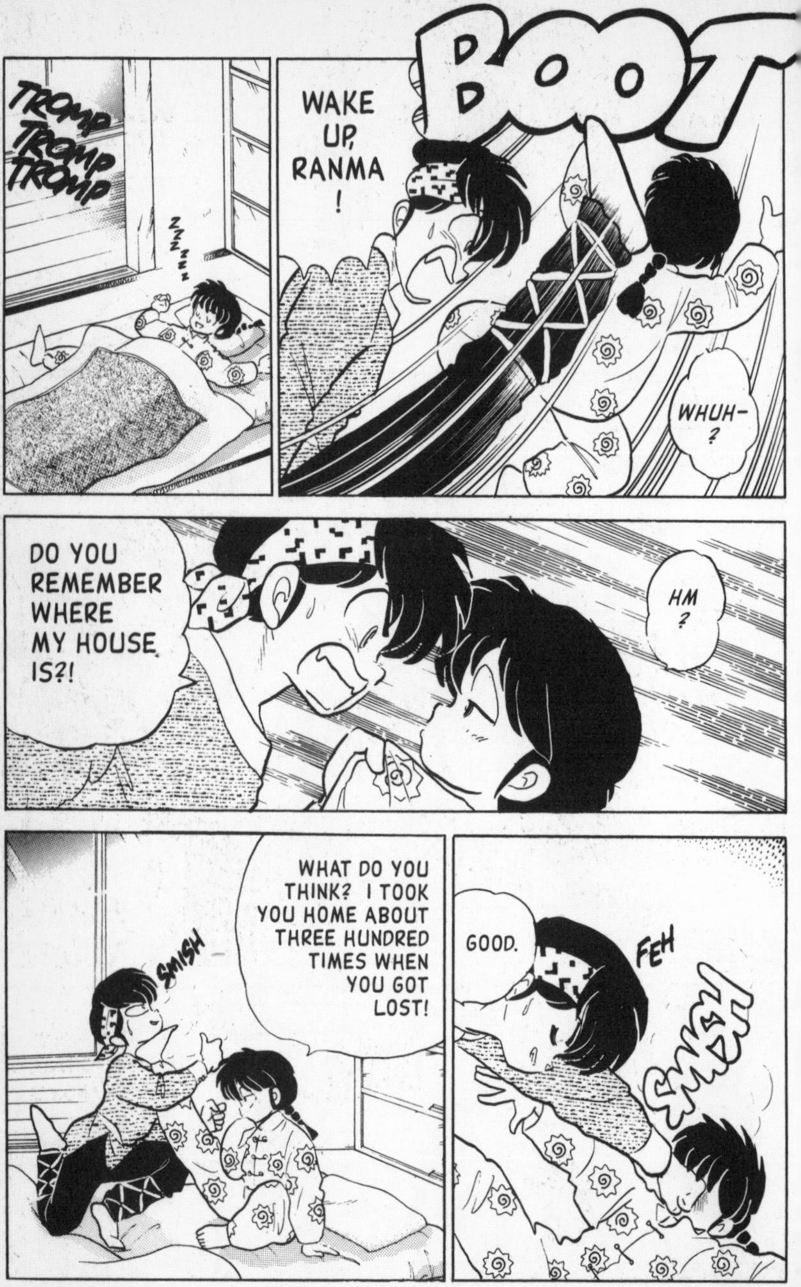
TROMP TROMP TROMP
ZZZZZZ
WAKE UP, RANMA!
BOOT
WHUH-?
DO YOU REMEMBER WHERE MY HOUSE IS?!
HM?
SMISH
WHAT DO YOU THINK? I TOOK YOU HOME ABOUT THREE HUNDRED TIMES WHEN YOU GOT LOST!
GOOD.
FEH
SMISH SMISH

IF YOU WANT TO PAY ME BACK...

...I'D GET OVER TO MY HOUSE AS SOON AS POSSIBLE.

LATER.

SEE YA

PAY YOU BACK?

WHY WAIT? I'D RATHER SETTLE THE SCORE RIGHT HERE AND NOW.

GOOK

I SAID, LET'S SETTLE THIS AT MY HOUSE!

SCRITCH SCRATCH

SO BASICALLY...

PAAM

...WHAT YOU'RE SAYING...

SMASH

...IS THAT YOU WANT *ME* TO TAKE *YOU* HOME!

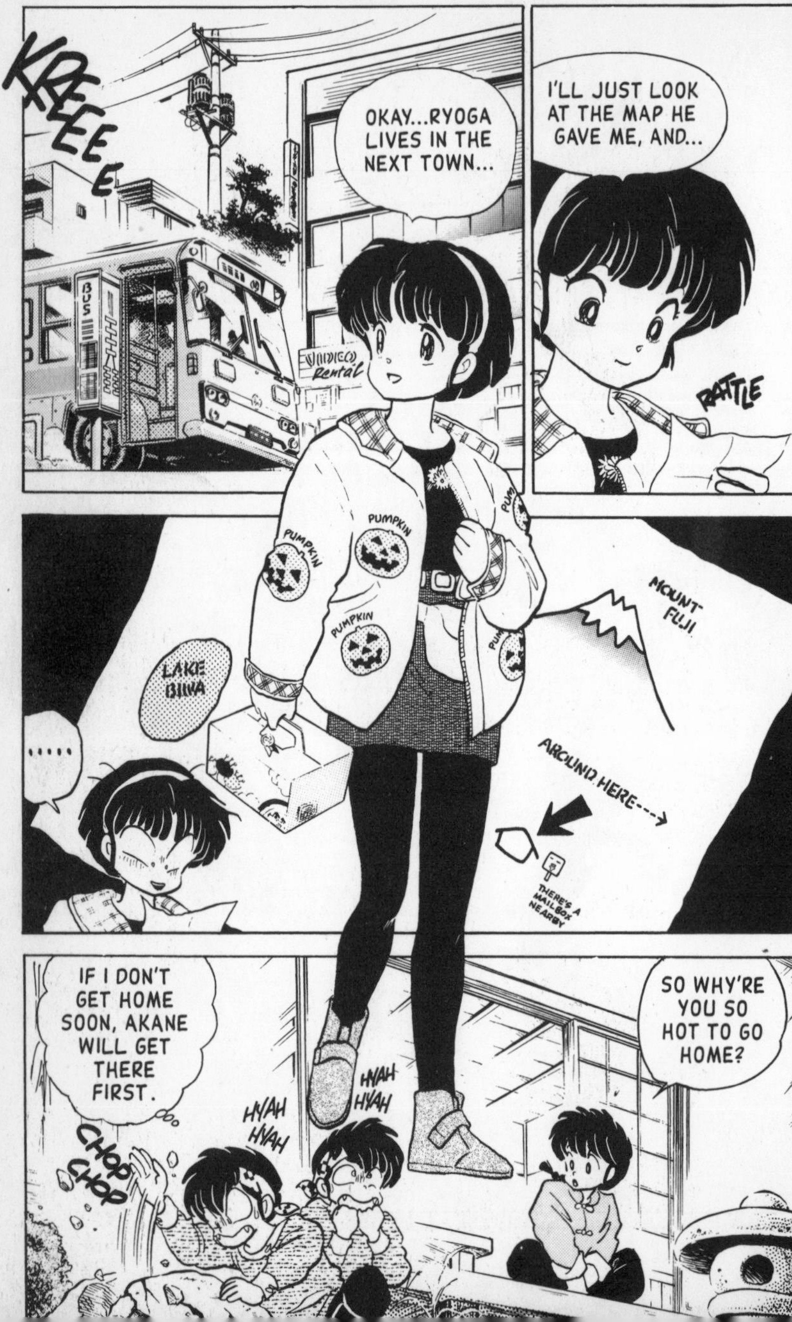
KREEEEE
OKAY...RYOGA LIVES IN THE NEXT TOWN...
VIDEO Rental
BUS
I'LL JUST LOOK AT THE MAP HE GAVE ME, AND...
RATTLE
PUMPKIN
......
LAKE BIWA
MOUNT FUJI
AROUND HERE--->
THERE'S A MAILBOX NEARBY
IF I DON'T GET HOME SOON, AKANE WILL GET THERE FIRST.
CHOP CHOP
HYAH HYAH
HYAH HYAH
SO WHY'RE YOU SO HOT TO GO HOME?

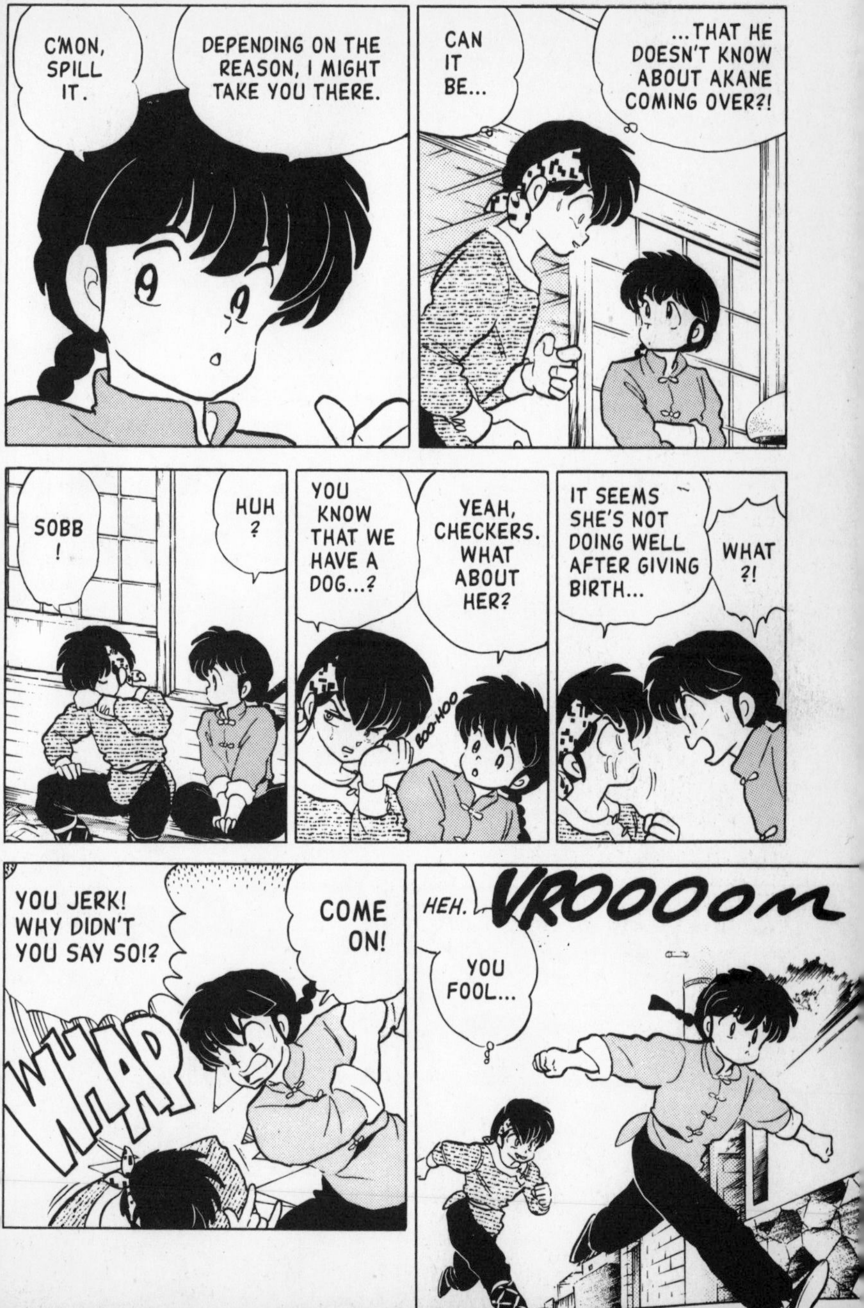
C'MON, SPILL IT.
DEPENDING ON THE REASON, I MIGHT TAKE YOU THERE.
CAN IT BE...
...THAT HE DOESN'T KNOW ABOUT AKANE COMING OVER?!
SOBB!
HUH?
YOU KNOW THAT WE HAVE A DOG...?
YEAH, CHECKERS. WHAT ABOUT HER?
BOO-HOO
IT SEEMS SHE'S NOT DOING WELL AFTER GIVING BIRTH...
WHAT?!
YOU JERK! WHY DIDN'T YOU SAY SO!?
COME ON!
WHAP
HEH.
VROOOOM
YOU FOOL...

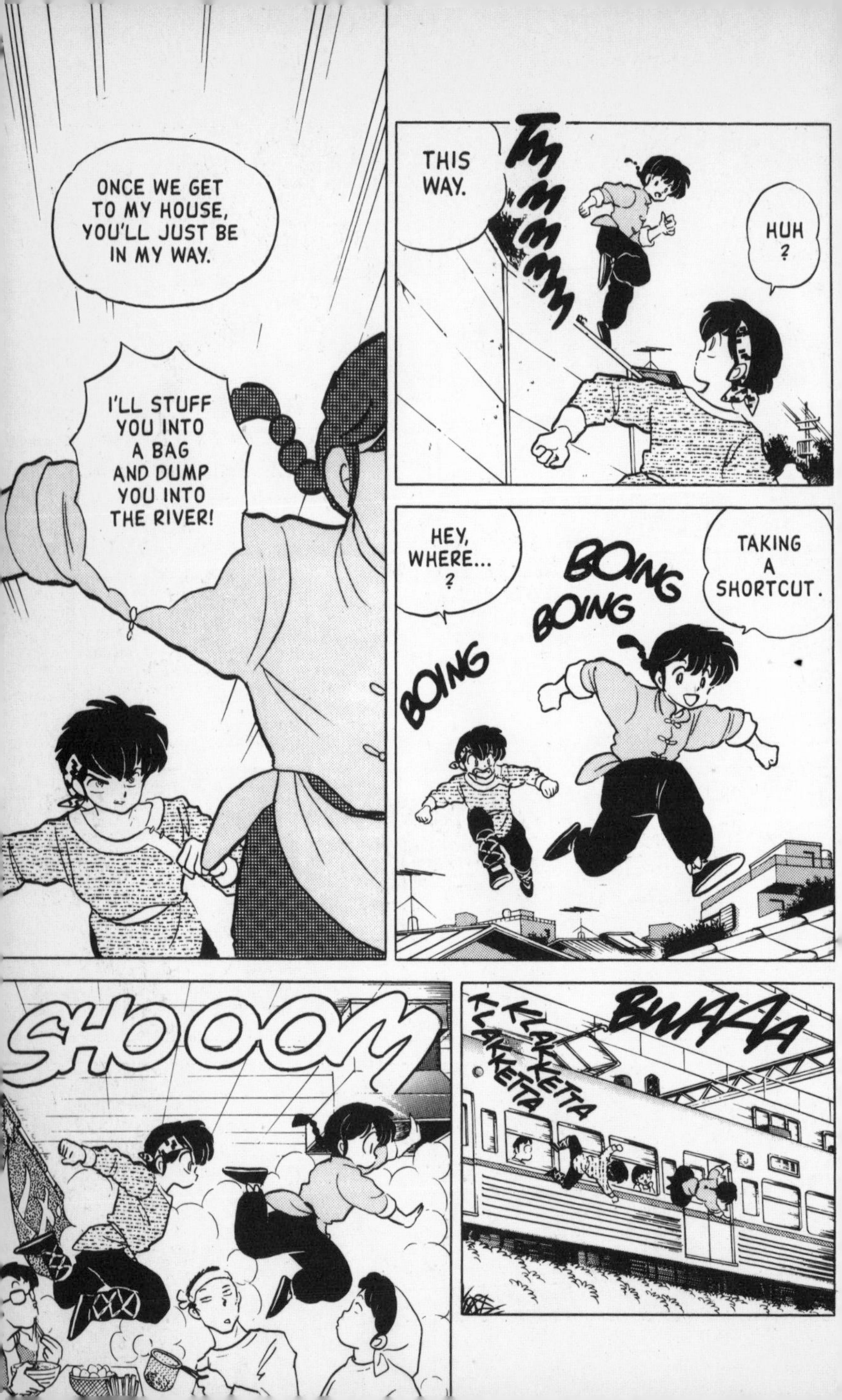
ONCE WE GET TO MY HOUSE, YOU'LL JUST BE IN MY WAY.
I'LL STUFF YOU INTO A BAG AND DUMP YOU INTO THE RIVER!
THIS WAY.
HUH?
HEY, WHERE...?
BOING
BOING
BOING
TAKING A SHORTCUT.
SHOOOM
KLAKKETTA
KLAKKETTA
BWAAAA

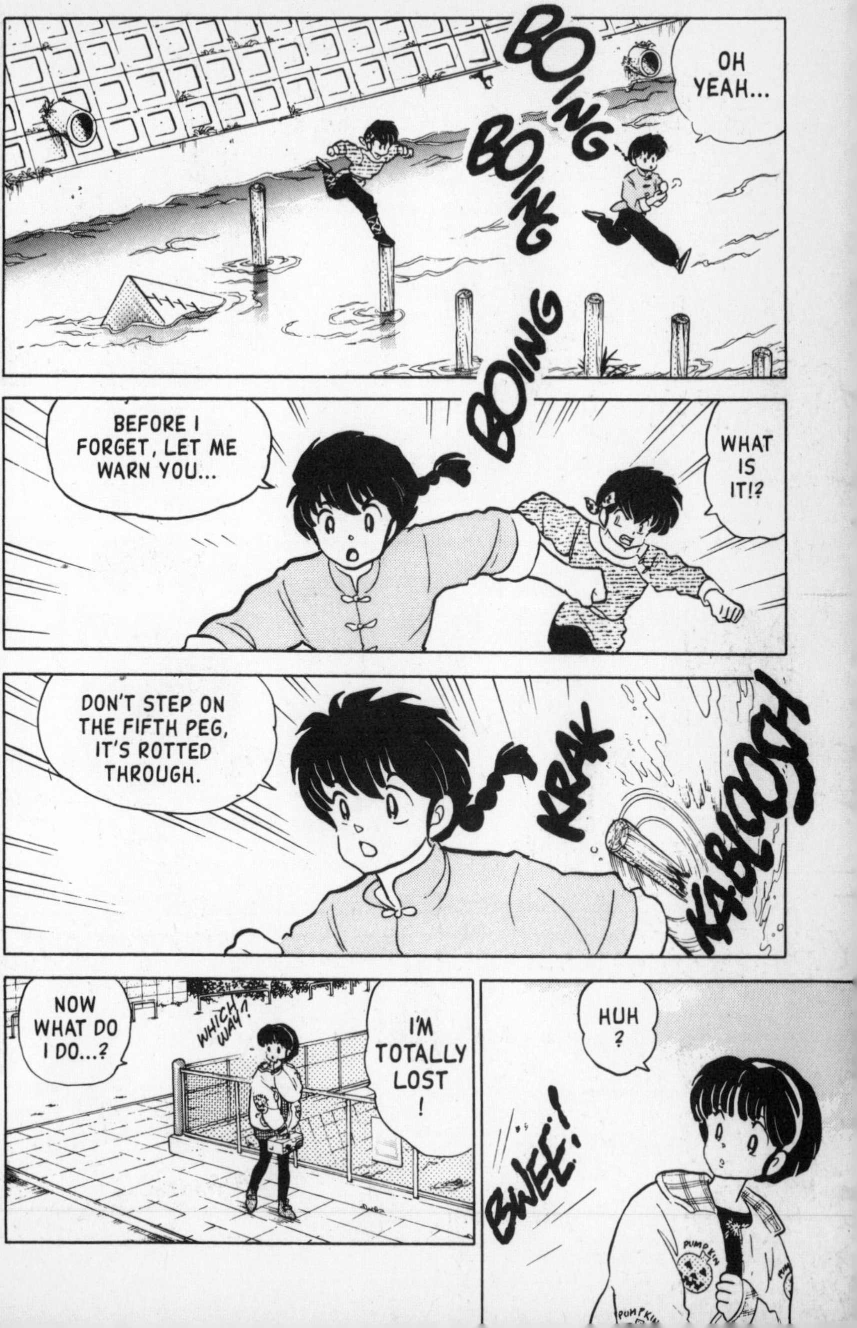
BOING
BOING
OH YEAH...
BOING
BEFORE I FORGET, LET ME WARN YOU...
WHAT IS IT!?
DON'T STEP ON THE FIFTH PEG, IT'S ROTTED THROUGH.
KRAK
KABLOOSH
NOW WHAT DO I DO...?
WHICH WAY?
I'M TOTALLY LOST!
HUH?
BWEE!
PUMPKIN

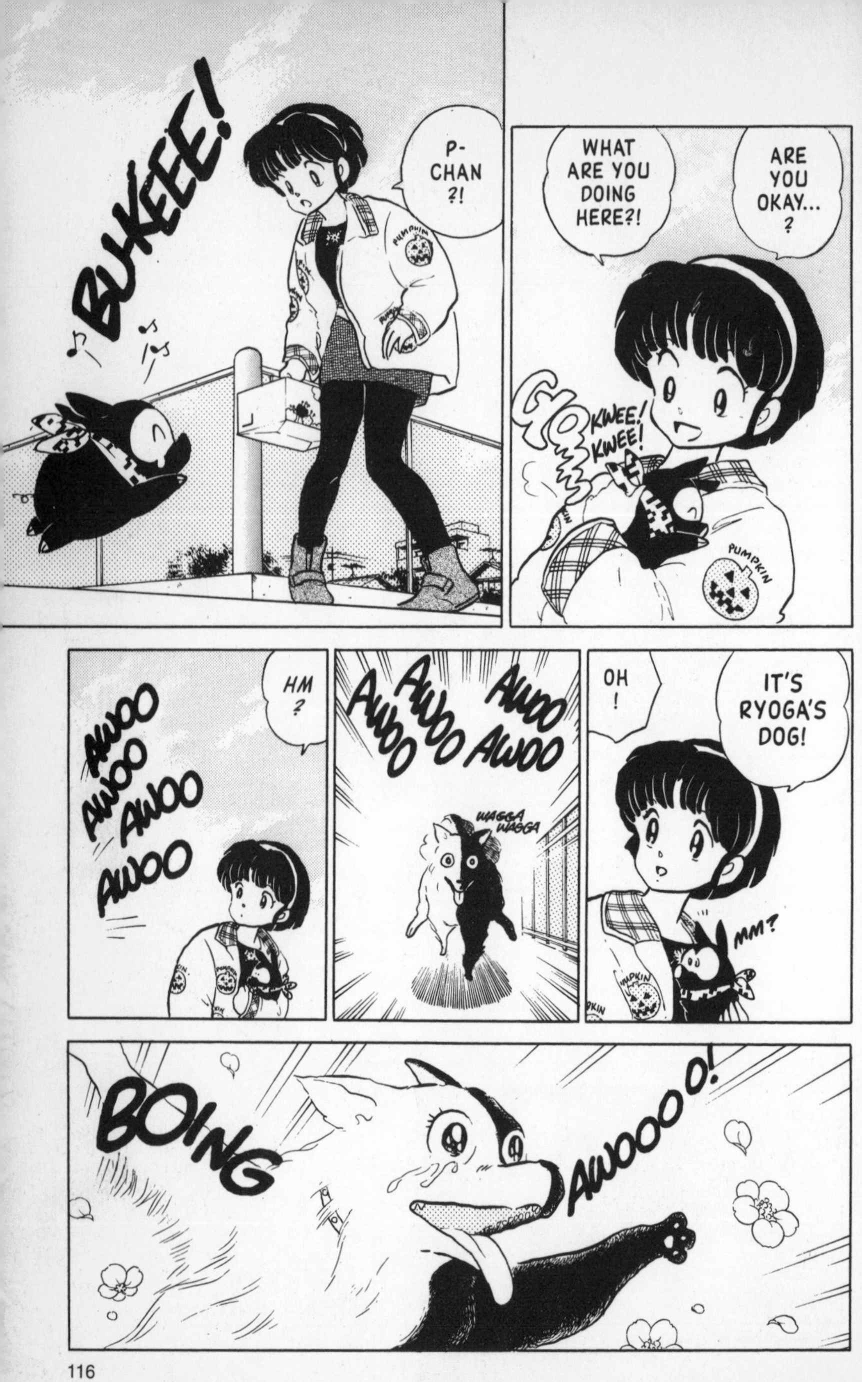

BUKEEE!
P-CHAN ?!
WHAT ARE YOU DOING HERE?!
ARE YOU OKAY... ?
GLOMP
KWEE! KWEE!
PUMPKIN
AWOO AWOO AWOO AWOO AWOO
HM ?
AWOO AWOO AWOO AWOO AWOO
WAGGA WAGGA
OH !
IT'S RYOGA'S DOG!
MM?
BOING
AWOOOO!

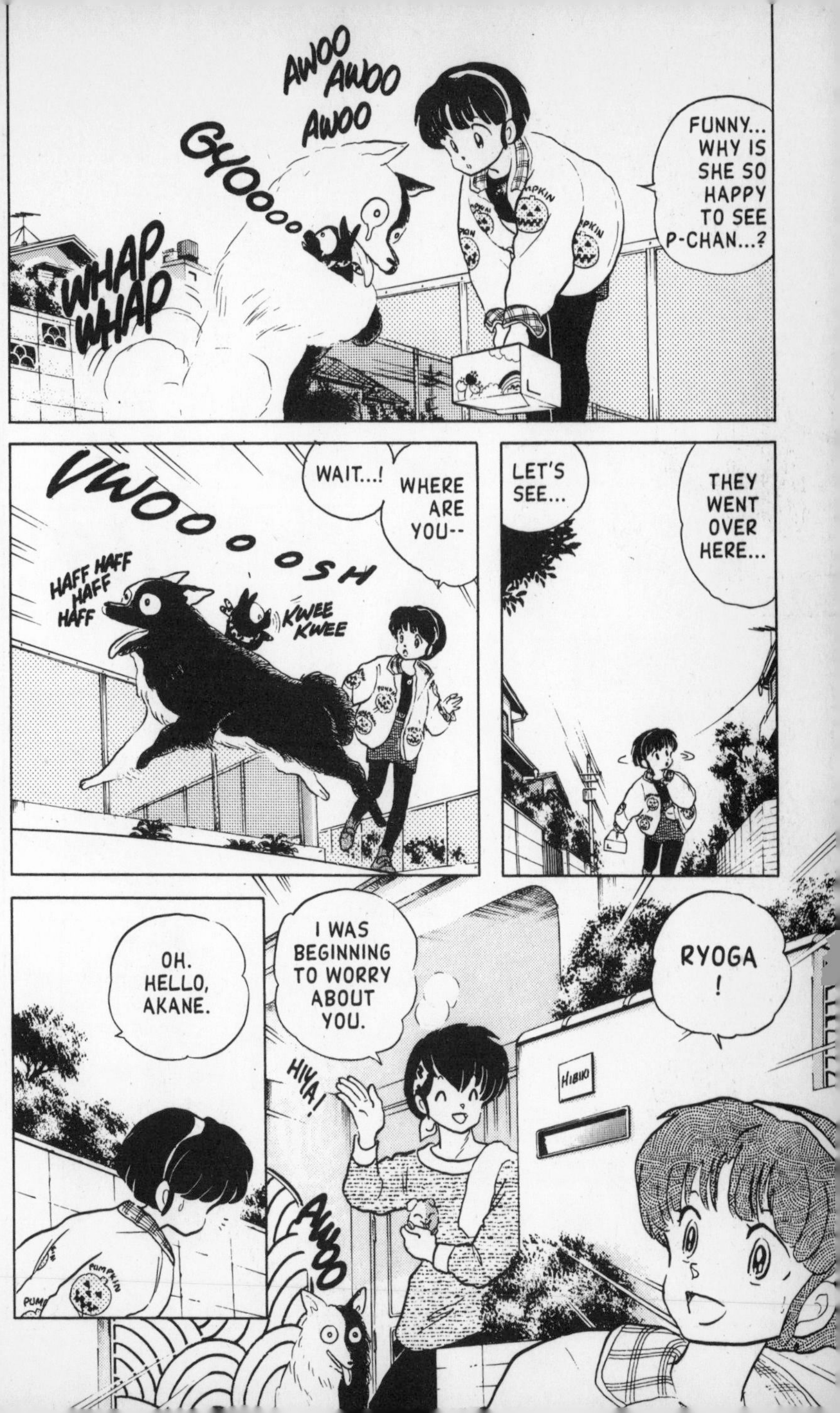

AWOO AWOO AWOO
GYOOOO...
WHAP WHAP
FUNNY... WHY IS SHE SO HAPPY TO SEE P-CHAN...?
VWOOOOOOSH
WAIT...!
WHERE ARE YOU--
HAFF HAFF HAFF HAFF
KWEE KWEE
LET'S SEE...
THEY WENT OVER HERE...
OH. HELLO, AKANE.
PUMPKIN
I WAS BEGINNING TO WORRY ABOUT YOU.
HIYA!
AWOO
HIBIKI
RYOGA!

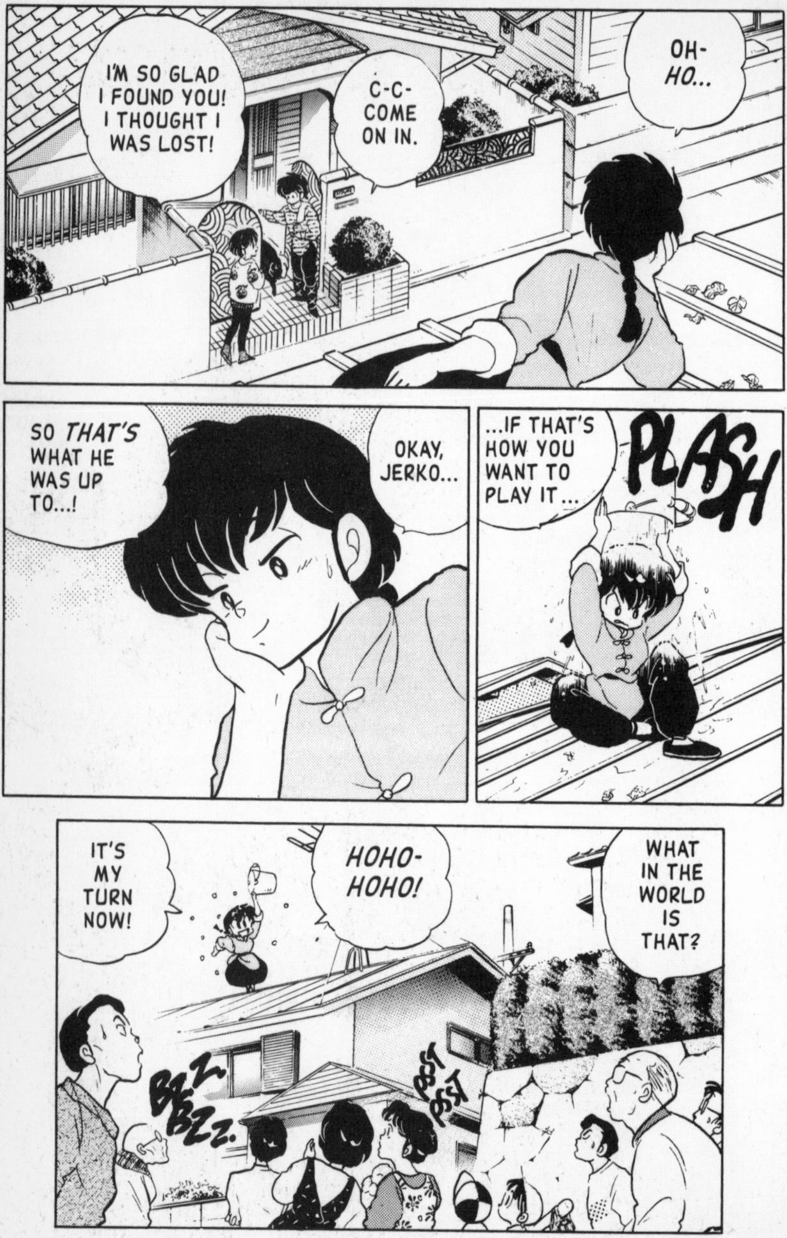
I'M SO GLAD I FOUND YOU! I THOUGHT I WAS LOST!
C-C-COME ON IN.
OH-HO...
SO THAT'S WHAT HE WAS UP TO...!
OKAY, JERKO...
...IF THAT'S HOW YOU WANT TO PLAY IT...
PLASH
IT'S MY TURN NOW!
HOHO-HOHO!
WHAT IN THE WORLD IS THAT?
BZZ BZZ.
PSST PSST

Part 8
OH, BROTHER!

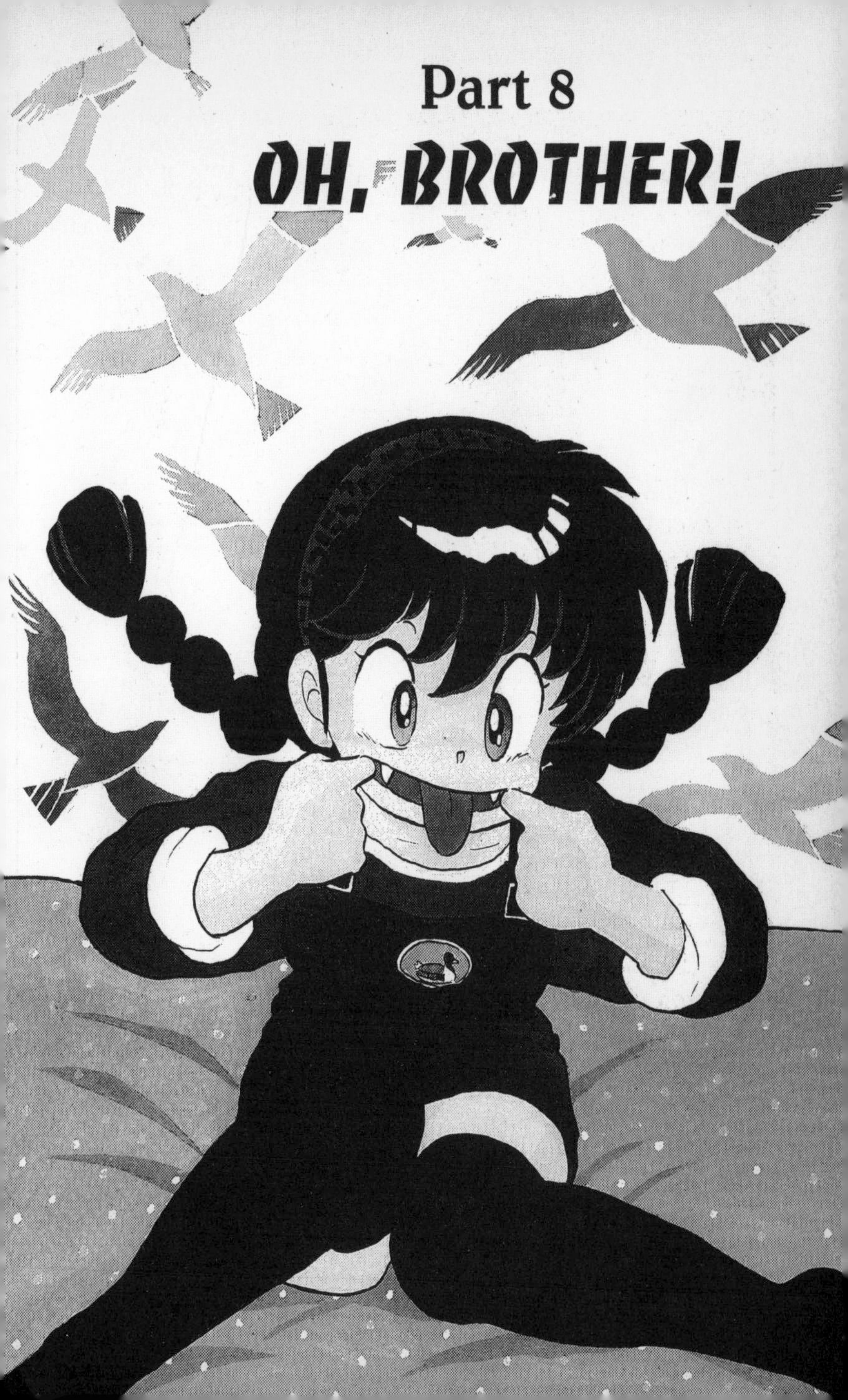

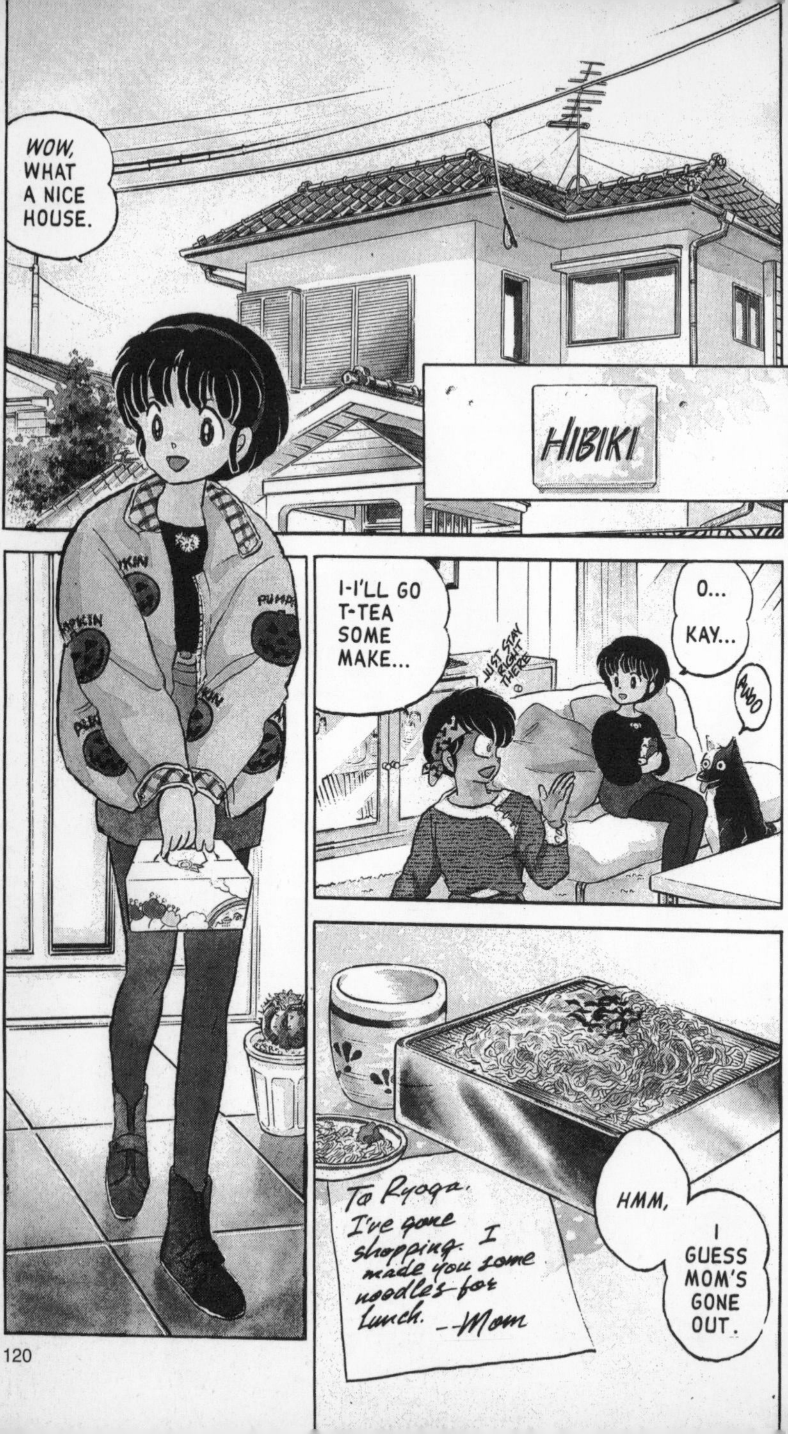
WOW, WHAT A NICE HOUSE.
HIBIKI
I-I'LL GO T-TEA SOME MAKE...
JUST STAY RIGHT THERE
O... KAY...
AWOO
To Ryoga. I've gone shopping. I made you some noodles for lunch. --Mom
HMM,
I GUESS MOM'S GONE OUT.

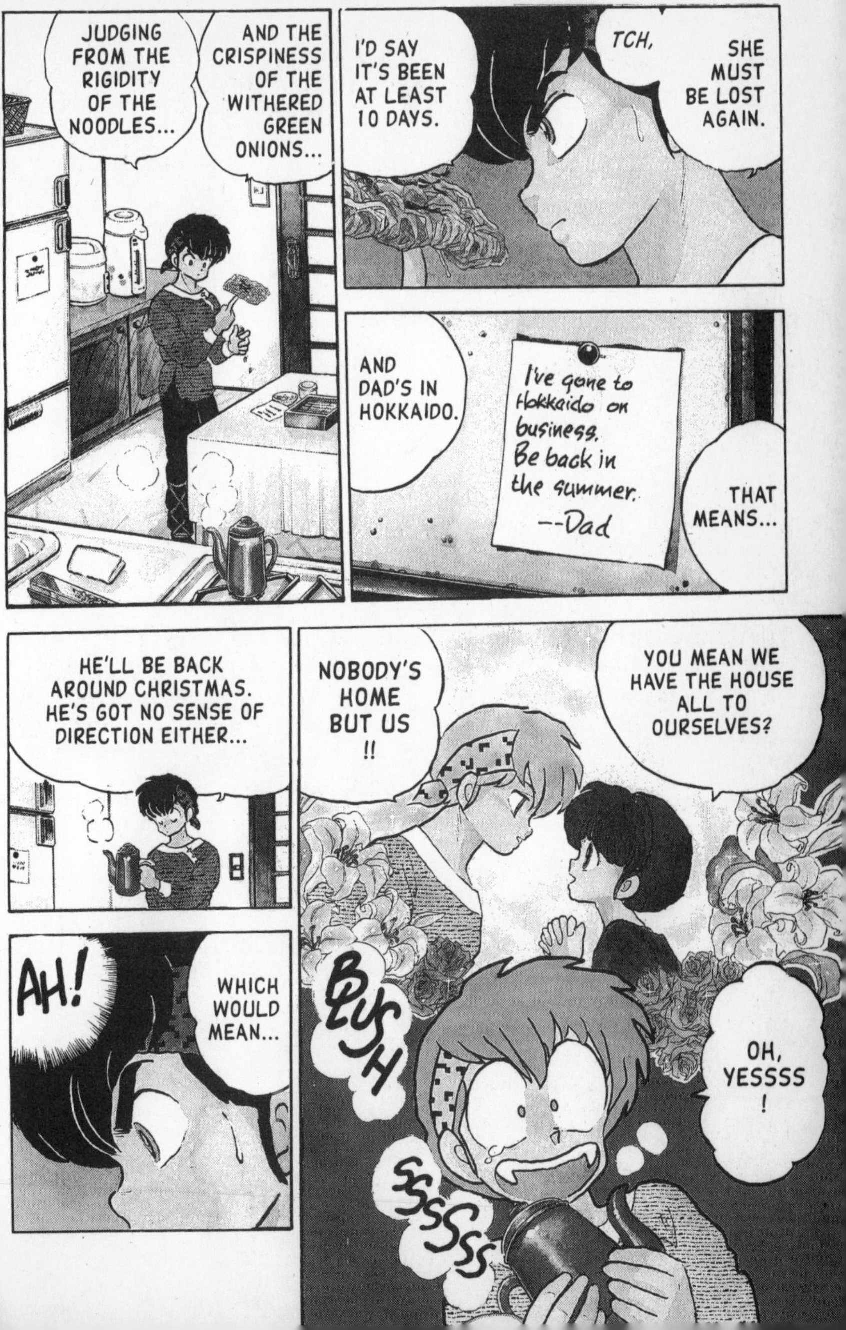
JUDGING FROM THE RIGIDITY OF THE NOODLES...
AND THE CRISPINESS OF THE WITHERED GREEN ONIONS...
I'D SAY IT'S BEEN AT LEAST 10 DAYS.
TCH,
SHE MUST BE LOST AGAIN.
AND DAD'S IN HOKKAIDO.
I've gone to Hokkaido on business. Be back in the summer. --Dad
THAT MEANS...
HE'LL BE BACK AROUND CHRISTMAS. HE'S GOT NO SENSE OF DIRECTION EITHER...
AH!
WHICH WOULD MEAN...
NOBODY'S HOME BUT US !!
YOU MEAN WE HAVE THE HOUSE ALL TO OURSELVES?
BLUSH
OH, YESSSS !
SSSSSS

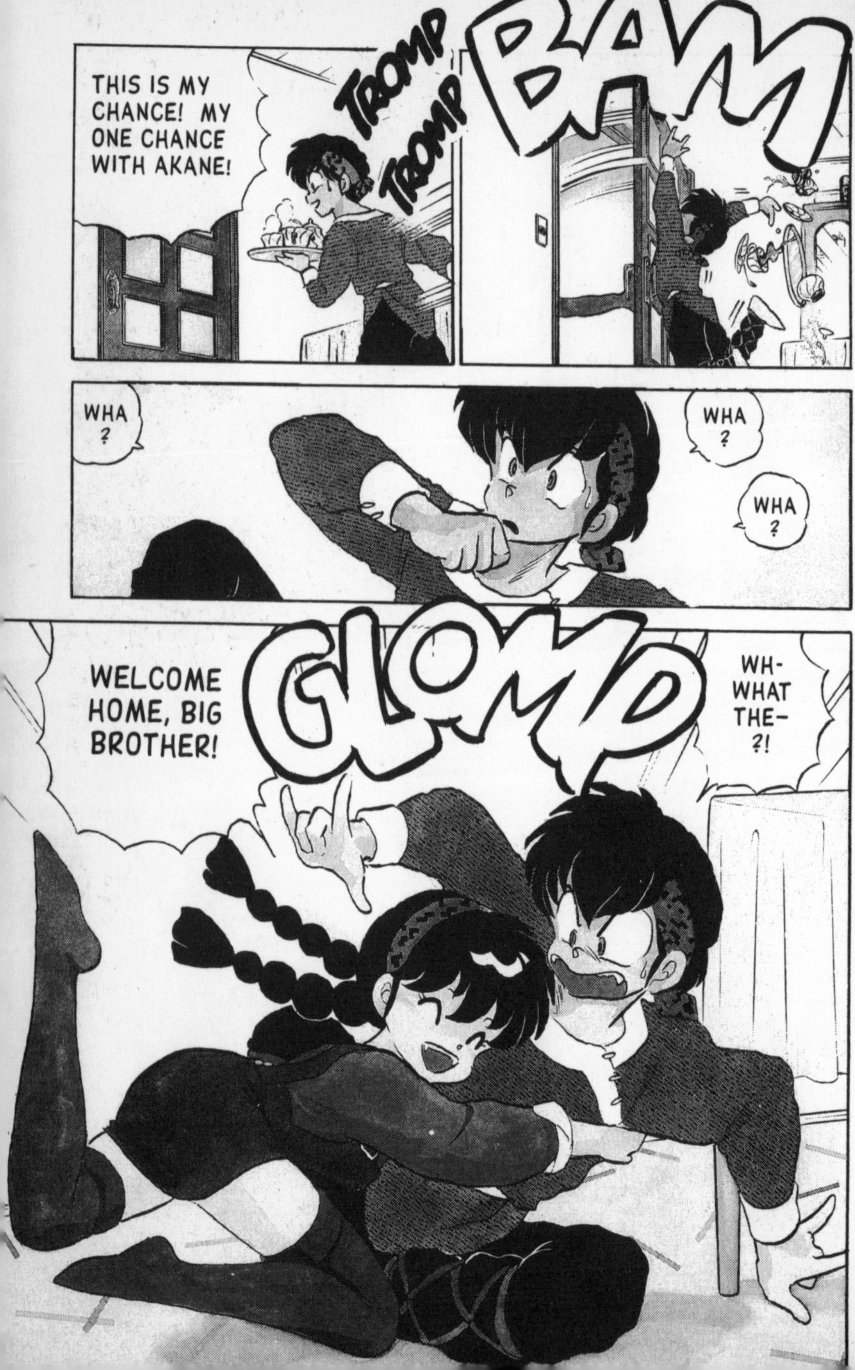
THIS IS MY CHANCE! MY ONE CHANCE WITH AKANE!
TROMP TROMP
BAM
WHA ?
WHA ?
WHA ?
WELCOME HOME, BIG BROTHER!
GLOMP
WH- WHAT THE- ?!

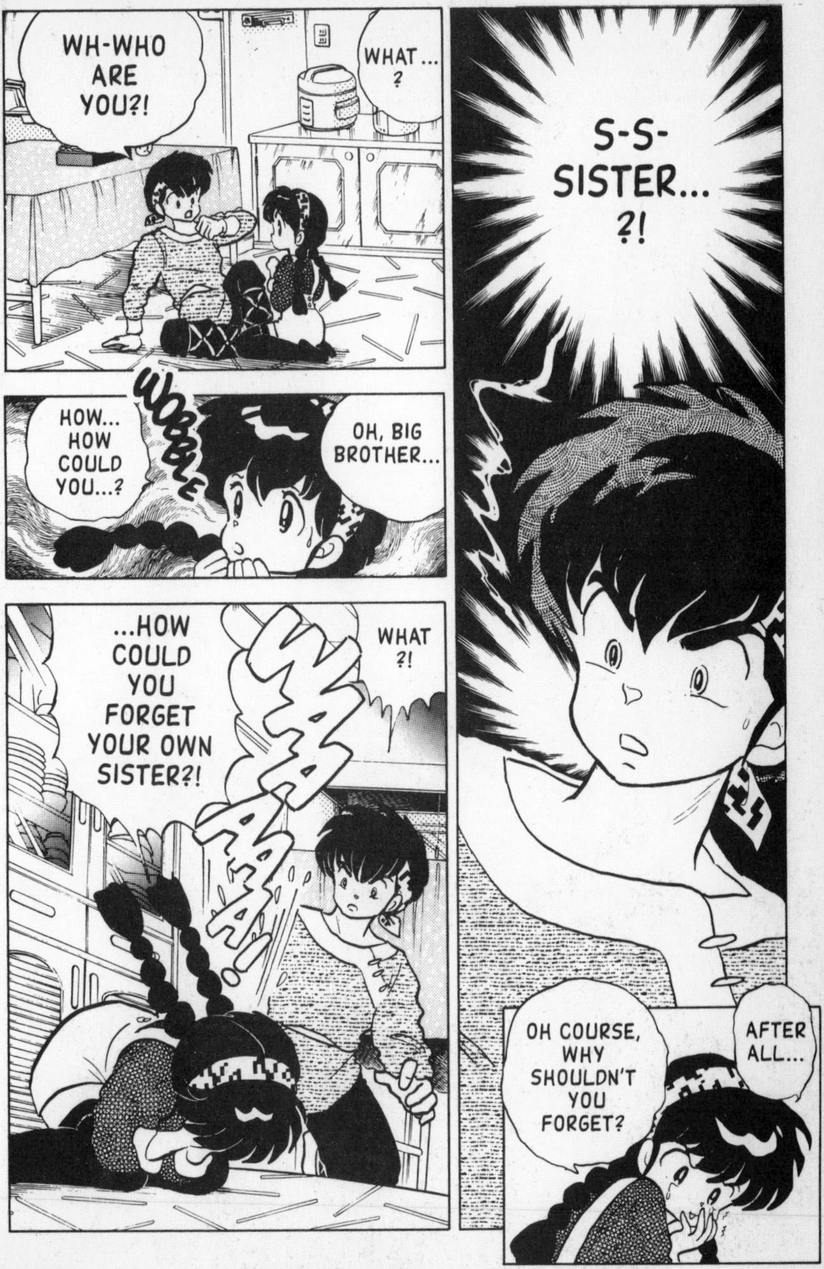
WH-WHO ARE YOU?!
WHAT... ?
HOW... HOW COULD YOU...?
WOBBLE
OH, BIG BROTHER...
...HOW COULD YOU FORGET YOUR OWN SISTER?!
WAAAAAA!
WHAT ?!
S-S-SISTER... ?!
OH COURSE, WHY SHOULDN'T YOU FORGET?
AFTER ALL...

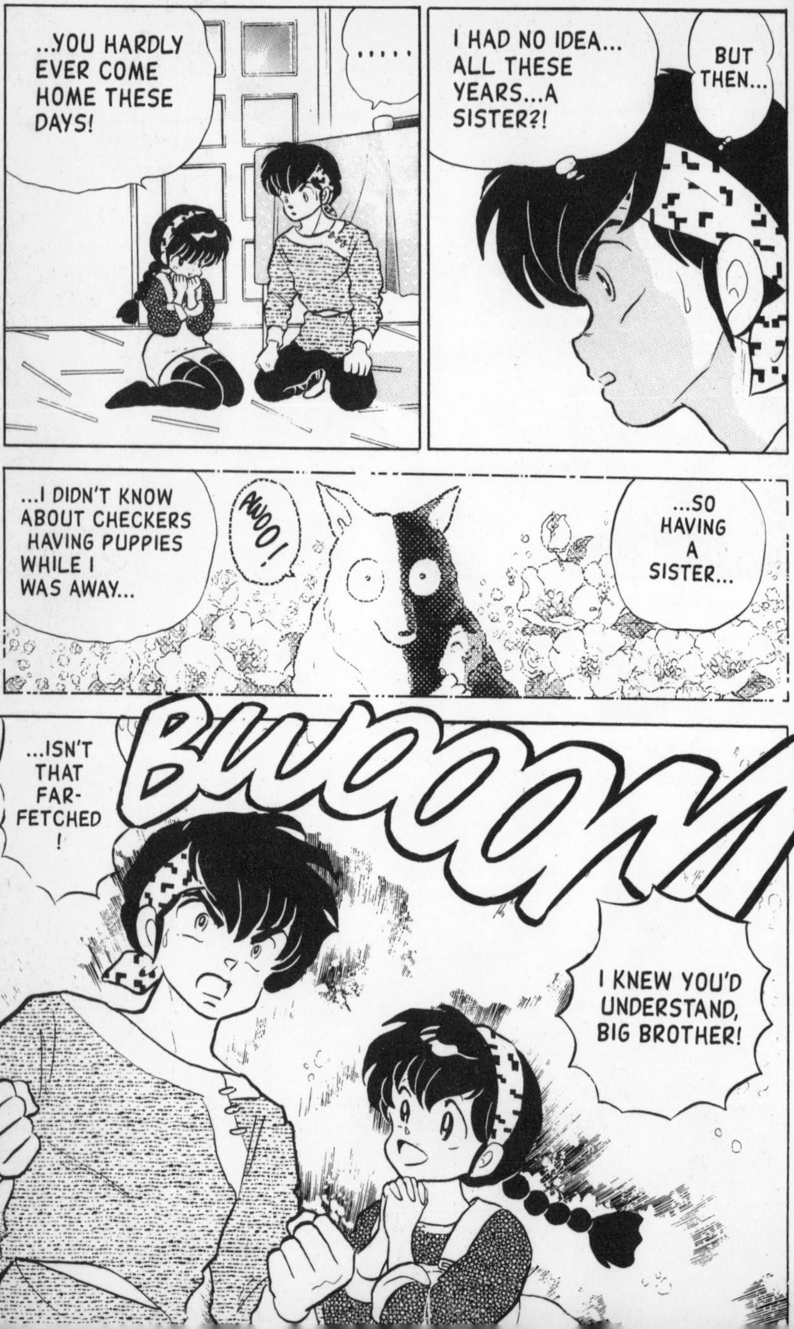
...YOU HARDLY EVER COME HOME THESE DAYS!
.....
I HAD NO IDEA... ALL THESE YEARS...A SISTER?!
BUT THEN...
...I DIDN'T KNOW ABOUT CHECKERS HAVING PUPPIES WHILE I WAS AWAY...
AWOO!
...SO HAVING A SISTER...
...ISN'T THAT FAR-FETCHED!
BUOOM
I KNEW YOU'D UNDERSTAND, BIG BROTHER!

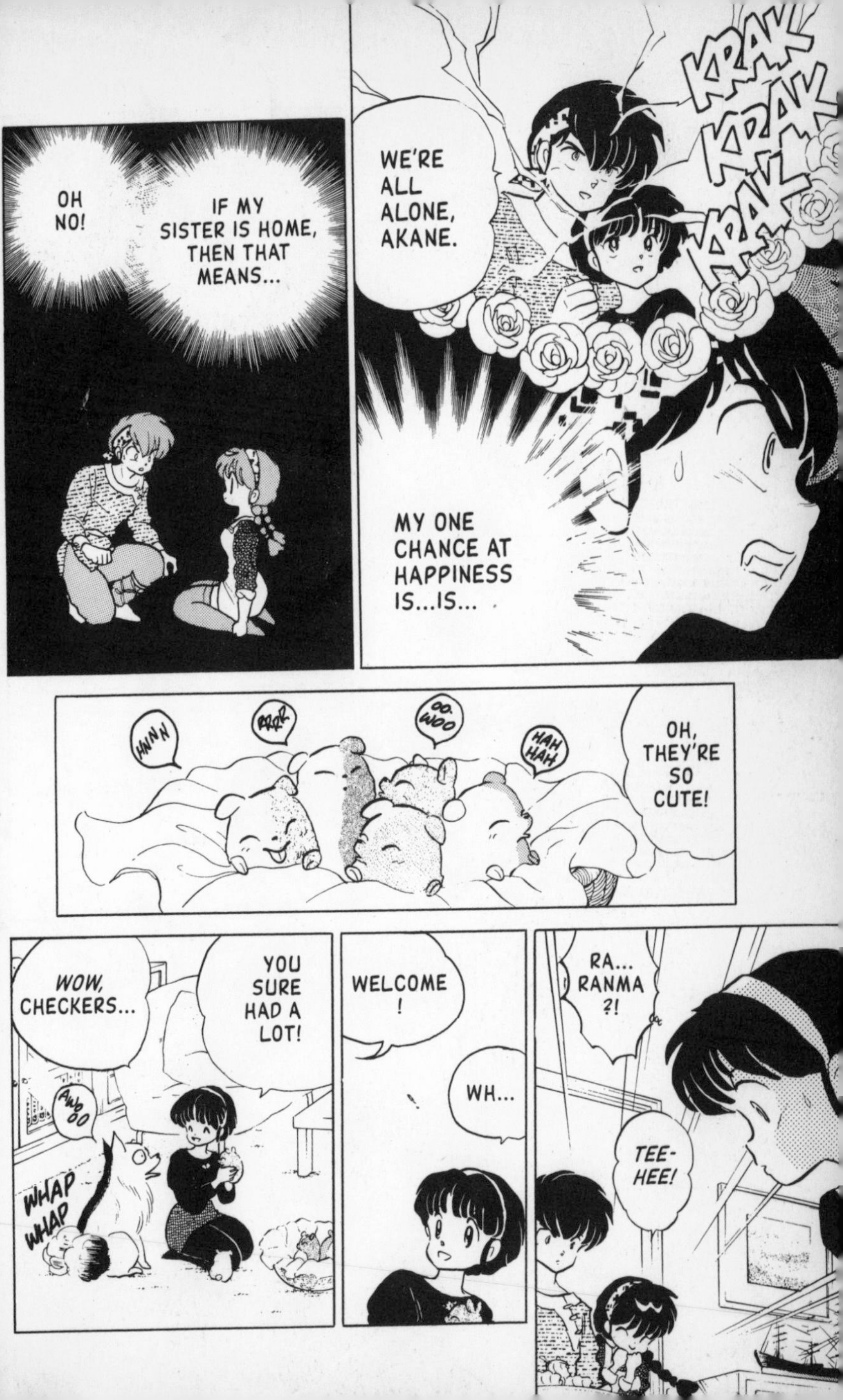
OH NO!
IF MY SISTER IS HOME, THEN THAT MEANS...
WE'RE ALL ALONE, AKANE.
KRAK KRAK KRAK
MY ONE CHANCE AT HAPPINESS IS...IS...
HNNN
HAH HAH
OH, THEY'RE SO CUTE!
WOW, CHECKERS...
YOU SURE HAD A LOT!
AWOOO
WHAP WHAP
WELCOME!
WH...
RA... RANMA?!
TEE-HEE!

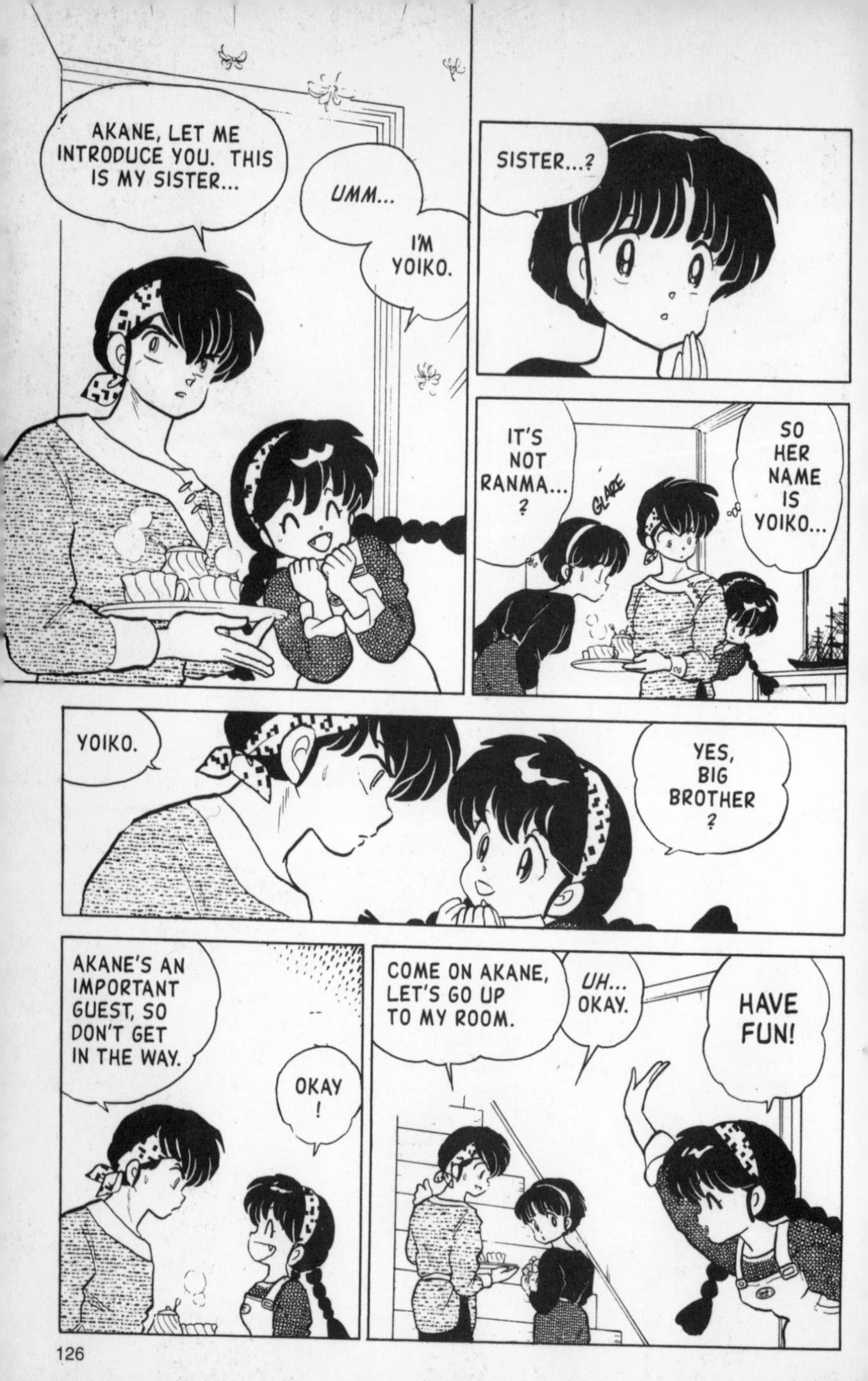
AKANE, LET ME INTRODUCE YOU. THIS IS MY SISTER...
UMM...
I'M YOIKO.
SISTER...?
IT'S NOT RANMA...?
GLARE
SO HER NAME IS YOIKO...
YOIKO.
YES, BIG BROTHER?
AKANE'S AN IMPORTANT GUEST, SO DON'T GET IN THE WAY.
OKAY!
COME ON AKANE, LET'S GO UP TO MY ROOM.
UH... OKAY.
HAVE FUN!

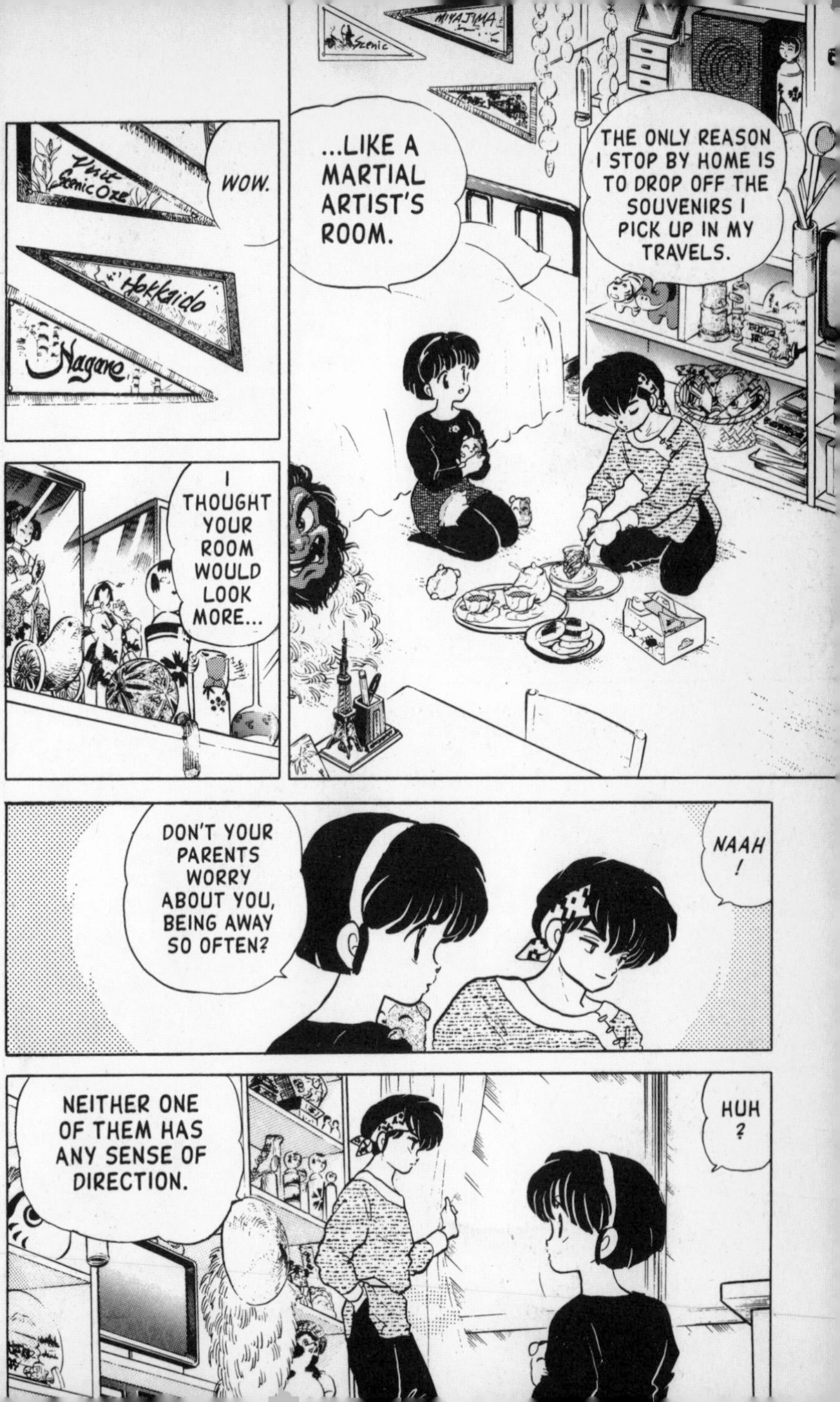
Visit Scenic Oze
Hokkaido
Nagano
WOW.
I THOUGHT YOUR ROOM WOULD LOOK MORE...
Scenic
MIYAJIMA
...LIKE A MARTIAL ARTIST'S ROOM.
THE ONLY REASON I STOP BY HOME IS TO DROP OFF THE SOUVENIRS I PICK UP IN MY TRAVELS.
DON'T YOUR PARENTS WORRY ABOUT YOU, BEING AWAY SO OFTEN?
NAAH!
NEITHER ONE OF THEM HAS ANY SENSE OF DIRECTION.
HUH?

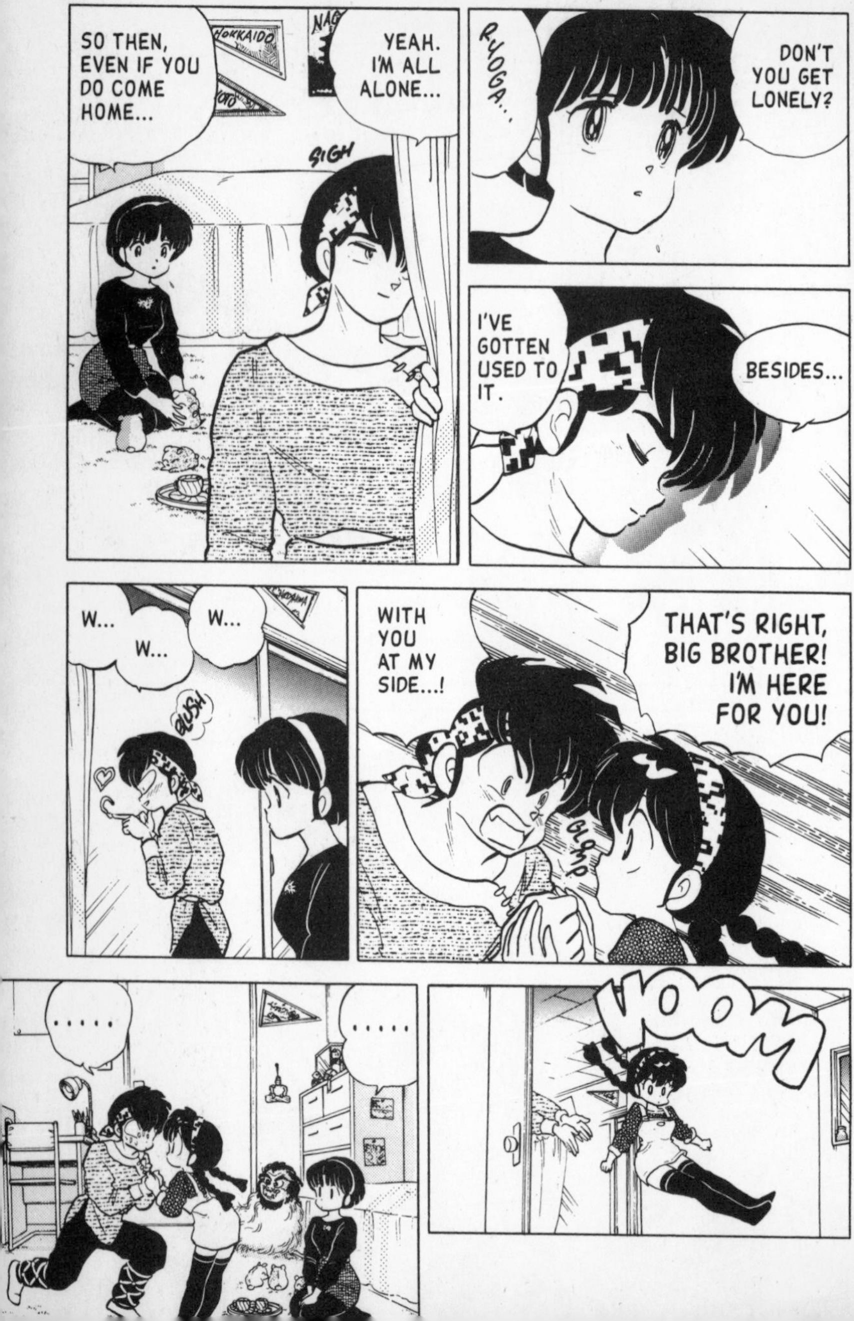
SO THEN, EVEN IF YOU DO COME HOME...
YEAH. I'M ALL ALONE...
SIGH
RYOGA...
DON'T YOU GET LONELY?
I'VE GOTTEN USED TO IT.
BESIDES...
W...
W...
W...
BLUSH
WITH YOU AT MY SIDE...!
THAT'S RIGHT, BIG BROTHER! I'M HERE FOR YOU!
GLOMP
.....
.....
VOOM

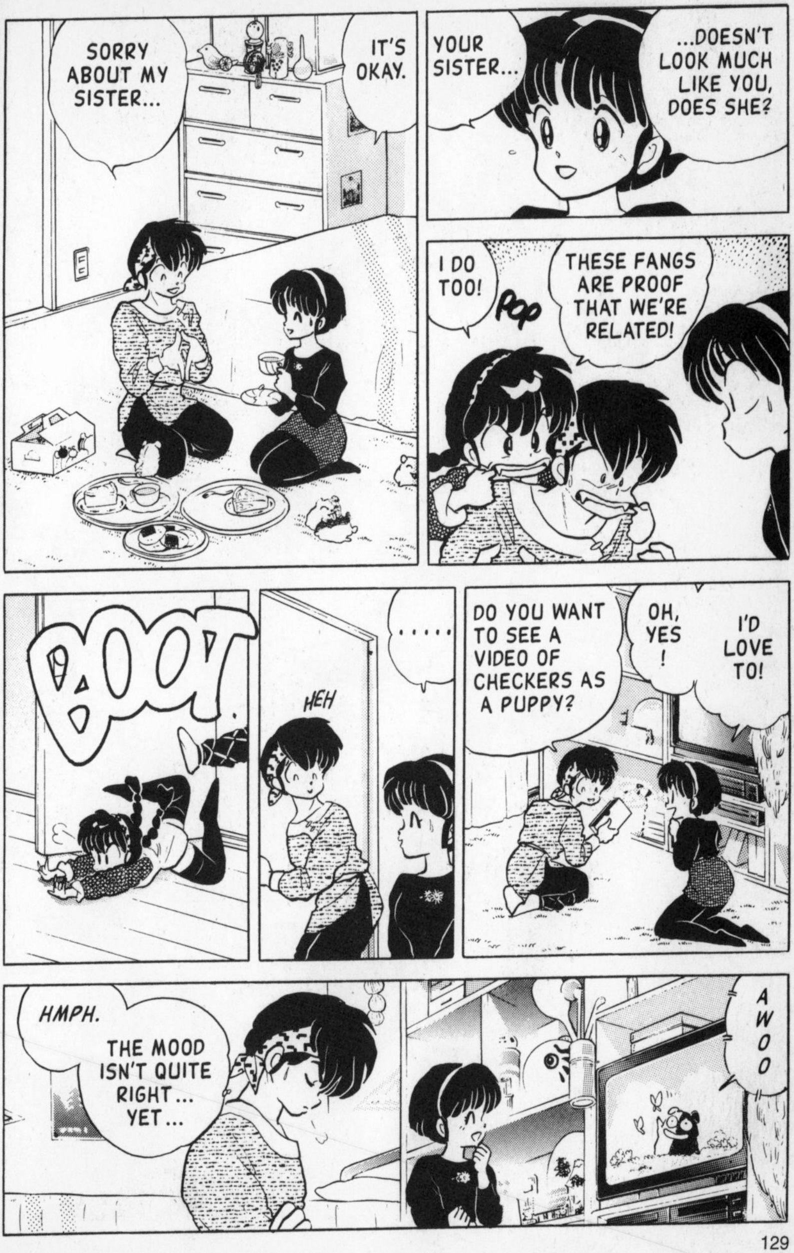
SORRY ABOUT MY SISTER...
IT'S OKAY.
YOUR SISTER...
...DOESN'T LOOK MUCH LIKE YOU, DOES SHE?
I DO TOO!
POP
THESE FANGS ARE PROOF THAT WE'RE RELATED!
BOOT
HEH
.....
DO YOU WANT TO SEE A VIDEO OF CHECKERS AS A PUPPY?
OH, YES!
I'D LOVE TO!
HMPH.
THE MOOD ISN'T QUITE RIGHT... YET...
AWOO

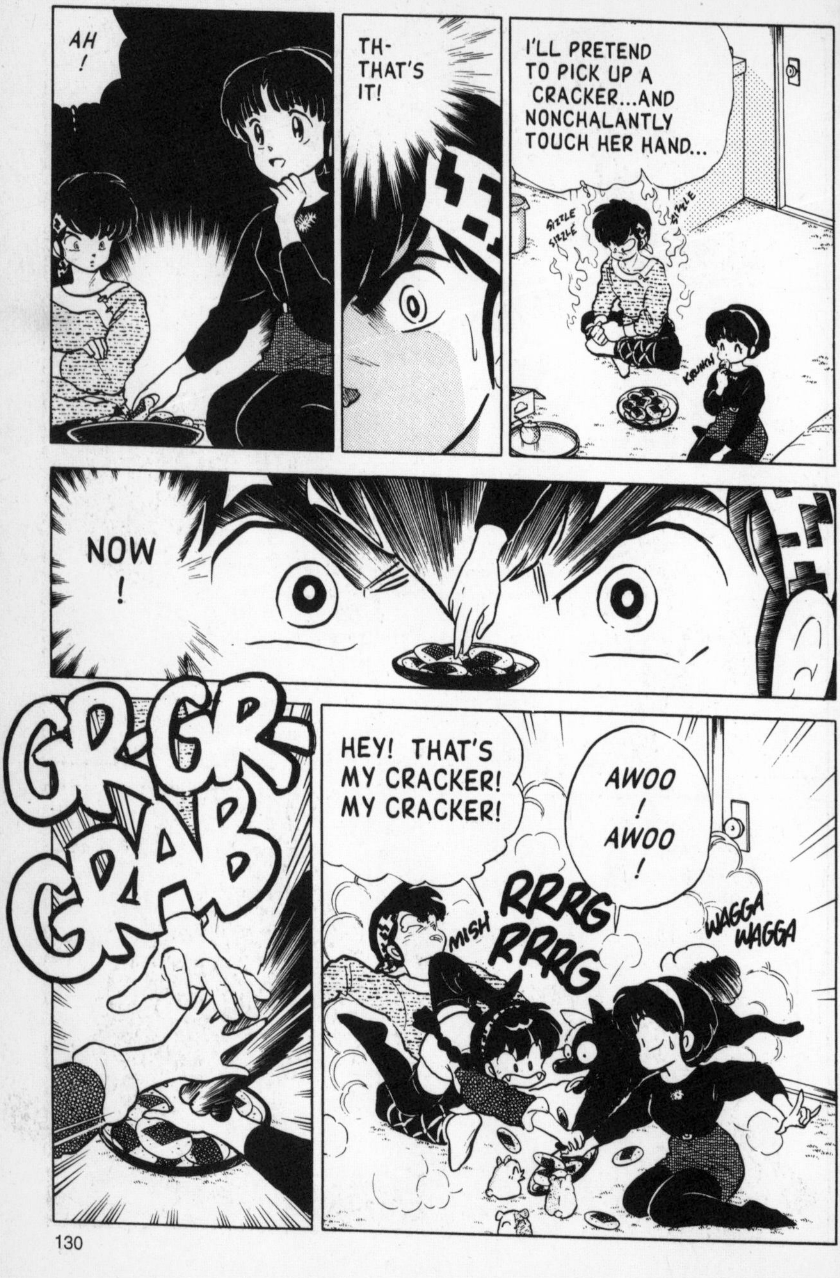
AH!
TH- THAT'S IT!
I'LL PRETEND TO PICK UP A CRACKER...AND NONCHALANTLY TOUCH HER HAND...
SIZZLE SIZZLE
SIZZLE
KRUNCH
NOW!
GR-GR-GRAB
HEY! THAT'S MY CRACKER! MY CRACKER!
AWOO! AWOO!
MISH
RRRG RRRG
WAGGA WAGGA

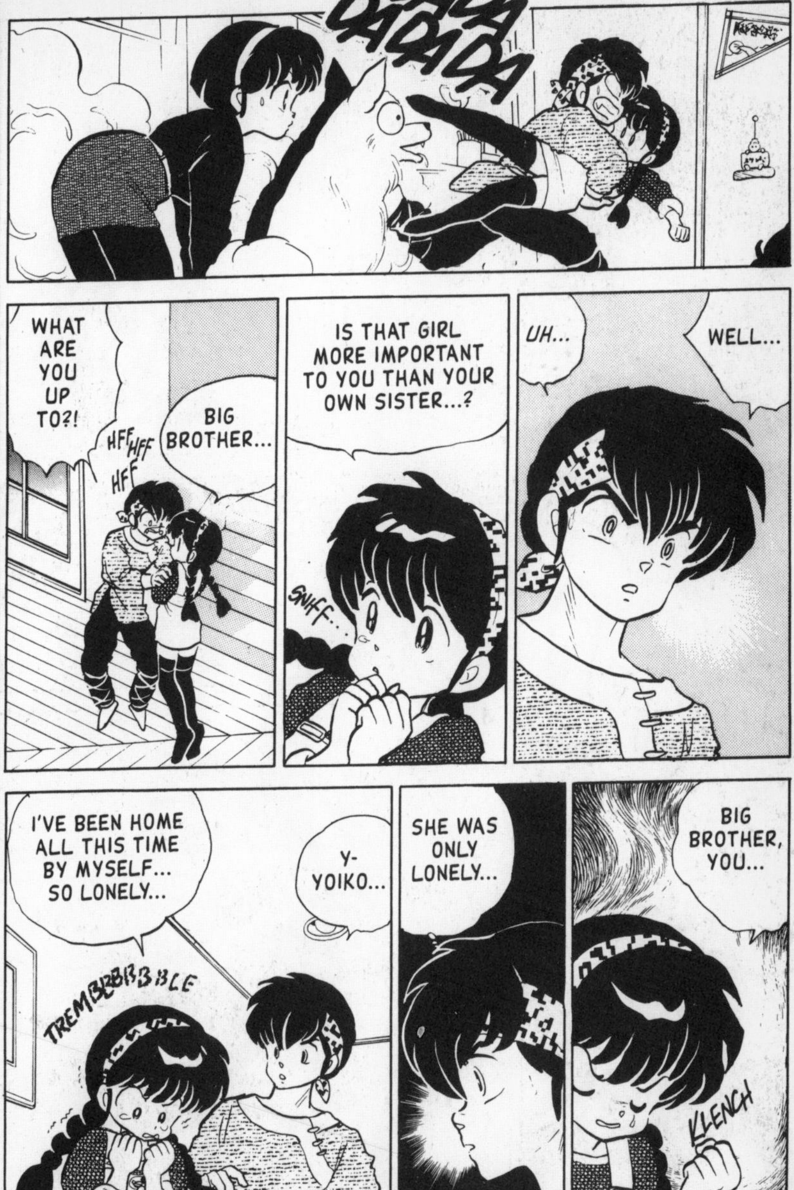
DADADA DADADA
WHAT ARE YOU UP TO?!
HFF HFF HFF
BIG BROTHER...
IS THAT GIRL MORE IMPORTANT TO YOU THAN YOUR OWN SISTER...?
SNIFF...
UH...
WELL...
I'VE BEEN HOME ALL THIS TIME BY MYSELF... SO LONELY...
TREMBBBBBBLE
Y-YOIKO...
SHE WAS ONLY LONELY...
BIG BROTHER, YOU...
KLENCH

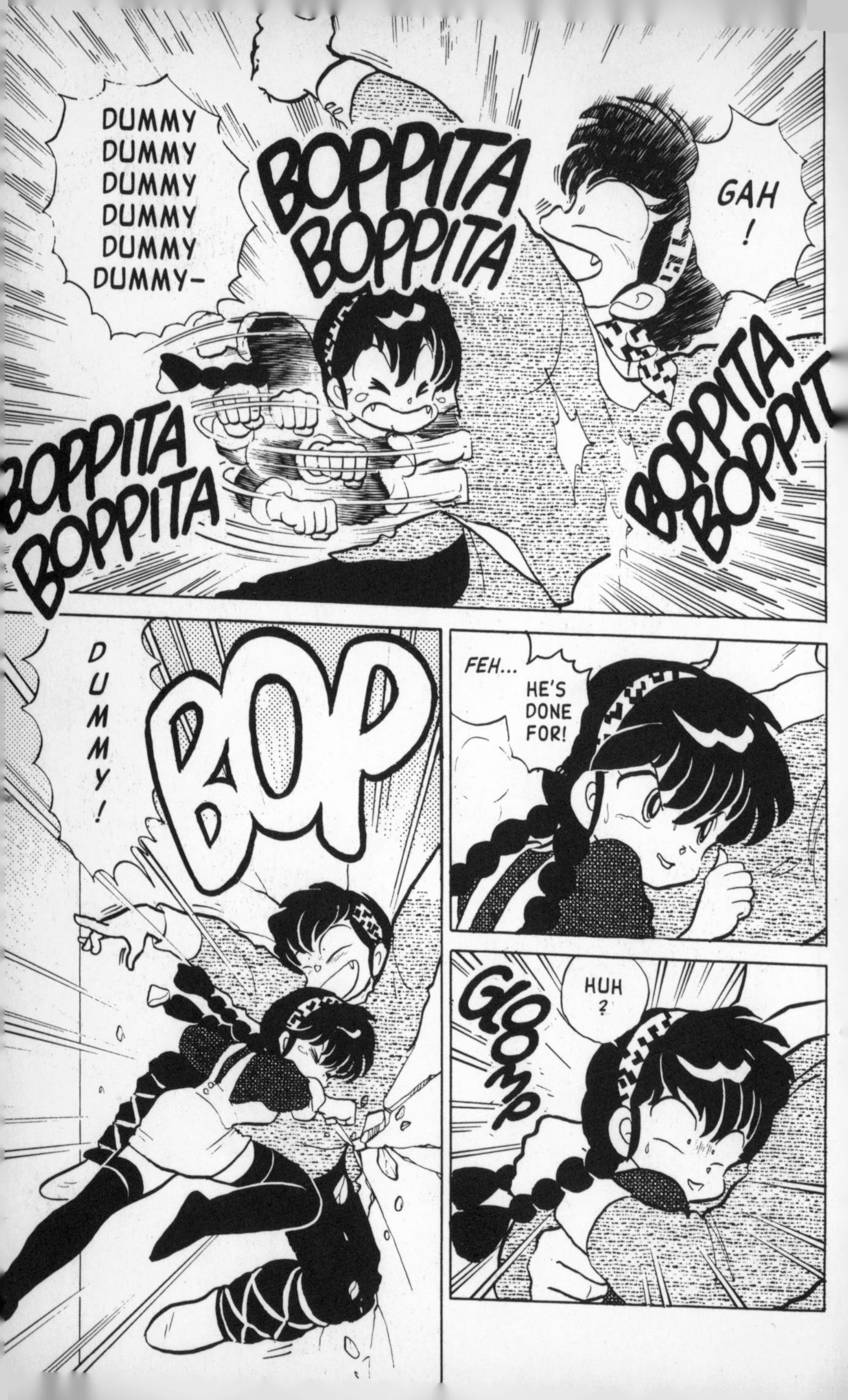
DUMMY DUMMY DUMMY DUMMY DUMMY DUMMY–
BOPPITA BOPPITA
GAH!
BOPPITA BOPPITA
BOPPITA BOPPIT
DUMMY!
BOP
FEH...
HE'S DONE FOR!
GLOMP
HUH?

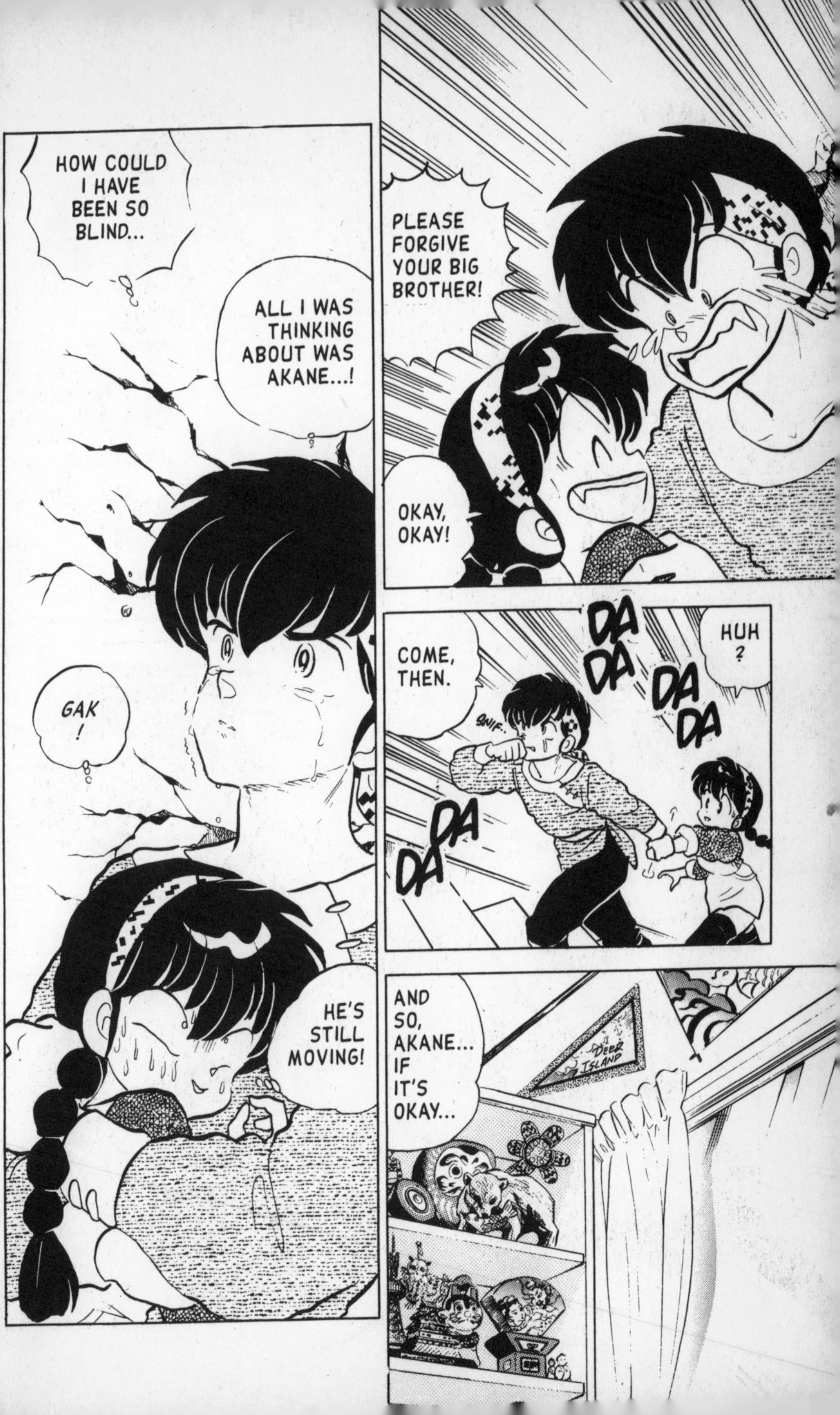
HOW COULD I HAVE BEEN SO BLIND...
ALL I WAS THINKING ABOUT WAS AKANE...!
GAK!
HE'S STILL MOVING!
PLEASE FORGIVE YOUR BIG BROTHER!
OKAY, OKAY!
COME, THEN.
SNIF.
DA DA
HUH?
DA DA
DA DA
AND SO, AKANE... IF IT'S OKAY...
DEER ISLAND

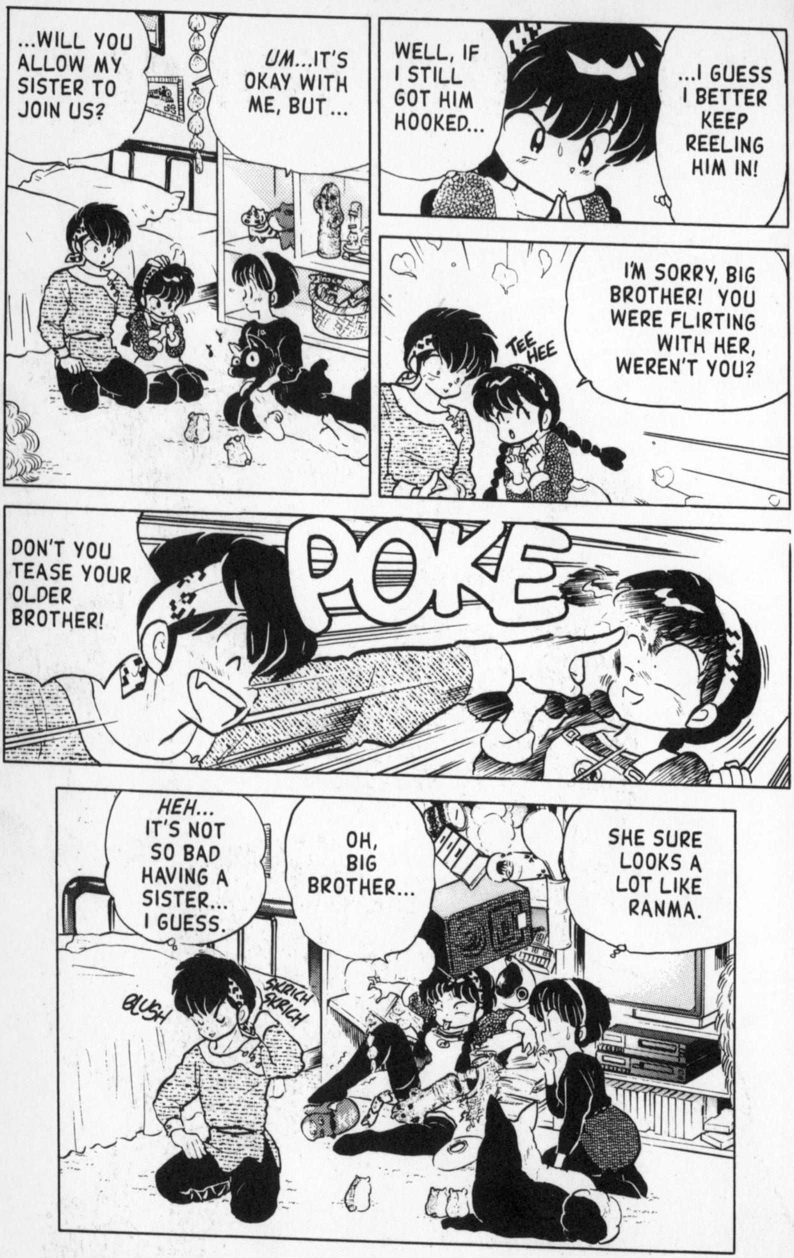
...WILL YOU ALLOW MY SISTER TO JOIN US?
UM...IT'S OKAY WITH ME, BUT ...
WELL, IF I STILL GOT HIM HOOKED...
...I GUESS I BETTER KEEP REELING HIM IN!
TEE HEE
I'M SORRY, BIG BROTHER! YOU WERE FLIRTING WITH HER, WEREN'T YOU?
DON'T YOU TEASE YOUR OLDER BROTHER!
POKE
HEH... IT'S NOT SO BAD HAVING A SISTER... I GUESS.
BLUSH
SKRICH SKRICH
OH, BIG BROTHER...
SHE SURE LOOKS A LOT LIKE RANMA.

Part 9

GET LOST, YOIKO!

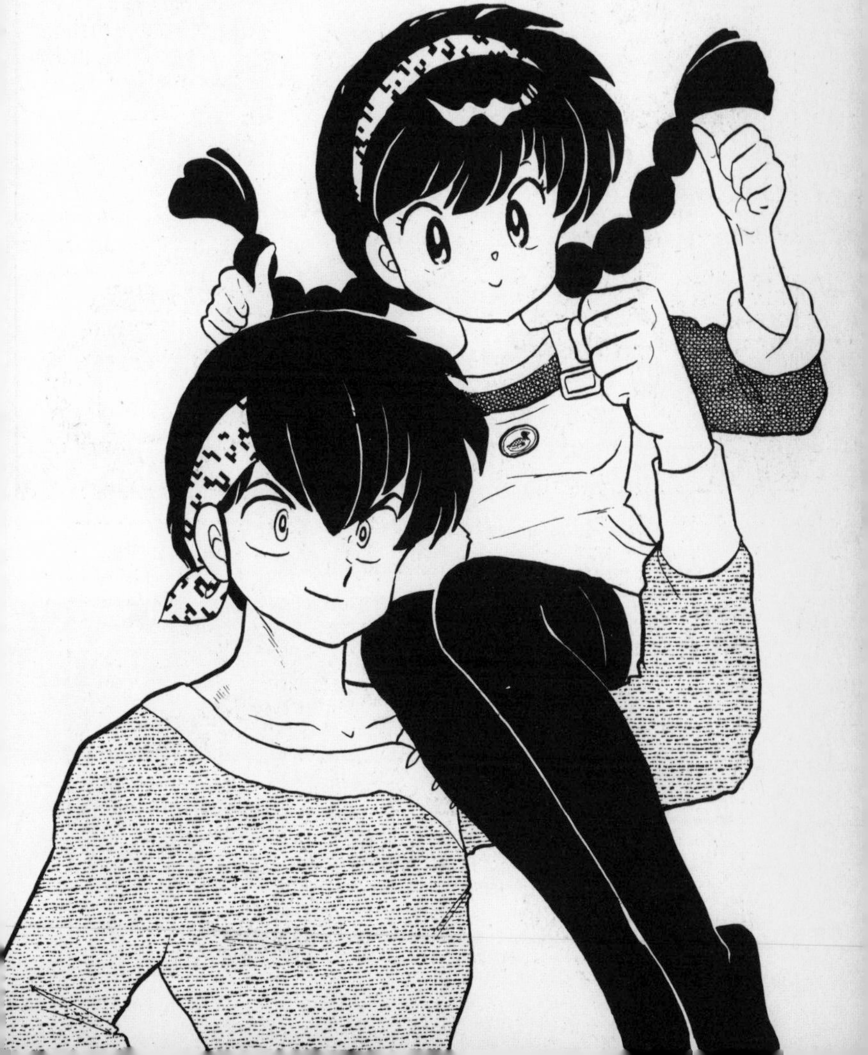

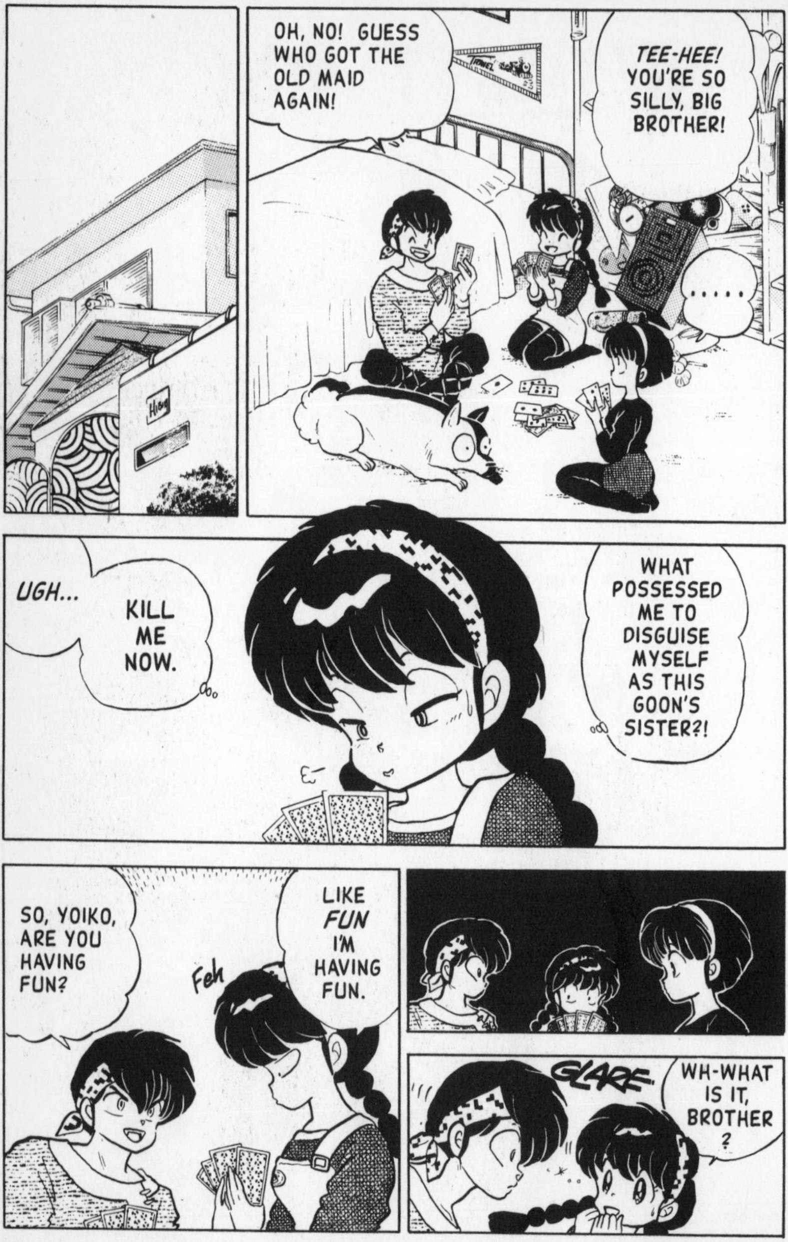
OH, NO! GUESS WHO GOT THE OLD MAID AGAIN!
TEE-HEE! YOU'RE SO SILLY, BIG BROTHER!
.....
UGH...
KILL ME NOW.
WHAT POSSESSED ME TO DISGUISE MYSELF AS THIS GOON'S SISTER?!
SO, YOIKO, ARE YOU HAVING FUN?
Feh
LIKE FUN I'M HAVING FUN.
GLARE
WH-WHAT IS IT, BROTHER?

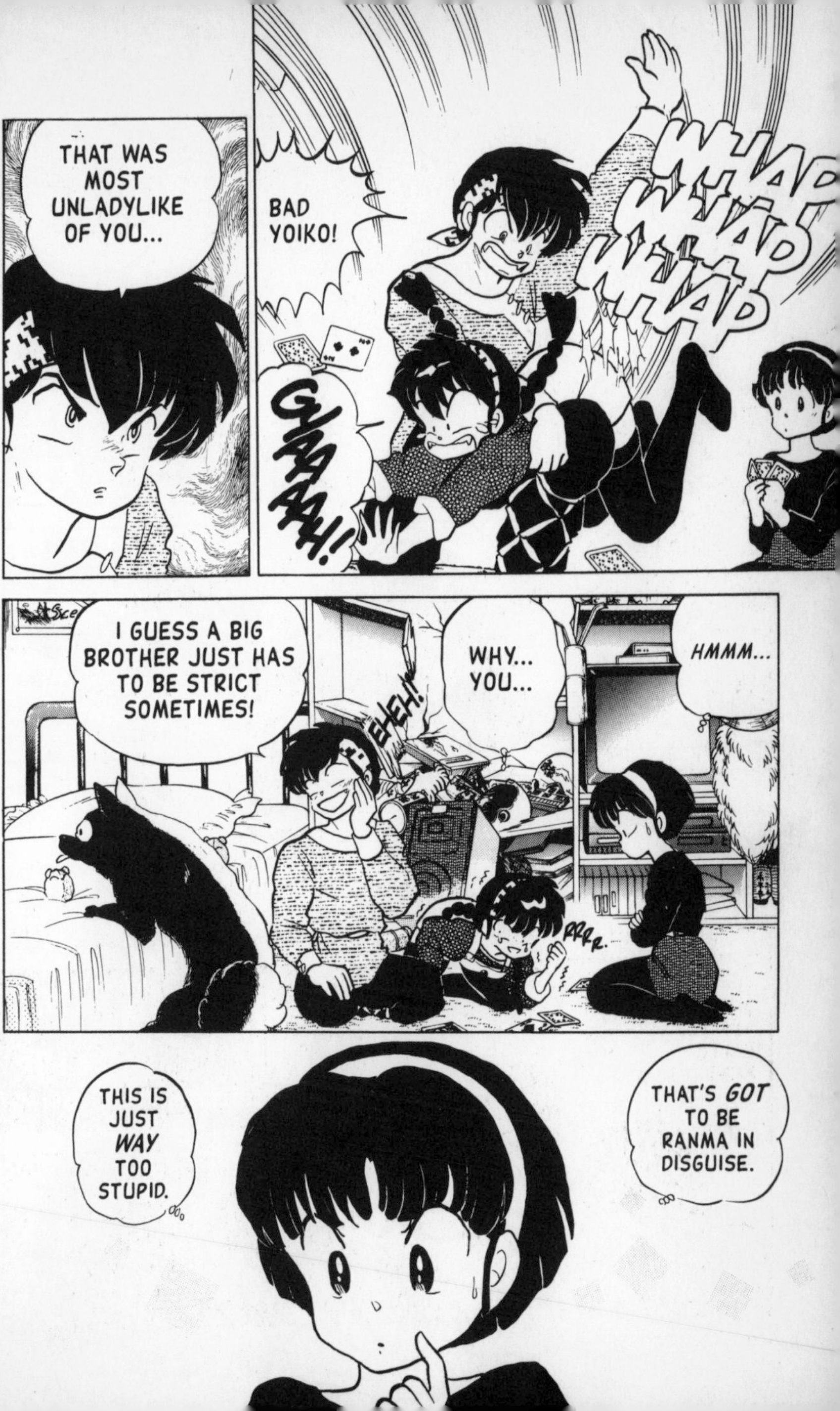
THAT WAS MOST UNLADYLIKE OF YOU...
BAD YOIKO!
WHAP WHAP WHAP WHAP
GWAAAAAH!!
I GUESS A BIG BROTHER JUST HAS TO BE STRICT SOMETIMES!
EHEH!
WHY... YOU...
RRRR.
HMMM...
THIS IS JUST WAY TOO STUPID.
THAT'S GOT TO BE RANMA IN DISGUISE.

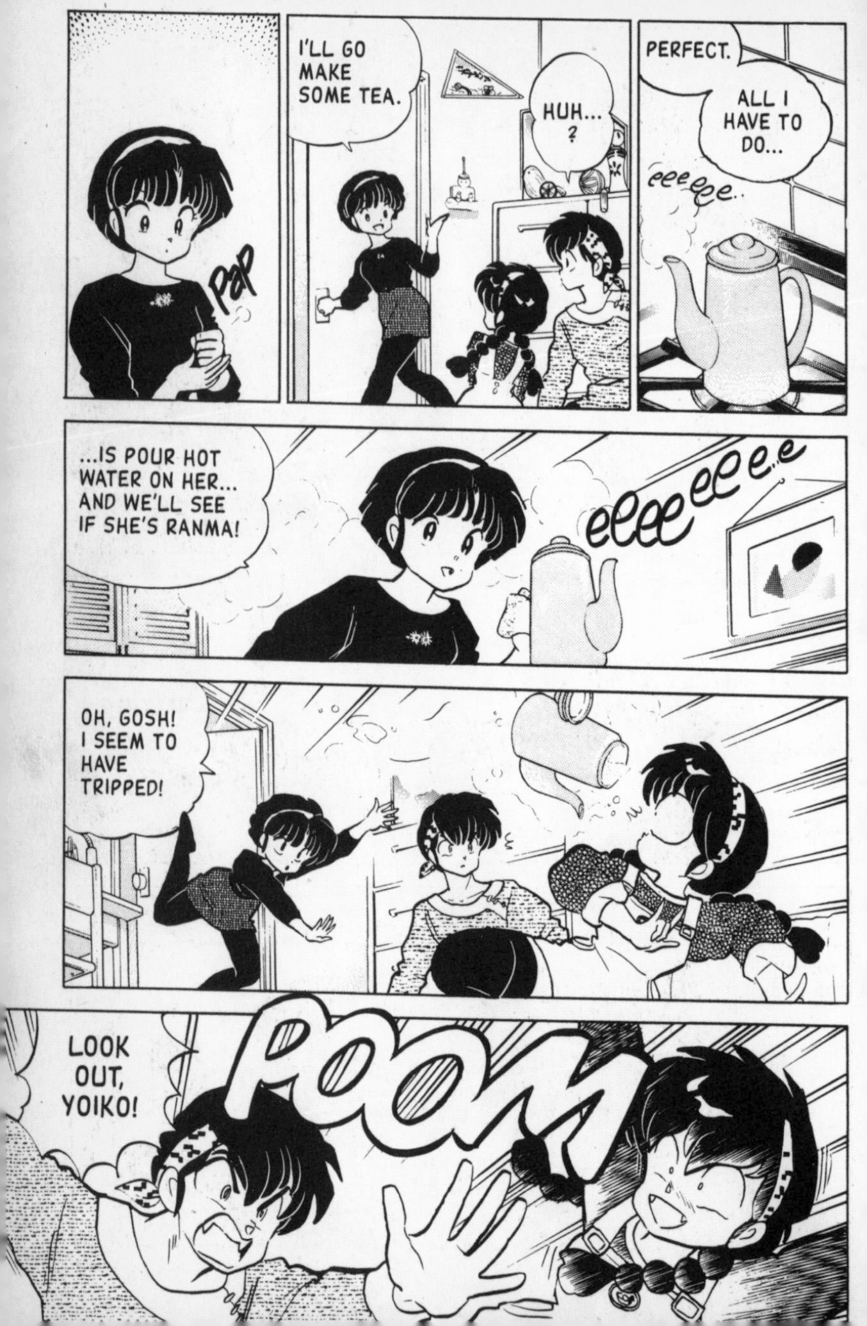
PAP
I'LL GO MAKE SOME TEA.
HUH...?
PERFECT.
ALL I HAVE TO DO...
eeeeee..
...IS POUR HOT WATER ON HER... AND WE'LL SEE IF SHE'S RANMA!
eeeeeeeee..e
OH, GOSH! I SEEM TO HAVE TRIPPED!
LOOK OUT, YOIKO!
POOM

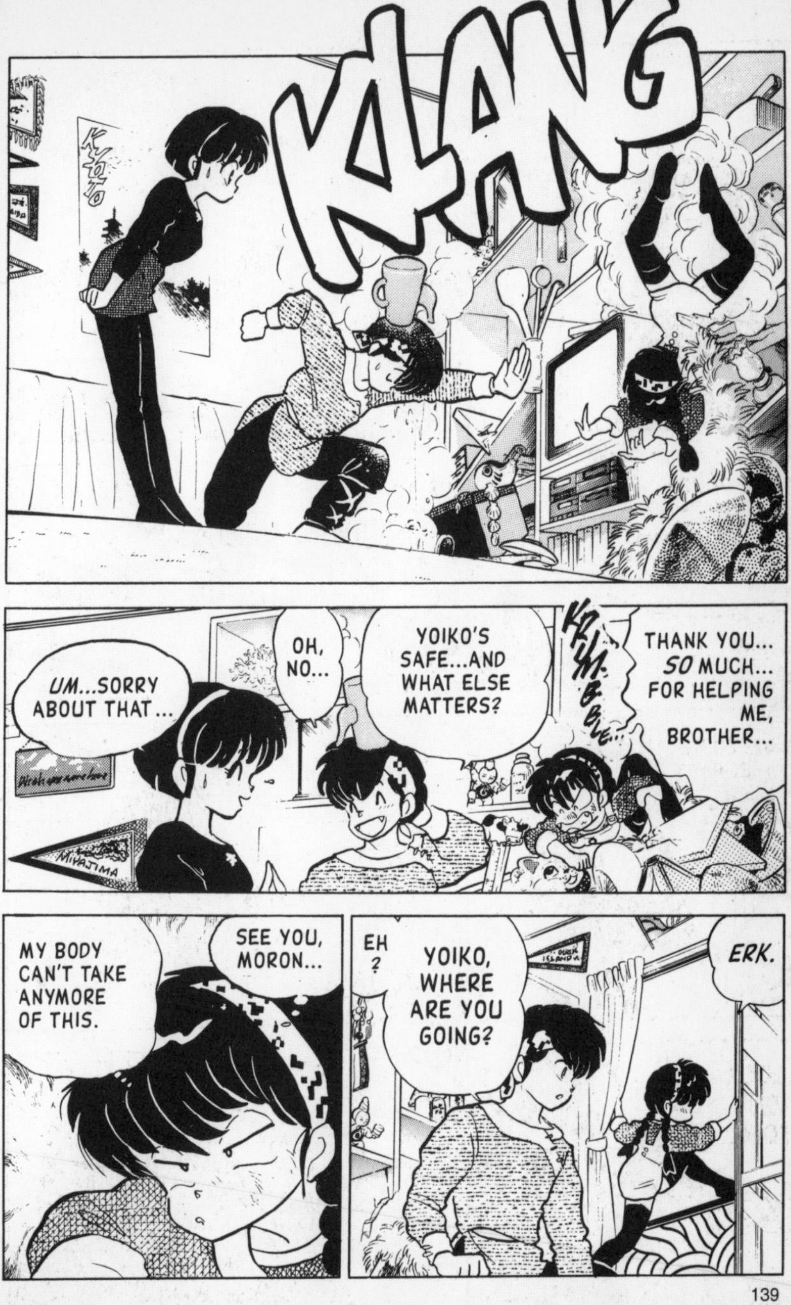
KLANG
UM...SORRY ABOUT THAT...
MIYAJIMA
OH, NO...
YOIKO'S SAFE...AND WHAT ELSE MATTERS?
KRUMBBLE...
THANK YOU... SO MUCH... FOR HELPING ME, BROTHER...
MY BODY CAN'T TAKE ANYMORE OF THIS.
SEE YOU, MORON...
EH ?
YOIKO, WHERE ARE YOU GOING?
ERK.

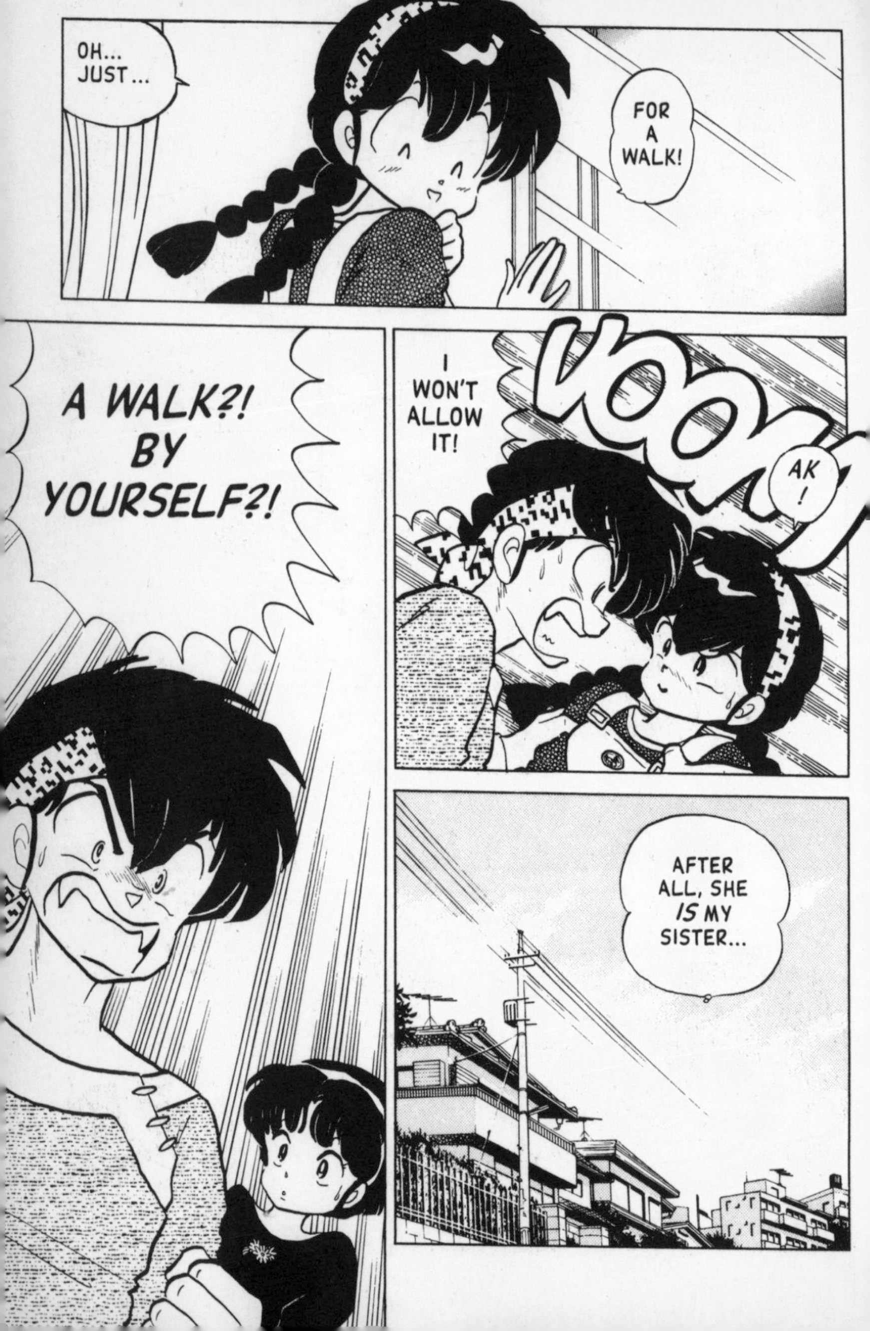
OH... JUST...
FOR A WALK!
A WALK?! BY YOURSELF?!
I WON'T ALLOW IT!
VOOM
AK!
AFTER ALL, SHE IS MY SISTER...

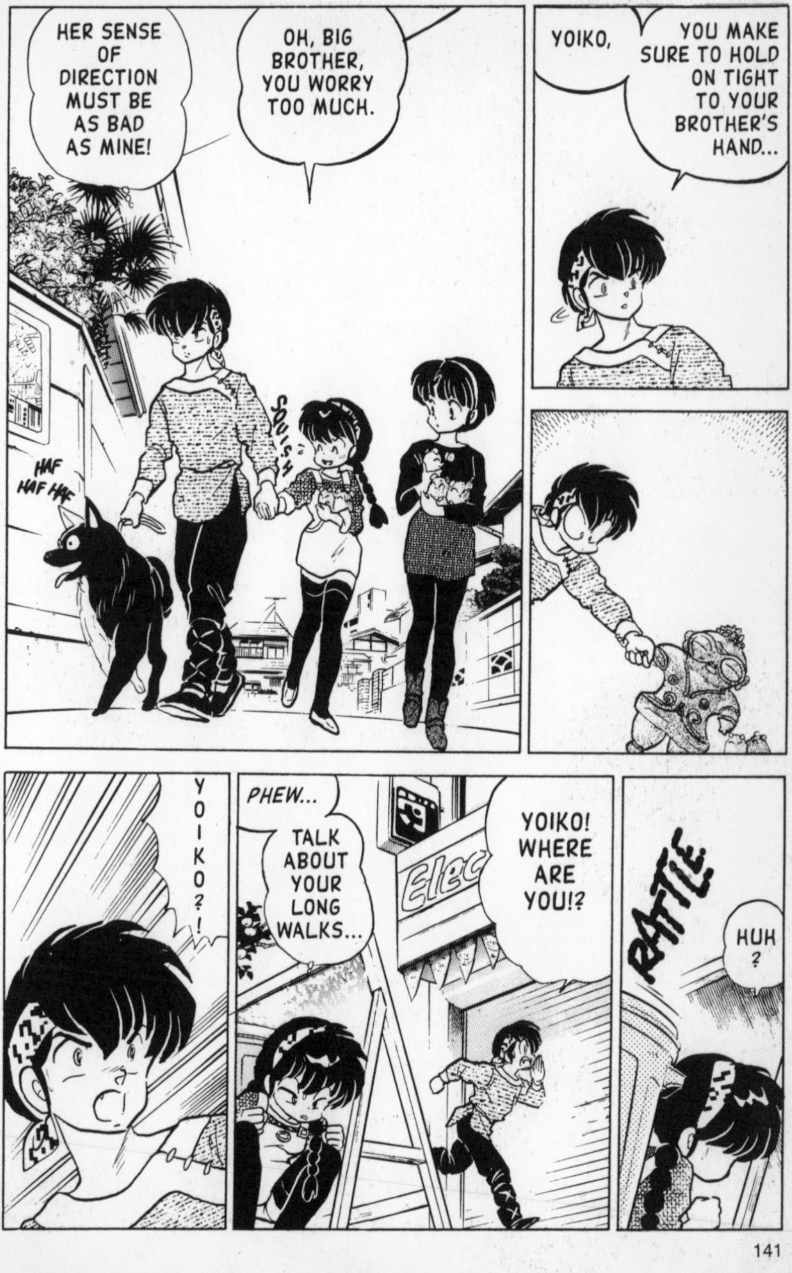
HER SENSE OF DIRECTION MUST BE AS BAD AS MINE!
OH, BIG BROTHER, YOU WORRY TOO MUCH.
HAF HAF HAF
SQUISH
YOIKO,
YOU MAKE SURE TO HOLD ON TIGHT TO YOUR BROTHER'S HAND...
YOIKO?!
PHEW...
TALK ABOUT YOUR LONG WALKS...
YOIKO! WHERE ARE YOU!?
RATTLE
HUH?

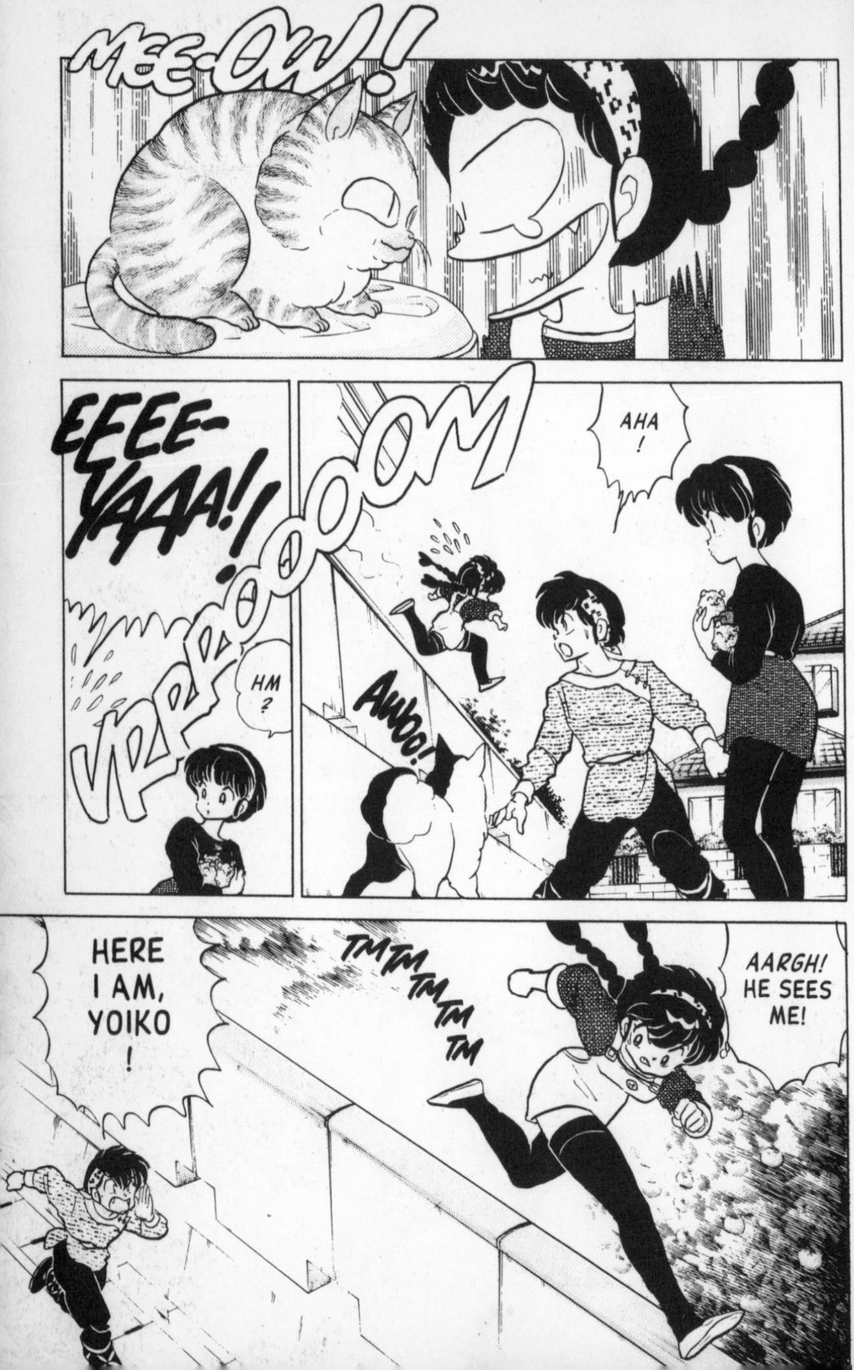
MEE-OW!!
AHA!
AWOO!
EEEE-YAAA!!
VRRROOOOOOM
HM?
AARGH! HE SEES ME!
TM TM TM TM TM TM TM
HERE I AM, YOIKO!

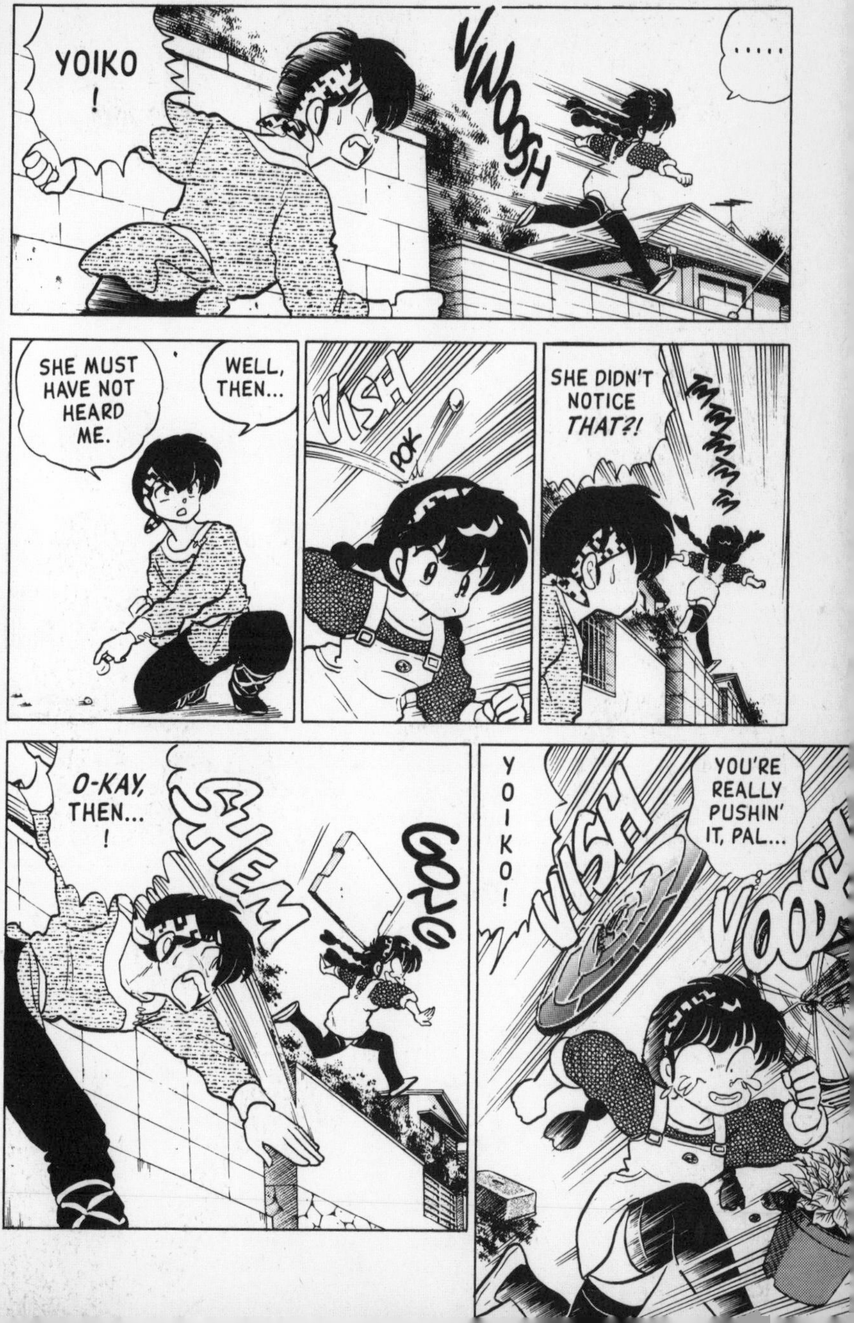
YOIKO !
VWOOSH
.....
SHE MUST HAVE NOT HEARD ME.
WELL, THEN...
VISH
POK
SHE DIDN'T NOTICE THAT?!
TMTMTMTMTM
O-KAY, THEN... !
CHEM
GONG
YOIKO!
VISH
YOU'RE REALLY PUSHIN' IT, PAL...

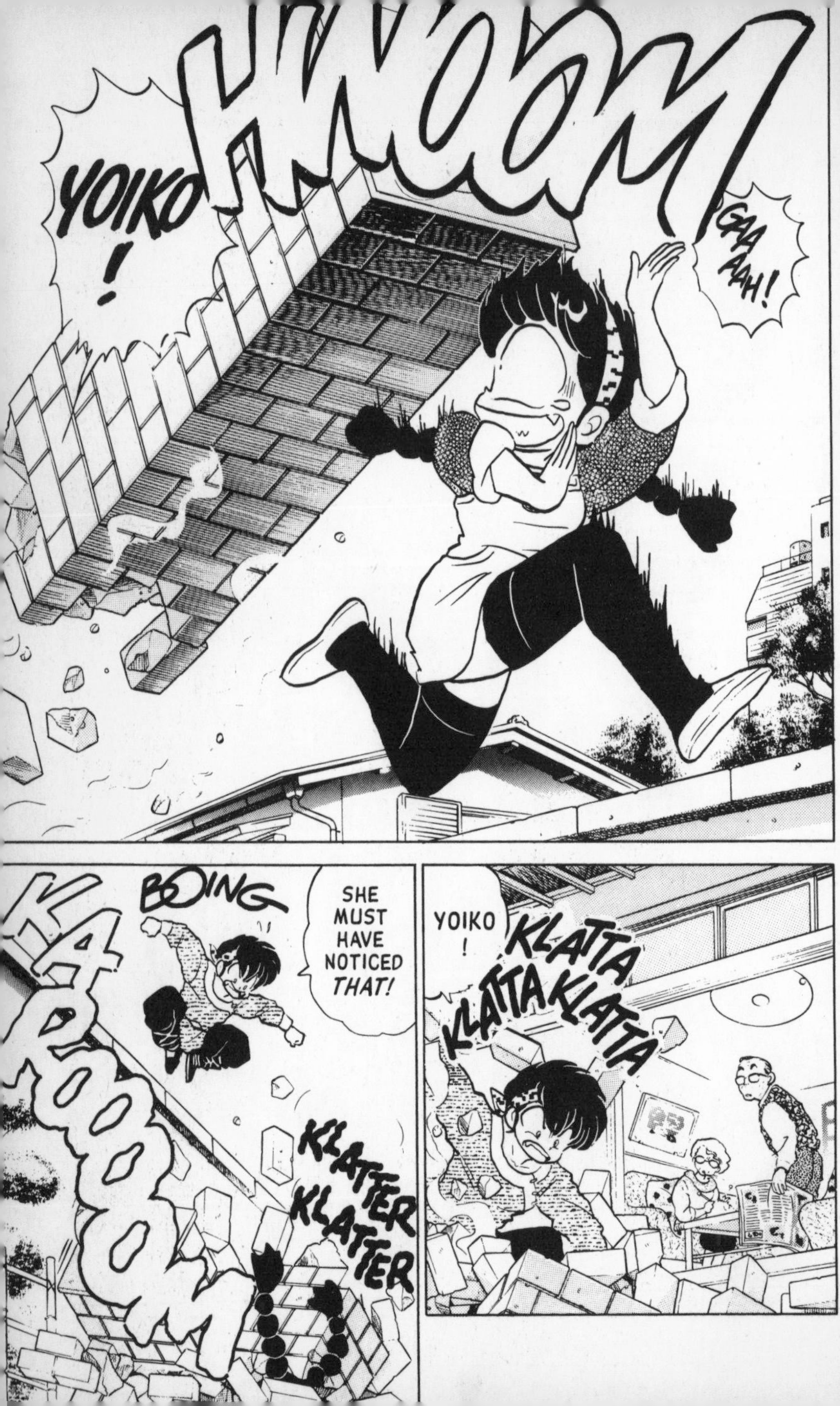
YOIKO!
WHOOM
GAAAAH!
KABOOOOM
BOING
SHE MUST HAVE NOTICED *THAT!*
KLATTER KLATTER
YOIKO!
KLATTA KLATTA KLATTA KLATTA

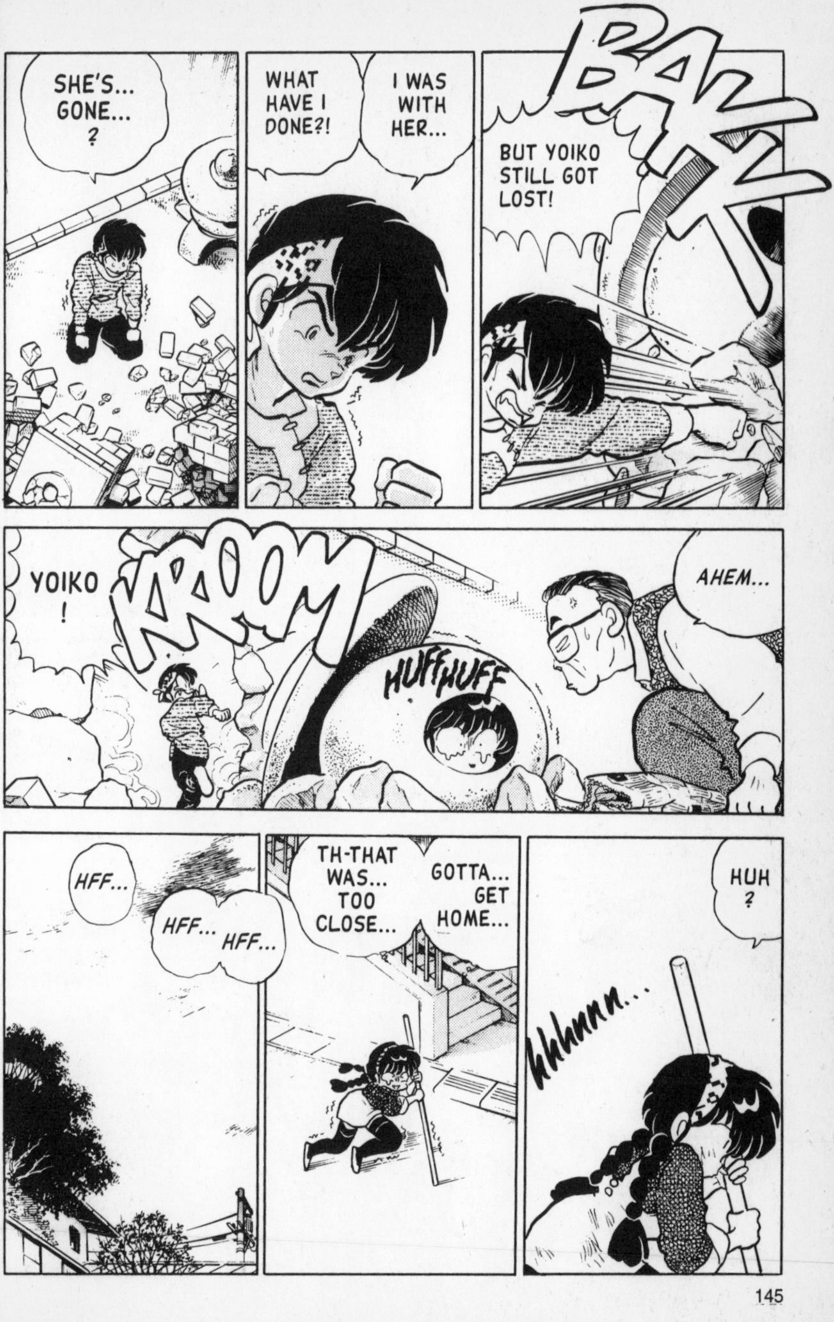
SHE'S... GONE... ?
WHAT HAVE I DONE?!
I WAS WITH HER...
BAKK
BUT YOIKO STILL GOT LOST!
YOIKO !
KABOOM
HUFF HUFF
AHEM...
HFF...
HFF... HFF...
TH-THAT WAS... TOO CLOSE...
GOTTA... GET HOME...
HUH ?
hhhnnn...

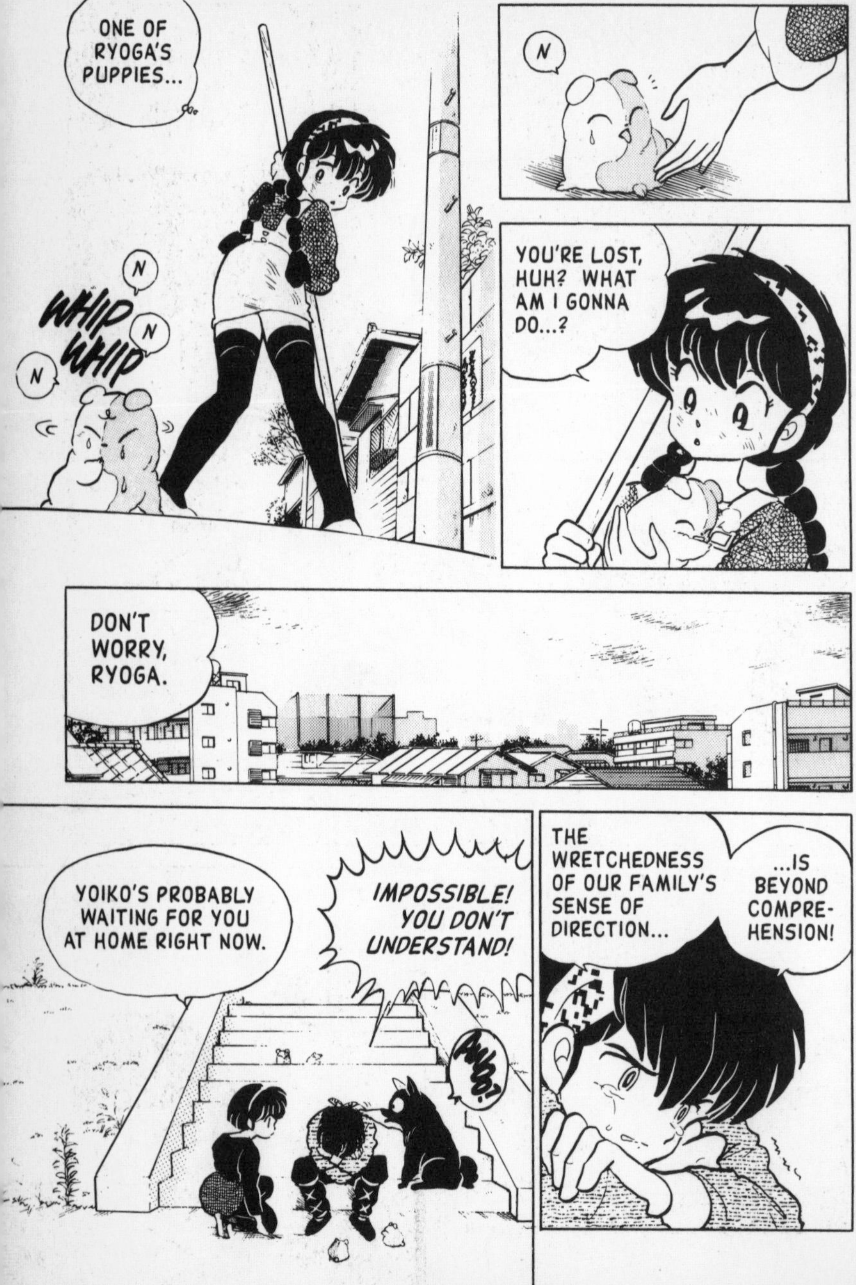
ONE OF RYOGA'S PUPPIES...
N
WHIP WHIP
N
N
N
YOU'RE LOST, HUH? WHAT AM I GONNA DO...?
DON'T WORRY, RYOGA.
YOIKO'S PROBABLY WAITING FOR YOU AT HOME RIGHT NOW.
IMPOSSIBLE! YOU DON'T UNDERSTAND!
AWOO?
THE WRETCHEDNESS OF OUR FAMILY'S SENSE OF DIRECTION...
...IS BEYOND COMPRE-HENSION!

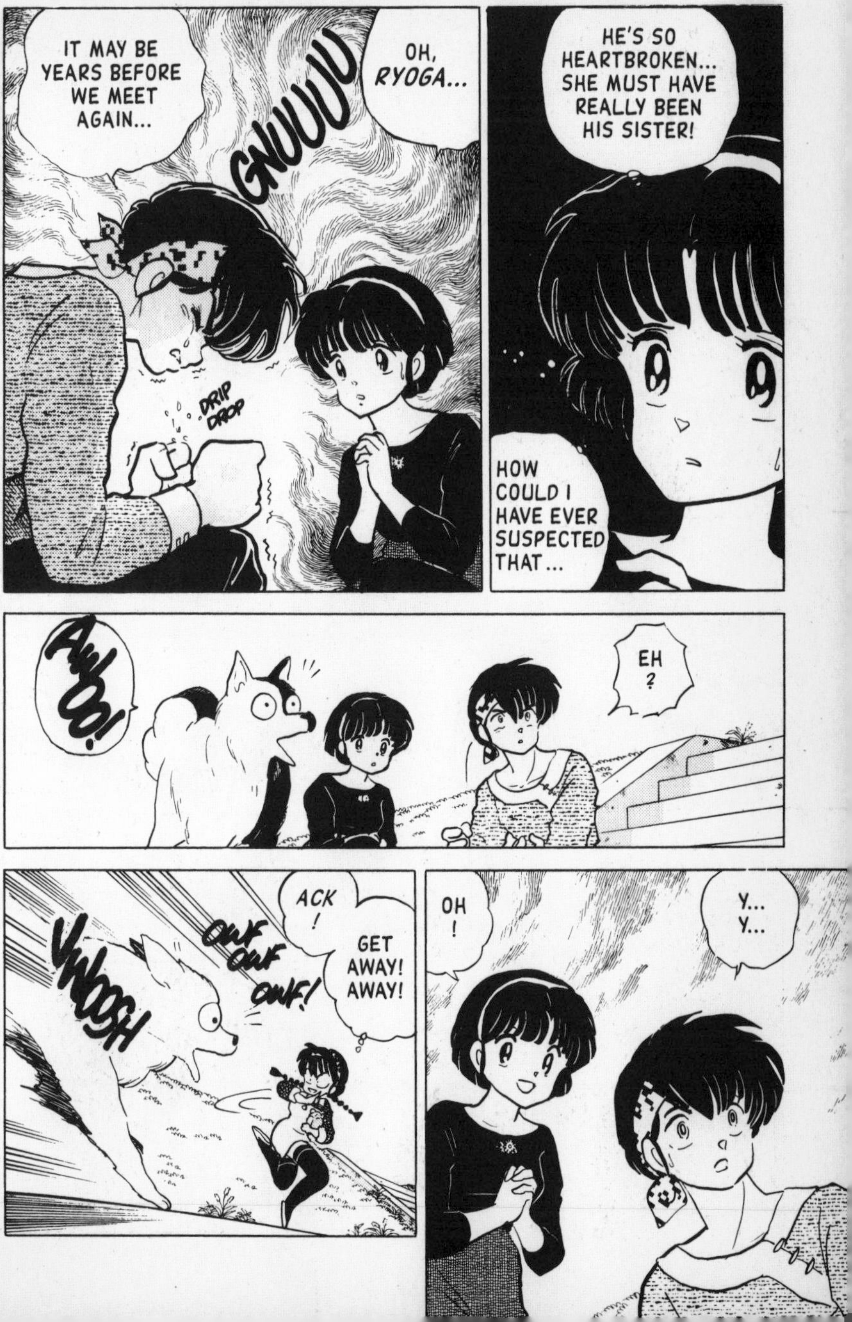
IT MAY BE YEARS BEFORE WE MEET AGAIN...
GNUUUU
OH, *RYOGA*...
HE'S SO HEARTBROKEN... SHE MUST HAVE REALLY BEEN HIS SISTER!
HOW COULD I HAVE EVER SUSPECTED THAT...
AWOO!
EH?
VWOOSH
OWF OWF OWF!
ACK!
GET AWAY! AWAY!
OH!
Y... Y...

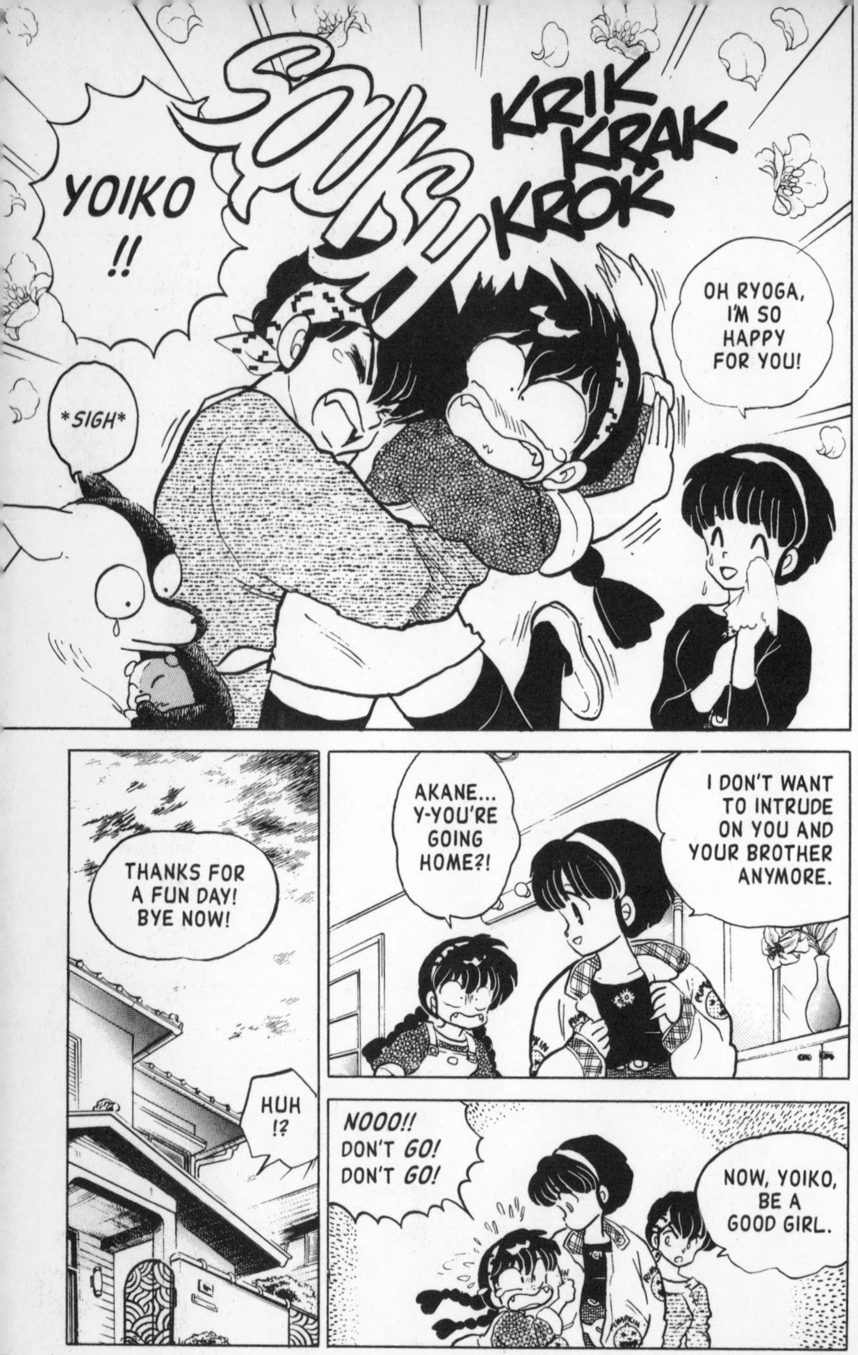
YOIKO !!
KRIK KRAK KROK
SIGH
OH RYOGA, I'M SO HAPPY FOR YOU!
THANKS FOR A FUN DAY! BYE NOW!
HUH !?
AKANE... Y-YOU'RE GOING HOME?!
I DON'T WANT TO INTRUDE ON YOU AND YOUR BROTHER ANYMORE.
NOOO!! DON'T GO! DON'T GO!
NOW, YOIKO, BE A GOOD GIRL.

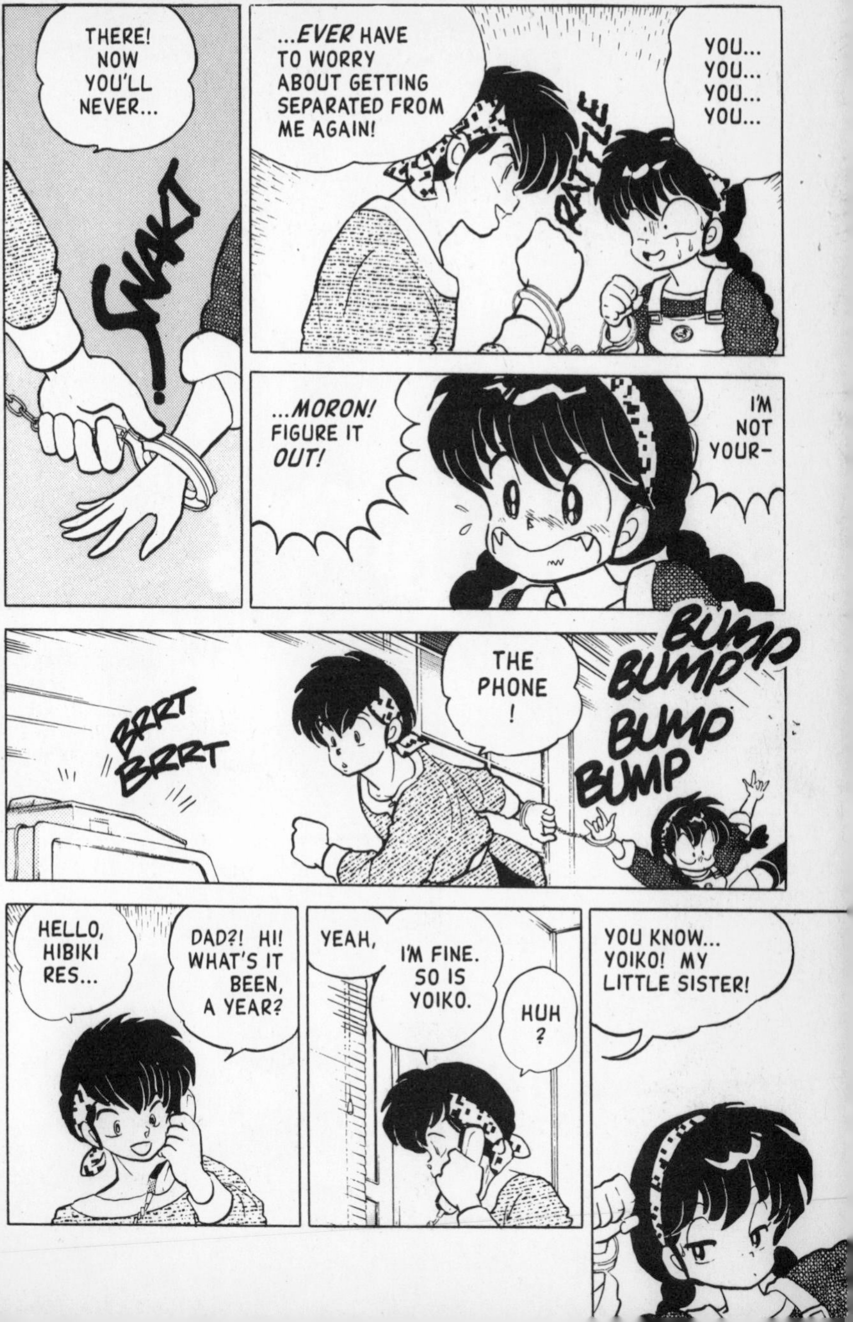
THERE! NOW YOU'LL NEVER...
SNAP!
...EVER HAVE TO WORRY ABOUT GETTING SEPARATED FROM ME AGAIN!
RATTLE
YOU... YOU... YOU... YOU...
...MORON! FIGURE IT OUT!
I'M NOT YOUR-
BRRT BRRT
THE PHONE!
BUMP BUMP BUMP BUMP
HELLO, HIBIKI RES...
DAD?! HI! WHAT'S IT BEEN, A YEAR?
YEAH,
I'M FINE. SO IS YOIKO.
HUH?
YOU KNOW... YOIKO! MY LITTLE SISTER!

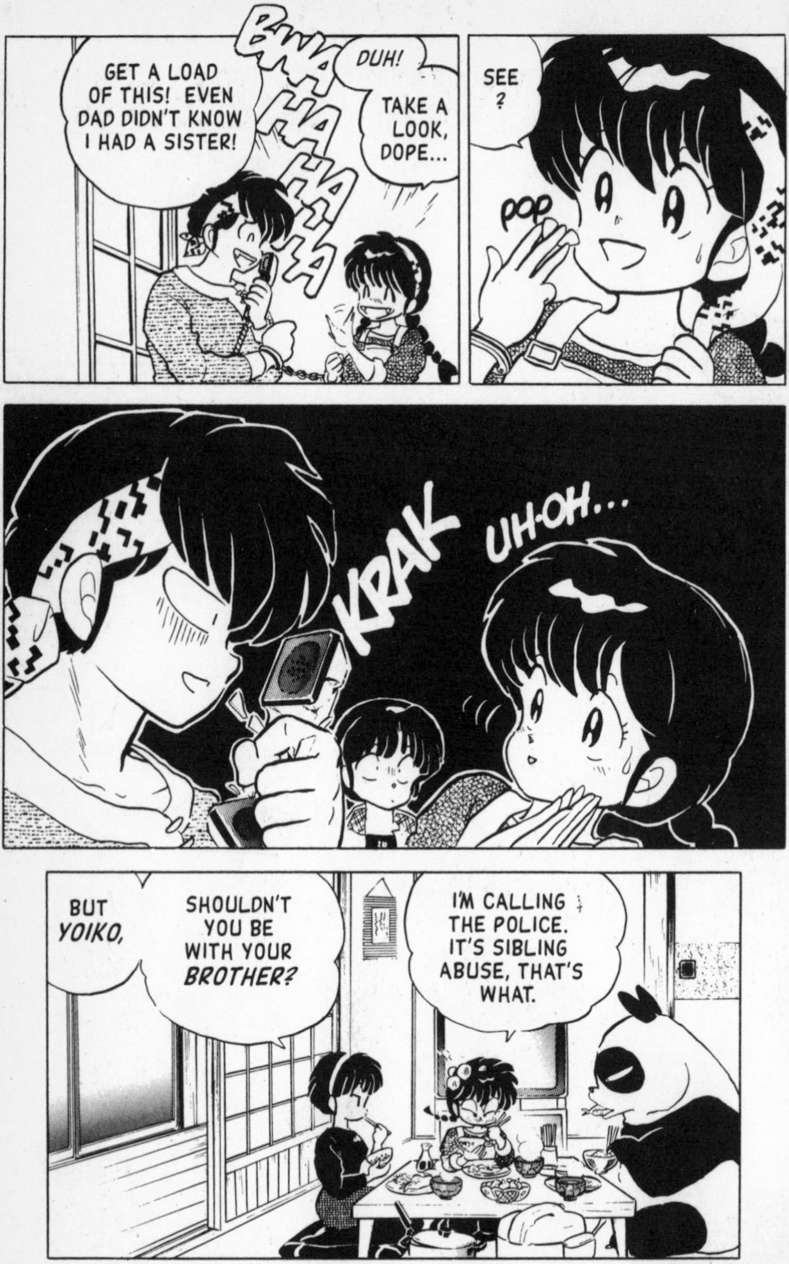
GET A LOAD OF THIS! EVEN DAD DIDN'T KNOW I HAD A SISTER!
BWAHAHAHAHA
DUH!
TAKE A LOOK, DOPE...
SEE?
POP
KRAK
UH-OH...
BUT YOIKO,
SHOULDN'T YOU BE WITH YOUR BROTHER?
I'M CALLING THE POLICE. IT'S SIBLING ABUSE, THAT'S WHAT.

Part 10
THE ULTIMATE TECHNIQUE

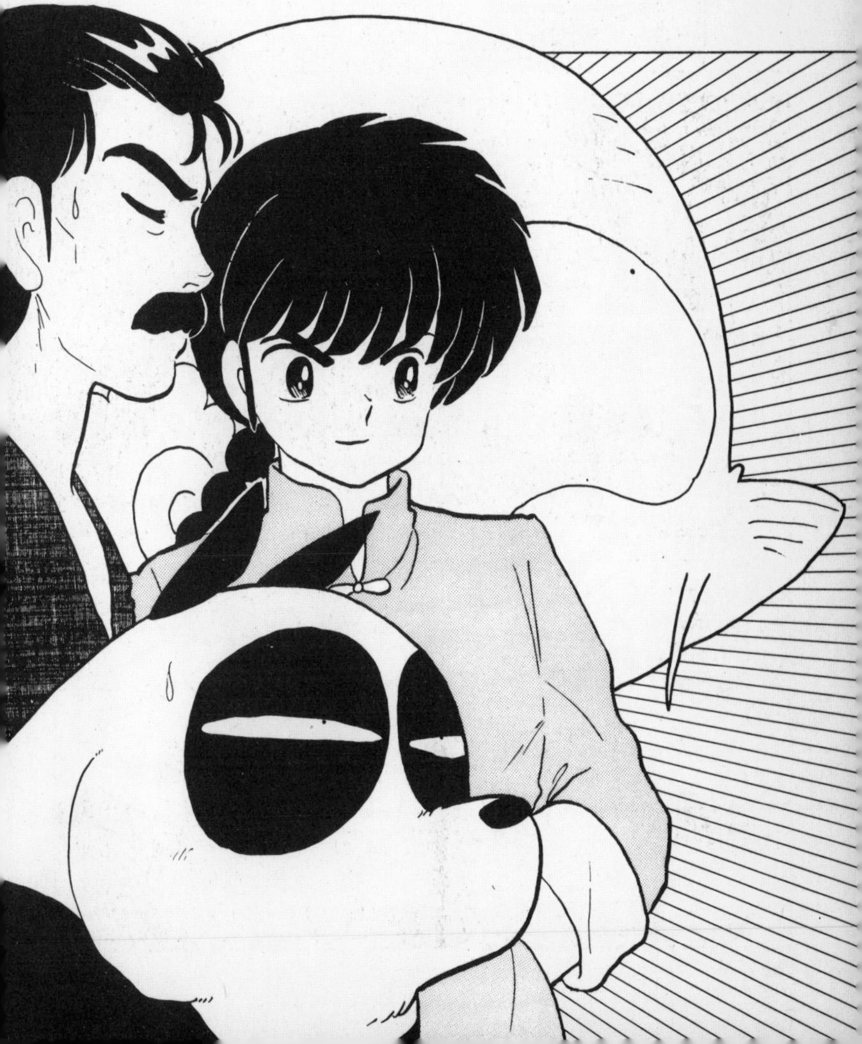

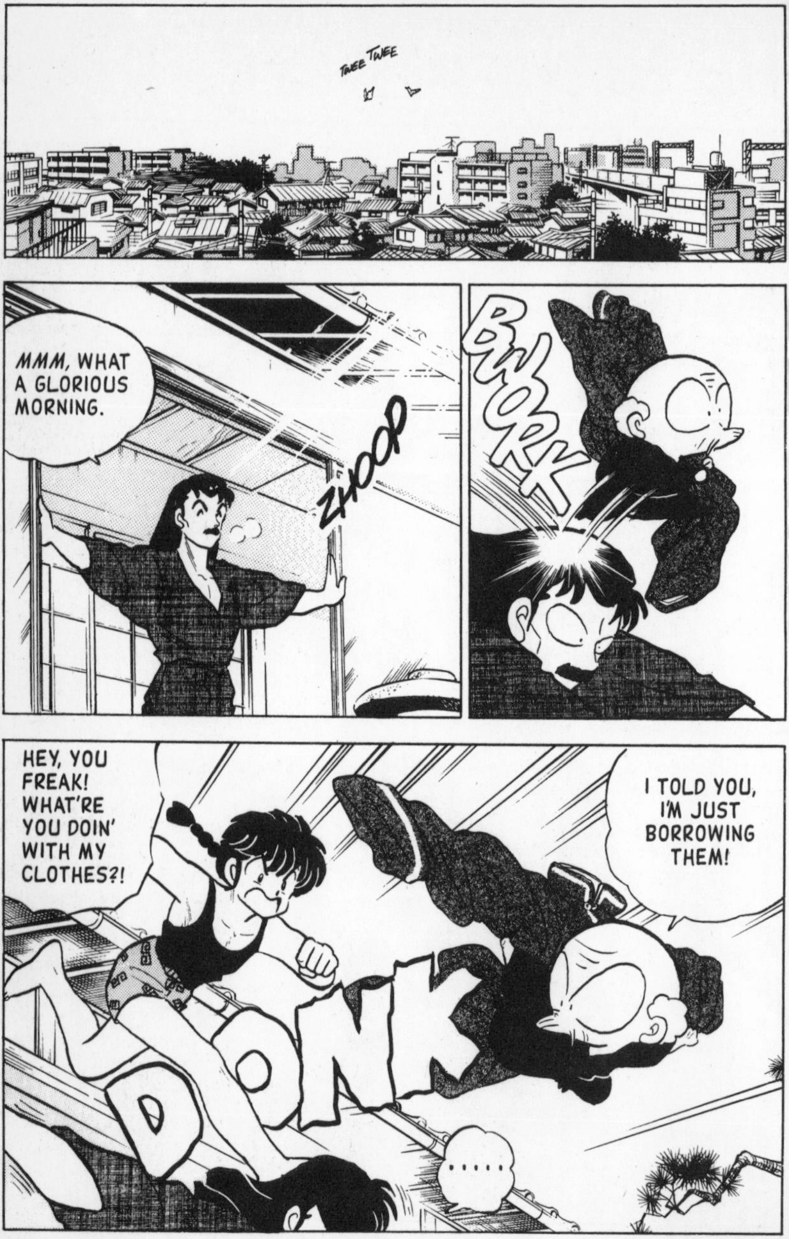
TWEE TWEE
MMM, WHAT A GLORIOUS MORNING.
ZHOOP
BWORK
HEY, YOU FREAK! WHAT'RE YOU DOIN' WITH MY CLOTHES?!
I TOLD YOU, I'M JUST BORROWING THEM!
DONK
.....

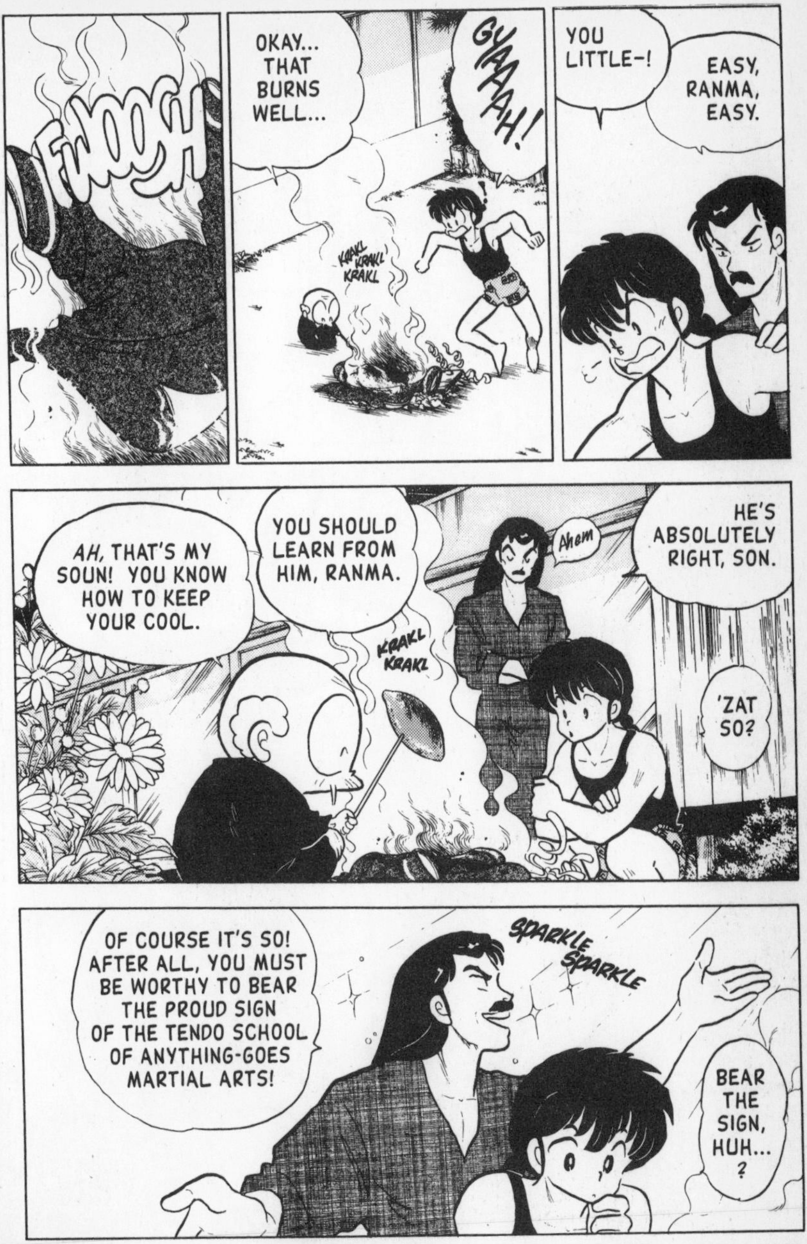
FWOOSH
OKAY... THAT BURNS WELL...
GYAAAAH!
KRAKL KRAKL KRAKL
YOU LITTLE-!
EASY, RANMA, EASY.
AH, THAT'S MY SOUN! YOU KNOW HOW TO KEEP YOUR COOL.
YOU SHOULD LEARN FROM HIM, RANMA.
KRAKL KRAKL
Ahem
HE'S ABSOLUTELY RIGHT, SON.
'ZAT SO?
OF COURSE IT'S SO! AFTER ALL, YOU MUST BE WORTHY TO BEAR THE PROUD SIGN OF THE TENDO SCHOOL OF ANYTHING-GOES MARTIAL ARTS!
SPARKLE SPARKLE
BEAR THE SIGN, HUH...?

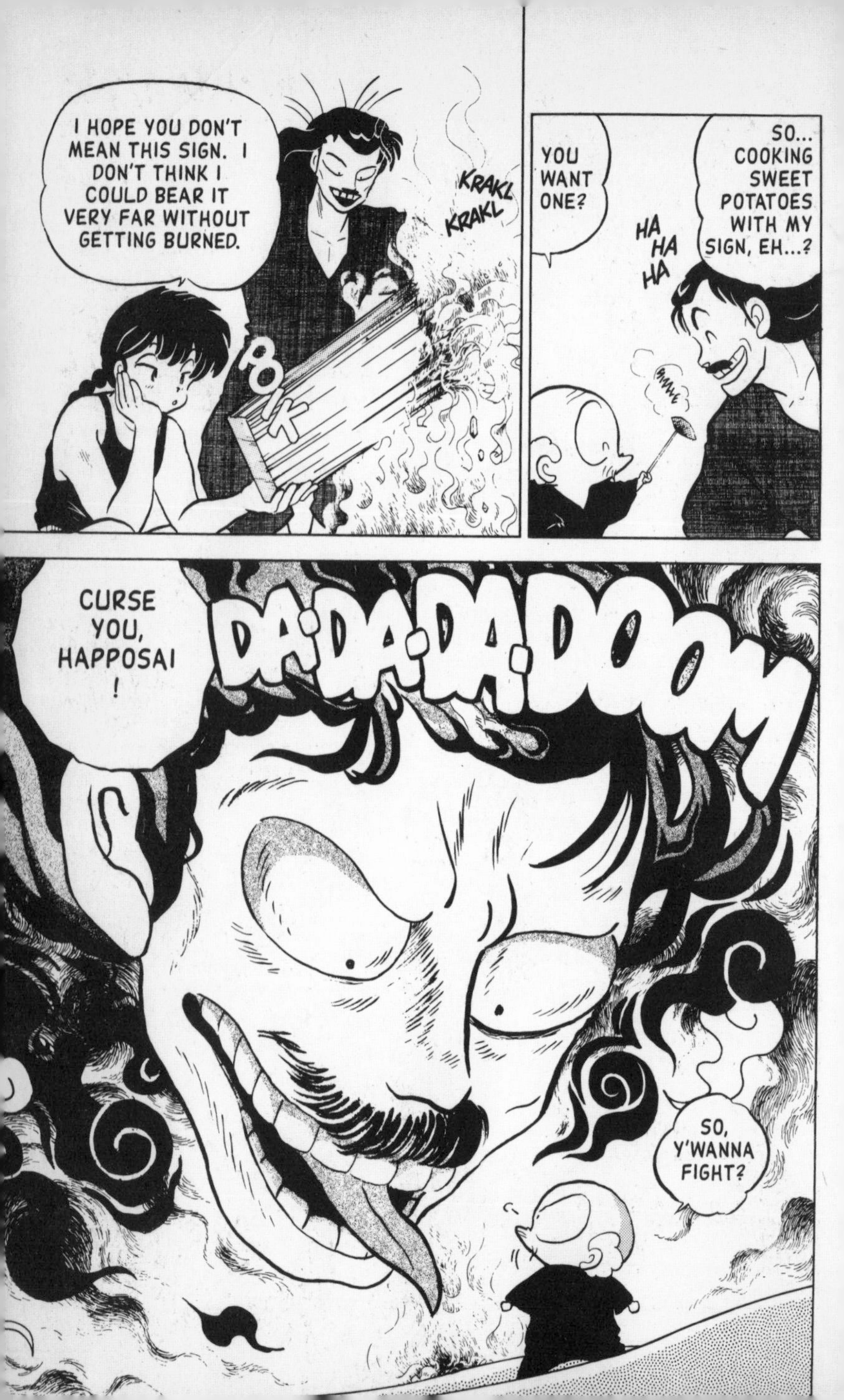
I HOPE YOU DON'T MEAN THIS SIGN. I DON'T THINK I COULD BEAR IT VERY FAR WITHOUT GETTING BURNED.
KRAKL
KRAKL
POK
YOU WANT ONE?
SO... COOKING SWEET POTATOES WITH MY SIGN, EH...?
HA HA HA
CURSE YOU, HAPPOSAI!
DA-DA-DA-DOOM
SO, Y'WANNA FIGHT?

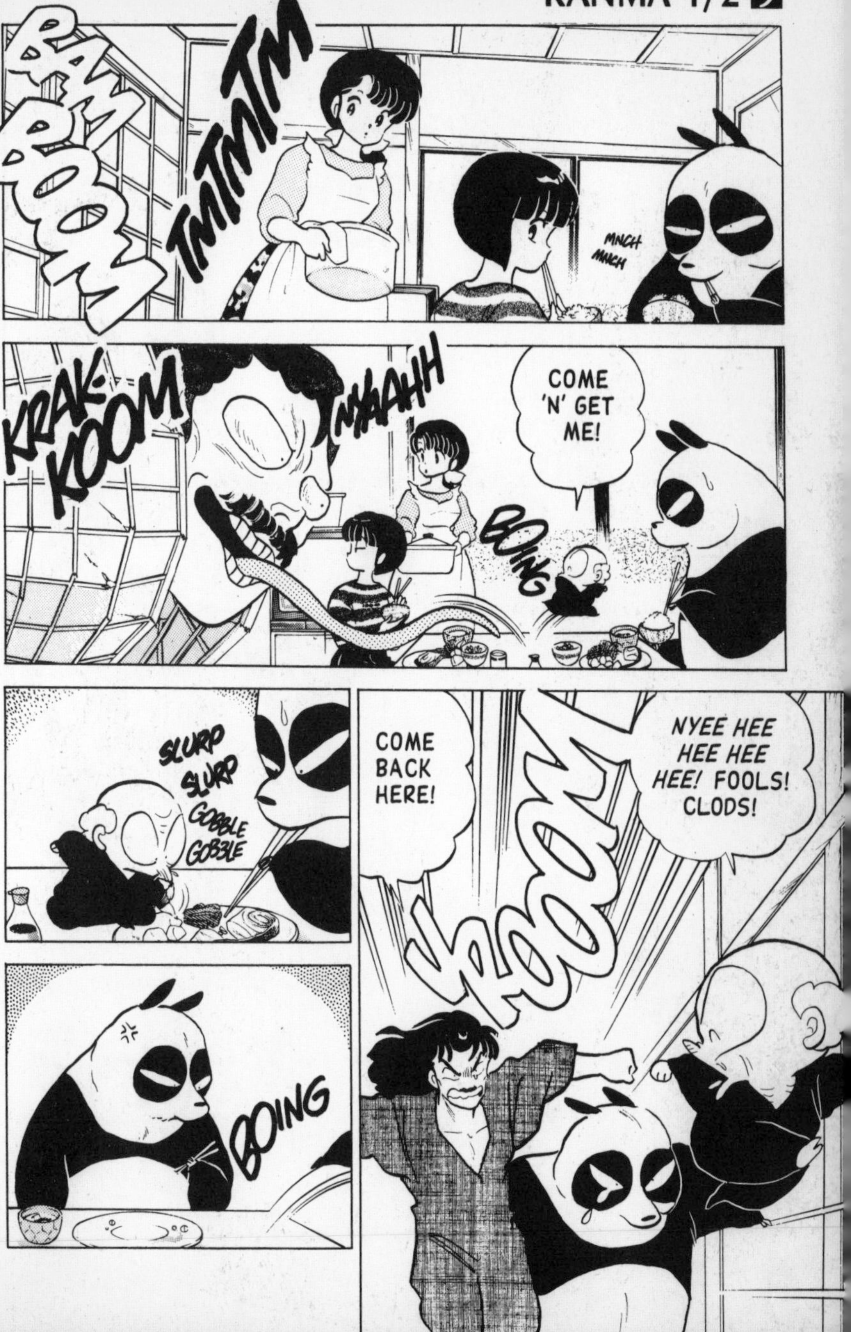
BAM BOOM
TMTMTMTM
MNCH MNCH
KRAK-KOOM
NYAAHH
COME 'N' GET ME!
BOING
SLURP SLURP
GOBBLE GOBBLE
COME BACK HERE!
NYEE HEE HEE HEE HEE! FOOLS! CLODS!
KBOOOM
BOING

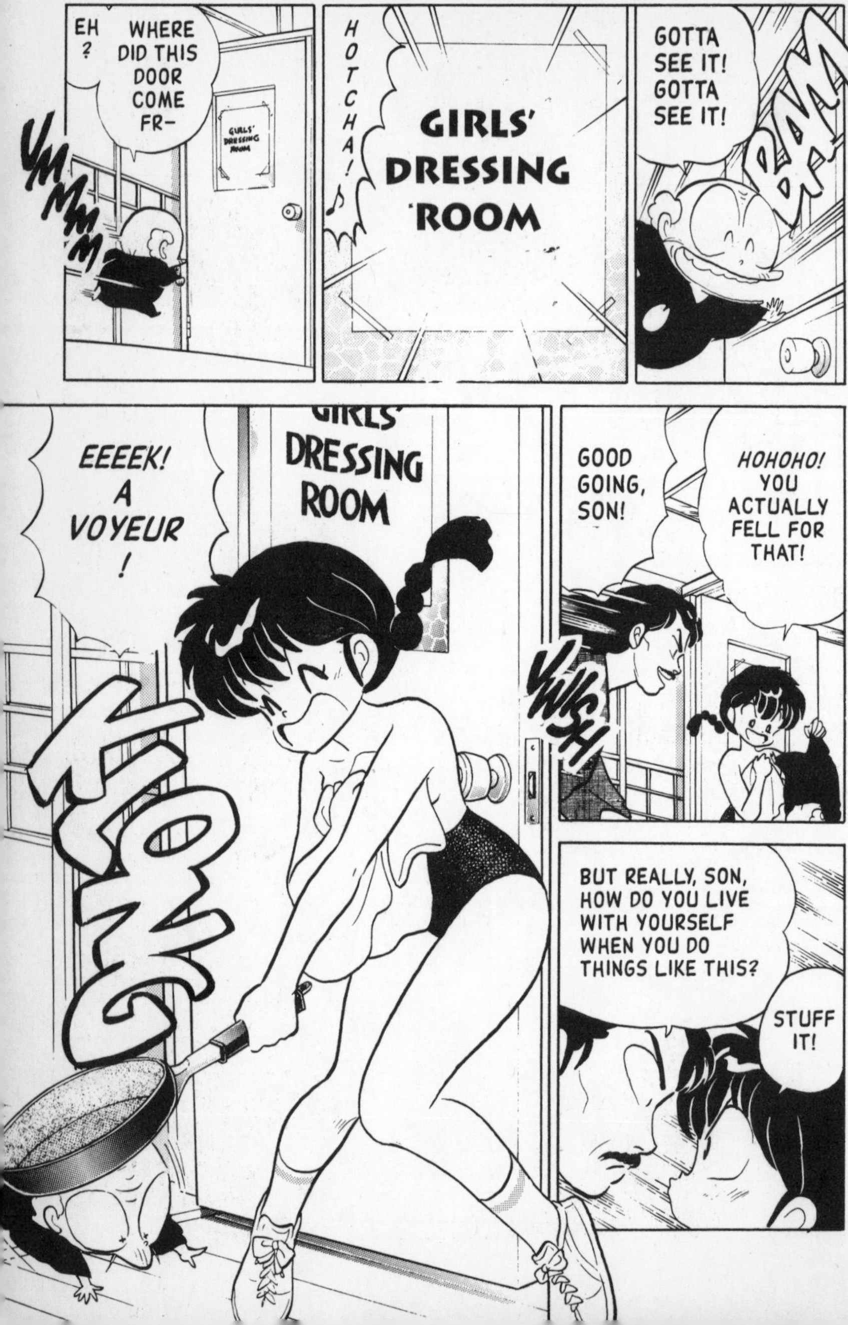
EH?
WHERE DID THIS DOOR COME FR-
GIRLS' DRESSING ROOM
HOTCHA!
GIRLS' DRESSING ROOM
GOTTA SEE IT! GOTTA SEE IT!
BAM
EEEEK! A VOYEUR!
GIRLS' DRESSING ROOM
KLONG
GOOD GOING, SON!
HOHOHO! YOU ACTUALLY FELL FOR THAT!
VWISH
BUT REALLY, SON, HOW DO YOU LIVE WITH YOURSELF WHEN YOU DO THINGS LIKE THIS?
STUFF IT!

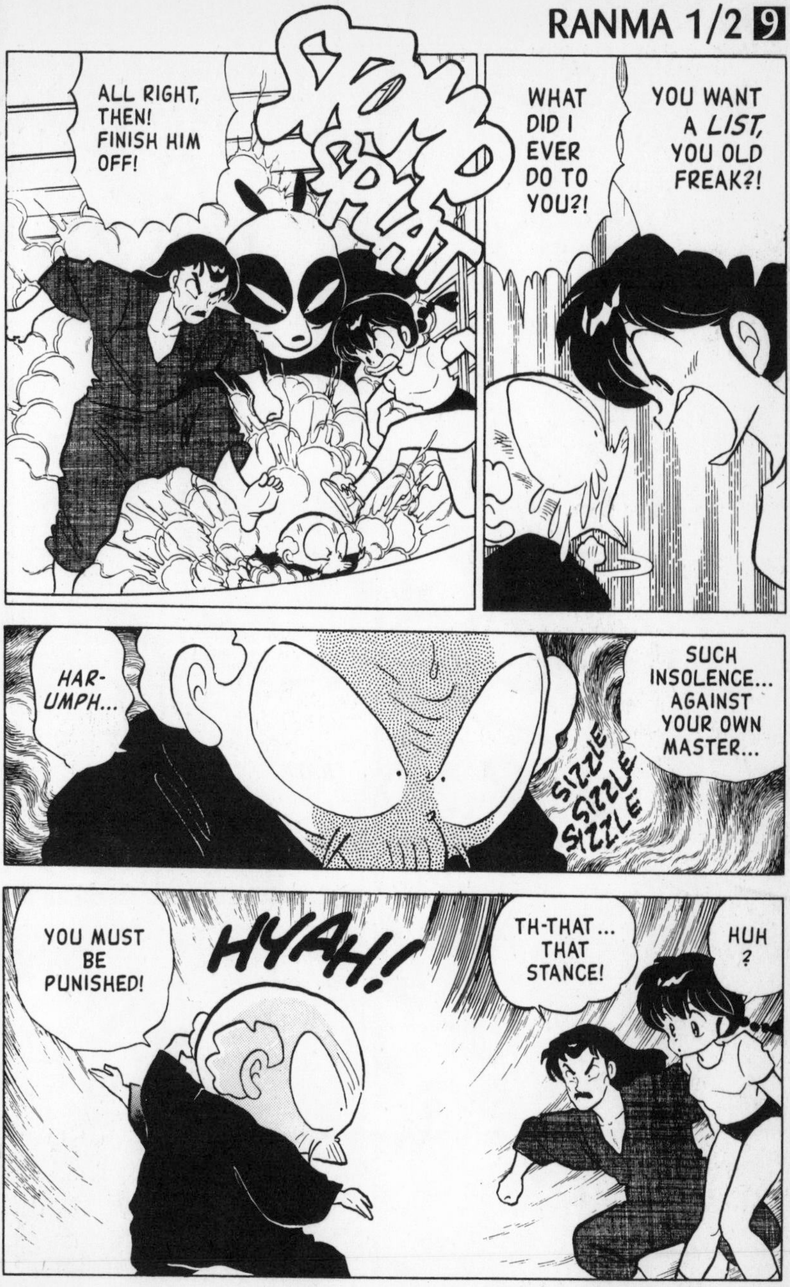
ALL RIGHT, THEN! FINISH HIM OFF!
STOMP SPLAT
WHAT DID I EVER DO TO YOU?!
YOU WANT A *LIST,* YOU OLD FREAK?!
HAR-UMPH...
SUCH INSOLENCE... AGAINST YOUR OWN MASTER...
SIZZLE SIZZLE SIZZLE
YOU MUST BE PUNISHED!
HYAH!
TH-THAT... THAT STANCE!
HUH?

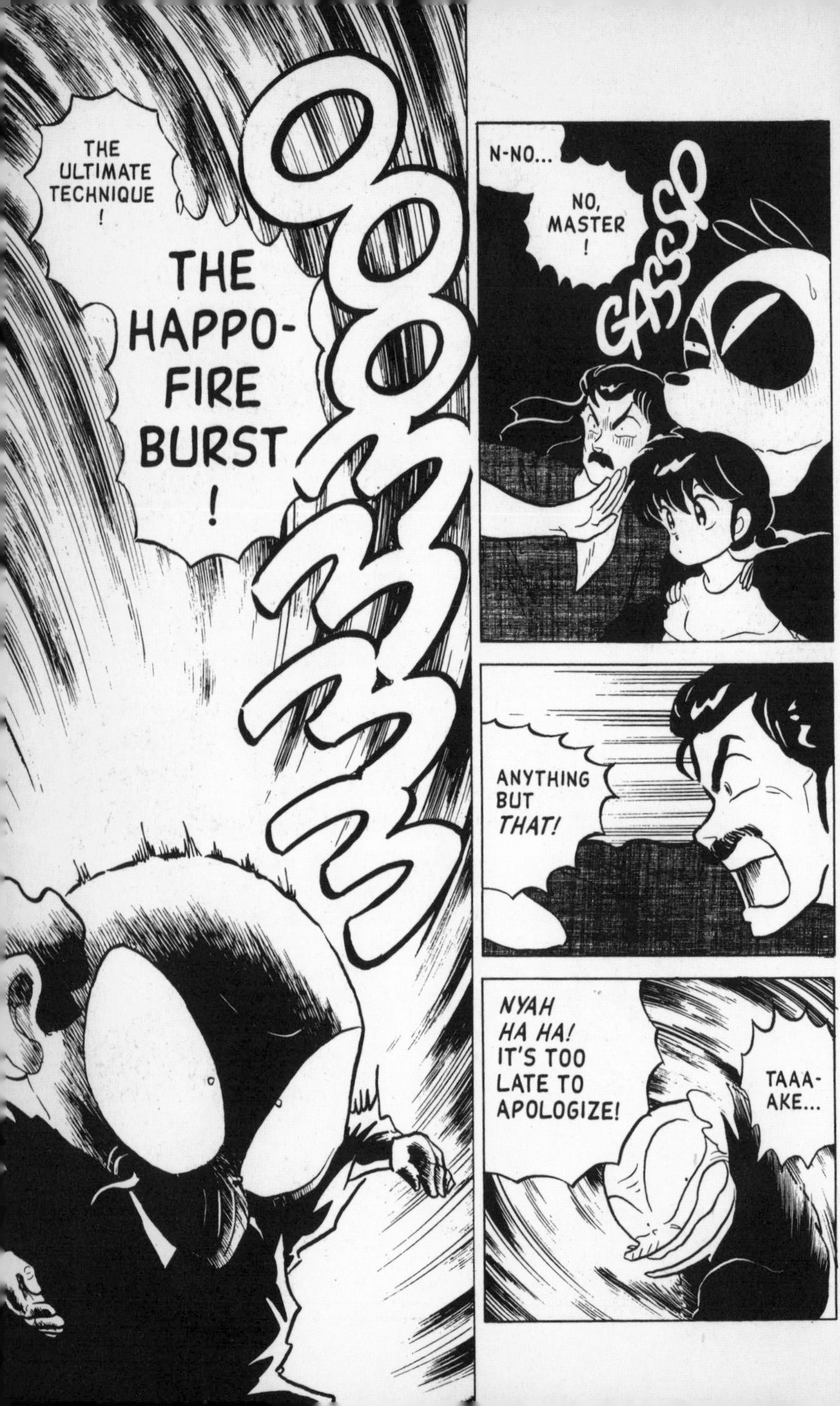
THE ULTIMATE TECHNIQUE!
THE HAPPO-FIRE BURST!
OOOOMMM
N-NO...
NO, MASTER!
GASSSP
ANYTHING BUT *THAT!*
NYAH HA HA! IT'S TOO LATE TO APOLOGIZE!
TAAA-AKE...

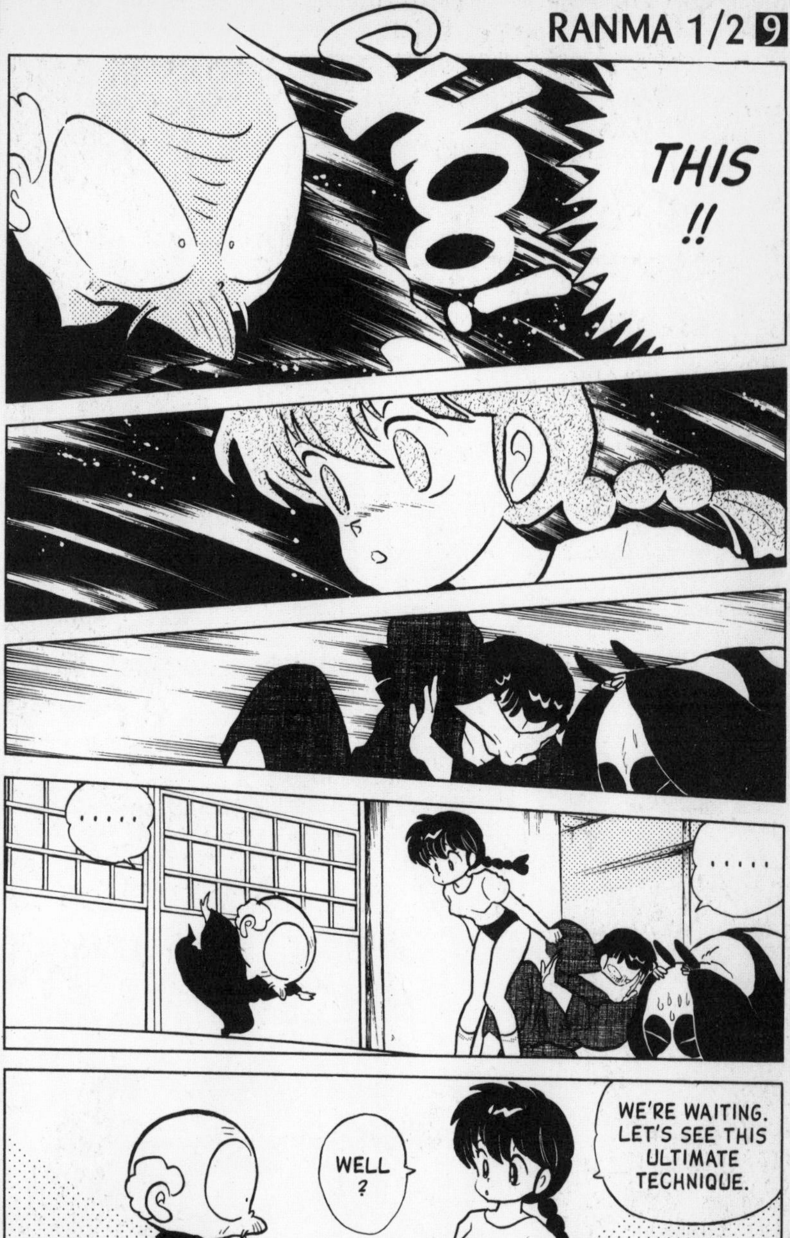
THIS !!
.....
.....
WELL ?
WE'RE WAITING. LET'S SEE THIS ULTIMATE TECHNIQUE.

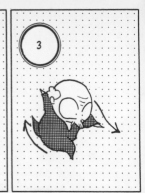

I FORGOT!

TOMP TOMP TOMP

POOM

THE ULTIMATE TECHNIQUE...

THE HAPPO-FIRE BURST...

JUST THINKING ABOUT IT MAKES MY HAIR STAND ON END.

YOU'VE ACTUALLY SEEN IT?

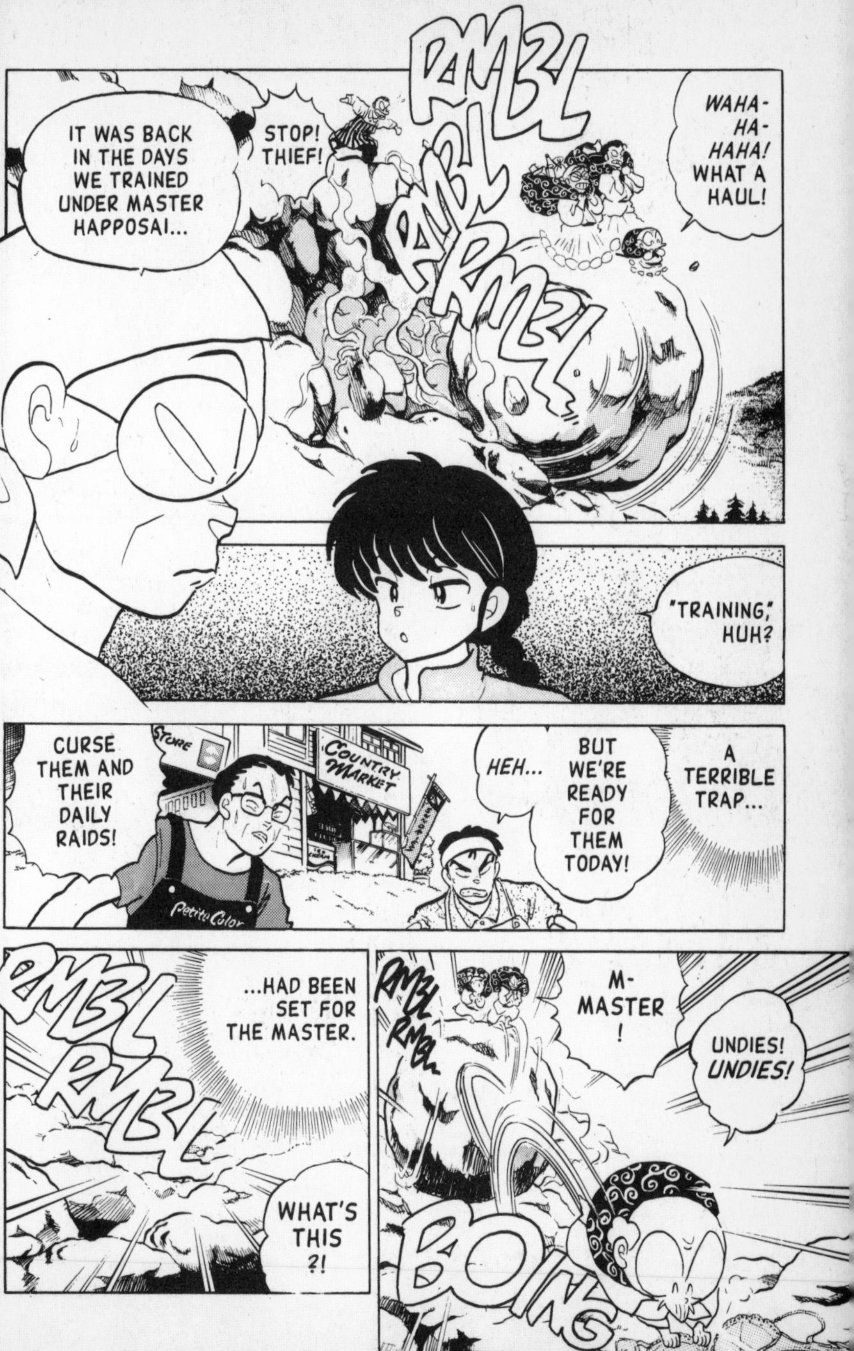
IT WAS BACK IN THE DAYS WE TRAINED UNDER MASTER HAPPOSAI...
STOP! THIEF!
RAMBL
RAMBL
RMBL
RMBL
WAHA-HA-HAHA! WHAT A HAUL!
"TRAINING," HUH?
CURSE THEM AND THEIR DAILY RAIDS!
STORE
COUNTRY MARKET
Petite Color
HEH...
BUT WE'RE READY FOR THEM TODAY!
A TERRIBLE TRAP...
RMBL
RMBL
...HAD BEEN SET FOR THE MASTER.
WHAT'S THIS?!
RMBL
RMBL
M-MASTER!
UNDIES! UNDIES!
BOING

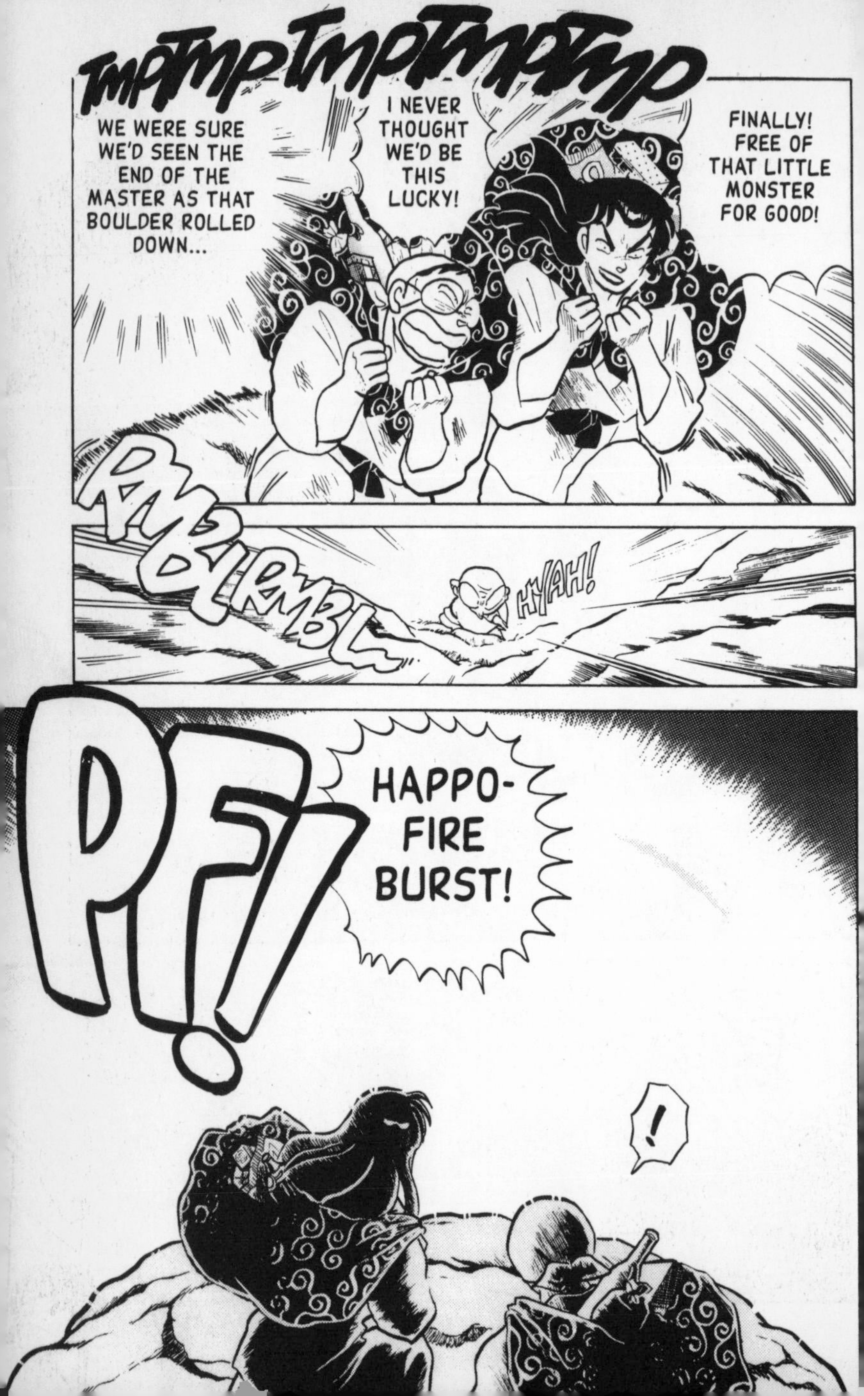
TMP TMP TMP TMP TMP TMP
WE WERE SURE WE'D SEEN THE END OF THE MASTER AS THAT BOULDER ROLLED DOWN...
I NEVER THOUGHT WE'D BE THIS LUCKY!
FINALLY! FREE OF THAT LITTLE MONSTER FOR GOOD!
RMBLRMBL
HYAH!
PF!
HAPPO-FIRE BURST!
!

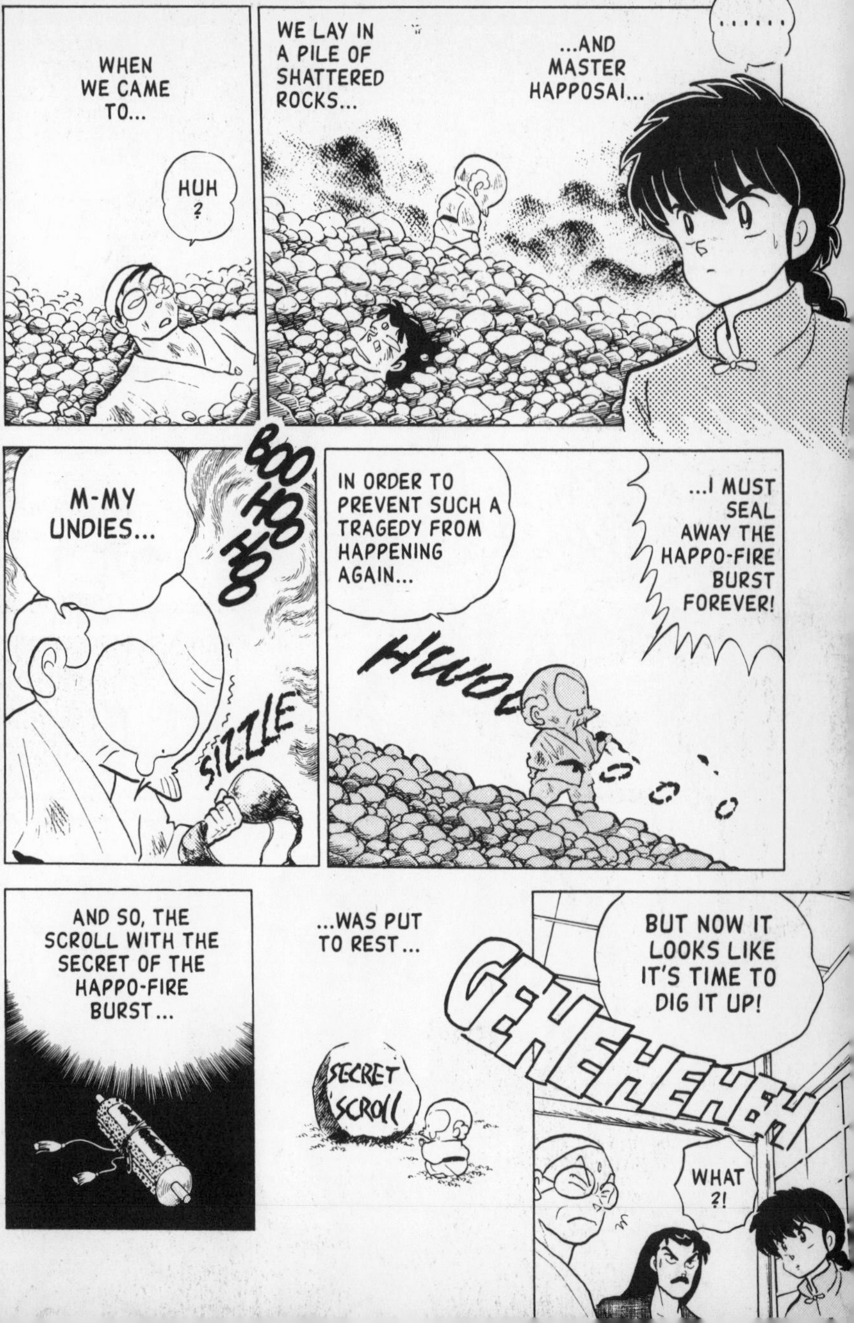

WHEN WE CAME TO...
HUH ?
WE LAY IN A PILE OF SHATTERED ROCKS...
...AND MASTER HAPPOSAI...
......
M-MY UNDIES...
BOO HOO HOO
SIZZLE
IN ORDER TO PREVENT SUCH A TRAGEDY FROM HAPPENING AGAIN...
...I MUST SEAL AWAY THE HAPPO-FIRE BURST FOREVER!
HWOO
AND SO, THE SCROLL WITH THE SECRET OF THE HAPPO-FIRE BURST...
...WAS PUT TO REST...
SECRET SCROLL
BUT NOW IT LOOKS LIKE IT'S TIME TO DIG IT UP!
GEHEHEHEH
WHAT ?!

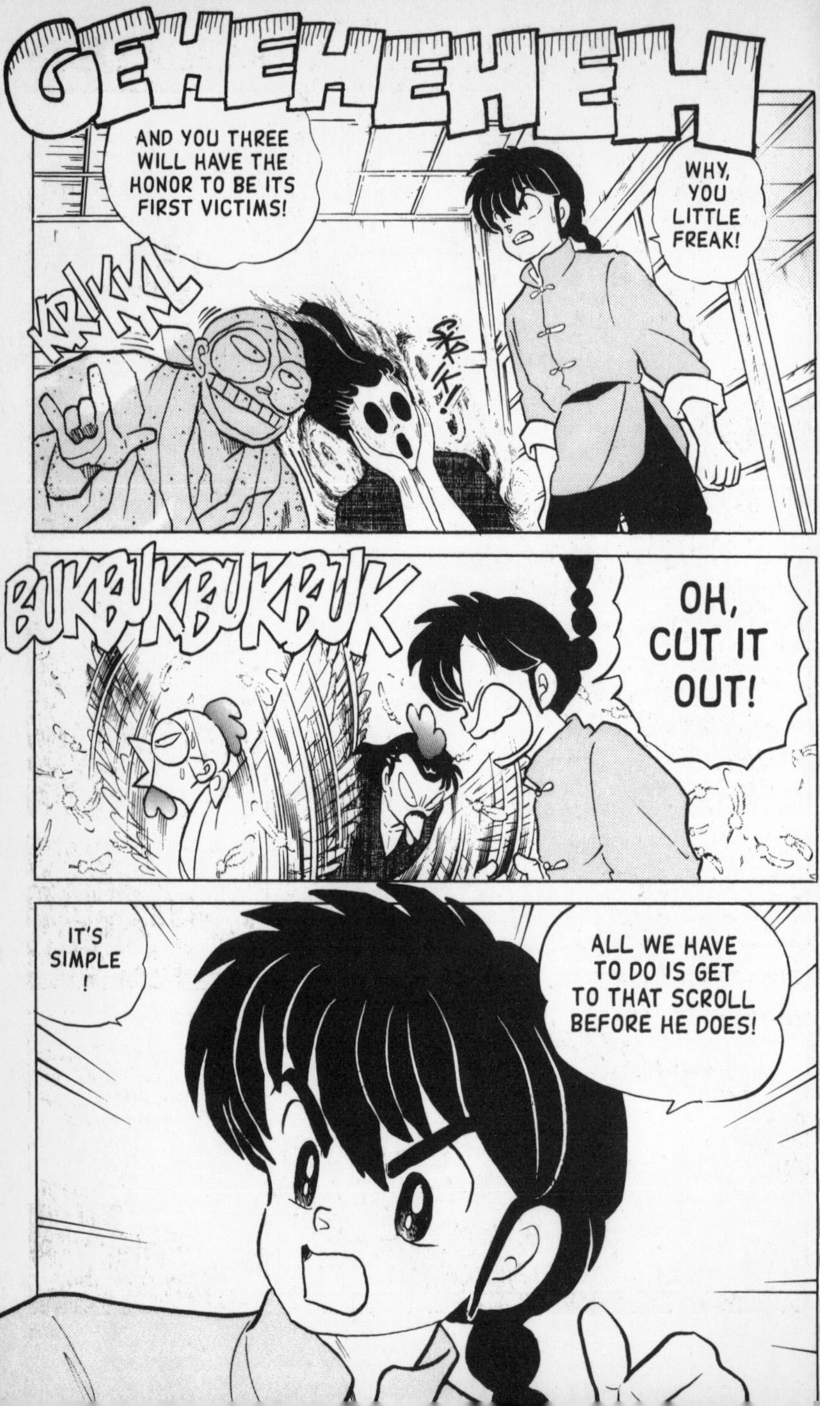
GEHEHEH
AND YOU THREE WILL HAVE THE HONOR TO BE ITS FIRST VICTIMS!
WHY, YOU LITTLE FREAK!
BUKBUKBUKBUK
OH, CUT IT OUT!
IT'S SIMPLE!
ALL WE HAVE TO DO IS GET TO THAT SCROLL BEFORE HE DOES!

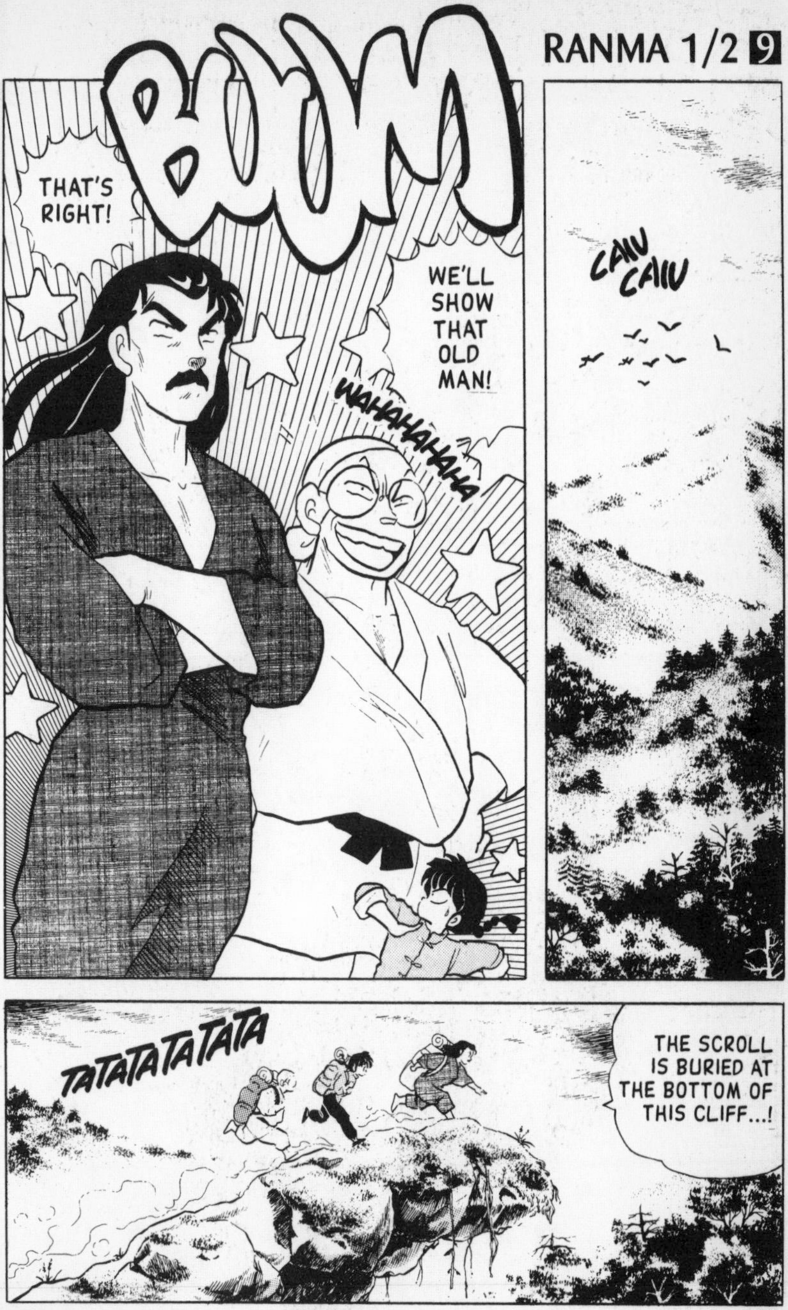
BUUM
THAT'S RIGHT!
WE'LL SHOW THAT OLD MAN!
WAHAHAHAHAHA
CAW CAW
TATATATATATA
THE SCROLL IS BURIED AT THE BOTTOM OF THIS CLIFF...!

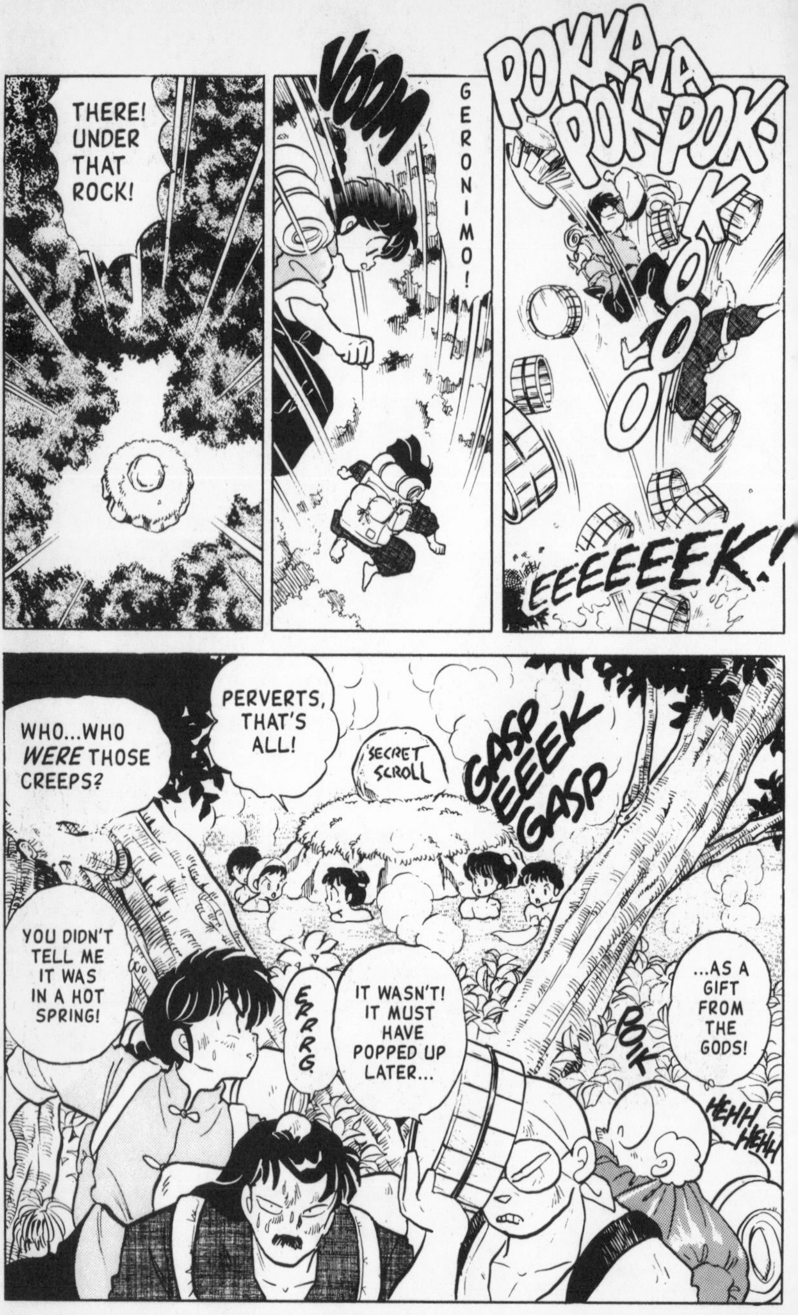
THERE! UNDER THAT ROCK!
VOOM
GERONIMO!
POKKALA POK POK POK
KOOOOO
EEEEEEEK!
WHO...WHO WERE THOSE CREEPS?
PERVERTS, THAT'S ALL!
SECRET SCROLL
GASP EEEK GASP
YOU DIDN'T TELL ME IT WAS IN A HOT SPRING!
ERRRG.
IT WASN'T! IT MUST HAVE POPPED UP LATER...
BOIK
...AS A GIFT FROM THE GODS!
HEHH HEHH

Part 11
GET THE SECRET SCROLL!

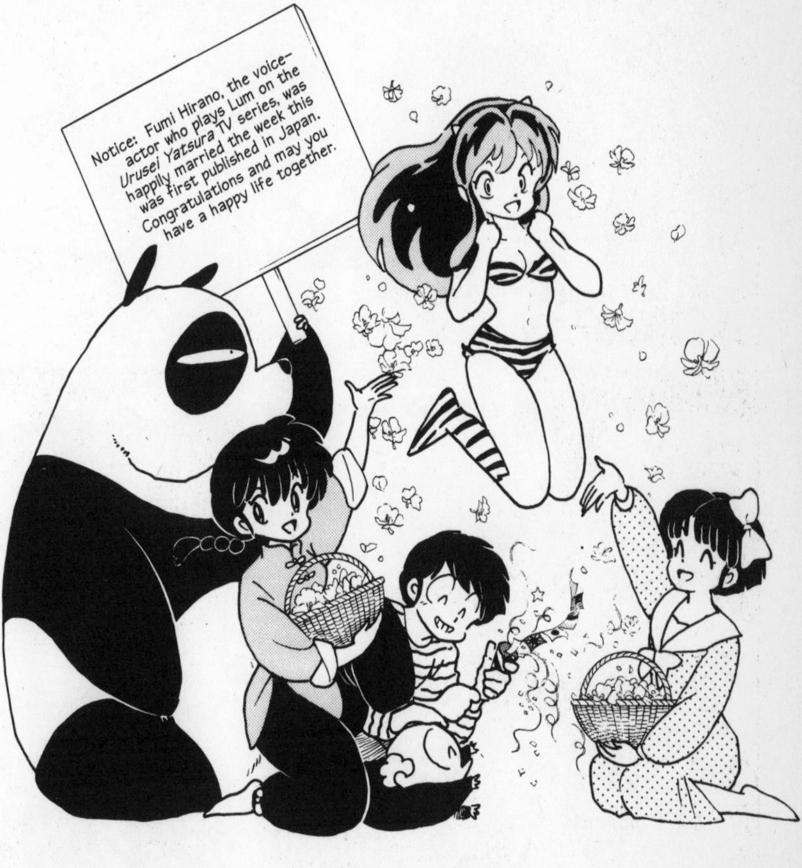
Notice: Fumi Hirano, the voice-actor who plays Lum on the Urusei Yatsura TV series, was happily married the week this was first published in Japan. Congratulations and may you have a happy life together.

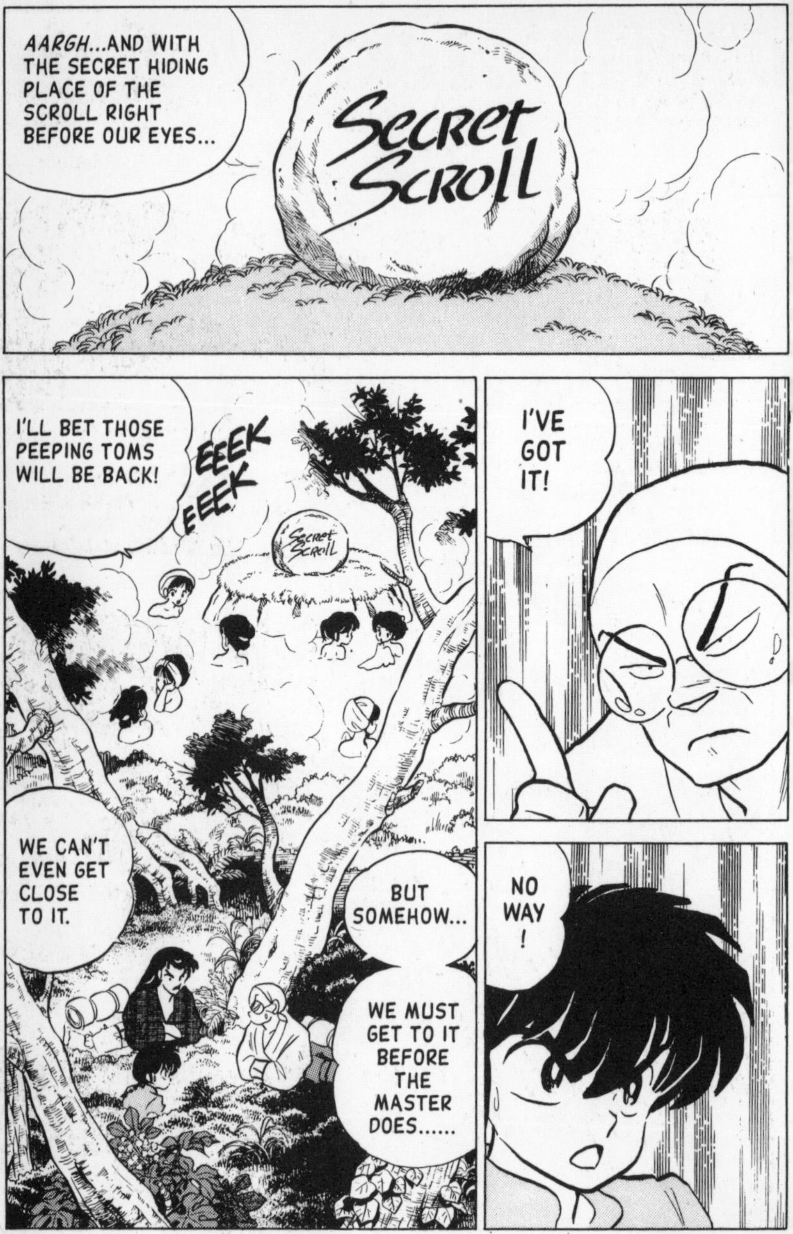
AARGH...AND WITH THE SECRET HIDING PLACE OF THE SCROLL RIGHT BEFORE OUR EYES...
Secret Scroll
I'LL BET THOSE PEEPING TOMS WILL BE BACK!
EEEK EEEK
Secret Scroll
WE CAN'T EVEN GET CLOSE TO IT.
BUT SOMEHOW...
WE MUST GET TO IT BEFORE THE MASTER DOES......
I'VE GOT IT!
NO WAY !

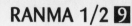

IF YOU TURN ME INTO A GIRL, I'M GONNA TURN BACK AS SOON AS I HIT THAT HOT SPRING!

PLOOSH

Heh heh heh! Get a load of this disguise!

HUH?

OF COURSE! BY DISGUISING YOURSELF WITH PAINT...

PAINT

...EVEN A CUTE LI'L PANDA CAN BE MADE TO LOOK LIKE A FEROCIOUS BEAR!

EEEEEE!

THEN, WHILE THE GIRLS SCREAM AND FLEE IN TERROR, WE MAKE OUR MOVE...

HEH HEH HEH

...AND GET THE SECRET SCROLL!

A PERFECT PLAN!

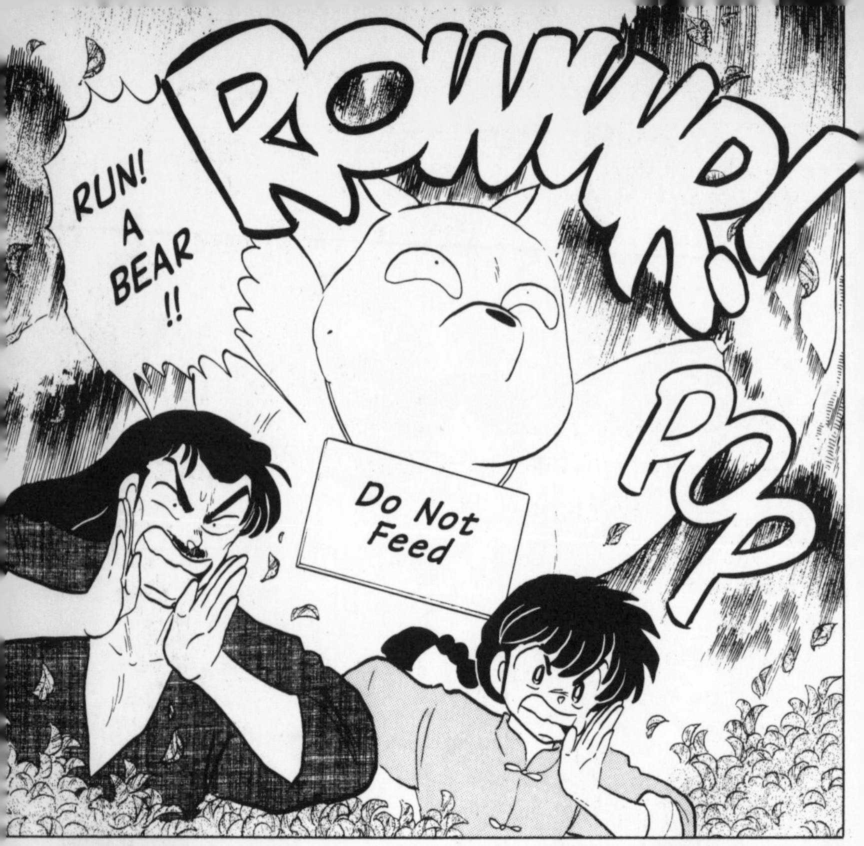
ROWR!
RUN! A BEAR !!
Do Not Feed
POP
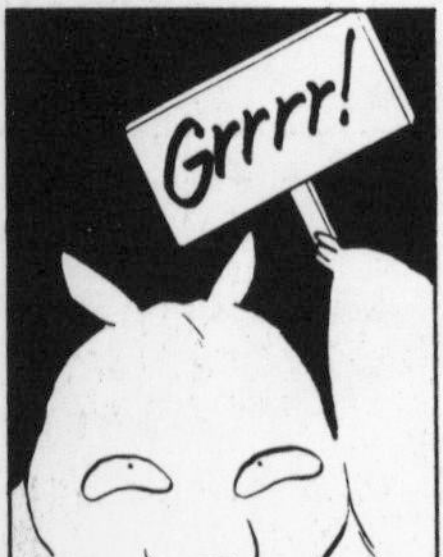
Grrrr!
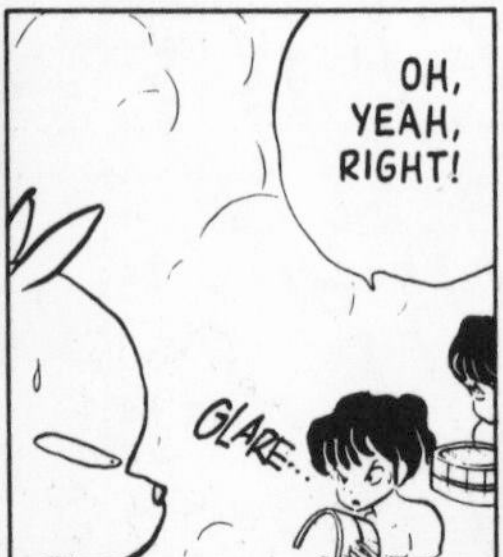
OH, YEAH, RIGHT!
GLARE...
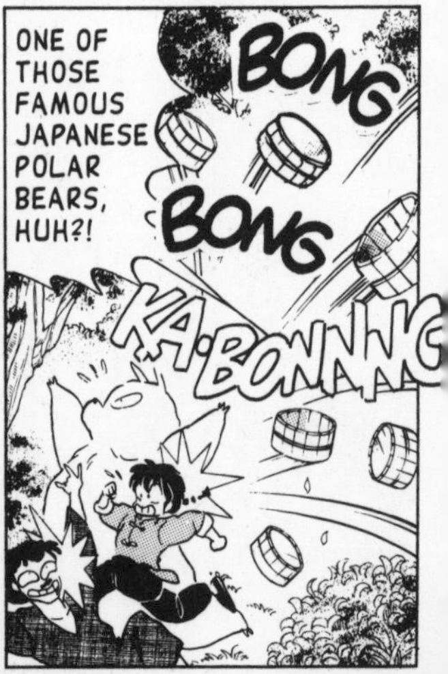
ONE OF THOSE FAMOUS JAPANESE POLAR BEARS, HUH?!
BONG
BONG
KA-BONNNG

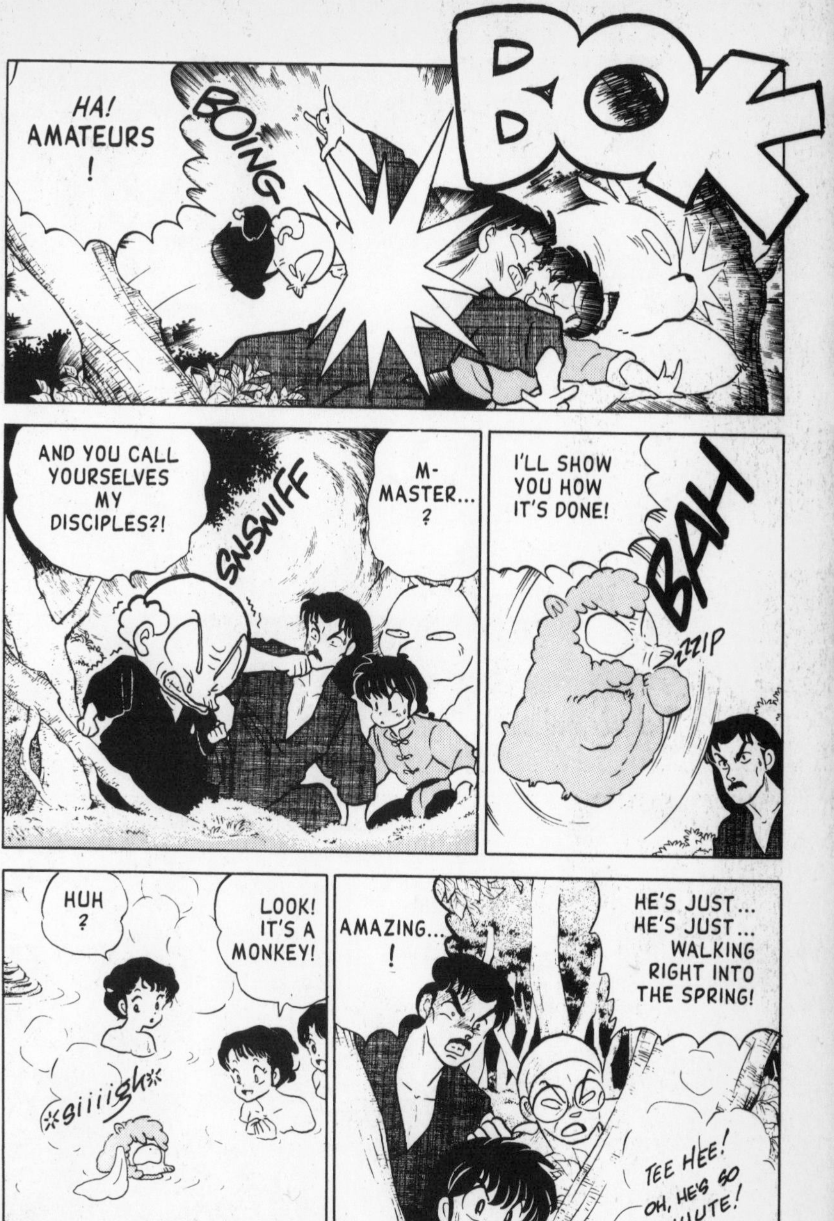

HA! AMATEURS !
BOING
BOK
AND YOU CALL YOURSELVES MY DISCIPLES?!
SN-SNIFF
M-MASTER... ?
I'LL SHOW YOU HOW IT'S DONE!
BAH
ZZZIP
HUH ?
LOOK! IT'S A MONKEY!
siiiigh
AMAZING... !
HE'S JUST... HE'S JUST... WALKING RIGHT INTO THE SPRING!
TEE HEE! OH, HE'S SO CUUUTE! ♪♪

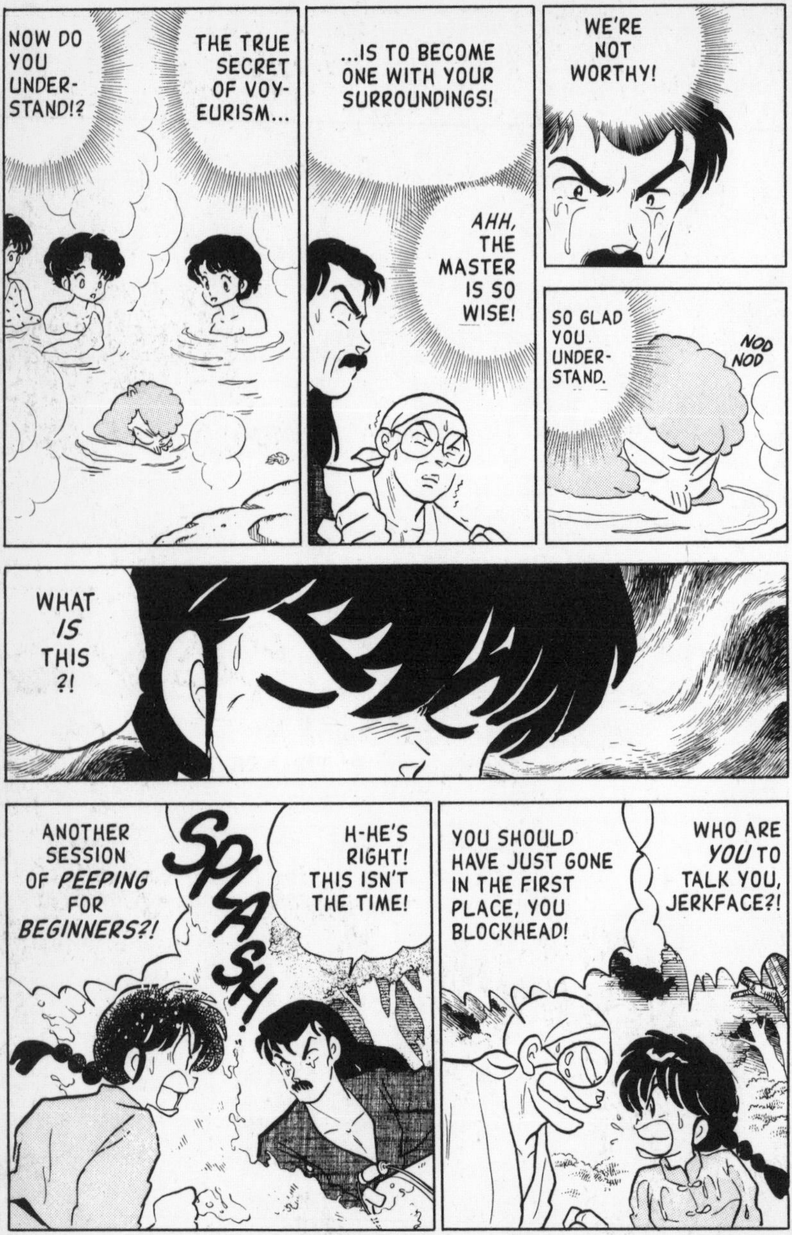
NOW DO YOU UNDER-STAND!?
THE TRUE SECRET OF VOY-EURISM...
...IS TO BECOME ONE WITH YOUR SURROUNDINGS!
AHH, THE MASTER IS SO WISE!
WE'RE NOT WORTHY!
SO GLAD YOU UNDER-STAND.
NOD NOD
WHAT IS THIS ?!
ANOTHER SESSION OF PEEPING FOR BEGINNERS?!
SPLASH!
H-HE'S RIGHT! THIS ISN'T THE TIME!
YOU SHOULD HAVE JUST GONE IN THE FIRST PLACE, YOU BLOCKHEAD!
WHO ARE YOU TO TALK YOU, JERKFACE?!

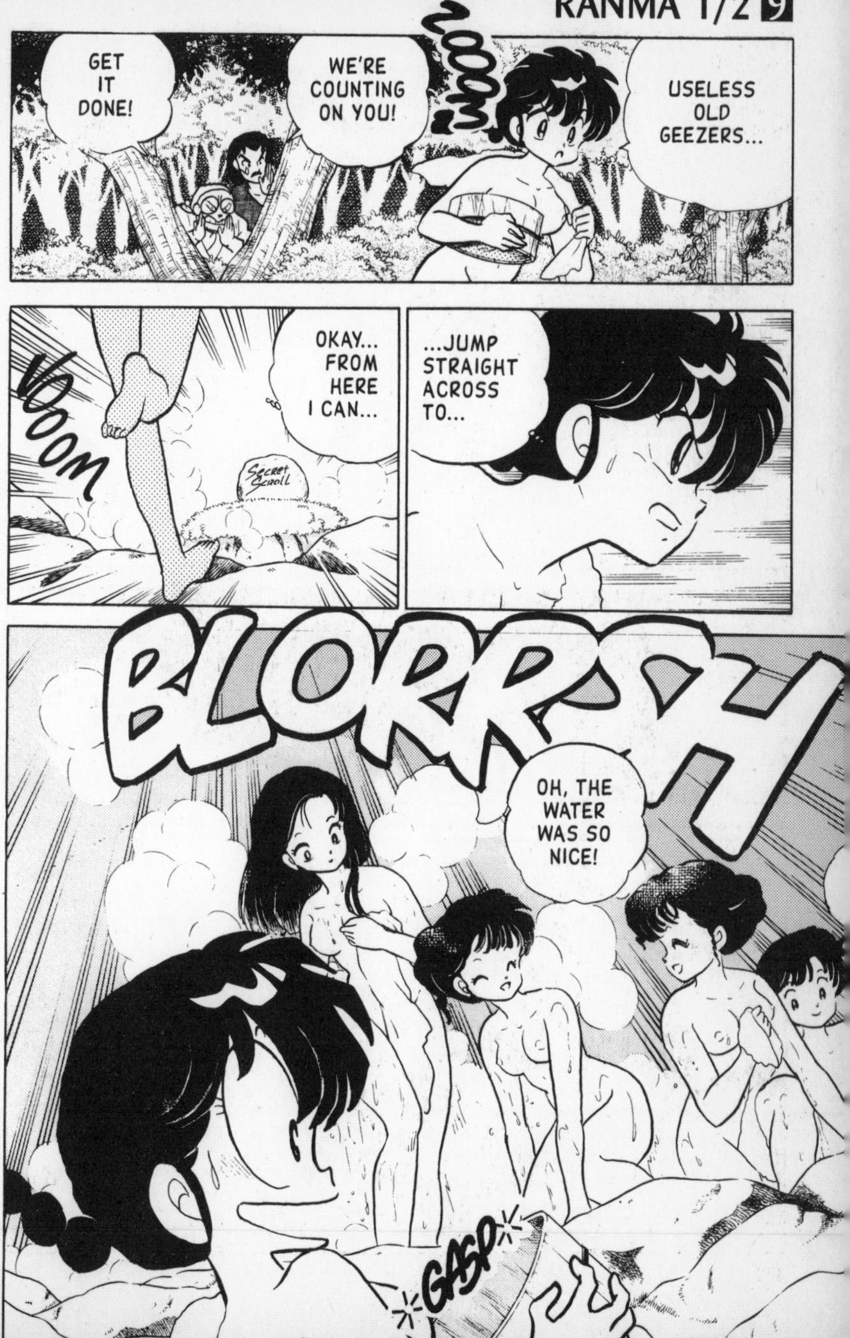
GET IT DONE!
WE'RE COUNTING ON YOU!
ZOOOOM
USELESS OLD GEEZERS...
VOOOM
OKAY... FROM HERE I CAN...
Secret Scroll
...JUMP STRAIGHT ACROSS TO...
BLORRSH
OH, THE WATER WAS SO NICE!
GASP

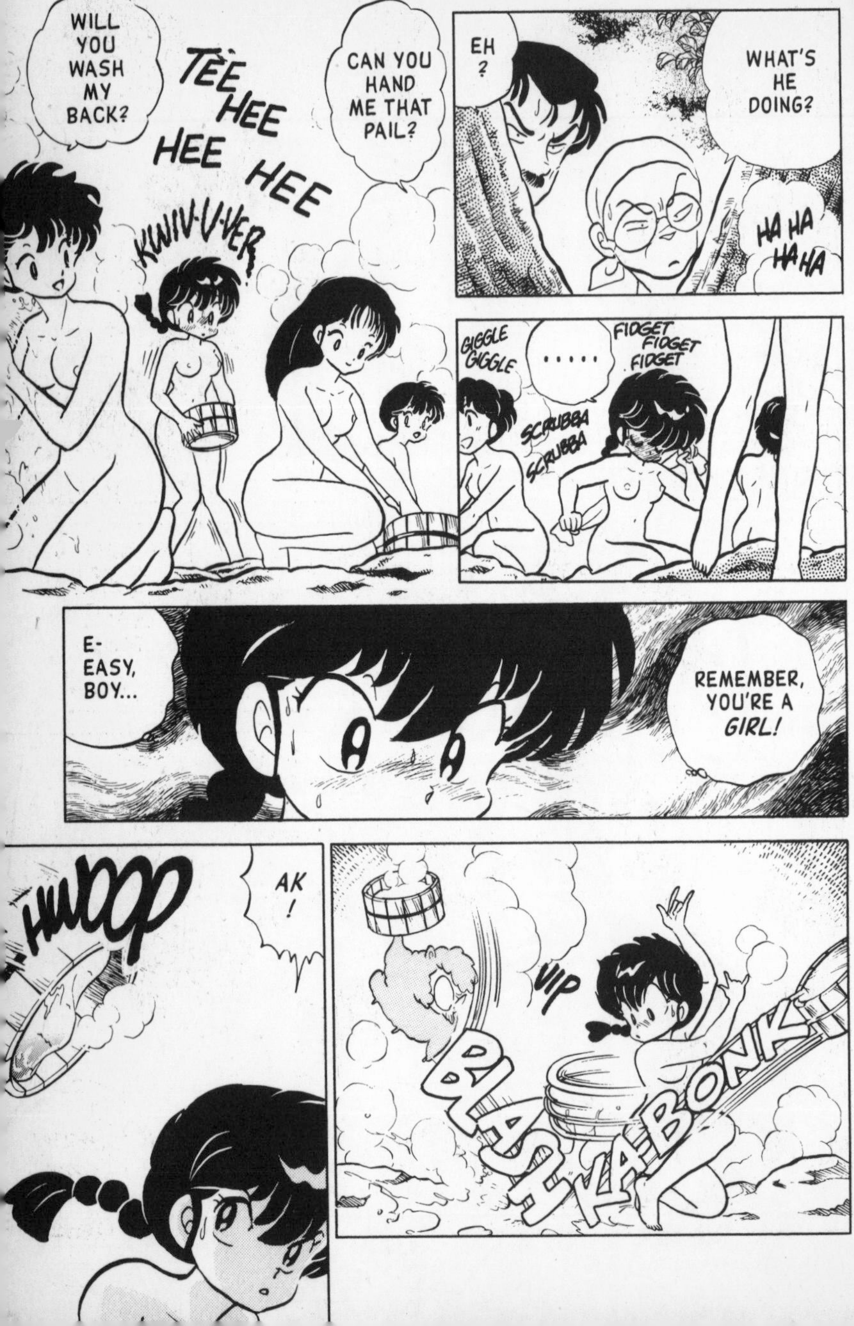
WILL YOU WASH MY BACK?
TÈE HEE HEE HEE
CAN YOU HAND ME THAT PAIL?
KWIVV-V-VER
EH?
WHAT'S HE DOING?
HA HA HA HA
GIGGLE GIGGLE
......
FIDGET FIDGET FIDGET
SCRUBBA SCRUBBA
E- EASY, BOY...
REMEMBER, YOU'RE A *GIRL!*
HWOOP
AK!
VIP
BLASH-KA-BONK

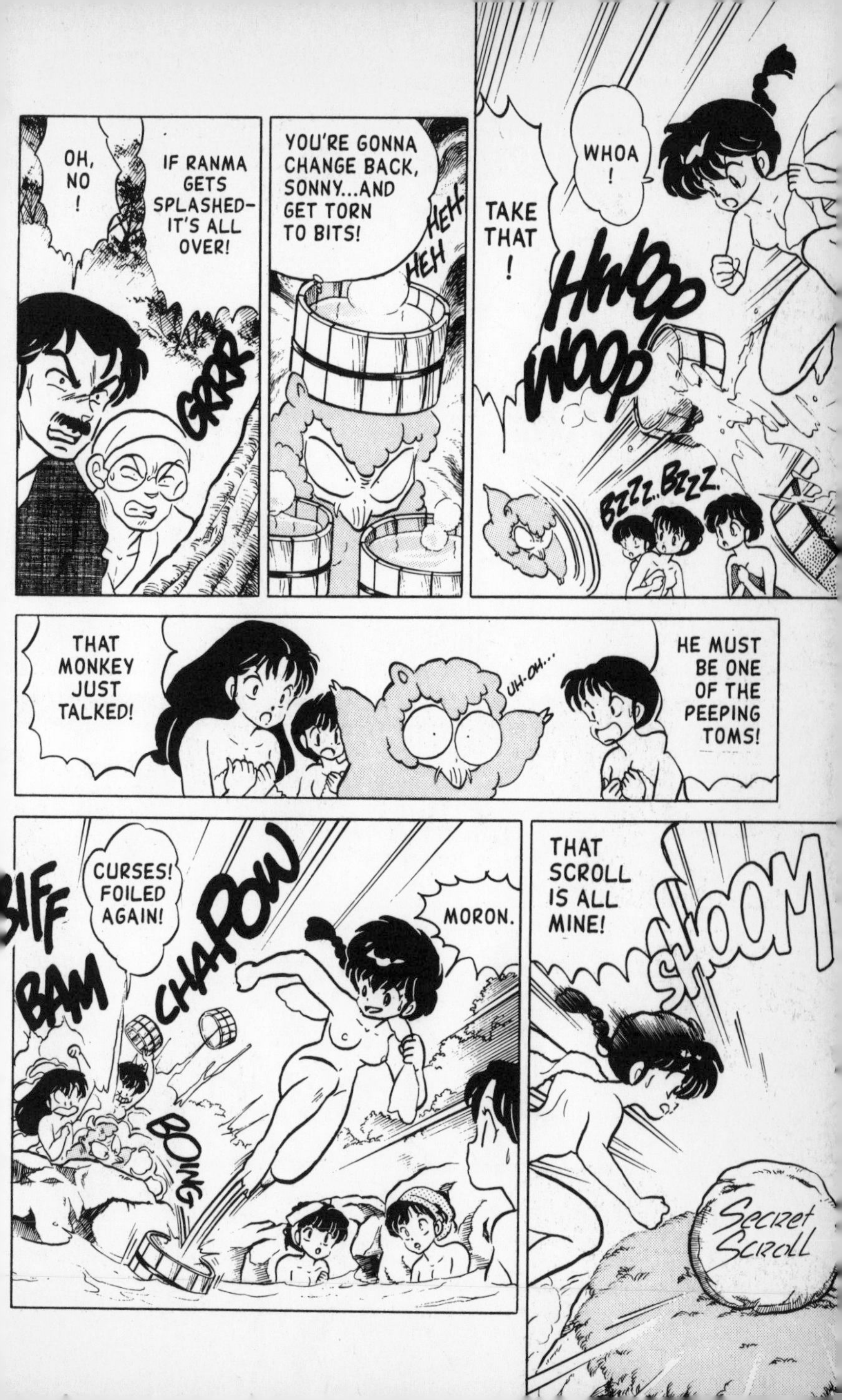
OH, NO!
IF RANMA GETS SPLASHED—IT'S ALL OVER!
GRRR
YOU'RE GONNA CHANGE BACK, SONNY...AND GET TORN TO BITS!
HEH HEH
WHOA!
TAKE THAT!
HWOOP WOOP
BZZZ..BZZZ.
THAT MONKEY JUST TALKED!
UH-OH...
HE MUST BE ONE OF THE PEEPING TOMS!
BIFF
BAM
CURSES! FOILED AGAIN!
CHAPOW
MORON.
BOING
THAT SCROLL IS ALL MINE!
SHOOM
Secret Scroll

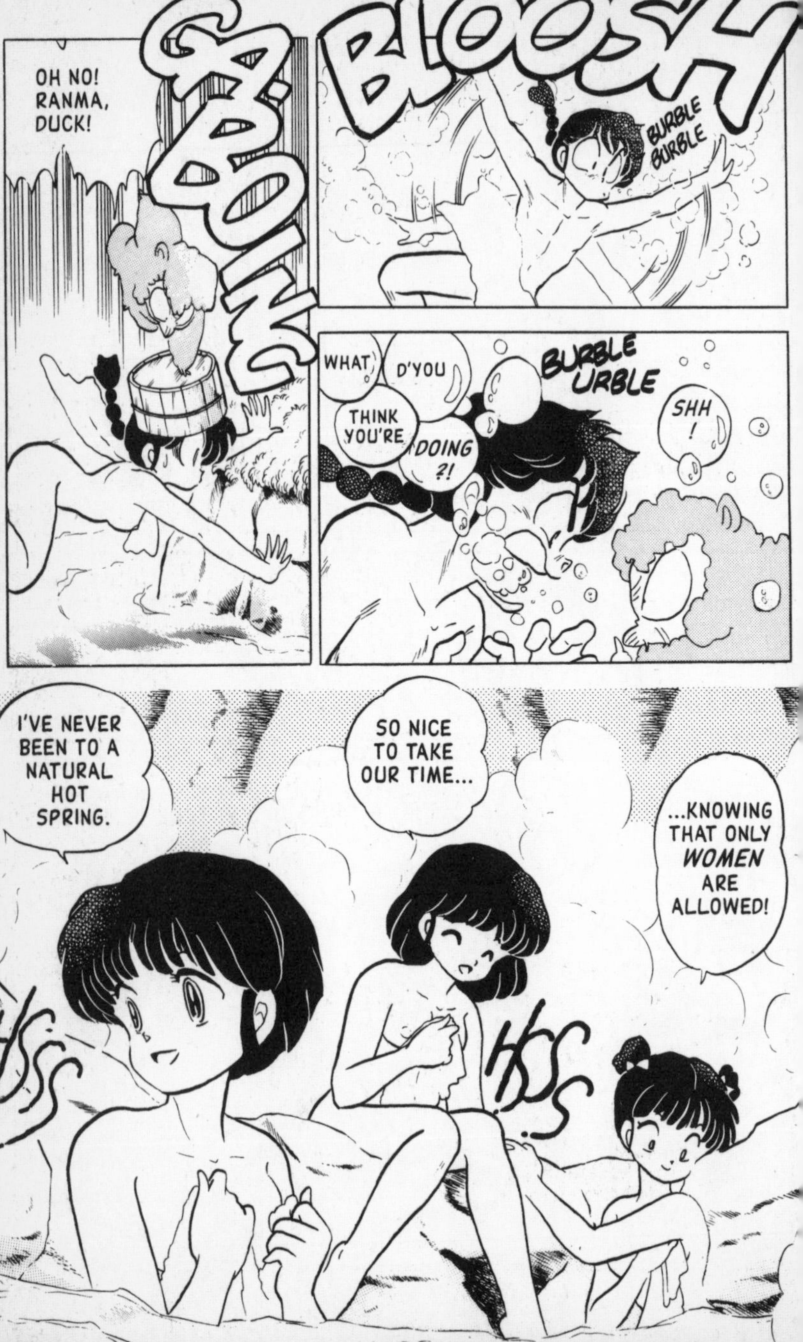
GA-BOING
OH NO! RANMA, DUCK!
BLOOSH
BURBLE BURBLE
WHAT D'YOU THINK YOU'RE DOING ?!
BURBLE URBLE
SHH !
I'VE NEVER BEEN TO A NATURAL HOT SPRING.
SO NICE TO TAKE OUR TIME...
...KNOWING THAT ONLY *WOMEN* ARE ALLOWED!
HSSS
HSSS

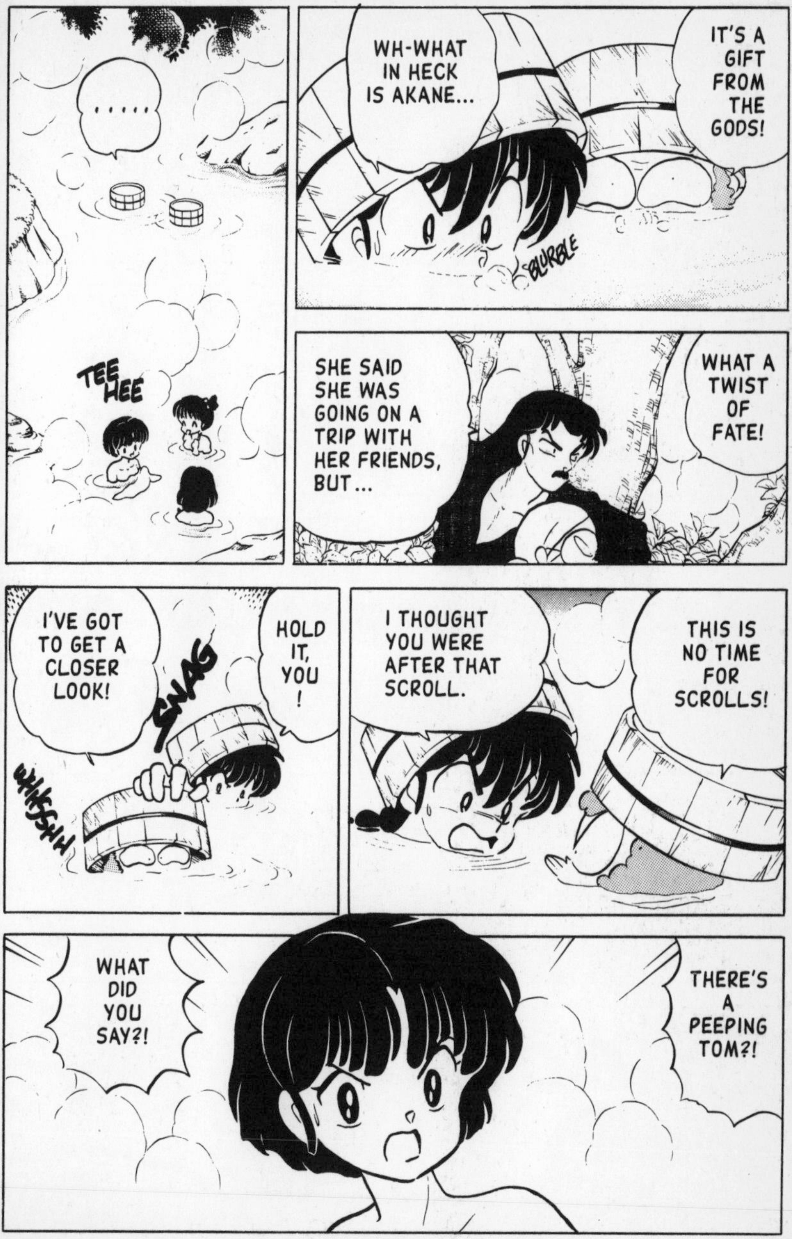
.....
TEE HEE
WH-WHAT IN HECK IS AKANE...
IT'S A GIFT FROM THE GODS!
BLURBLE
SHE SAID SHE WAS GOING ON A TRIP WITH HER FRIENDS, BUT...
WHAT A TWIST OF FATE!
I'VE GOT TO GET A CLOSER LOOK!
HOLD IT, YOU!
SNAG
WHISSH
I THOUGHT YOU WERE AFTER THAT SCROLL.
THIS IS NO TIME FOR SCROLLS!
WHAT DID YOU SAY?!
THERE'S A PEEPING TOM?!

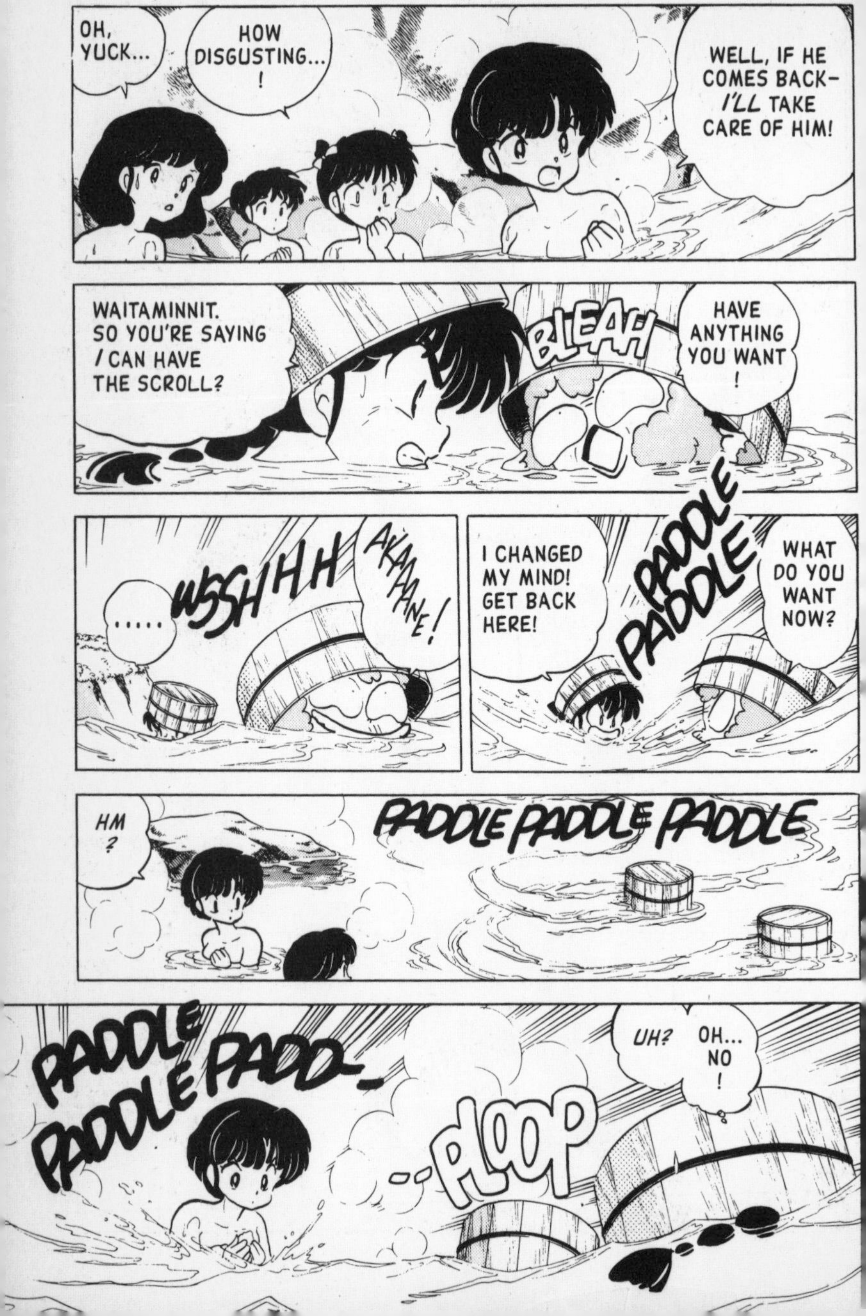
OH, YUCK...
HOW DISGUSTING...!
WELL, IF HE COMES BACK– I'LL TAKE CARE OF HIM!
WAITAMINNIT. SO YOU'RE SAYING I CAN HAVE THE SCROLL?
BLEAH
HAVE ANYTHING YOU WANT!
.....
WSSHHH
AKANNNE!
I CHANGED MY MIND! GET BACK HERE!
PADDLE PADDLE
WHAT DO YOU WANT NOW?
HM?
PADDLE PADDLE PADDLE
PADDLE PADDLE PADD–
--PLOOP
UH?
OH... NO!

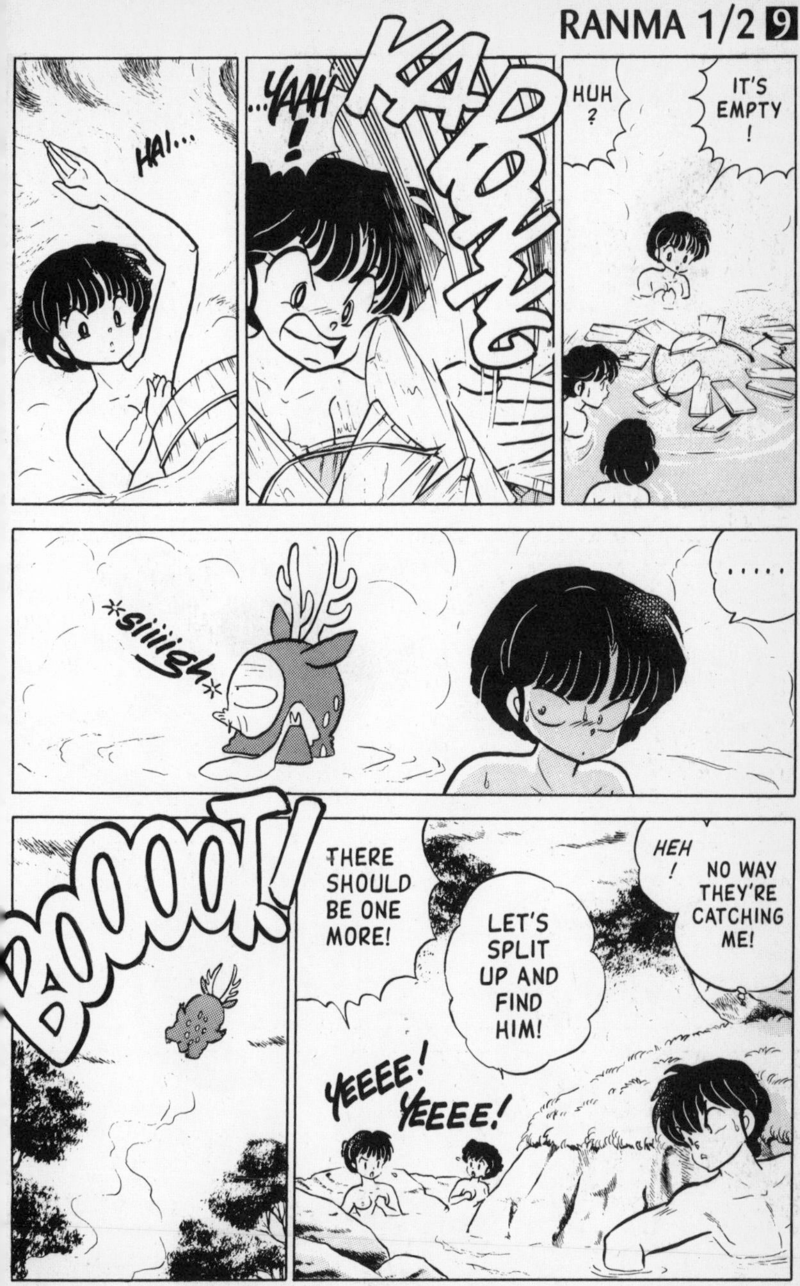
HAI...
...YAAH!
KA-BOWMG
HUH?
IT'S EMPTY!
siiiigh
.....
BOOOOT!
THERE SHOULD BE ONE MORE!
LET'S SPLIT UP AND FIND HIM!
HEH!
NO WAY THEY'RE CATCHING ME!
YEEEE!
YEEEE!

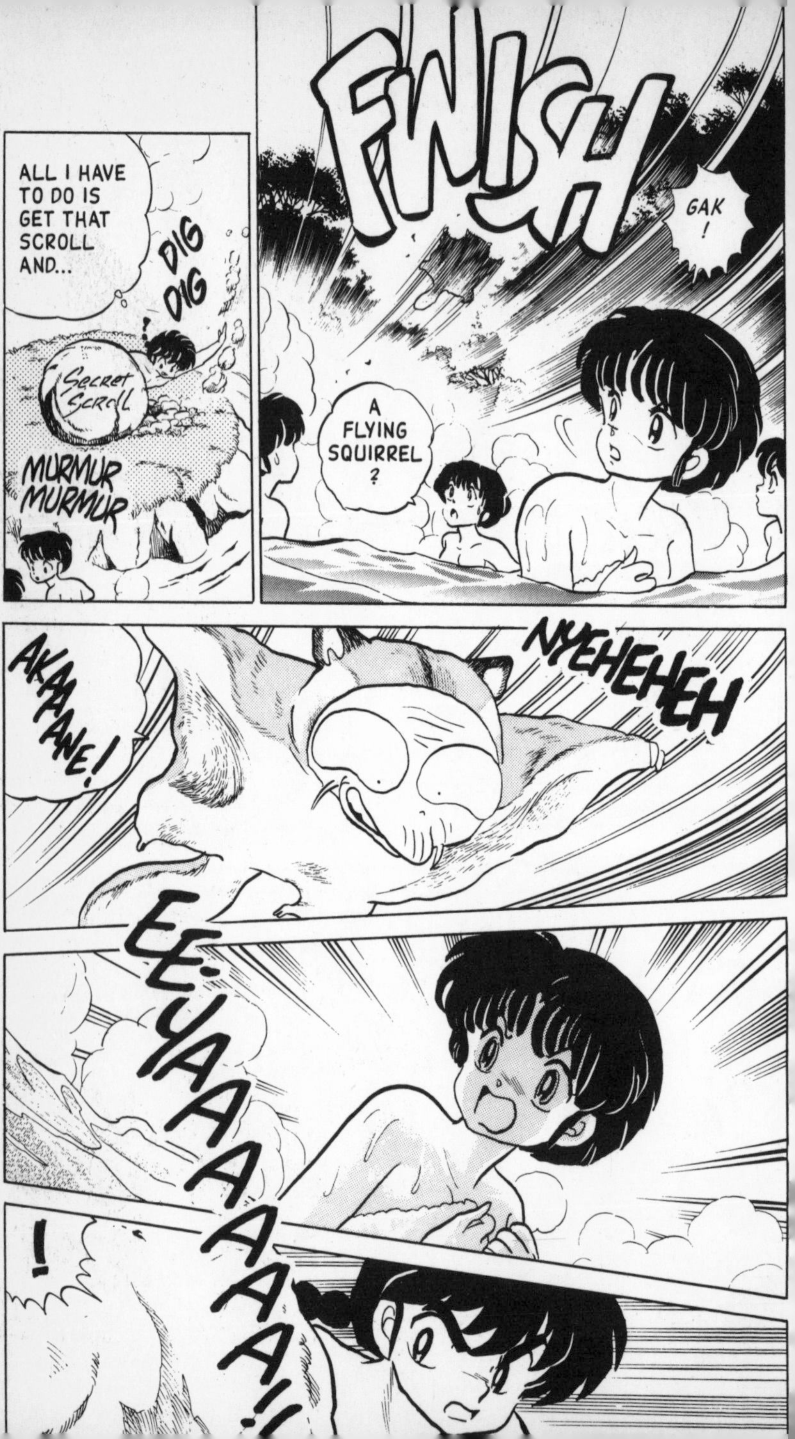
ALL I HAVE TO DO IS GET THAT SCROLL AND...
DIG DIG
Secret Scroll
MURMUR MURMUR
FWISH
GAK!
A FLYING SQUIRREL?
AKAAANE!
NYEHEHEH
EE-YAAAAAAA!!
!

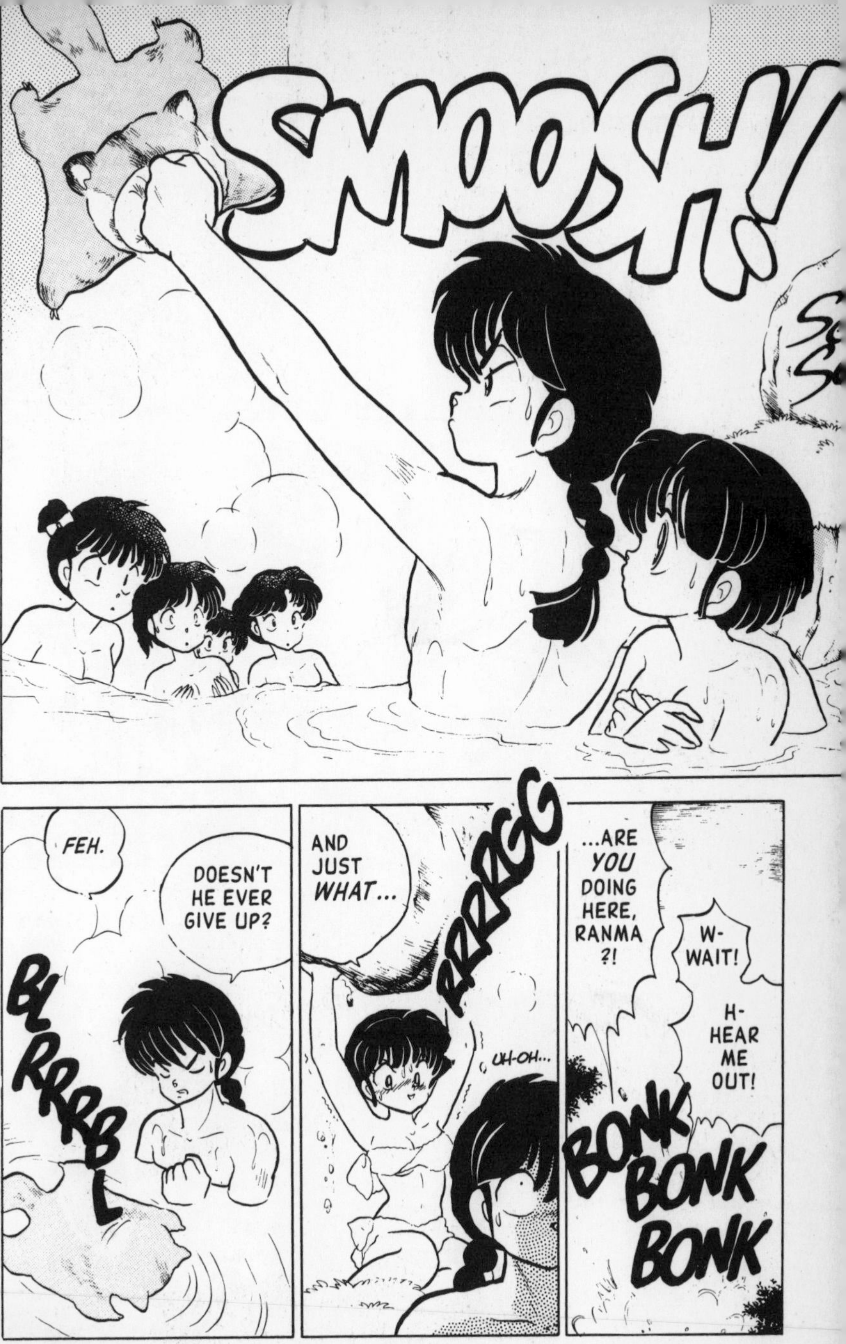
SMOOCH!
FEH.
DOESN'T HE EVER GIVE UP?
BLRRRBL
AND JUST *WHAT*...
RRRRGG
UH-OH...
...ARE *YOU* DOING HERE, RANMA ?!
W-WAIT!
H-HEAR ME OUT!
BONK
BONK
BONK

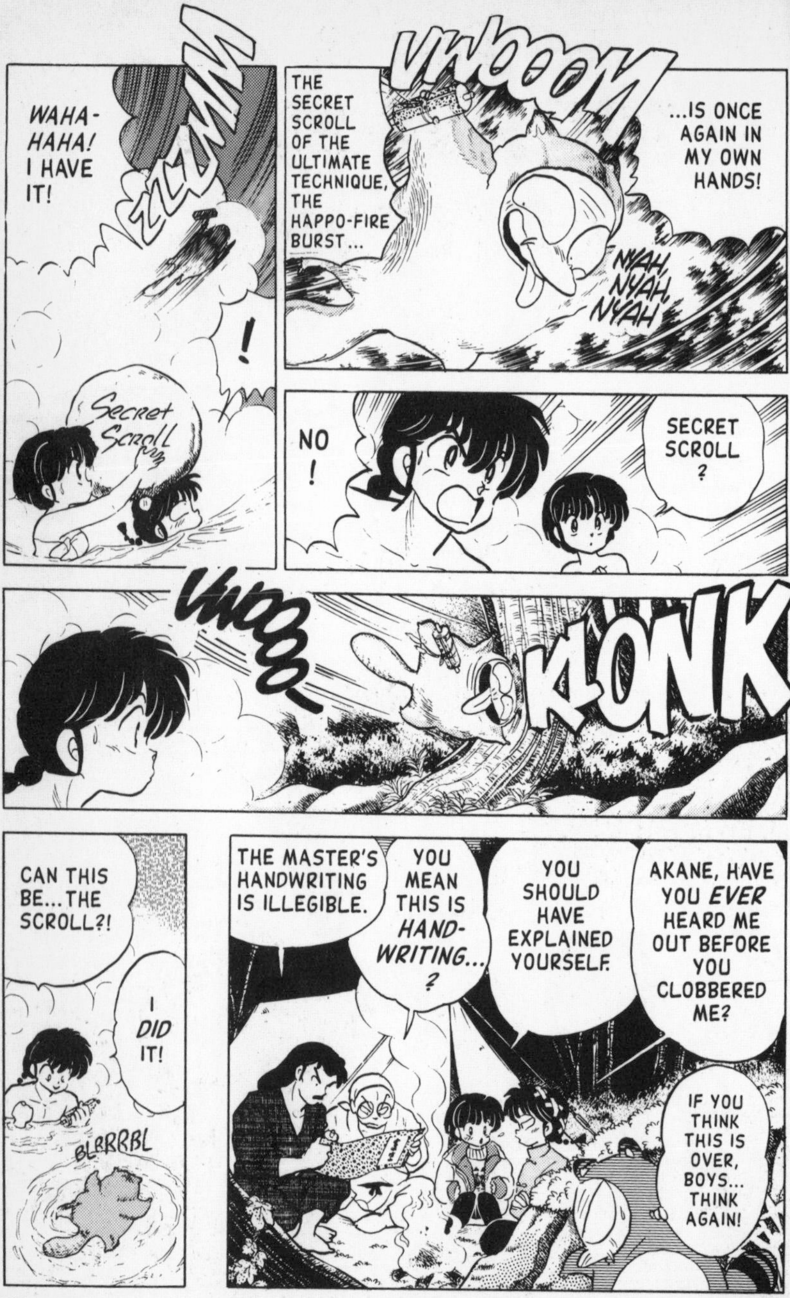

ZZZWM
WAHA-HAHA! I HAVE IT!
!
Secret Scroll
VWOOOM
THE SECRET SCROLL OF THE ULTIMATE TECHNIQUE, THE HAPPO-FIRE BURST...
...IS ONCE AGAIN IN MY OWN HANDS!
NYAH, NYAH, NYAH
NO !
SECRET SCROLL ?
VWOOOO
KLONK
CAN THIS BE...THE SCROLL?!
I DID IT!
BLBRRBL
THE MASTER'S HANDWRITING IS ILLEGIBLE.
YOU MEAN THIS IS HAND-WRITING... ?
YOU SHOULD HAVE EXPLAINED YOURSELF.
AKANE, HAVE YOU EVER HEARD ME OUT BEFORE YOU CLOBBERED ME?
IF YOU THINK THIS IS OVER, BOYS... THINK AGAIN!

Part 12
THE FIRE-BURST OF TERROR!

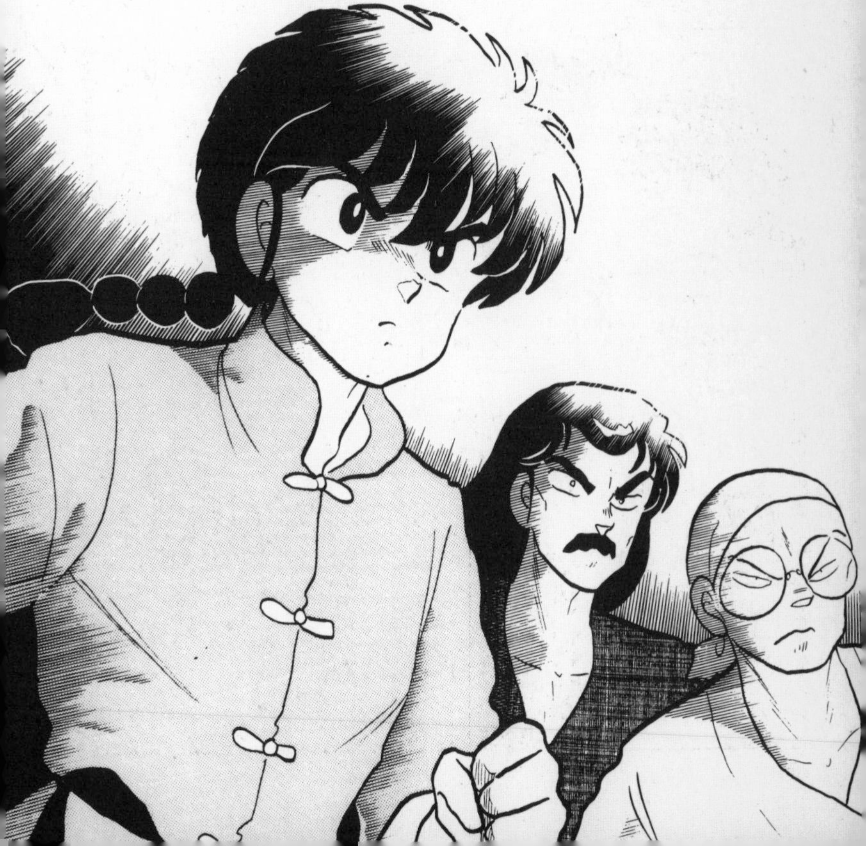

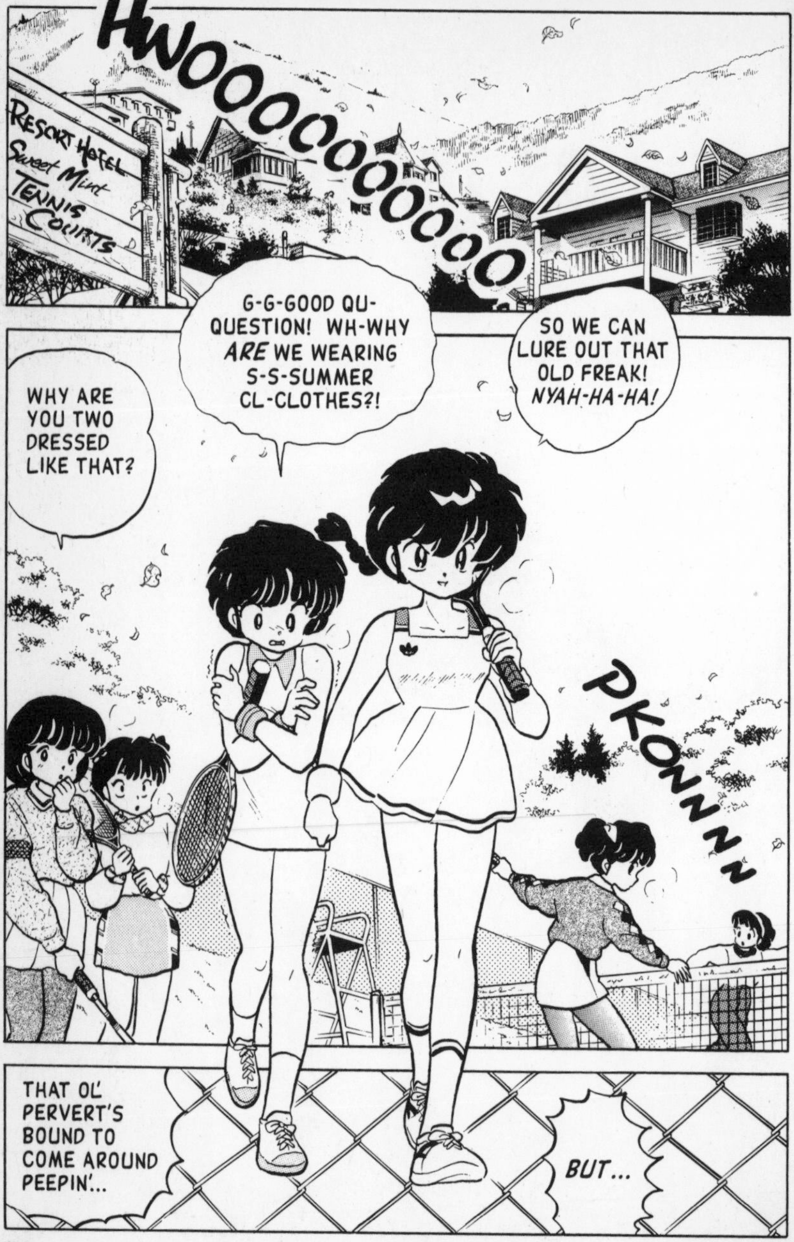
HWOOOOOOOOOOOOOO
RESORT HOTEL Sweet Mint TENNIS COURTS
WHY ARE YOU TWO DRESSED LIKE THAT?
G-G-GOOD QU-QUESTION! WH-WHY *ARE* WE WEARING S-S-SUMMER CL-CLOTHES?!
SO WE CAN LURE OUT THAT OLD FREAK! *NYAH-HA-HA!*
PKONNNNN
THAT OL' PERVERT'S BOUND TO COME AROUND PEEPIN'...
BUT...

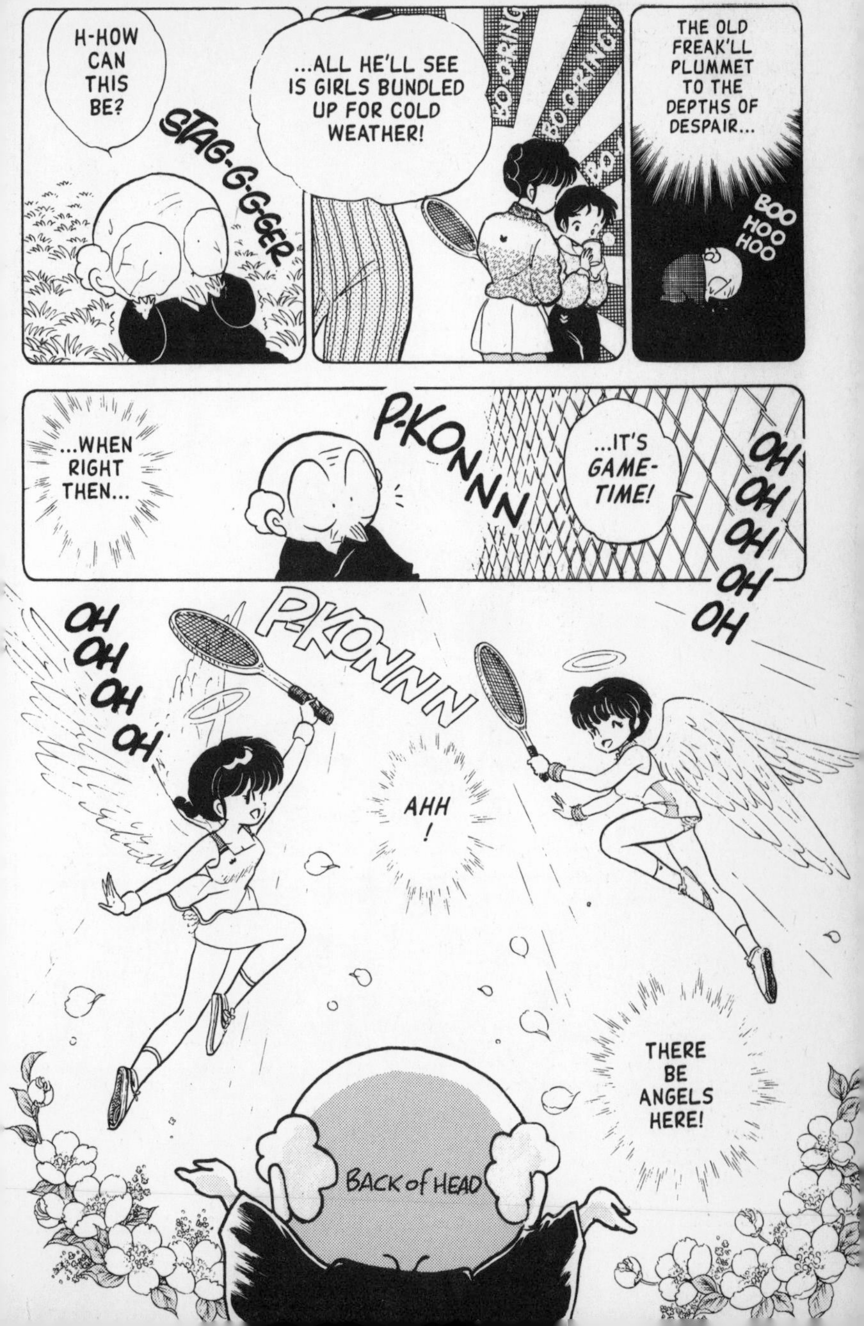
H-HOW CAN THIS BE?
STAG-G-G-GER
...ALL HE'LL SEE IS GIRLS BUNDLED UP FOR COLD WEATHER!
BOORING
BOORING!
BO
THE OLD FREAK'LL PLUMMET TO THE DEPTHS OF DESPAIR...
BOO HOO HOO
...WHEN RIGHT THEN...
P-KONNNN
...IT'S GAME-TIME!
OH OH OH OH OH OH
OH OH OH OH
P-KONNNN
AHH!
THERE BE ANGELS HERE!
BACK of HEAD

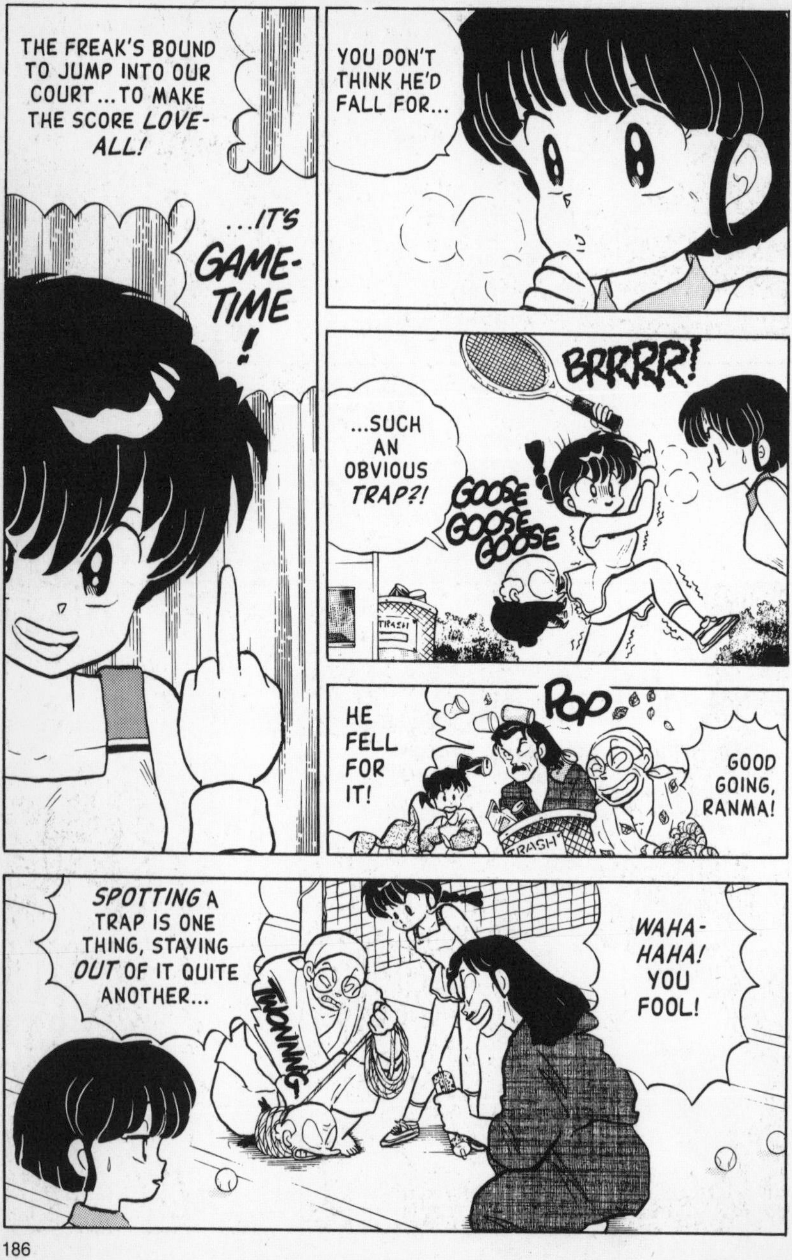
THE FREAK'S BOUND TO JUMP INTO OUR COURT...TO MAKE THE SCORE LOVE-ALL!
...IT'S GAME-TIME!
YOU DON'T THINK HE'D FALL FOR...
BRRRR!
...SUCH AN OBVIOUS TRAP?!
GOOSE GOOSE GOOSE
TRASH
HE FELL FOR IT!
POP
GOOD GOING, RANMA!
TRASH
SPOTTING A TRAP IS ONE THING, STAYING OUT OF IT QUITE ANOTHER...
TWONNNG
WAHA-HAHA! YOU FOOL!

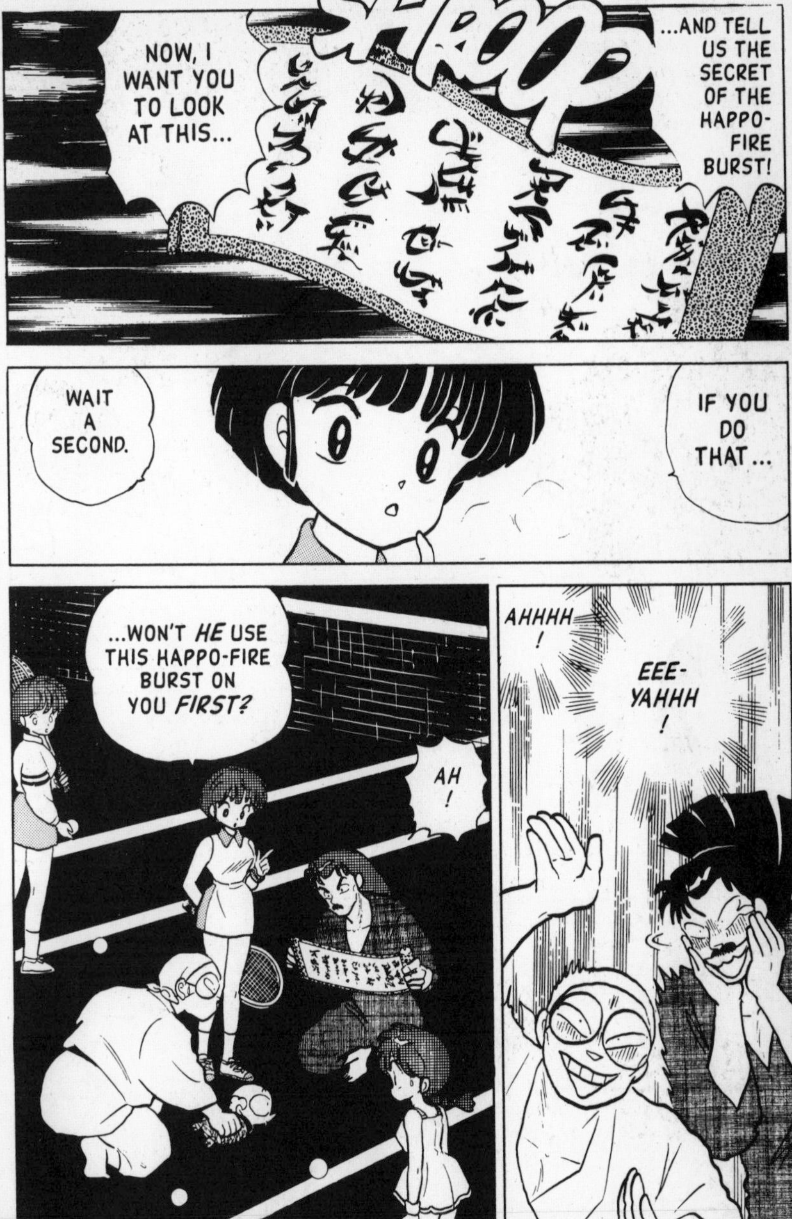
NOW, I WANT YOU TO LOOK AT THIS...
SHROOP
...AND TELL US THE SECRET OF THE HAPPO-FIRE BURST!
WAIT A SECOND.
IF YOU DO THAT...
...WON'T *HE* USE THIS HAPPO-FIRE BURST ON YOU *FIRST*?
AH!
AHHHH!
EEE-YAHHH!

RUN AWAAAAAY!

HUH? WHAT ARE WE RUNNING FROM?

YEEEE

YEEEE

KLATTA KLATTA KLATTA

HWOOOOOOO

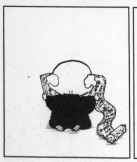

HMM?

HEY, OL' FREAK... WHAT'S UP?

BRRR BRRR

I...I CAN'T READ IT!

188

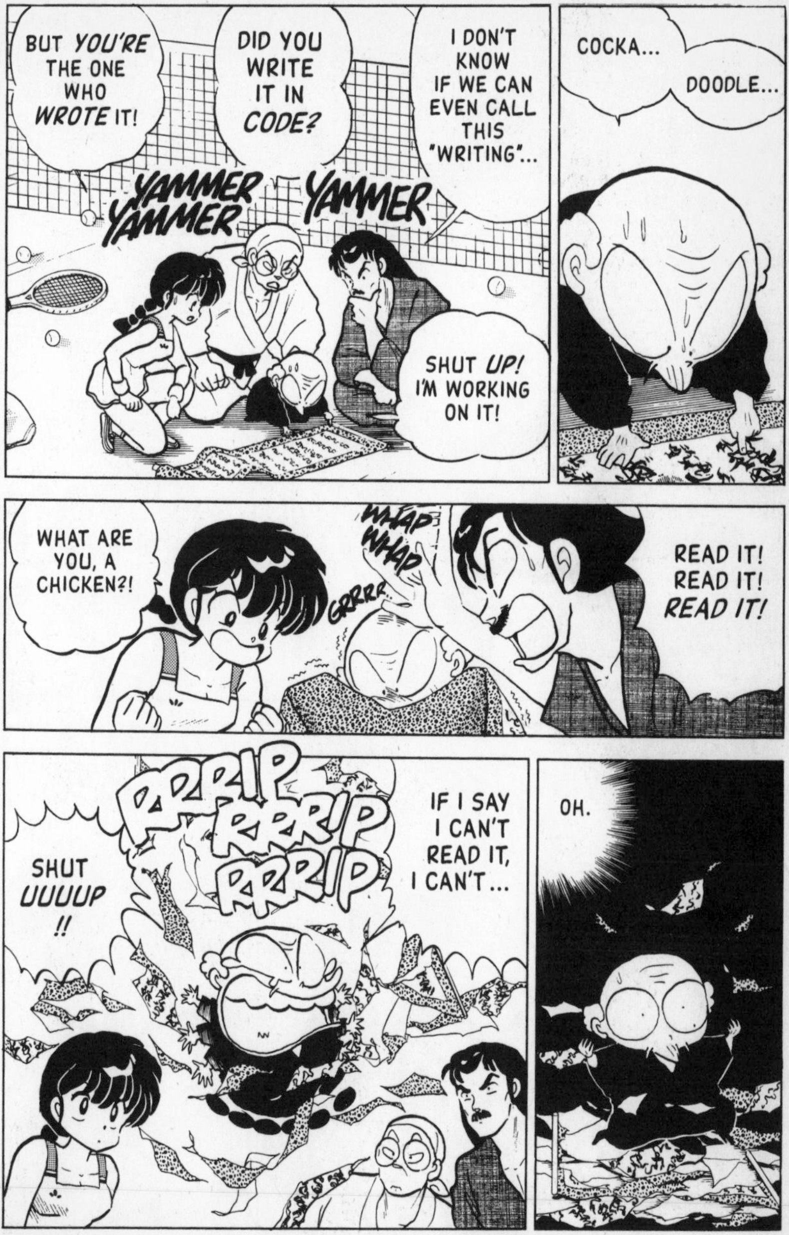
BUT YOU'RE THE ONE WHO WROTE IT!
DID YOU WRITE IT IN CODE?
I DON'T KNOW IF WE CAN EVEN CALL THIS "WRITING"...
YAMMER YAMMER
YAMMER
SHUT UP! I'M WORKING ON IT!
COCKA...
DOODLE...
WHAT ARE YOU, A CHICKEN?!
WHAP WHAP
GRRRR
READ IT! READ IT! READ IT!
SHUT UUUUP !!
RRRIP RRRIP RRRIP
IF I SAY I CAN'T READ IT, I CAN'T...
OH.

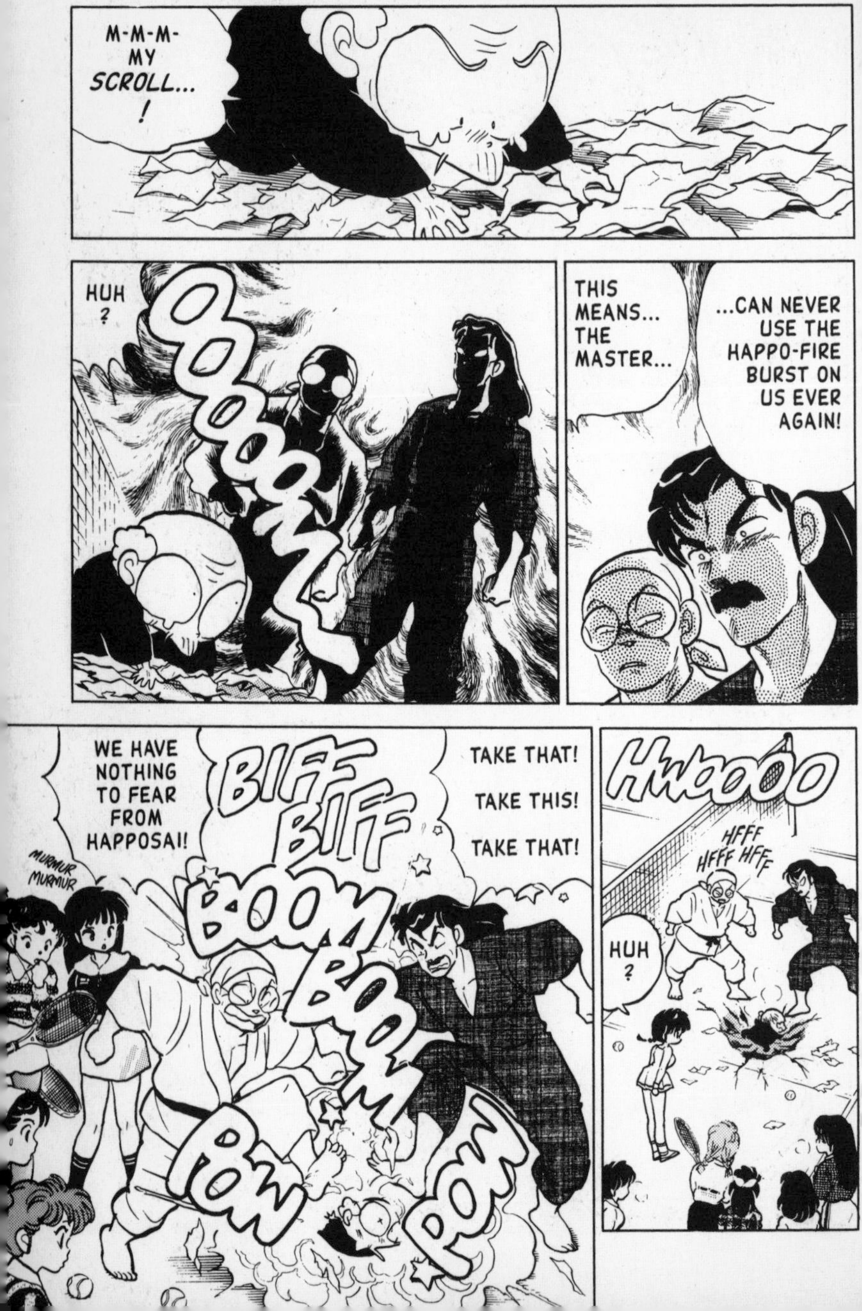
M-M-M-MY SCROLL...!
HUH?
OOOOOM
THIS MEANS... THE MASTER...
...CAN NEVER USE THE HAPPO-FIRE BURST ON US EVER AGAIN!
WE HAVE NOTHING TO FEAR FROM HAPPOSAI!
MURMUR MURMUR
BIFF BIFF
TAKE THAT!
TAKE THIS!
TAKE THAT!
BOOM BOOM
POW POW
HWOOOO
HFFF HFFF HFFF
HUH?

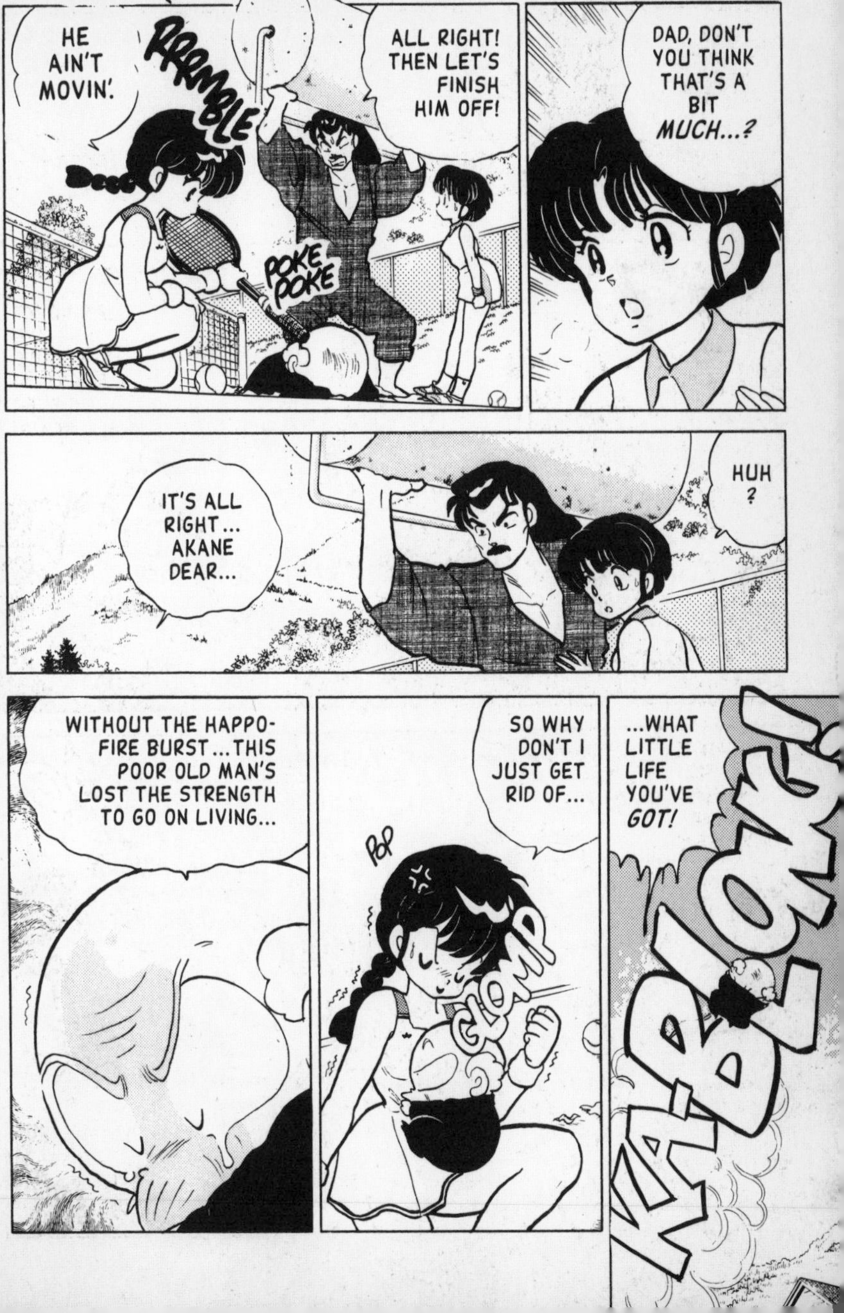
HE AIN'T MOVIN'.
RRRMBLE
ALL RIGHT! THEN LET'S FINISH HIM OFF!
POKE POKE
DAD, DON'T YOU THINK THAT'S A BIT *MUCH...?*
IT'S ALL RIGHT... AKANE DEAR...
HUH ?
WITHOUT THE HAPPO-FIRE BURST... THIS POOR OLD MAN'S LOST THE STRENGTH TO GO ON LIVING...
SO WHY DON'T I JUST GET RID OF...
POP
GLOMP
...WHAT LITTLE LIFE YOU'VE *GOT!*
KABLONG!

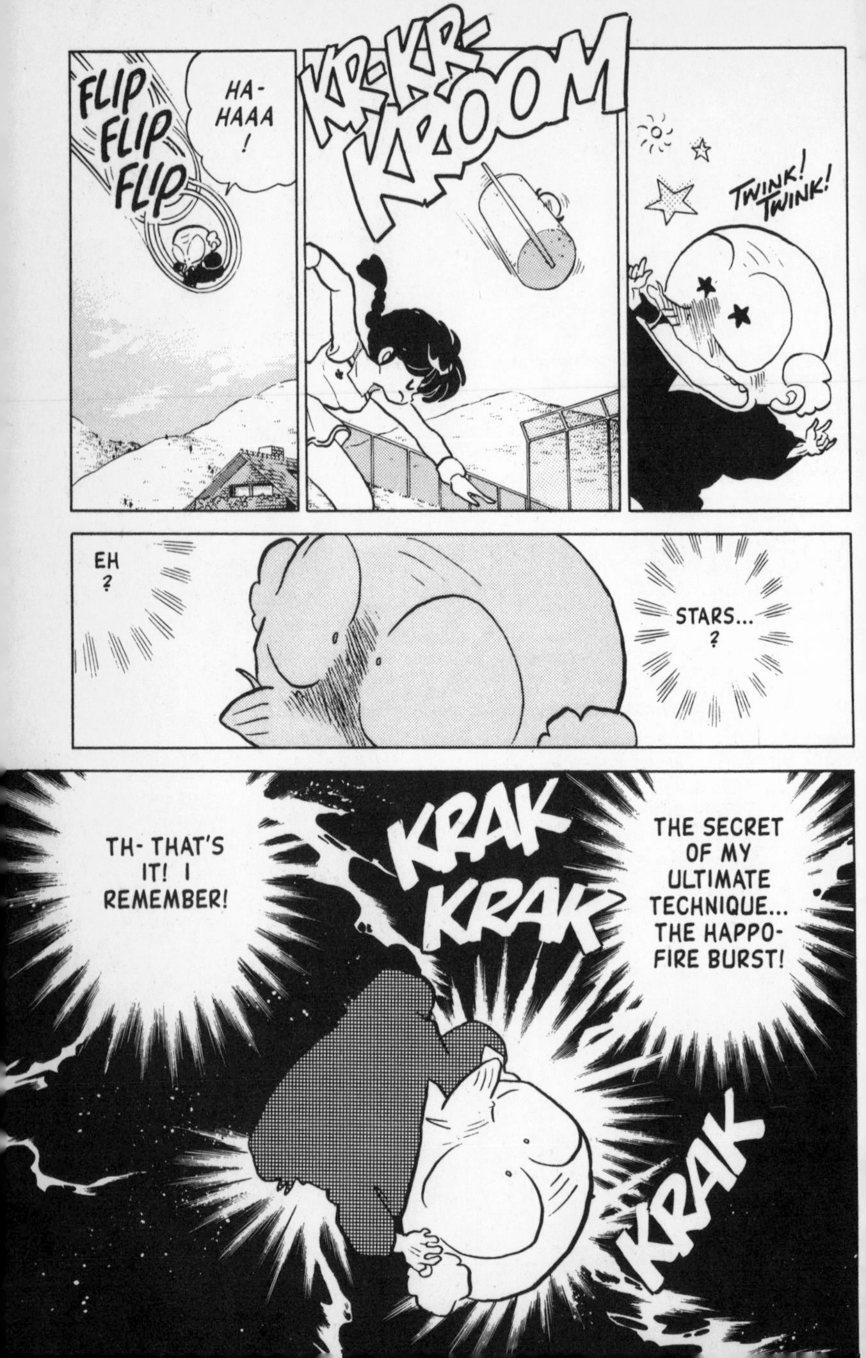
FLIP FLIP FLIP
HA-HAAA!
KR-KR-KABOOM
TWINK! TWINK!
EH?
STARS...?
TH- THAT'S IT! I REMEMBER!
KRAK KRAK
THE SECRET OF MY ULTIMATE TECHNIQUE... THE HAPPO-FIRE BURST!
KRAK

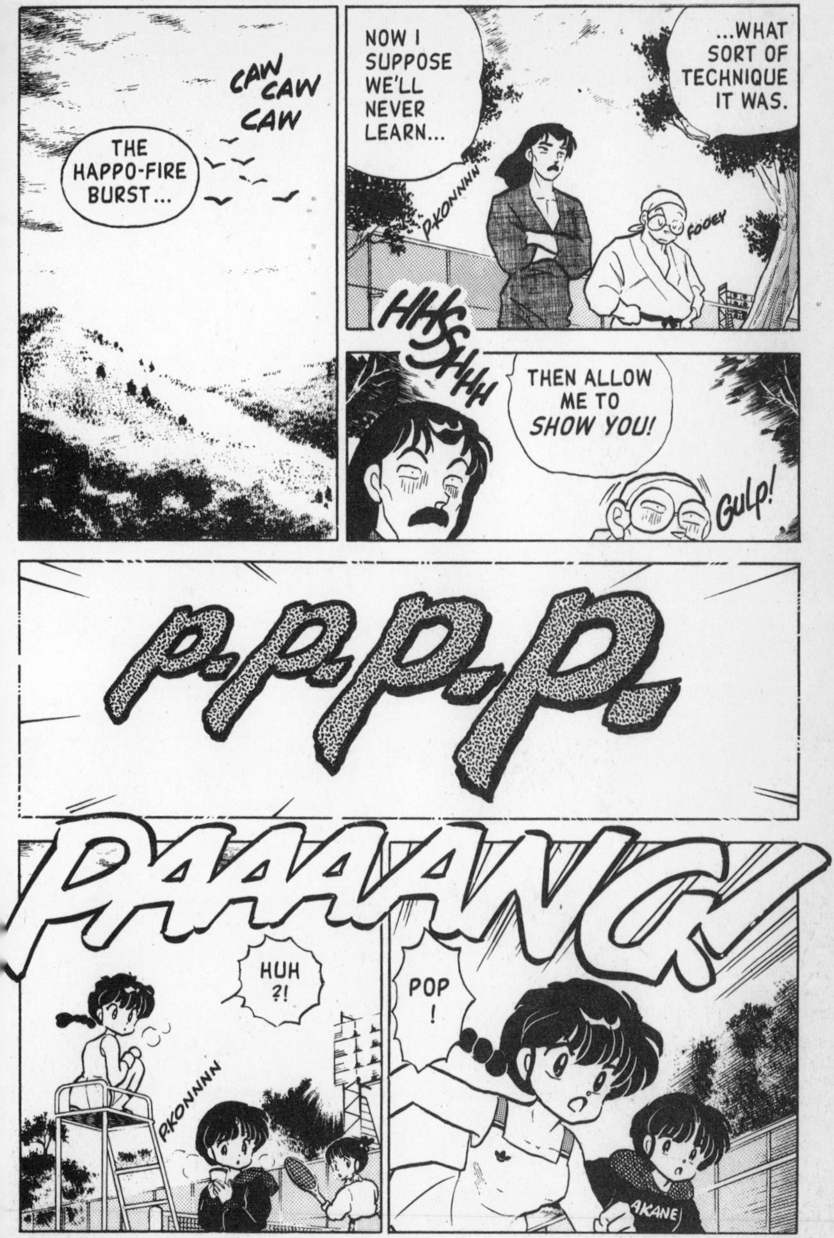
CAW CAW CAW
THE HAPPO-FIRE BURST...
NOW I SUPPOSE WE'LL NEVER LEARN...
...WHAT SORT OF TECHNIQUE IT WAS.
P-KONNNN
FOOEY
HHSSHHH
THEN ALLOW ME TO SHOW YOU!
GULP!
P.P.P.P.
PAAAANG!
HUH ?!
P-KONNNN
POP !
AKANE

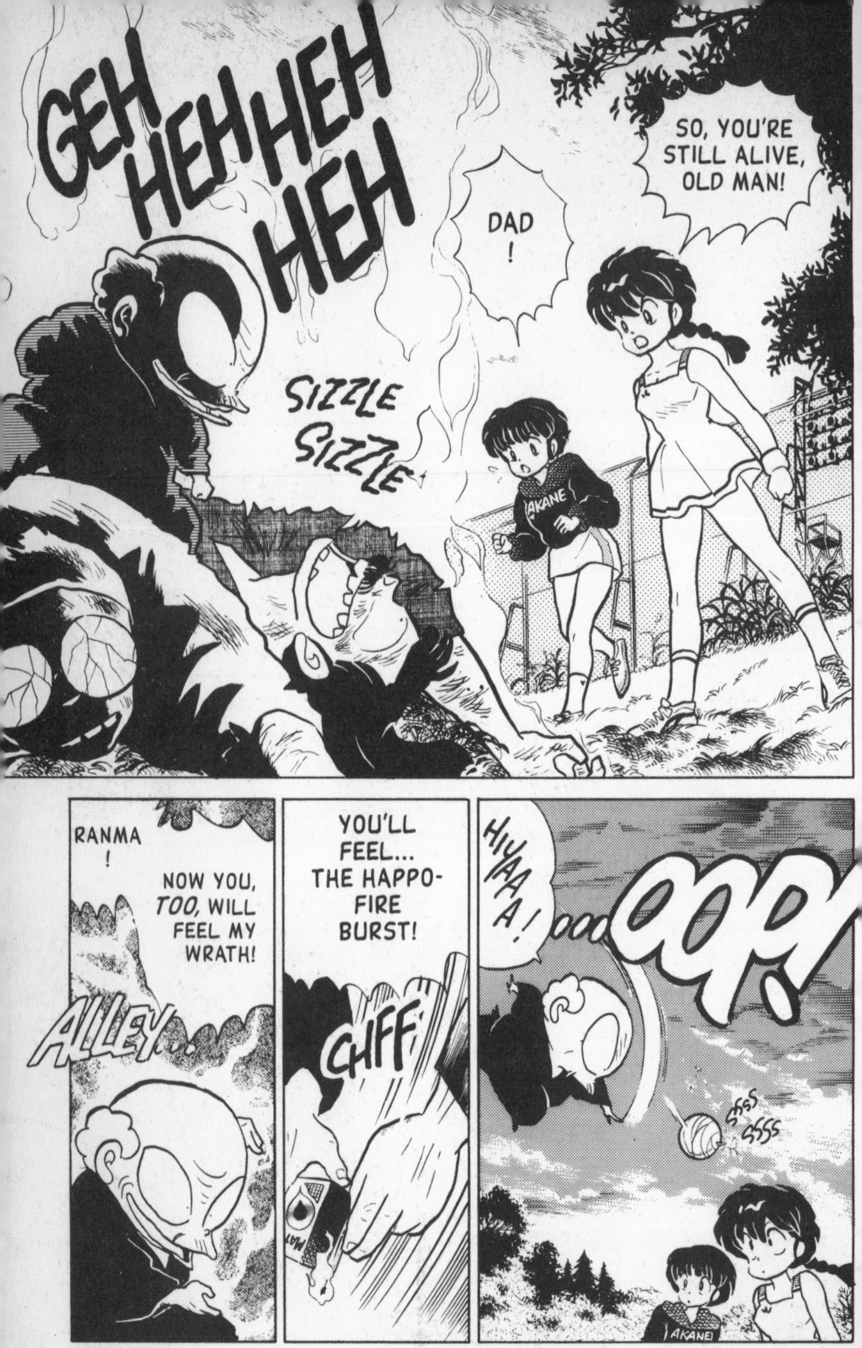
GEH HEHHEH HEH
SIZZLE SIZZLE
DAD !
SO, YOU'RE STILL ALIVE, OLD MAN!
AKANE
RANMA !
NOW YOU, *TOO,* WILL FEEL MY WRATH!
ALLEY...
YOU'LL FEEL... THE HAPPO-FIRE BURST!
CHFF
HIYAAAA!
...OOP!
SSSS SSSS
AKANE

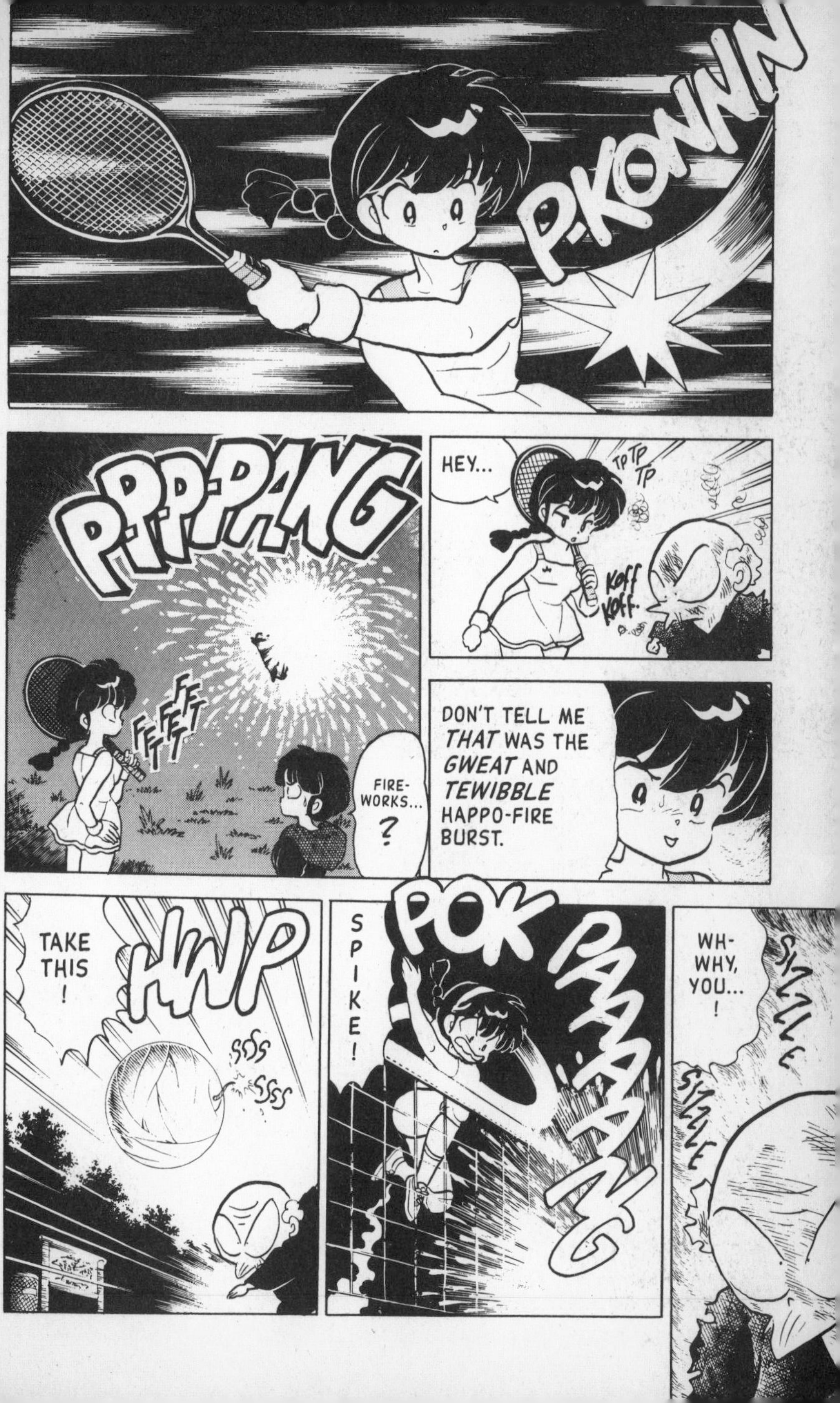
P-KONNN
P-P-P-P-ANG
FFT FFT FFT
FIRE-WORKS...?
HEY...
TP TP TP
KOFF KOFF
DON'T TELL ME *THAT* WAS THE *GWEAT* AND *TEWIBBLE* HAPPO-FIRE BURST.
TAKE THIS!
HNP
SSS SSSS
SPIKE!
POK PAAAAANG
WH-WHY, YOU...!
SIZZLE SIZZLE

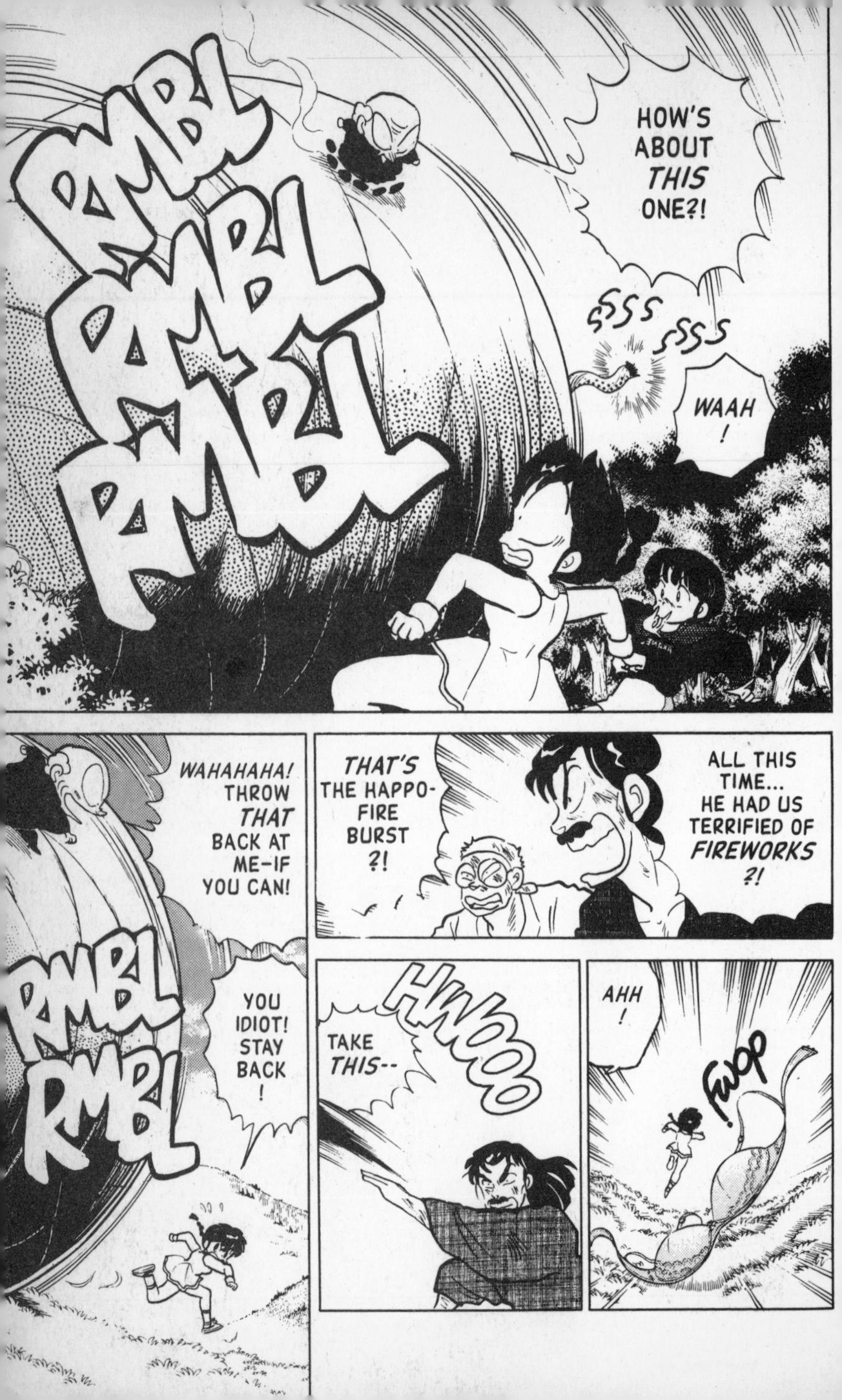
RMBL RMBL RMBL
HOW'S ABOUT THIS ONE?!
SSSS SSSS
WAAH!
WAHAHAHA! THROW THAT BACK AT ME—IF YOU CAN!
THAT'S THE HAPPO-FIRE BURST ?!
ALL THIS TIME... HE HAD US TERRIFIED OF FIREWORKS ?!
RMBL RMBL
YOU IDIOT! STAY BACK!
HWOOO
TAKE THIS--
AHH!
FWOP

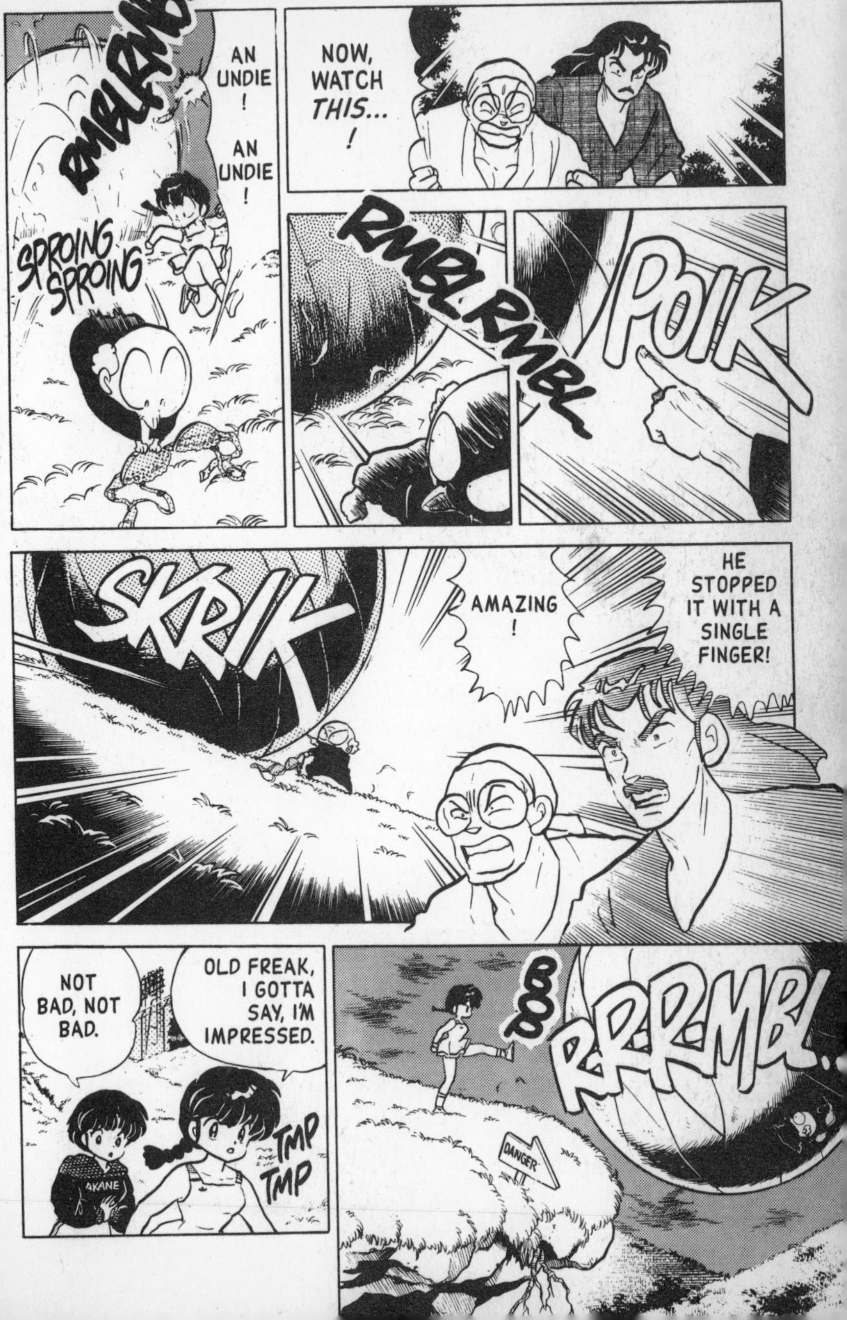
RMBLRMBL
AN UNDIE !
AN UNDIE !
SPROING SPROING
NOW, WATCH THIS... !
RMBLRMBL
POIK
SKRIK
AMAZING !
HE STOPPED IT WITH A SINGLE FINGER!
NOT BAD, NOT BAD.
OLD FREAK, I GOTTA SAY, I'M IMPRESSED.
AKANE
TMP TMP
DOOO
RRRRMBL...
DANGER

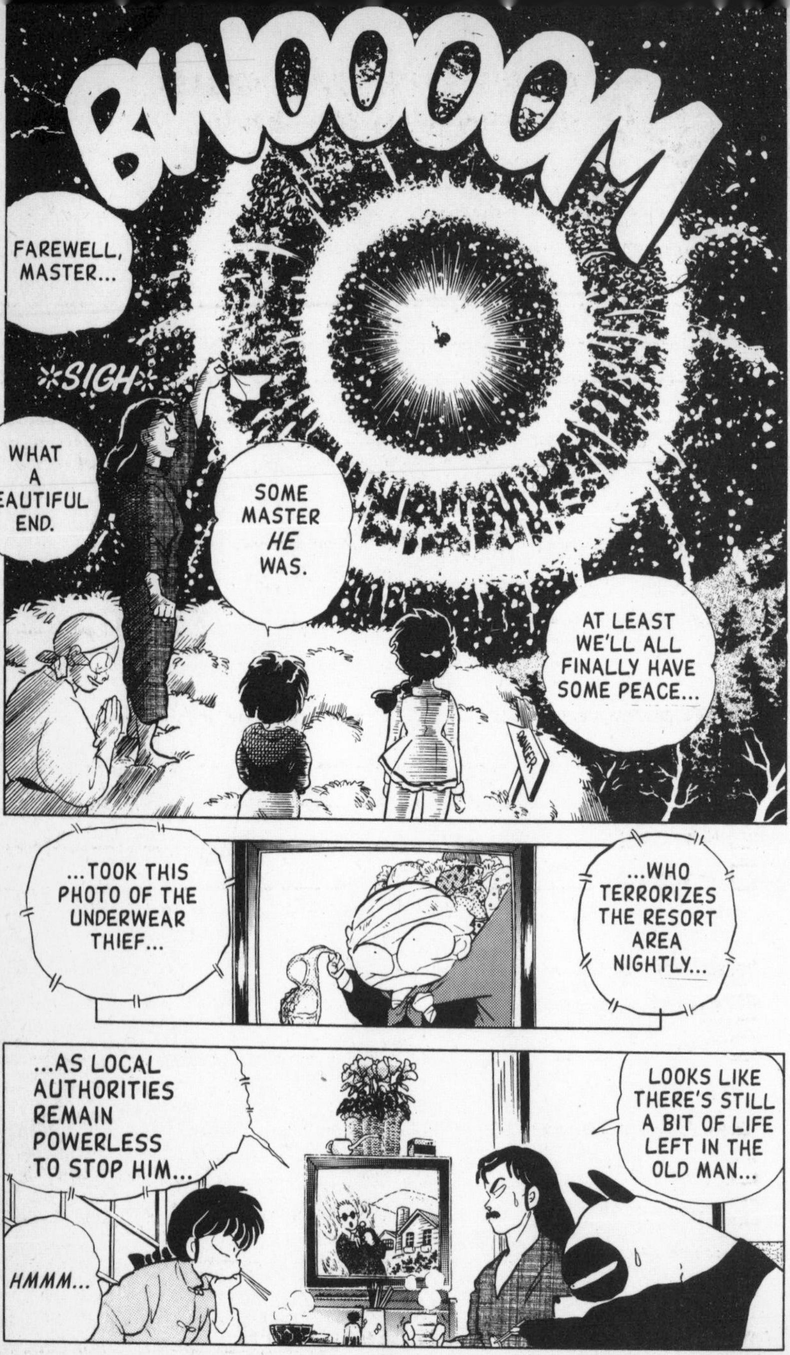
BWOOOOM
FAREWELL, MASTER...
SIGH
WHAT A BEAUTIFUL END.
SOME MASTER *HE* WAS.
AT LEAST WE'LL ALL FINALLY HAVE SOME PEACE...
DANGER
...TOOK THIS PHOTO OF THE UNDERWEAR THIEF...
...WHO TERRORIZES THE RESORT AREA NIGHTLY...
...AS LOCAL AUTHORITIES REMAIN POWERLESS TO STOP HIM...
HMMM...
LOOKS LIKE THERE'S STILL A BIT OF LIFE LEFT IN THE OLD MAN...

END OF RANMA 1/2 VOLUME 9.

COMPLETE OUR SURVEY AND LET US KNOW WHAT YOU THINK!

☐ Please do NOT send me information about VIZ products, news and events, special offers, or other information.

☐ Please do NOT send me information from VIZ's trusted business partners.

Name: _____

Address: _____

City: _____ **State:** _____ **Zip:** _____

E-mail: _____

☐ Male ☐ Female **Date of Birth** (mm/dd/yyyy): ___ / ___ / ___ (Under 13? Parental consent required)

What race/ethnicity do you consider yourself? (please check one)

☐ Asian/Pacific Islander ☐ Black/African American ☐ Hispanic/Latino

☐ Native American/Alaskan Native ☐ White/Caucasian ☐ Other: _____

What VIZ product did you purchase? (check all that apply and indicate title purchased)

☐ DVD/VHS _____

☐ Graphic Novel _____

☐ Magazines _____

☐ Merchandise _____

Reason for purchase: (check all that apply)

☐ Special offer ☐ Favorite title ☐ Gift

☐ Recommendation ☐ Other _____

Where did you make your purchase? (please check one)

☐ Comic store ☐ Bookstore ☐ Mass/Grocery Store

☐ Newsstand ☐ Video/Video Game Store ☐ Other: _____

☐ Online (site: _____)

What other VIZ properties have you purchased/own? _____

_____

How many anime and/or manga titles have you purchased in the last year? How many were VIZ titles? (please check one from each column)

ANIME	MANGA	VIZ
☐ None	☐ None	☐ None
☐ 1-4	☐ 1-4	☐ 1-4
☐ 5-10	☐ 5-10	☐ 5-10
☐ 11+	☐ 11+	☐ 11+

I find the pricing of VIZ products to be: (please check one)

☐ Cheap   ☐ Reasonable   ☐ Expensive

What genre of manga and anime would you like to see from VIZ? (please check two)

☐ Adventure   ☐ Comic Strip   ☐ Science Fiction   ☐ Fighting

☐ Horror   ☐ Romance   ☐ Fantasy   ☐ Sports

What do you think of VIZ's new look?

☐ Love It   ☐ It's OK   ☐ Hate It   ☐ Didn't Notice   ☐ No Opinion

Which do you prefer? (please check one)

☐ Reading right-to-left

☐ Reading left-to-right

Which do you prefer? (please check one)

☐ Sound effects in English

☐ Sound effects in Japanese with English captions

☐ Sound effects in Japanese only with a glossary at the back

THANK YOU! Please send the completed form to:

NJW Research
42 Catharine St.
Poughkeepsie, NY 12601

All information provided will be used for internal purposes only. We promise not to sell or otherwise divulge your information.